To Brielle
with love
yours
Oma a. Opa

STUDIES IN
VICTORIAN LIFE AND LITERATURE

THE LION
AND THE
CROSS

Early Christianity in Victorian Novels

Royal W. Rhodes

Ohio State University Press
Columbus

Library of Congress Cataloging-in-Publication Data

Rhodes, Royal W.
The lion and the cross : early Christianity in Victorian novels /
Royal Rhodes.
p. cm. — (Studies in Victorian life and literature)
Includes bibliographical references (p. xxx–xxx) and index.
ISBN 0–8142–0648–4 (cloth : alk. paper).
—ISBN 0–8142–0649–2 (pbk. : alk. paper)
1. English fiction—19th century—History and criticism.
2. Christianity and literature—Great Britain—History—19th century.
3. Church history—Primitive and early church, ca. 30–600—
Historiography. 4. Historical fiction, English—History and criticism.
6. Fiction—Religious aspects—Christianity. 7. History, Ancient, in literature.
8. Church history in literature. 9. Christianity in literature. I. Title. II. Series.
PR878.R5R46   1995
823'.809382—dc20   94–26139
CIP

Text designed by John Delaine.
Type set in Bembo.
Printed by Bookcrafters, Chelsea, MI.

9 8 7 6 5 4 3 2 1

In memory of my grandparents,
Booker Lee and Olga Donaghe Rhodes
and
William Francis and Lillian Kelley Welch

The last of the merry Victorians

CONTENTS

PREFACE

ON 22 OCTOBER 1978, Pope John Paul II celebrated the inaugural Mass
of his pontificate. During his homily he mentioned in passing the nineteenth-century novel *Quo Vadis?* by the Polish author Henryk Sienkiewicz, thus alluding to the Petrine traditions of the See of Rome and
the new pontiff's nationality. The use of novels to make religious statements or claims has a tradition that found its fullest embodiment in Victorian England, when literary talents were enlisted to defend or attack
the ramparts of ecclesiastical authority.

The question of authority, especially in regard to Scripture and tradition, was in the early 1960s the concern of many, myself included, who
witnessed the panoply and politics of Vatican Council II. It was said then
that the unseen "Father of the Council" was John Henry Cardinal
Newman, many of whose views were vindicated in that ecclesiastical assembly. My own study of Newman drew me back to the sources he studied, Scripture and the Fathers, which he had hoped would be sources of
unity, if not ecclesial union, among divided Christians. That interest in
Newman and the two Churches in which he is an enduring ornament
promoted this present study.

I am grateful to Professor Jaroslav Pelikan of Yale, who shared in the
course of seminars and tutorials his understanding of the tangled history
of doctrine and of Newman's impassioned intellect: *cor ad cor loquitur.*
Professor Robert Kiely of Harvard provided guidance in the history and
criticism of the Victorian novel. The late Professor Robert Lee Wolff of
Harvard was the source of numerous suggestions and helpful criticisms.
His work on the religious dimensions of Victorian fiction for adults and
children, providing not only the sources themselves but also a comprehensive interpretation of them, leaves every student of this subject in his
debt. Professor John E. Booty generously shared his insights into the

thought and ethos of the Anglican Church, imbuing the theological issues with his own literary sensitivity and humanity. Hollis Professor
Emeritus George Huntston Williams was a compassionate guide to the
continuities and discontinuities of Church history, uniting the disparate
historical periods that are the subject of this study. His understanding of
history and the critical role of personalities in eras of historical change assisted me in beginning and completing this task. I want to thank Pat
Bosch, Nancy Davis, and Teri Severns for their time and skill in typing
early versions of this work. Special thanks go to Sharon Duchesne, who
used her computer wizardry to type and assemble the completed manuscript. Finally, I owe the full measure of my gratitude to my late parents
and grandparents, who nurtured and encouraged me, giving me their
unending love and raising me "to worship the Lord in the beauty of
holiness."

INTRODUCTION

The Church of the Fathers
and Victorian Religious Controversy

For all who might wish to acquire the current controversial small-talk without the labor of reading grave works of theology, the press was about to provide abundant instruction in the shape of novels and story-books, illustrating the doctrines and practices of the newly-risen "ism." And now a very extensive literature of this kind has grown up among us, exhibiting the "movement" and the "development" in all their phases, and adding largely to the materials which must be mastered by the future Church historian who would qualify himself for describing the workings of the late controversies on the mind of our generation.

—George Eliot, "Religious Stories," *Fraser's Magazine* (1848)

So WROTE THE Victorian author George Eliot (Mary Ann Evans, 1819–80) in surveying the growing number of didactic novels and tales by writers of different religious persuasions. Within that body of literature, the Early Church novel is a distinct subgenre that has been commented upon by a variety of literary historians and critics. As helpful as their work is, their understanding of the Victorian religious novel needs revision. A neglected aspect of this literature, but one that remains the chief reason for undertaking the continued study of these novels, is their preoccupation with the controverted doctrines and partisan religious issues of the period, masked by antique settings. No Victorian writer was untouched by these contemporary issues, whether they identified themselves or have been identified as "religious" authors. A number of writers, however, can be identified in terms of their specific churchmanship. The disputed theological questions of the day became in the hands of such authors—Anglicans, Dissenters, and Roman Catholics—the

1

substance of novels meant to portray the distinctive features of the ideal Church, conceived variously by the contending religious parties. Delineating the polemical and propaganda value of the many novels in this category, showing their links to particular issues, and marking the shifting stances of individual authors and religious groups within the period put a strain on both the writer and the reader of this study. If one approaches the novels in terms of the churchmanship of their authors, however, one can use this material as an array of highly significant and articulate documents for the study of Church history, documents that show vividly the rapid pace of movements of thought within the Victorian Age and the highly charged emotional pulse of the religious debate. Those churchly issues grew, root and branch, as a direct result of the Oxford Movement, blending theology and Romanticism and raising the level of religious disputation by its heightened historical consciousness. In the Early Church novel High Church Anglican writers found a valuable instrument for their program of religious reform; it is necessary, therefore, to examine the complex relationships between the Oxford Movement and the literary program undertaken by various theological writers. For authority they appealed to Scripture and the tradition of antiquity; it is necessary, then, to discuss their understanding of those sources, of antiquity, and of contemporary criticism of that appeal.

THE OXFORD MOVEMENT AND LITERATURE

The Oxford Movement (1833–45), that flowering of the Anglo-Catholic Revival in the Church of England, continues to be a rich source of scholarly investigation as a religious, social, and political phenomenon. This is true partly because the movement attracted the attention and sometimes the allegiance of the best minds and most dynamic personalities of nineteenth-century Britain. The important historiographical interpretations of the movement, beginning in the Victorian era itself, reemerging with new vigor for the centennial, and continuing with altered perspectives to our own day, demonstrate the range of approaches to the study of the Anglo-Catholic Revival as a dramatic episode in Church history. The movement has also been seen by both its adherents and opponents as an exercise of formidable literary virtuosity; Walter E. Houghton's masterful elucidation of the rhetorical toils of John Henry

Newman's *Apologia*, for example, confirmed that evaluation. Although some critics have stressed discontinuity with the literary aspirations of the epoch, generally the movement is now readily understood as an influential channel, in both its aesthetic forms and sensibilities, for transmitting Romanticism throughout the nineteenth century. In the partisan view of Newman's close friend Frederic Rogers, Tractarianism offered, in place of the aesthetic and emotional famine of the Evangelical school, "a religion which did not reject, but aspired to embody in itself, any form of art and literature . . . which could be pressed into the service of Christianity."[1] Therefore, an important task of the Church historian, investigating those personal, confessional, and ecclesiastical questions that shaped the revival, remains to examine portions of that massive literary productivity and to relate it to the personal and religious concerns of the various authors and to their culture and society at large. This is exactly the challenge set by George Eliot in 1848.

The present investigation will deal with specific examples of religious-historical novels in Victorian England, novels and tales depicting the Roman Empire and the Early Church from New Testament times down to the sixth-century mission of Augustine to Britain. This subgenre of Romantic literature, popularized by Edward Bulwer-Lytton and Walter Pater among others, has received some attention from those literary historians interested in the development of the novel. This has been part of a more extensive critical examination of the theoretical base of historical fiction and the revolutionary development of historical consciousness in the nineteenth century with its new historical outlook: historicism. It is enough to remark that historical trends played a crucial role in enlivening the understanding of Victorian England about its organic unity with the historical phenomena of its past. Thus, in 1850 Lord Palmerston defended in Parliament his gunboat diplomacy by voicing this Romantic sense of national identity and imperial aspiration in the ringing phrase: "Civis Romanus sum." The mantle of empire had been transferred to the last outpost of that empire; in some respects the Britons were more Roman than the Romans. Such an awareness, fed by popular culture as well as by the traditions of classical education, merged with religious interests to promote a wide readership for this type of novel, in which the Victorians "looked upon the face of Caesar."[2]

While recognizing religious elements in many of the novels produced during this period, only a few investigators have tried to relate systematically this fictionalized material to the theological concerns of their authors or to the pressing religious questions of the day. Some have related these questions only in general terms to major movements and trends of ideas, for example, Raymond Chapman's theoretical identification of such fiction with the Oxford Movement. But historical novels, rooted not only in historiographical works but also in "tracts for the times," pamphlets, sermons, cautionary tales, personal memoirs, and converts' confessions, should be aligned with the particular concerns of the Victorian pulpit and political platform.[3]

From the great number of religious-historical novels produced during the Victorian era, this study treats selectively re-creations of the Ancient or Primitive Church from Apostolic and Subapostolic times down through the first six Christian centuries, the Church of the Fathers, East and West. These examples are used as literary-historical sources to track shifts in the religious understanding and sensibilities of the nineteenth century. They share concerns found in secular or nonconfessional examples of historical fiction: criticism of contemporary culture and society, a sense of historical nostalgia, a deep sense of nationhood, various Romantic literary devices, and a proclivity toward sensationalism, to name a few corresponding elements. But the religious or churchly novels reflect much more their authors' theological concerns and the changing questions of the contemporary religious debate: the authority of Church and Scripture, tradition and apostolic succession, conversion and apostasy, faith and doubt, and the relation of Church and State. Regarding the question of authority alone, the important, though not exclusive, appeal to Christian antiquity and the Apostolic Church finds dynamic, imaginative response in these works. This has to be related, not only to the broad movements of thought, such as the Oxford Movement or Ritualism, but also to the specific concerns of the various authors, concerns and study not purely theological but historical as well. The ecclesiastical authors examined here should be viewed as literary witnesses, sometimes programmatic, sometimes unwitting, to controverted theological positions, to the deepest concerns within their own or other Church parties, and specifically to various aspects of the Anglican/Roman Catholic debate. Religious issues, not purely historiographical or literary ones, generated this literature and set it inevitably in a polemical context.[4]

In the Victorian era earlier historical epochs had become badges of religious party; for example, the seventeenth-century Civil War and the figures of King Charles I and Oliver Cromwell functioned in that emblematic way, as did the Reformation period and the perennially riveting personalities of the Tudor dynasty. On one side, James Anthony Froude, sometime Tractarian sympathizer, in the first of four volumes of his *History of England from 1529 to the Death of Elizabeth* (1856–70) defended the English Reformers against the Whig interpretations of Hallam and Macaulay and the disdain of some Tractarians, including his deceased older brother Hurrell, the close friend of Newman. Froude, largely innocent of dogmatic theology, saw the Reformation in political and philosophical terms as England's unshackling from a foreign potentate and from intellectual enslavement.[5] Against Norman and Stewart absolutism, Froude and later historians, at times quite tendentiously, raised the standard of Saxon democratic institutions down through English history.[6] Later in the century, E. A. Freeman reiterated this view: "We have reformed by calling to life again the institutions of earlier and ruder times, by setting ourselves free from the slavish subtleties of Norman lawyers, by casting aside as an accursed thing the innovations of Tudor tyranny and Stewart usurpation."[7] Therefore, reform, whether of the sixteenth or nineteenth century, was viewed by many influential Victorians in politicized terms, not without definite repercussions for the state of religion in the land. On the other side of the question, the appeal to the Caroline divines and beyond them to antiquity became the particular badge of the Tractarians, who were intent on fostering a "new Reformation" in the State Church. Various historical projects, for example, the Library of the Fathers of the Holy Catholic Church (St. Bartholomew's Day, 1838 to 1885), begun under the joint editorship of John Henry Newman, John Keble, and Edward Bouverie Pusey, provided an enduring contribution to theological scholarship. At times uncritical and unhistorical in their use of the past,[8] the Tractarians sought to defend a particular historical view, contributing to the general appeal to history. Although Newman in 1844 admonished himself in the front of the preliminary notebooks for his *Essay on Development*, "Write it historically, not argumentatively," the use of history by him and others was inherently and by necessity polemical.[9]

As religiously minded people in the Victorian era looked for the bases of belief and religious authority, concerned with certainty and security, an anachronistic view and portrayal of the Ancient Church played an important role. Even as tastes changed through this period, readers looked for no mere costume dramas, but for the type of tales of religious introspection and confession they were enjoying in other "theological romances" and even "boilers down."[10] On the other hand, this return to the Early Church was mutually understood as an attempt to judge, respectively, the Roman and Reformation churches against the purity of the ancient and undivided Christian community: "Our appeal was to antiquity—to the doctrine which the Fathers and Councils and Church universal had taught from the creeds."[11] Such historical appeals were sometimes viewed by Evangelicals as an ignominious betrayal of Protestant principles. Liberal churchmen considered them irrelevant to the pressing social and religious needs of the nineteenth century.

These novels, however, cannot be viewed merely as tendentious history or sentimental expressions of piety. Although many of them are both, they are also important glosses on the diverse theological and historical books of their authors, on the popular and critical views of religious issues, on the hagiographical style and archaeological interests of the nineteenth century, and on the spirituality of the age. In terms of what peculiar insights they give into this age generally, they provide fresh evidence for the view that Newman's departure from the Anglican church in 1845 was only a false ending to the Oxford Movement. What had begun as a defense of the high Anglican doctrine of the Church vis-à-vis its subjection to the parliamentary State took on new colors in a continuing theological and ecclesiastical effort to develop the Anglo-Catholic understanding of the English Church. That understanding, shaped by confrontation with an intellectually combative Roman Catholicism and renewed hierarchy in England and by party debate within the Anglican Church, continued to turn to antiquity for justification, just as did the opponents of both groups. That historical appeal, satirized by Newman in the alleged titles of books appropriate for an Anglo-Catholic library—"Lays of the Apostles," "The English Church Older Than the Roman," and "Anglicanism of the Early Martyrs"—developed and sharpened after 1845.[12] This study examines those ecclesiastical motivations which have been incompletely explained or ignored in purely literary studies and will treat a variety of little known Anglican and Roman Catholic authors. Because the Non-Conformists stressed Scripture alone, their spokesmen were not conspicuously involved in the development of literary treatments of the Subapostolic age, although a few will be mentioned in passing.

In particular, the novels provide valuable information not immediately identifiable in the other theological and historical works of the authors. They show the angle, sometimes direct, more often oblique, at which Victorians pursued the major religious questions of the day through crisis and calm. One ready example is the Gorham case (1848–50), which is not so important for an understanding of Victorian belief about baptismal regeneration in infants, the doctrinal point that initiated the dispute, but is essential for understanding the Erastian relationship of State and Established Church, whether bishops or Parliament should decide which doctrines must be affirmed by a duly ordained priest in the Church of England. The dynamics of the claim to apostolic, independent spiritual authority that occupied a variety of church bodies in Britain and the Continent during this period appears in the novels in terms of the doctrines, ritual, and polity of the Christian Church confronting the Roman Empire and the emerging barbarian nations. The rival religions to Christianity in that empire, pagan cults, Hellenistic philosophy, and proselytizing Judaism are transmogrified in the novels from the secularism, philosophical humanism, and Jewish/Zionist questions of the day. The contemporary Victorian debate over asceticism, ritualism, and biblical-historical criticism is articulated afresh with an appeal to antiquity. And just as Edward Gibbon and the Enlightenment had largely deeschatologized the Christian message, so the novels reflect in a unique way the nineteenth century's reeschatologizing of that gospel, raising new perspectives on the questions of prophecy, revelation, miracles, and martyrdoms by using a variety of literary skills to introduce apocalyptic themes and images into Victorian religious discourse. Perhaps most important, the novels document a historic shift in the consciousness of Christian believers facing the growing secularism and humanistic challenge to orthodoxy; the appeal to the ancient apologetics of a minority church is seen as a direct parallel to the Victorian condition. The Early Church of the Fathers, then, addresses Christians across the millennia with a new immediacy. Like the Victorians themselves, we must now turn to the Fathers in order to examine the varied methods and complex motives that pressed the churchly authors to re-create the

Early Church in novels. Why, apart from treatments in sermons, tracts, and theological treatises, were the authors compelled to portray the Church of the Fathers in this genre? What gains and losses did this strategy engender? To answer these questions it will be necessary to survey briefly the positions of Victorian proponents and opponents of an appeal to antiquity and then comment on possible reasons why the novel was chosen as a suitable vehicle for ecclesiastical programs and propaganda.

THE APPEAL TO ANTIQUITY

The appeal to antiquity, formulated during the Victorian religious debate, can be mapped in two distinct ways. First, one can catalogue the tremendously important discoveries of new texts, which provided fresh information about the past. The discovery in 1875 of the *Didache*, rich in detailed instructions for the life and liturgy of an Early Christian community, is one prime example. The information from such discoveries, however, did not always enter into the novels. An extensive bibliography could also be done showing the new editions and translations made available to the informed Victorian public. For this learned circle the Church of the Fathers as a concept changed significantly between 1845 and 1875. The second way to penetrate into this area is to trace the shifting meanings that contemporary writers applied to such key terms as *the Primitive Church, the Apostolic Church,* and *the Church of the Fathers.* What this study will refer to generally as Early Christianity was referred to by Victorian writers in several ways, undergoing redefinition throughout the period. There is, moreover, a pronounced oscillation in their use of such language. Whereas High Church novelists used the *Ancient Church, Primitive Church,* and *Church of the Fathers* interchangeably—as did Roman Catholic writers, who also employed the term *Patrology* almost exclusively—Evangelicals and the more liberal Broad Churchmen had long adopted the vocabulary and distinctions used on the Continent in Protestant circles. In referring to the Primitive Church, what German theologians called the "Urkirche," the Evangelical and Broad Church novelists meant the Christian Church up to the close of the New Testament Canon. The place of the second-century Apologists, such as Justin Martyr and Irenaeus, is hard to define without the modern understanding of strata in Scripture, even strata in the strata shown by form criticism and redaction criticism. Broad Churchmen, however, were more willing than their Evangelical colleagues to argue for the continued inspiration of the Apologists. The High Church inclusiveness in terminology was part of a doctrinal stance in regard to the apostolicity of the entire epoch of the Early Church; Evangelicals and Broad Churchmen demonstrated by their exclusive distinctions their leaning toward Scripture alone and their opposition to Anglo-Catholic beliefs.

A striking feature of the Oxford Movement, a feature commented on in studies and interpretations of the era, was its appeal to the Fathers, a bipartite appeal immediately to the seventeenth-century Caroline divines and mediately through them to the Fathers of the Primitive Church.[13] They were by no means the first or sole advocates of such an appeal. Thomas Chalmers, the leader of the Great Disruption in Scotland (1843), argued from similar authorities in *On Respect Due to Antiquity* as his basis for the church's independence from Erastian programs, which placed the church in the control of the State. The spiritual heirs of the Scottish Non-Jurors, the Hutchinsonians, and later the Hackney Phalanx, all historic opponents to state control, were the fathers of the Tractarians in such appeals. Even the rationalist prime minister Lord Melbourne (1779–1848) dabbled in patristic literature as a hobby. With an earnest intensity characteristic of the age, the thought of the Fathers was mined to answer the burning new questions of the day, questions on the best form of church government, on the nature of prophecy and revelation, and on the nature and function of Christ. Any investigation of the sort presented here should remind the reader of how much still remains to be known about the Victorian use of the Fathers in terms of sources and texts available, methods of interpretation, and theological utility as they conceived it.

Using an inverted form of the canon found in the *Commonitory* of Vincent of Lerins (ca. 434), "quod semper, quod ubique, quod ab omnibus" [what is believed always, everywhere, and by all],[14] as the criteria for what constituted orthodox tradition, the Tractarians attempted to make the English branch of the Catholic Church a *via media* between what they regarded as Protestant neglect of tradition and Roman Catholic innovations. Another signal contribution of the Tractarians in this regard was the extensive publication of extracts of the Fathers, *catenae* of quotations addressing controverted doctrinal points, and the larger enterprise of patristic translations, The Library of the Fathers, continued under the editorship of Dr. Pusey and Charles Marriott after Newman's departure. The Library constituted the first comprehensive corpus of patristic texts in English translation.[15] A wide audience could thus read the Fathers for themselves and test the doctrines and practices contained therein.

What were the Victorians finding when they did look into the storehouse of antiquity? First of all, they thought they could without difficulty grasp the "mind and purpose of the old Fathers" and from this clear perspective establish the measure by which to judge or vindicate controverted theological points in the present age. Of equal importance, they found that the Fathers confirmed the Articles, liturgy, and canons of the Anglican Church in terms of its "Antiquity, Catholicity, and Universality." While the Church of England diverged from this ancient model on some points, felt by the investigators to be therefore external and not of the *esse*, the vital essence, of the church, they found the Fathers and the Church of England speaking with one voice on the continuity of received truth in Scripture, protected and maintained by the apostolic succession of bishops, dubbed the "historic episcopate" later in the century.

Based on the patristic sources, the Tractarians, Evangelicals, and Broad Churchmen, with varying degrees of emphasis, accepted one canon of Scripture, two testaments of equal authority and plenary inspiration, three creeds (the Apostles', Nicene, and Athanasian), and four Ecumenical Councils (Nicaea, Constantinople, Ephesus, and Chalcedon). To this array Tractarians added emphasis on five centuries of purity, the *consensus quinquesaecularis* down to the mission of Augustine of Canterbury in 597, six Ecumenical Councils "allowed and received" (Constantinople II and III were added to the earlier list), seven ecclesiastical centuries "of great authority and credit," and eleven centuries of Christian unity between East and West.

Richard Hooker's (ca. 1554–1600) understanding of the intimate relationship of Scripture, reason, and tradition was a convenient shorthand for these Victorians sorting out the respective claims of Fathers and Reformers. The Fathers were honored because they came in time near the composition of Scripture, demonstrated the mind of that Scripture, and received uncorrupted the apostolic traditions. Although by the 1850s Anglicans recognized the divergence in local traditions of the historic pentarchy, the five ancient patriarchates, an awareness brought by research into and contact with the Eastern Orthodox churches, they still tended to homogenize their view of the several centers of early Christianity under the rubric *the undivided Church*. Along with the Vincentian canon and the Ecumenical Councils, the consensus of the Fathers was seen as a representative guide but not an infallible one. In contrast to the company of the apostles, there was no parity of authority among respective Fathers. Moderate Churchmen picked up and read Augustine with more impact than when they might chance to read Ephraem the Syrian. Even the language of orthodox Fathers was thought to present dangers in the Victorian age, since it could be misconstrued to encompass Roman "corruptions." Pusey's university sermon (14 May 1843) on the "Real Objective Presence of Christ in the Eucharist," written chiefly in the language of the Fathers—in particular Cyril of Jerusalem and John Chrysostom—was condemned by university authorities and Pusey was suspended from preaching for two years.

The position of the Council of Trent (1545–63), which Anglicans understood to set up the Fathers as an authoritative source independent of Scripture, was rejected. Nor were the Fathers to be viewed as providing an exact pattern of church life and worship binding for all time. Even the old High Church liturgiologists had freely deviated from ancient usages to create their own patterns of celebration. The Fathers were considered a positive force in shaping the English Reformation but were not a binding theological authority. This attitude was vividly expressed in the decision of Stephen Lushington, Dean of Arches, the magistrate in the case of Rowland Williams under prosecution for his allegedly heterodox article regarding biblical criticism in *Essays and Reviews* (1860). The earlier ecclesiastical censure was nullified, since the court could make a determination only on the basis of the legal formularies of the Establishment, and not on the basis of Scripture, the doctrines of the Ancient Church, or the consensus of divines.[16] For decades controversialists had asked whether the Anglican Church could be said to possess the Christian faith as transmitted by the Fathers. In 1846 T. W. Allies, a Tractarian, had resolved the question in the affirmative in his work *The Church of England Cleared from the Charge of Schism*, and then turned dramatically volte-face in 1850. The final legal decisions over the Gorham case (1848–50), involving the linked questions of baptismal regeneration and Erastianism; the Denison case (1856–58), concerning eucharistic worship and belief in a real presence; and the turmoil over *Essays and Reviews* (1860–62), involving the new criticism, forced a number of Anglicans to accept Newman's verdict that the via media and its continuity with the Church of the Fathers was only a "paper system," at best a mere creature of the State. They were forced to this extreme because it seemed to them that the courts had systematically excluded the Fathers as a basis for Anglican belief; and it was believed by some that Church authorities in condemning the Tractarians had inadvertently condemned the Fathers. Other Anglicans, however, continued to implement changes based on patristic models that had not been immediately conceptualized or systematized into a theology of Anglo-Catholicism of the type seen later in Charles Gore (1853–1932), Henry Scott Holland (1847–1918), Darwell Stone (1859–1941), and Charles Lindley Wood—Viscount Halifax (1839–1934).

Froude, Keble, and Pusey

The Tractarians and their early sympathizers were far from unanimous about the appeal to the consensus of Anglican divines and the Early Church. Samuel Wilberforce, the bishop of Oxford (1845–69) and termed by some "the High Church incarnate," agreed for a time with the Tractarians and admitted the validity of such an appeal to the Caroline divines and the initial three centuries of the Christian era, before cautiously reconsidering.[17]

R. Hurrell Froude (1803–36), the Fellow of Oriel who brought Newman and John Keble to understand each other and sealed their mutual friendship, was, according to Frederic Rogers, the one who first christened the members of the movement "Apostolicals." Along with another Oriel Fellow, John Davison, Froude sought from the early Fathers a general perspective as well as specific vindication of his own theological ideas. In 1827 he found support for his affirmation of celibacy in the works of Ignatius of Antioch; the Fathers were seen, then, as supportive and regulative insofar as they confirmed the present religious outlook of the inquirer.[18] Although he encouraged Newman's own patristic research, Froude diverged on the prominence of the role to be played by the Church of the Fathers. "[H]e was," says Newman, "powerfully drawn to the Medieval Church, but not to the Primitive."[19]

John Keble (1792–1866), whose Assize Sermon of 1833 defending the "successors of the Apostles" in the suppressed Irish bishoprics is credited with launching the Oxford Movement, believed the Anglican Church was the one true representative in England of the whole Church, Catholic and Apostolic; it was not an impersonal institution but "one's own Nursing Mother and one-third of Christendom." On the other hand, since he admitted the broken nature of that Catholic identity, it is sometimes easy to caricature Keble's position as a defense of "the one true parish." His Assize Sermon was not, however, merely an attack on the "National Apostasy" resulting from or causing the government's suppression of redundant dioceses in Ireland. It was a declaration of the "external security" served by the apostolic succession, safeguarding an unwavering communion with the Church of the Apostles and preventing Roman "novelties" (e.g., the doctrine of transubstantiation) and Protestant infidelity, which were both due to excessive "rationalism."[20] After 1827 enforced leisure permitted him to study the early Fathers, such as Cyprian, and allusions to these authors appeared in his momentously best-selling collection of verses, _The Christian Year_ (1827).[21] That verse, likened by some critics to Wordsworth rewritten for pious ladies, and his Latin lectures as professor of poetry at Oxford (1831–41) point out the relationship between Romantic epistemology and Keble's sometimes quirky brand of Tractarian sacramentalism.

The theory of language and symbol contained in the works of Bishop Butler and William Wordsworth (a historical and hereditary usage transmitted in analogy, metaphor, and symbol, compared to the ahistoric, analytic use of language in Bacon and Hobbes) was for Keble preparation for a reclamation of the symbolic mode of thought of the Fathers, especially the Alexandrians.[22] Along with his editorship of The Library of the Fathers, Keble also published a translation of Irenaeus' _Against Heresies_ (1872). Early on he was requested to do the volume on Bede in the Lives of the English Saints.[23] Keble was, of course, more actively engaged in the new edition of Richard Hooker, praising the judicious Elizabethan divine who withdrew from Thomas Cranmer's position and drew near William Laud: through that latter worthy archbishop, Providence, by overruling the _sola scriptura_ excesses of the Reformation, left the way open to a restoration of ante-Nicene antiquity.[24] Apostolic succession, the sacrificial nature of the Eucharist, and the triune God were doctrines not found systematically manifest in Scripture, but nonetheless binding on the faithful. In the summer of 1836 Keble preached his famous sermon at Winchester Cathedral "Primitive Tradition Recognized in Holy Scripture." He declared that the tradition of the Fathers was parallel to, and not merely derivative from, Scripture. It was the Fathers who provided the context of the composition and reception of those writings; "the Scriptures themselves," he stated, "do homage to the tradition of the Apostles."[25] For Keble that tradition was complete and authoritative from primitive times. He followed the understanding of both the Magdeburg *Centuries* and the *Annales*: truth is immutable; it has not, indeed cannot, improve, evolve, change, or develop. The modern age only rediscovers that original deposit of faith. He criticized Robert Isaac Wilberforce in 1850 for adopting the "abstract," "metaphysical," and "legal" theory of development of Newman "instead of clinging to Scripture and to primitive antiquity."[26] When Keble finally did read Newman's *Essay on Development* for himself in 1863, his horror was confirmed: "It must come to development after all . . . to a pretty theory instead of Catholic Tradition."[27] The vicar of Hursley had reworked Newman's charge that the via media was not real but only a "paper system" into what, for Keble, was a telling argument against Newman.

The Library of the Fathers remains a monument, *aere perennius*, to the financial sacrifice as well as to the scholarly care of Edward Bouverie Pusey (1800–82), the first "name" to be joined to the Tracts, since he was then professor of Hebrew at Oxford (1828–82). For many the name of Pusey itself meant antiquity, as Keble explained to Bishop Wilberforce in 1851.[28] The Fathers illuminated for Pusey correct theological opinion but were not themselves authoritative. In Tract 18, "Thoughts on the Benefits of the System of Fasting, Enjoined by Our Church" (1833), Pusey viewed the 1549 Edwardian Prayer Book as a visible link uniting the English Church with "the Primitive Catholic Church." Like the Fathers, the Prayer Book had no independent authority but transmitted faith and devotions to the contemporary Church. This connection between the Fathers and the formularies and authorized texts of the English Church is reiterated in Pusey's reason for choosing selections from the Fathers to be read by the Anglican Sisterhood revived under his direction. The Fathers are those "whom our Homilies so praise."[29] On this point Pusey and most of the other Tractarians parted ways. To Pusey, as to the Reverend Sir George Prevost among others, the Reformation was a true reform, repudiating Roman corruption and recalling the purity of the Primitive Church. Pusey could with equanimity offer to subscribe to the Martyrs' Memorial (1838–41) to the sixteenth-century bishops Cranmer, Latimer, and Ridley, looked upon by most as a scheme to exalt the Reformation and deliberately embarrass the Tractarians; he showed none of Froude's shuddering contempt for the Reformers. As he told Newman: "We owe our peculiar position as adherents of primitive antiquity to them."[30] There were certain elements Pusey unearthed in the fervid course of his "high-pitched devoted patristicism," such as the prayers of ancient martyrs to and for the dead, that ran counter to Reformation principles and that shocked his Anglican contemporaries.[31] But late in the century, especially as he mulled over the dangerous principles he detected in the First Vatican Council decrees, Pusey lamented the "lull" in theological debate and the general neglect of the Fathers by "the young clergy so ignorant of antiquity as not to know the difficulty."[32] When the vast publishing project of the Library of the Fathers reached its conclusion, fewer people were bothering to read the Fathers provided for them.

NEWMAN AND THE ROMAN CATHOLICS

When Ignaz Döllinger (1799–1890), the scholarly Roman Catholic opponent of Ultramontanism, described John Henry Newman (1801–90) as the greatest living authority on the first three centuries of the Christian era, it was in response to the latter's *Essay on Development* and the seventeen years of patristic research behind it, research that exploded the unhistorical notions of the reactionary Catholic Ultramontanists.[33] Since boyhood Newman had been fascinated with the Fathers; at the time of his conversion in 1816, a conversion to Evangelical faith, a copy of Joseph Milner's five-volume *History of the Church of Christ* (1794–1819) had delighted him with extensive extracts from Augustine, Ambrose, and others.[34] At the same time, a reading of Thomas Newton's *Dissertations on the Prophecies* (1754) convinced him that the pope was the predicted Antichrist. Renewing his interest in these sources in the late 1820s, he started to read chronologically, beginning with Ignatius and Justin

Martyr. But as he later observed, he approached them the wrong way: "I had read them simply on Protestant ideas, analyzed and catalogued them on Protestant principles of division, and hunted for Protestant doctrines and usages in them." The one vivid impression he kept from that initial foray into the dense patristic literature had profound meaning for contemporary ecclesiological questions: the divine institution of the episcopate.

In 1831, requested by Hugh Rose, the High Church rector of Hadleigh, to write on the early Councils, Newman concentrated on Nicaea, the beginning of a "drama in three acts."[35] The result was published in 1833 as *The Arians of the Fourth Century*. That same year, after the Assize Sermon, he likened John Keble confronting the power of the State to Ambrose opposing the emperor Theodosius. This dramatic use of "realized" analogy, where likeness becomes identity, simile becomes symbol, was Newman's distinctive style in treating the Fathers. No other Anglican was startled awake from haunted dreams to see in his own looking glass the grim visage of an Arian or Monophysite.[36] What had startled Newman, he later claimed, was the aggressive Catholic apologetics of Nicholas Wiseman, beginning in 1836 and culminating in an article in the *Dublin Review*, "Anglican Claims to Apostolical Succession" (1839), which contained the magical phrase of Augustine, "securus judicat orbis terrarum." To Newman this appeared as a simpler method of deciding ecclesiastical questions, but he responded publicly to Wiseman that Augustine's principle was not a rigorous regulation without damaging exceptions. The only sure guide for the English Church, Newman decided, was its own traditional via media in adhering to Scripture and Christian antiquity alone. After his conversion he included a contradictory note in the revised edition (1877, 1883) of his work the *Via Media* that "history and patristical writings do not absolutely decide the truth and falsehood of all important theological propositions, any more than Scripture decides it . . . all that we can say is that history and the Fathers look in one determinate direction. The definition of the Church is commonly needed to supply the defects of logic."[37]

By 1840 Newman saw his task as one of adversary to Protestants who opposed the Church of the Fathers to the Apostolic Church or to those who said the Apostolic system was irretrievably lost. At the same time, since the Anglican Church was a branch of the one Catholic Church, it was necessary to demonstrate that its formularies could be interpreted according to the doctrine and practice of the Catholic Church since antiquity. He took it for granted that because the Church was founded by Christ, there never was a time since antiquity when it was not. "The Catholic Fathers and Ancient Bishops" had been lauded by the formulators of the Thirty-Nine Articles, so that formulary had to be at least "patient" of Catholic understanding. The explosive Tract XC resulted. The document and its hostile reception launched Newman and his disciples Romeward. Because the Anglican episcopate condemned the tract and seemingly its Catholic understanding of antiquity, Newman concluded that they had disinherited the English Church from the Early Church and broken the apostolic bond of antiquity, the rule of inward holiness and divine faith that had for so long been "miraculously preserved." Newman later unctuously criticized his Anglo-Catholic colleagues as "Patristico-Protestants" who had to use "private judgment" (the name at which every High Church knee quaked) in regard to the Fathers, since there was no formal ecclesial approbation by their bishops.[38]

In order to lay the ghost of his turmoil and to account for the apparent variations in the history of Christian dogma, during his retirement at Littlemore he began work on the *Essay on Development* (1845). He concluded that Protestantism was not historic Christianity, but the historical evidence was too fragmentary to identify it positively with Roman Catholicism. Using seven rigorous "tests" that he later amended to "notes," he concluded, "Primitive Christian history could only be understood in the light of later Christian history. . . . isolated, the [early] expressions formed no system and pointed no where."[39] But since Christ founded an unfailing Divine Society, there must exist a visible Church in the nineteenth century that was historically the successor of the Church of the Fathers. That had to be the Church of Rome. Moving from intimations to accumulated probabilities to certainty, a process he later codified in his *Grammar of Assent* (1870), Newman made his leap of faith from this platform. It should be noted in passing that this process is a theological movement and not a strictly historical one. That is confirmed in the *Essay on Development* (chap. 2, sec. 3:5) by the introduction of those divine twins Ambrose and Athanasius, who are marvelously resuscitated to pass judgment hypothetically on the Victorian Church. Both were properly orthodox and both had bearded the State for interfering in ecclesiastical matters. Newman undoubtedly chose them as *examples* of the living "mind" of the Church; they would recognize not Canterbury but Rome as the living Catholic system. Newman substituted this "mind" for the Anglican use of the canon of Vincent of Lerins.

On the Continent, Roman Catholics were also deeply engaged in the study of the Fathers and Christian antiquities as part of a widespread Catholic Revival. The textual work of J.-P. Migne's *Patrologia* of Latin (1844–55) and Greek (1857–66) Fathers—built on and continuing the work of the Maurists Mabillon, Martène, and Ruinart and the archaeological discoveries and publications of J. B. DeRossi (1822–94), including the famed excavation of the catacomb of St. Callistus in 1852—provided the raw material for generations of other scholars.[40] Both Catholics and Protestants could warmly applaud Ignaz Döllinger's encyclopedic survey of the world of antiquity, his *Vestibule of Christianity*, which Newman had had translated at the Oratory, and his conservative study *The First Age of Christianity and the Church* (1860).[41] On the other hand, the Fathers of the Church were of particular usefulness in the confessional apologetics of this revived Continental Catholicism. Albert DeBroglie composed his painstaking history, *The Church and the Empire in the Fourth Century* (1856–66), because contemporary France required conversion, he thought, like the Roman Empire.[42] And François Auguste, vicomte de Chateaubriand (1768–1848), the grand Romantic author and statesman, used the literary and architectural remains of antiquity to "prove" the incompatibility of Protestantism with Primitive Christianity.[43]

The most famous name in this apologetic endeavor was, of course, Johann Adam Möhler (1796–1838), whose reading of the Fathers had been a personal revelation of an organic, spontaneous Christianity. Möhler made a mystical identification of contemporary believers and the Fathers and saw Enlightenment Deism as Arianism and Romantic Pantheism as Sabellianism.[44] He wrote in 1825, "He who truly lives in the Church will also live in the first age of the Church and understand it; and he who does not live in the present Church will not live in the old and will not understand it, for they are the same."[45] In his *Symbolik* (1832) he aimed to prove that Protestantism was unfaithful to primitive Christianity. Although Newman cites Möhler in the *Essay on Development* (introduction, sec. 21) as a distinguished example of the use of the Fathers in controversial works, it seems unlikely that Newman read much of the Tübingen scholar during his Anglican career.[46] Newman's Romanizing disciples, W. G. Ward and Frederic Oakeley, whom Tom Mozley likened to the pugilistic Castor and Pollux, read the Romantic *Einheit* and dogmatic *Symbolik* with enthusiasm, finding there the notion that the only true test of Catholic doctrine was the moral experience to be had living that teaching.[47] It was this idea of a living and authoritative Church, in which the past was absorbed, perhaps consumed, by the present, that set off the understanding of dogma and ecclesiology of Continental Roman Catholicism from the movement in England. W. G. Ward's inflammatory *Ideal of a Christian Church* (1844) was as far from William Palmer's *Treatise on the Church* (1838) as the nineteenth century was from the fourth.

THE ARNOLDS, TAYLOR, SAVILLE

Of course not everyone was as sanguine as the Tractarians about the usefulness of patristic texts and study. Thomas Gaisford, dean of Christchurch and a director of the Oxford University Press, called the volumes of the Fathers in the House Library "sad and rubbish."[48] Benjamin Jowett (1817–93), master of Balliol and Broad Church Platonist, thought Voltaire had contributed more than all the Fathers. In 1839 Mark Pattison, who later contributed with Jowett to *Essays and Reviews*, lamented the time he squandered on "degenerate and semi-barbarous Christian writers of the Fourth Century."[49] The bitterness in Pattison's observation betrays the intensity of emotions involved in his own spiritual movement from Newmanism to skepticism, a movement critics of the Tracts claimed was inevitable. Even the publication of patristic texts, albeit with forceful, even tendentious notes, elicited sharp responses. The foundation of the Parker Society in 1844, named for the staunchly Protestant Matthew Parker (1504–75), archbishop of Canterbury, was with the Martyrs' Memorial a move to set the Reformers against the Fathers. Perhaps a desire to avoid such theological entanglements, as well as a scholarly bias, prompted the Oxford Press to print only Latin and Greek texts, but no English translations, of the Fathers.[50]

Other opponents saw this appeal as a "limited historicism," which seemed to be "a fear of development as a stubborn refusal to consider different opinions."[51] To these critics the appeal to the Fathers appeared as an inability to address or cope with the modern age, just as surely as the revived cult of asceticism was merely a mask for morbid hatred of the body and life, destroying the family and the State. Charles Kingsley satirized the archaicizing influence of the Tractarians in the fictional character Lord Vieuxbois, who states, "I do not think that we have any right in the nineteenth century to contest an opinion which the fathers of the Church gave in the fourth."[52] In such a case liberal churchmen believed that backward-glancing Victorian Christianity would become only a dead letter.

The Tractarian quest *ad fontes* enlisted the interest, if not always the allegiance, of numerous thoughtful enquirers into religious topics. Such immersion in the sources had profound effects, since it forced the investigators to "reflect on the psychology of historians and chroniclers; . . . exposed mere hagiography and pious tradition; . . . increased the student's sensitiveness to historic evidence and its presentation."[53] Primitive Christianity could appear to such minds as so much chaos as well as cosmos, horror as well as holiness. George Eliot (1819–80)—who among numerous accomplishments translated David Strauss's *Das Leben Jesu* (1846) and wrote a historical novel, *Romola* (in *Cornhill*, 1862–63) about Savonarola's Florence—attempted to construct, based on a linear theory of history, a chart of Early Church history with dates and names. Her research proved personally unedifying and undercut for her the notion of the absolute truth of Christianity.[54] For Eliot, as for other Victorians, once the received sense of the unity and coherence of the Early Church was disturbed, all ground of authority and truthfulness fell away. The supposed purity of the Early Church was taken quite literally; when evidence contradicted it they threw off the entire system. Newman had recognized the danger inherent in such total immersion in the sources: "To imbibe into the intellect the ancient Church as a fact, is either to be a Catholic or an infidel."[55] Two works by Isaac Taylor, *Natural History of Enthusiasm* (1829), a rationalistic critique of Evangelicalism continued in his book *Fanaticism* (1833), and *Ancient Christianity and the Doctrines of the Oxford Tracts for the Times* (1839–40), a progressively more shrill reply to the Puseyites, inadvertently helped Eliot slip the restraints of orthodoxy.[56] The doubts Taylor raised in her mind about the security of using the Fathers as a moral or doctrinal guide were pushed by Eliot back to the apostles. Were they any safer? That question of authority pressed through Fathers to Scripture and the apostles to Jesus himself is characteristic of the age, especially after the 1860s and the rise of biblical criticism.

Not all Anglicans were ready or willing to throw out the Fathers because of reputed Puseyite excesses or inapplicability of patristic doctrine to the present age. Thomas Arnold (1795–1842), for one, believed that while the Primitive Church, even less the post-Nicene Church, had little special authority in current circumstances, it still played a valuable role in the preservation of Christianity.[57] There were, he concluded in his *Fragment on the Church* (published 1844), three, perhaps overlapping, phases in Church history: (1) the first and perfect state of purity when institutions were subordinate to the Spirit; (2) an intermediate phase when forms, such as Councils and Creeds (Arnold himself rejected the Athanasian Creed), were provisionally necessary to preserve the initial Spirit; and (3) ossification of these temporary forms. But in his own day, at least following 1830, the Spirit of Christianity was self-evident, he believed, and older forms must be discarded as unnecessary. His descendants took opposing sides in relation to the Church of the Fathers. Tom Junior (1823–1900), who converted back and forth between Anglicanism and Roman Catholicism, was attracted by the stories of the martyrs of Lyons and the heroic deaths of Ignatius and Polycarp; he saw the "idea" of the Church as a historical fact in the lives of ordinary people being schooled in holiness. Tom's eldest daughter, Mary—Mrs. Humphry Ward (1851–1920), the author of the successful novel of religious crisis *Robert Elsmere* (1888)—was, much like Eliot, turned against traditional Christianity on historical grounds, based on her own systematic and intense reading of fourth- and fifth-century authors in the course of her research on Visigothic Spain.[58]

Isaac Taylor (1787–1865), a former Dissenter regarded by some contemporaries as the most important English lay theologian since Samuel Taylor Coleridge and credited with coining the English term *patristic,* had become convinced of the corruptions of the Primitive Church after reading the graphic accounts in the works of Sulpicius Severus, the fifth-century biographer of Martin of Tours.[59] In *Ancient Christianity and the Doctrines of the Oxford Tracts for the Times* (originally published 1838–40) Taylor assembled his private reading to oppose the Tracts in general and Newman in particular with "the present UNITY, purity, and spiritual

vitality of protestant christendom," embodied in the English Church.[60]
He also attacked "the Paparchy," the "'bible alone' outcry," and latitudi-
narian infidelity (which was the reason in 1863 he berated John William
Colenso, bishop of Natal, for his revolutionary critical approach to the
Pentateuch). The Church of England and the Fathers themselves hold
forth the sole authority of the canon of Scripture (the "WRITTEN CA-
NONICAL REVELATION," as Taylor impressed on his audience, 2:151).
This was the only sure guide, since "preposterous errors and sad delin-
quencies" had crept into both the Early Church and the present one, errors to be expunged by "our *modern* good sense." The Tractarians, he
felt, had sought "GENUINE APOSTOLIC TRADITIONS," on the basis of the
"Scanty (not to say vapid) writings" of the Subapostolic age, and in place
of "Catholic truth," embraced "every element of papal tyranny, cruelty,
profligacy, and spiritual apostasy" (2:143, 1:426). The Newmanites had
begun "not indeed to *cleanse* the stables of monkish pietism, but to deluge
the land with their filth" (1:64). The result was a reexcrescence of
"Monkery and Miracle." The "ascetic institute of the nicene Church"
and the "ghostly tyranny of unmarried priests," set against the simple idea
of the Church in the Sermon on the Mount, were related to a disordered
social condition. Taylor amplified Thomas Arnold's position that such
visible and arbitrary distinctions among Christians were necessarily fatal
to piety and morals. Miracles were directly linked to Monkery, since a
taste for the marvelous was characteristic of the ascetic life. Jerome, the
prime mover in such corruption, is seen as the cause of more human mis-
ery than the hordes of Tamerlane (1:346). Taylor ominously indicates
that miracles and the cult of saints and martyrs "were employed as the
means of COAXING THE MOB TO SUPPORT THE CHURCH IN OPPRESSING
THE SEVERAL BODIES OF SEPARATISTS" (2:376). Such saint worship
("demolatry"), which is conducive to unbounded credulity or universal
skepticism, is carried over into the modern age in the "gaudy polytheism" observed by every "rightminded traveller" in Spain, Italy, and Ireland (2:376). Taking the age of Pope Gregory the Great as the undisputed *terminus ad quem* of accumulated corruption and superstition,
Taylor divides Church history into stages—from Gregory to the Nicene
Age, the Nicene Age to Cyprian, and Cyprian to the Apostolic Age—
positing on the basis of "historical *probability*, a proportionate corruption" for the various stages. Opposed to this progressive idolatry and

degeneracy is the patriarchal/Mosaic/prophetic witness of the Protestant ministry. Whereas the Tractarians attempt to Judaize the Church in external practices and forms, the Protestant clergy are the true continuators of the Aaronic hierarchy, "modestly observant of its subordinate place in the social system."[61] Scripture, again, is the proof of this in its apocalyptic predictions, sustaining the true Aaronic structures and denouncing Roman usurpations and political intrigues. Taylor was an important and influential early critic of the Tractarians, respected as an authority because of his knowledge of patristic sources.[62] Questions and objections he raised were used by various authors later in the century who shared his indignation, if not his scholarship.

An example of that is found in Bourchier Wrey Saville (1817–88), the Evangelical rector of Shillingford Exeter, who composed his work *The Primitive and Catholic Faith* (1875) in response to both Ritualism and Vaticanism. He writes: "The chief object of this present work is to show the resemblance between the doctrines of the Reformed Church of England, as interpreted by the 'Evangelical' party, and those held and taught by the Primitive Church in the earliest and purest days of her existence; as well as to urge upon all the duty of cultivating a closer communion with other Protestant Churches who hold the same faith with ourselves, though not under Episcopal government."[63] That primitive faith is summarized in a quotation from Cyril of Alexandria: "Evangelical teaching is grace by faith; justification in Christ; and sanctification through the power of the Holy Ghost" (x, 10). The pan-Protestantism this faith nourishes is "the Gospel of the grace of God" described in Ephesians, while the Ritualistic preach "another Gospel" described in Galatians. The Vatican Council (1869–70) was manifestly predicted by the Holy Ghost as Babylon the Great, the Mother of Harlots. Papists unable to recognize the Pope as Antichrist similarly would not have recognized Christ as the Messiah; Saville cites Christopher Wordsworth, the conservative bishop of Lincoln (1869–85), as the authority that the prophecies linking the bishop of Rome to Apocalyptic Babylon were as true as the Old Testament predictions of the Messiah fulfilled in Jesus.[64] Saville's emphasis is always on apocalyptic texts and evidence. Likening the Ritualists themselves to the forty assassins pursuing Paul (Acts 23:21), Saville construes Ritualism as an unacceptable return to Jewish ordinances. The analogy he uses is that of a weak Peter of Antioch confronting Paul, who was "better taught in the truth of Evangelical religion." Saville spurns any Jewish connections, just as he later did in *Anglo-Israelism and the Great Pyramid* (1880), a rejection of the alleged Jewish origin of the English nation. On the other hand, he supports the Pauline foundation of Christianity in England: *The Introduction of Christianity into Britain: An Argument on the Evidence in Favour of St. Paul Having Visited the Extreme Boundary of the West* (1861). Arthur P. Stanley, the Broad Church dean of Westminster (1864–81), had warned in the same year about attaching too much importance to missionaries before Augustine, but the idea of the apostolic foundation of the ancient British Church as a remedy to Romanism had a wide and continuing appeal. Until the year 600, the British Church enjoyed purity and independence; then Augustine introduced syncretistic practices and demonology (i.e., saint worship) in order to win over the Saxons, as reported by Bede (*Eccl. Hist.* 1.30), thus bringing on the "Egyptian darkness" of the Middle Ages.[65]

The variety of authors and of positions taken on the Church of the Fathers tells a great deal. A large number of clergy and laity of all church parties and those who finally rejected any church affiliation were searching the Fathers, as well as the Scriptures, to justify or condemn contemporary religious movements. Even those who proclaimed "the Bible alone" as the guide to faith and practice were compelled to bolster their position by an appeal to the Early Church. By the 1870s no one could simply ignore the mass of patristic evidence; this was the lasting effect brought by the Oxford Movement's appeal to the Primitive Church.

THE EARLY CHURCH

With such a varied and complex appropriation of the Fathers, constructed over time by a multitude of sermons and other theological works, the question remains why Victorian authors chose the novel to present the Church of the Fathers to their readership. Granted the immense popularity of the novel form during this period, was there something special the religious-historical novelist felt could be accomplished in that form with more facility than in the standard genres of theological discourse? And what, if any, was the theological justification they made of such use of novels?

When Thomas Carlyle and other eminent Victorians isolated the basis of the immense popularity of Sir Walter Scott's Waverley novels, they concluded with the truism that historical novels taught the modern age that the past was filled with "living men." In Christian terms, representatives of various church parties believed that "faith is illustrated more by the life of the character described than by mere theological terms by which it may be expressed."[66] Thus followed the literary galleries of portraits, memorials, and biographies illustrating the spirit and effects of Christianity since antique times. In 1840 Newman published the essays of *The Church of the Fathers* in order to present, as he says, in biographical sketches "the atmosphere, the sentiments, and customs of the Early Church." But these fragments did not prove artistically or theologically satisfying; a longer format, capable of presenting the varied richness of the congeries of atmosphere, sentiments, customs, and beliefs, seen as they were lived and as they affected living agents in history, was necessary. The novel, religious writers found, was particularly suited to that end, since without excessive dryness (or perhaps even objectivity) they could present what they called the "facts" (the opposite of hypotheses and thus "objective") and the "ethos" of the Early Church. A "fact" was a snapshot of antiquity, the essence of "ethos" a moving picture.

The word *ethos,* or at least its freighted meaning, was minted and circulated by the Anglo-Catholics, replacing the term used by older High Churchmen: "the *genius* of Anglicanism." The term connotes for the modern reader, perhaps, the vague notion of Common Prayer piety and the cluttered tea-time atmosphere of John Keble's parsonages. For the Tractarians and Anglo-Catholics it denoted much more. The ethos of the Early Church they hoped to instill was not a mere "servile imitation of the past, but such a reproduction of it as is really new, while it is old."[67] By various means they sought the total "consciousness" of orthodoxy, not merely subscription to orthodox expressions. The modality of that reproduction was to be through holiness and prayer. Tractarians were concerned with the "notes" of the Church not only as "Catholic" and "Apostolic" but also as "Holy," the note left out of the Prayer Book version of the Nicene Creed. They shared this advertised quest for holiness as constitutive of the Church with Evangelicals and Methodists who cherished the classic model of Wesley's "Holiness Club." The publication of martyrs' and saints' lives was to them no mere pious exercise but a practical pattern of moral examples for contemporary imitation. They also helped give historic meaning to the proper understanding of the early creeds, confessions, and Scripture itself. Both R. Hurrell Froude and Thomas Arnold Jr. found this pure ethos of the Early Church exemplified in the character of the second-century Polycarp.[68]

The connection between Newman's Tract XC, demonstrating the Catholic sense of the official formularies of the English Church, and his projected Lives of the English Saints (1844–45), demonstrating the Catholic sense of the spirituality and holiness of the English Church, is direct and formally necessary. Martyrology tales, "spiced with sensationalism," enjoyed along with hagiographical collections an extended vogue. First, martyrs were employed by opposing churchmen as well to demonstrate the horrific effects of the Catholic system; in 1875 John Foxe's sixteenth-century *Book of Martyrs* was published in London in yet another edition and used in the ongoing antipopery campaign. Second, liturgy was a source and expression of this ethos and was painstakingly re-created in the novels. A distinction often made in this regard between the Tract writers and the later Ritualists or Ecclesiologists is hard to maintain. Härdelin and others have convincingly demonstrated the importance of the liturgy to the early Tractarians. They felt that liturgical customs were visible signs of Catholic doctrine, both expressing and preserving that doctrine and its continuity with the Primitive Church's understanding of Scripture, since liturgy is doctrine and Scripture lived out.[69] The historic visibility of the Church and its doctrine is another vital component of ethos. Third, for men such as Frederic Oakeley and W. G. Ward, ethos had an ethical edge; since the religious experience is historical and societal in nature, conscience and its necessary concomitant, a living moral guide, must exist and so constitute the ground of any appeal to authority. They found this in a spiritually independent, authoritatively teaching Church: *ubi auctoritas, ibi ecclesia.* This combination of Romantic feeling and communal conscience—more in harmony, they felt, with the mysteriousness of the living, revealed truth—was opposed by them to the spartan logical reason of the Oxford Noetics and other liberalizing theologians. Fourth, the sense of ethos must be seen in terms of contemporary considerations of propriety. The "reserve in communicating religious knowledge," the *disciplina arcani* of the Early Church, was an idea Tractarians revamped, causing such great misunderstanding. This sense

of reserve was as much revulsion at the enthusiastic methods and interminable, emotional witnessing of new waves of Evangelicalism as anything else. And the notion of ethos constituted an equal revulsion toward
the present supposed worldliness of the Church of England. Figures as
diverse as James Anthony Froude and Richard W. Church viewed with
sad eye the "lazy carriages and fashionable families" of English bishops
and the "'smug parsons,' and pony-carriages for their wives and daughters" against the Tractarian ideal of "holy life, prayer, fasting, the confessional."[70] This multileveled understanding of ethos, then, exemplified
the life of the Church of England and the consequences of the appeal to
antiquity much more articulately than any formal theory of authority.
But even that most formal theory, the Vincentian Canon, was looked
upon basically as a test of that ethos, a "moral or spiritual principle," displayed in the "outward manifestations of a holy community."[71]

This quest for a holy "ethos" that characterized the movement in
general had particular importance for Newman. In 1837 he wrote that he
found a defect in the novels of Jane Austen: "What vile creatures her parsons are! She has not a dream of the high Catholic ἤθοσ."[72] This sense of
ethos as a comprehensive worldview was articulated later when, speaking
of his historical work, he wrote:

> What I should like would be to bring out the ἤθοσ of the Heathen
> from St. Paul's day down to St. Gregory, when under the process, or in
> the sight of the phenomenon, of conversion; what conversion *was* in
> those times, and what the position of a Christian in that world of sin,
> what the sophistries of philosophy viewed as realities influencing men.
> But besides the great difficulty of finding time, I don't think I could do
> it from History. I despair of finding facts enough—as if an imaginary
> tale could alone embody the conclusions to which existing facts *lead*.[73]

While recognizing the incompleteness of any depiction and the need to
rely on the Church as a doctrinal guide, the search for the proper expression of ethos was phrased in his continual personal query "What would
the Fathers have done?"[74] It was his attempt to see what the Fathers *had*
done in analogous situations that turned him to the straight "record of
facts" in his three-volume translation of Claude Fleury's *Ecclesiastical*

History. In a memorable phrase, Newman commented that Fleury "presented a sort of photograph of ecclesiastical history" with a minutely detailed narrative not found in the Church histories of Johann Mosheim (1693–1755), August Neander (1789–1850), Joseph Milner (1744–97), or Henry H. Milman (1791–1868).[75] And although Fleury's presentation "unsettled" him, Newman was personally convinced that holiness was possible in the English Church, apart from the specific Catholic doctrines which it seemed only Rome visibly manifested. Newman saw in the age of the martyrs a visible sign of this demonstration of principles even before the formulation of doctrines. By 1839 in his essay "Prospects of the Anglican Church" he had already moved from the general Tractarian understanding of ethos to the developing *"mind* of the church." "We cannot," he wrote, "if we would, move ourselves literally back into the times of the Fathers: we must in spite of ourselves, be churchmen of our own era, not of any other, were it only for this reason, that we are born in the nineteenth century, not in the fourth."[76] But in Newman's response to Nicholas Wiseman following 1839 he concluded that he had aligned himself with the Donatists, who made the unity of the Church depend on holiness, whereas now, following Augustine, he believed the only sure way to salvation was the reverse, the dependence of holiness on formal unity in the Church. This was the new "mind" he put on while composing the *Essay on Development.* Decades later in response to Kingsley's query "What does Dr. Newman mean?" he went beyond the simple question in terms that help us unravel his perception of both "ethos" and "mind." In the *Apologia* he wrote: "He asks what I mean; not about my words, not about my arguments, not about my actions, as his ultimate point, but about that living intelligence, by which I write, and argue, and act. He asks about my Mind and its Beliefs and its sentiments; and he shall be answered."[77] The progressive use of the terms *ethos, Mind,* and *meaning* recapitulates important stages in Newman's own development. *Ethos* pertains to the present reduplication of a standard established in the past, which is recovered or rediscovered for the present. *Mind* reflects the near suppression of the past for a present, living authority, such as Ward's "Ideal" Church. And *meaning* signifies a shift to an emphasis on persons and human experiences, connecting past and present, memory and observation, using personalist terms and historical analogy. That larger *meaning*, a grammar of belief and practice, behaving, as it were, as though a living intelligence, generated by the theological disputes of the Oxford Movement, intimately linked in its unfolding Newman's novel of the Early Church with other religious forms used by Roman Catholics, Anglo-Catholics, and their opponents.

1

EGYPTIANS, DRUIDS, GLADIATORS, AND EPICUREANS

Historical Novels on Early Christian Times

THE NINETEENTH CENTURY was an age obsessed with history writing. A popular and commercial vehicle for recent historical and archaeological research, especially in the 1830s and 1840s, was the historical novel, using the scholarly apparatus of formal histories to step from behind the clutter of pure costumery and to address, stage front, the complex historical causes and patterns of the events depicted.[1] Utilitarian criticism, led by periodicals such as the *Westminister Review*, and reforming sentiments mixed equal parts of unfulfilled expectations and propaganda, expressed in historical-sounding rhetoric. For the Early Church novel, as for other kinds of fictional history, the vogue lasted throughout the century, attracting "not only the public but les raffines,"[2] and was stimulated from time to time by the political, social, and religious questions of the age. The mere listing of those Early Church novels is an arduous task, since no complete catalog exists;[3] but a comprehensive categorization of those works is even more difficult. In general, any schematic arrangement should not be dependent entirely on formal periodization of composition and purely literary motives, such as radically distinguishing early from late Victorian examples on the basis of a literary motif or radically separating action novels from philosophical and meditative ones.[4] Most important, the novels were successive addresses, albeit indirect, to the age of the author and thus provide documentation of a continuing historical-literary critique of modern culture. That ad hominem dimension must be recognized in their composition and in the continuing critical interest they have for the modern reader.

While adopting Curtis Dahl's basic bipartite typology of Early Christian novels, and yet maintaining at the same time the interconnectedness of those violently active and meditative types, I find it necessary to distinguish in this study between the works of religious controversialists, considered in later chapters, and the works of nonchurchly, or avowedly secular, authors. This does not deny the significant concerns of many of the latter group for moral, philosophical, or religious ideas, or even the concern of the former group for political and social questions beyond the theological pale. Indeed, the secular writings at times indicate far better the current theological taste and opinions than do the tendentious posturings of clerical authors. But the difference is the same as that between journalism and theology; one can report accurately the religious pulse of the times, while the other creates the pulse, provides the vocabulary and rules for discourse. The nonchurchly writers, unlike the ecclesiastical ones, were not initiators of the public debate over theological questions raised in the aftermath of the Oxford Movement. They were not concerned or qualified to unravel the convoluted dogmatic and ritual points plaguing the age but could be effective indicators of the general religious and social unrest of the period. On the other hand, having said this, I should stress that both groups had the very same literary roots. E. Cornelia Knight's *Marcus Flaminius* (1792), a mixture of archaeological instruction and moralistic comment on contemporary court figures by a littérateuse in Samuel Johnson's circle, was part of a tradition of "seventeenth and eighteenth-century didactic prose fictions combining instruction about the ancient world, moral precepts, and political or satiric comment on the age in which they were written."[5] Later churchly and secular authors raided this common past and the contemporary work of each other as the genre developed and proved successful.

THE PERIOD FROM 1820 TO 1870

The opening decades of Victoria's life correspond to what is called the Age of Reform, or the Age of Improvement, encompassing politically the Regency and reigns of her royal uncles, George IV and William IV,

and socially the rapid population growth, urbanization, and industrializa-
tion of the nation. The Catholic Emancipation Act (1829) and the Reform Bill (1832) are signal instances of political and social realignment. At
the same time this was a period of continuing religious revival, partially at
least in response to the supposed moral and ecclesiastical laxity of Regency England. The age of railroads was brought into sudden confrontation with the age of martyrs.[6] Restoration of the past in some form in the
churches paralleled political movements to restore, amid the turmoil and
aftermath of revolution, the traditional privileges of the ancien régime,
producing examples as diverse as Young Englandism at home and legitimist conventicles abroad. The widespread sense of displacement and nostalgia, expressed and fostered by Romanticism, emerged with differing
perspective in the historical novels of Lockhart, Moore, Ogle, Smith,
and Lytton. They portrayed antiquity with a certain degree of accuracy,
although depending more consistently on the simple motifs of tradition and their own imaginative skills; but in the house of Caesar they
found the same issues that faced the sportive and confident House of
Hanover.

John Gibson Lockhart (1794–1854), the author of an Early Church
novel, *Valerius* (1821), is better known as the son-in-law and biographer
of Sir Walter Scott and as the squire of Abbotsford. It was as editor after
1825 of the critically severe *Quarterly Review*, known as a Tory voice for
the landed gentry and the Established Church as well as an energetic opponent of the Romantic tendencies of the age, that Lockhart became
publicly involved in religious debate. The *Quarterly* was cautiously supportive of the Oxford Tracts as an antidote to the "popular religionism of
the day" (i.e., Evangelicalism); but in response to Tract 80, "On Reserve," the old-fashioned High Church cleric and reviewer William
Sewell sounded the alarm "to keep them from going beyond the principles of our own Reformation." In highly charged language the periodical even defended the ascetic practices in Hurrell Froude's
posthumously published *Remains* (1838–39): "There is little fear in this
day from any stoicism of religion. . . . It is epicurism of heart and mind
. . . that is the plague and poison of this country."[7] By 1842, however, the
Quarterly had turned against the Puseyites and the "ultra-rubricious" faction, while still labeling the Latitudinarians as "Laodiceans" and the liberal Archbishop Whately of Dublin a "Mohametan." The *Quarterly*

continued to toast, in Tory style, "Church and King." On a more personal level, Lockhart was the agent behind Henry H. Milman's *History of Christianity* (1840), having suggested this forum to deal with questions about miracles raised by Milman's *History of the Jews* (1829). Lockhart's family in turn was deeply affected by the Oxford Movement and its aftermath; in 1851 his daughter Charlotte and her husband, James Hope-Scott, joined Edward Manning in converting to Roman Catholicism. Although eventually reconciled to this later in life and even enjoying in Rome the company of Cardinal Wiseman, decked out as though he were Cardinal Wolsey, Lockhart was not tempted to follow the younger generation in their religious, any more than their literary, adventures.

Valerius, the first Early Church novel of the nineteenth century in English, owed as much to *Ivanhoe* (1819) as to the earlier philosophical tales produced on the Continent.[8] Lockhart had a first-class degree, *literae humaniores*, from Oxford, which accounts in part for his expert handling of Roman topography; but his novel, as one critic put it, read like a translation.[9] Valerius, the titular hero, is the son of the Roman commander of the Ninth Legion under Agricola in Britain and a British mother. After his father's death he journeys to Rome to claim some legally entailed estates; the journey permits Lockhart to display his knowledge of Roman place-names and, once in Rome, to explore with his young hero the topography and architectural monuments (e.g., the Flavian Amphitheatre). Similarly the world of barristers and legal maneuvers permits Lockhart to parade his own training in the law. This "honest Briton," Valerius, is exposed to "lying Greeks" and variations of Epicurean, Stoic, and Cynic philosophy, as well as pagan "imperial rites." Assisted by two faithful and comic servants, Boto "the Druid" and Dromo, characters out of Terence's comedies, and a variety of praetorians and gladiators, Valerius at last wins the love of the "moderately" beautiful Athanasia and through her accepts Christianity. They escape from prison, marry (in a pagan wedding ceremony), and return to Britain in order to elude the persecution of Christians under Trajan, which has already claimed the martyr Thraso of Antioch. Trajan, Adrian [Hadrian], Pliny the Younger, and Tacitus are the historical figures introduced; the emperor even leads a symposium on Plato's *Timaeus* that is evocative of a Regency salon. In this rarified society, "the leaders of fashion change the style of their hairdressing continually, and it would be thought extremely barbarous to enter the theatre or the baths . . . without having care to follow their example in all such particulars" (*V*, 1:28).

Valerius is introduced to Christianity by Thraso, who reinforces the earlier impression made by pagans about the intimate link between Judaism and Christianity: their common Scripture, music, and sacred history. Thraso, the son of a Jewish mother and proselyte father, witnessed the siege and fall of Jerusalem and the desertion of the city by the Christian inhabitants following a series of minatory oracles confirming Christ's prediction; the Jews in turn intensified persecution of the Christians. Thraso became a Christian in Jerusalem, where he examined eyewitnesses to the miracles of Jesus and experts who attested to the fulfillment of Old Testament prophecies in Christ. Lockhart himself is a witness to the continuing appeal to miracle and prophecy for Christian apologetics, but with a typical post-Enlightenment insistence on using reason to test sources. The central teaching of early Christianity is "expiation by the cross," coupled with the admonition "to reverence, in all things that are lawful, the authority of Caesar" (*V*, 1:163). Christians in fact take up arms, but only to defend themselves, not for revolution; the treasonous knight Cotilius is condemned for such activity.[10] While stationed under Titus in Egypt, Thraso fell into the bondage of sin by sacrificing to the ox Apis (the symbol of the national religion, as the "Bull" was the emblem of Britain), but he was reconciled by a priest who "having publicly heard my confession in presence of the Church there, gave unto me absolution, and admitted me once more to be a partaker with them in the ordinances of the sanctuary" (*V*, 1:170). Although the novel predates the bitter controversies over the practice of auricular confession, Lockhart stresses that confession and absolution are lawful *public* acts of the Christian community, as opposed to private and "secret"—charges made later regarding such acts.

Two motives prompt the "atheistical" (i.e., nonsuperstitious) Briton Valerius to seek baptism. His revulsion from gladiatorial deaths in the Colosseum, "the place of guilt," is heightened, in sentiments quite Victorian, by the sight of one hundred "beautiful" children witnessing the carnage: "I saw the feet of so many tender and innocent ones placed there upon the same hot and guilty sand, which had so often drunk . . . the blood of the innocent" (*V*, 1:161–62). Second, his contemplation of death and longings for the soul's immortality, after the "intense convulsions of animal suffering," are reinforced by a conversation with Parmeno the Ionian, who is reading Heraclitus in the "Palatine Library" surrounded by the busts of Homer, Plato, Aristotle, the poets, and tragedians (in the fashion of the sixteenth-century Vatican library by that name). Love, Parmeno teaches, is the source of all knowledge and the final ordering principle of the universe. The "sublime" wisdom of Socrates, Plato, Egypt, and India have prepared Valerius for the "godlike loftiness" of precepts he finds later in reading the Gospel of Luke, "a plain and perspicuous [sic] narrative of facts," culminating in the simple witness of the Roman centurion (see Luke 7:1). Valerius made the identification between such all-ordering Love and Christ. A selection (Ps. 46) from the "Royal Poet of the Hebrews" is able to "sooth in sorrow and strengthen in tribulation," unlike the mere entertainment of pagan poets (V, 2:162). Plato's sublime obscurity of vision was a mysterious anticipation of this. Lockhart felt that the poetry of the Bible was meant to convey truth, not excite pleasure.[11]

The martyrdom of Thraso and veneration for his relics in the catacombs ("the Christian synagogue") move Valerius' shadowy conversion as much as any other factors. He receives the "symbol of regeneration," baptism, by stepping into a fountain and having water sprinkled on his forehead. He has already attended a morning communion service in which the Christians, kneeling in a circle, kiss a gold cross and silver goblet. And he anachronistically receives a passionflower as a symbol of his Christianity.[12] Christians use such natural symbols but maintain that the will of God is the only image of the Maker of All that is acceptable, a Hebraic notion that appealed to the strong moral conviction of the nineteenth century. While some pagans accuse Christians of eating "raw children," others, attracted by their Samaritan-like good works, defend them and ironically predict that Christians will supplant the religions of Palestine just as the worship of Isis and Cybele was supplanted, having themselves overcome the Olympian cults. Behind this statement are a linear view of history and a concept of the progressive education of the race, ideas generated by philosophical discussion in the seventeenth and eighteenth centuries. An appendix transcribes the well-known correspondence of Trajan and Pliny concerning Christians in Bithynia. Lockhart stresses throughout the novel Trajan's leniency and humaneness. One character observes, "Destiny has willed that Rome should be the Mistress of the World; but it seems neither necessary nor fitting, that she should carry her control into the secret parts of men's minds, and interfere with their notions of religious obligation" (*V*, 1:70). That enlightened concern for religious toleration, sounding like an Address from the Throne, found its political embodiment in Britain later in the decade in a series of enabling acts extending the franchise to Dissenters and Roman Catholics.

Born in Dublin of Roman Catholic parents, Thomas Moore (1779–1852) was admitted to Trinity College in 1794 to study for the bar; the partial removal of legal disabilities for Roman Catholics in 1793 made this possible. After 1799 various aristocratic patrons introduced him into literary circles and court life. He became a friend and biographer of Byron and knew Leigh Hunt, as well as other literary luminaries. Later he met Lord John Russell, Lord Lansdowne, and various Whig politicians with an interest in Irish affairs; Russell was eventually the editor of eight volumes of Moore's *Diary and Correspondence* (1853–56). Known for his haunting lyrics "Believe me if all those endearing young charms" and "The harp that once thro' Tara's halls," Moore's other writings, including history and satire, were grounded in Irish issues, disguised or apparent. He was disappointed by the prince regent's failure to fulfill hopes for Catholic Emancipation following 1811. Moore's fanciful tale *Lalla Rookh* (1817) was in fact an expression of Irish patriotic yearnings under the veil of the Romantic orientalism then so much the fad, as Newman's boyhood fascination with Arabian tales and Southey's *Thalaba* (1801) attests.[13] In 1824 he published the pseudonymous *Memoirs of Captain Rock*, an indictment of the Church of Ireland on the question of the tithe. In the same year he wrote further on this vexed question, signing himself "a Munster Farmer."[14] *Odes upon Cash, Corn, Catholics, and Other Matters* (1828) joined the flood of propaganda published concerning the questions of tariff, free trade, and the Corn Laws on the eve of Catholic Emancipation. Moore also wrote *Travels of an Irish Gentleman in Search of a Religion* (1834), in which he displayed how his nominal Catholicism was affected by the freethinking society in which he had moved, and a four-volume *History of Ireland* (1835–40). The concern for reform issues and their application to the Irish question can be legitimately called the central motif in Moore's authorship, including his Early Church novel, *The Epicurean* (1827).[15]

The reputed sensuousness of *The Epicurean*, the prose expansion of his poem of 1822 "Alciphron," created a stir upon the novel's publication. The various periodicals took up the critical and public response; the *Westminister Review* alone devoted thirty-three pages of comment to it.[16] Despite claims of sensationalism, the tale is a tame one of a young man's spiritual pilgrimage. Moore pretends to discover a Greek MS fragment in 1800 (just after Napoleon's expedition to Egypt) in the monastery of St. Macarius in Cairo, where it was being sold in shreds as amulets for Arab pigeon houses by the monks, "who are never slow in profiting by superstition." The manuscript is narrated by Alciphron, a twenty-four-year-old Athenian dissatisfied with the hedonistic, although refined, Epicurean sect, called "The Garden," of which he had been elected chief "Heresiarch" [*sic*]. He follows the instructions of a dream that he trusts "more than Divine Providence." And in the summer of A.D. 247 he sails to Alexandria to learn the secrets of immortality (a most un-Epicurean pursuit), which men claimed then as in modern times to be carved, along with all alchemical and antediluvian secrets of the Thrice-Great Hermes, in the hieroglyphics of the pyramids. Alciphron falls in love with Alethe, a priestess of Isis, and pursues this image of Psyche through a subterranean necropolis, moonlit cruises on the Nile accompanied by anachronistic fireworks, and esoteric initiation rites. His idea of paradise is an eroticized one: woman is the "deity of the Present," for whose sake alone was immortality desirable. And his triple test of Fire, Water, and Air imitates the Illuminist imagery of the Freemason ceremonial of Tamino's ordeal in Mozart's *Zauberflöte*. The hypocritical Memphis priests serve as vehicles for Moore's feelings about Freemasons, Orange Lodges, and the Established Church in Ireland. Just before the final lifting of the veil of Isis, the Epicurean learns that Alethe (her name means "Truth") is a secret Christian who has outwardly conformed to the established cult and whose mother, Theora ("One who consults an oracle"), was an amanuensis for the Christian philosopher Origen. The couple escape to the desert hermitage of Melanius, where Alciphron pretends initially to become a Christian in order to be espoused to Alethe. The persecution under Valerian claims her, but the authorities refuse to believe that the Epicurean has truly converted (the reverse of the situation Walter Pater's later hero Marius faced). The translator's note reports that Alciphron lived as a hermit and was condemned to the brass mines [*sic*] of Palestine, where he died in 297 during the persecution of Diocletian. It goes on to say that since Alciphron held opinions derived from Origen that were later maintained by Arius, the Athanasian chroniclers of a later date accused the hermit of addiction to Egyptian superstition when a bauble of the Isis cult, a memento of Alethe actually, was found among his relics.

Alciphron's Epicureanism, a refuge for the luxury loving and indolent, is seen by Moore as a via media between "the alarmed bigotry of the declining Faith, and the simple austerity of her rival" (*E*, 11). The indolent praise the "frugality and temperance" of Epicurus with untroubled hypocrisy and charm. As in a court masque, two youths habited as Eros (the celestial love of the Platonists) and Anteros (the earthly, Epicurean name of love) combat on flower boats.[17] This notion of Epicurean self-love (Anteros) was a standard interpretation early in the nineteenth century, supported by such eighteenth-century moralist works as those by Bishop Joseph Butler (1692–1752) in his *Three Sermons on Human Nature* and his *Dissertation on Virtue*. Alciphron turns from the "cold, mortal creed" of his sect and seeks immortality in Egypt, where it seems that Time will gaze from the pyramids when it expires (*E*, 36). He drinks the golden chalice of Lethe and life and is told by white-robed boys: "Thou shalt never die." This is an ironic contrast to a later Christian communion service, derived from a description by Tertullian. Finally, he is disillusioned not only by the trickery and priestcraft but also by the promises that eternal life is meant for a future world, "the airy pledges of all creeds."

Alciphron first learns of Christianity from Alethe when he sees her kiss a silver cross in the Gothic gloom of her mother's funerary chapel. "A cross [i.e., the Ankh]," Moore ironically observes, "was, among the Egyptians, the emblem of a future life" (*E*, 54), whereas for Christians it was "a substantial and assuring pledge." Theora, following the spiritual principles of Origen, had been able to extract from the pagan religion "those pure particles of truth which lie at the bottom of all religions," but those truths are "feelings, rather than doctrines." The special teaching of Origen, veiled in the theology of Egypt, is the unity and goodness of the creator; the preexistence, fall, and restoration (*apocatastasis*) of the human soul; and the sharp distinction between sensible objects of adoration and the spiritual, invisible deity, which is the root cause of the allegorical method of interpretation (*E*, 147, 149). From the "anchoret" Melanius, also a student of Origen, the Epicurean learns more about Christian brotherhood and belief. The hermit is a gentle holy man, pictured with a wild antelope asleep at his feet like the legends of the hermit Paul with his heraldic lion and the later Celtic solitaries and their domesticated beasts of paradise. This is a visible image of the spiritual quality of the hermit, a vocation that Moore nevertheless disapproves: "Less selfish, however, in his piety, than most of these ascetics, Melanius forgot not the world, in leaving it. He knew that man was not born to live wholly for himself; that his relation to human kind was that of the link to the chain, and that even his solitude should be turned to the advantage of others" (*E*, 185–86). This moderate view of the active monastic life was characteristic of English religious writers later in the century when Anglican religious orders for men and women were revived.

Alciphron has some knowledge of Christianity already from the "platonising refinements of Philo" and the Epicureans: Celsus and Lucien (always given the French spelling by novelists). They have prepared him. In the Hebrew Scripture, the "well of living waters," he reads the answer to his longing for immortality in the oracular verse "The Lord hath commanded the blessing, even Life for evermore." He was not prepared for the form of "simple majesty, the high tone of imagination," and the poetry of heaven. Yet its narrative could still be merely "a tissue of splendid allegories." The Book of the Law, Melanius explains, was a compound of prophecy and preparation, demonstrating miracles to the living and offering predictions about the future. God has kept the Jewish race intact to testify to the creation of the world by One Supreme Being and to be a memorial of His power. Their testament is incomplete, however, since it speaks of the descent of God, but not the ascent of Man. On the other hand, the Law underscores the important doctrine that rewards and punishments are all enacted on this side of the grave. The fascination with Origen during the nineteenth century was focused on this point; there is no eternal punishment for sinners. Moore and F. D. Maurice can be linked together here. Using the silver-lettered *Codex Cottonianus* of the New Testament (the *Codex Cottonianus* LXX was believed to be Origen's own copy), the hermit instructs the philosopher about redemption, seen as a restoration of mankind to purity and happiness. The transformation of the Bible into an aesthetic artifact, however, should be noted. Alciphron learns of the exalted Christ, inferior only to the one, self-existent Father, and of the miracles that authenticated Christ's divine mission. That verbal proto-Arianism in Origen is only apparent, but Moore quotes the Unitarian Joseph Priestley (1733–1804) to confirm that interpretation (*E*, 258).

The novel fits easily among the rational pleas for religious toleration in England and Ireland during the 1820s. Moore is as averse to the intolerance of Christian groups, monastic conventicles or dogmatists, as to "the bigots of the court." Viewing the miscellany of nations in Alexandria, he writes:

> Here Christianity, too, unluckily, had learned to emulate the vagaries of Paganism; and while, on one side, her Ophite professor was seen kneeling down gravely before his servant, on the other, a Nicosian was, as gravely, contending that there was no chance of salvation out of the pale of the Greek alphabet. Still worse, the uncharitableness of Christian schism was already distinguishing itself with equal vigour; and I heard of nothing, on my arrival, but the rancour and hate, with which the Greek and Latin Churchmen persecuted each other, because forsooth, the one fasted on the seventh day of the week, and the others fasted upon the fourth and sixth. (*E*, 27–28)

That Gibbon-like view of Christians in the third century, even more poignant because it is put in the mouth of a sensitive pagan, is plainly a comment on the confessional and party divisions of churches in the nineteenth. Throughout the later age, even between friends, olive branches could be discharged as if from a catapult. Moore adopts the enlightened tone of the reformer. One cannot help wondering, however, at his own distaste for the Memphis priesthood, clerics in the established religion, imposed by the government on the native population over an older religion and supported by local tithes. He has indirectly re-created nineteenth-century Ireland on the Nile.

Although not authors of Early Church novels as defined in this study, Nathaniel Ogle and Horace (later Horatio) Smith (1779–1849) were successful historical novelists of Palestine and Egypt just prior to the Apostolic era. They share so many of the concerns of the other secular novelists considered here that a brief notice would be beneficial. Ogle, following the example of Scott, published a three-volume novel *Miriamne: An Historical Novel of Palestine* (1825), delineating the homicidal intrigues of Herod, Salome, and Cleopatra. A confirmed Whig Protestant, Ogle became embroiled in controversy over the Corn Laws and opposed the place of distinctive catechisms (rather than the Bible alone) in school reform measures, exciting the ire of Herbert Marsh, the High Church bishop of Peterborough (1819–39).[18] Successively Lady Margaret Professor (1807) and bishop of Llandaff (1816–19) before his translation to Peterborough, Marsh was virulently anti-Calvinist and engaged in controversy with the Evangelicals Charles Simeon and Isaac Milner, dean of Carlisle, while purging his diocese of Calvinist clergy. Marsh claimed that the Quaker-founded Lancastrian Institution of education and the nondenominational British and Foreign Bible Society (founded 1804) were part of a plot to level the Established Church. Although concerned with ecclesiastical renewal, Marsh practiced nepotism and pluralism and was an eminent, if undauntable, target for reformers like Ogle.

Horatio Smith, poet, satirist, and friend of Shelley, Lockhart, Leigh Hunt, and the society hostess Lady Blessington, made his fortune on the stock exchange and retired to the Regency watering spot of Brighton, where he indulged his interests in dramatists, newspapers, and novels.[19] In the same year as George Croly's apocalyptic tale of the Wandering Jew, *Salathiel* (1828), Smith published *Zillah: A Tale of the Holy City*, recounting the siege and fall of Jerusalem to the Romans in 37 B.C.[20] Avoiding the "peculiar phraseology" of Scripture out of reverence, he narrates the story of Zillah, the sixteen-year-old daughter of the Jewish Sagan, the second high priest, who serves with disgust at the dissolute court of the perfumed and effeminate prince Antigonus. After many romantic adventures, including abduction, piracy, a slave market, a mysterious horseman, and a talisman, she arrives back at Jerusalem in time to put on armor and defend the city as "Judith Maccabeus." Along the way Mark Anthony, Cleopatra, and Octavius are introduced as important participants in the plot; and the history of the internecine warfare of the Pharisees, Sadducees, Essenes, and Zealots is explored. The fall of the city is depicted at the climax of a fierce battle, complete with rampaging elephants. The end is proclaimed by an omnipresent prophet, Nabal the Black Shadow. Zillah survives to wed her Roman lover Felix, who becomes a Jewish proselyte with an undogmatic view of religion: "In faith and doctrine no one can be quite sure that he is right, but in the practice of religion [i.e., philanthropy and universal toleration] none can err" (Z, 4:316).

The novel contains a number of literary conceits: the portraits of Virgil and Horace dining together can certainly be identified as Horace and his older brother James. Even the title of the novel has personal significance; the biblical Zillah was the mother of Tubal Cain, the first of the "smiths."[21] In his later satiric work *The Tin Trumpet* (1836), an alphabetical list of current words given with epigrammatic or tendentious definitions, Smith displays some of his reforming zeal untempered by the distance of fiction, although he uses a pseudonym. He lists among other "public wrongs": tithes and endowments, rotten boroughs, slavery of negroes ("the images of God in ebony"), Test acts and subscription, foxhunting and game laws, primogeniture and legitimist monarchies, and the tradition of flogging in schools and the military. He is against the Athanasian Creed ("a motley monster of bigotry"), the Articles of Religion ("a cat-o-thirty-nine-tails"), and ceremonial. The appeal to antiquity made by High Churchmen is just the use of dead bones "for the purpose of knocking down live flesh."[22] The bench of bishops is heaped with Edward Irving's charismatic followers, a growing number in the 1830s, as self-proclaimed "Apostles" who rant in the "Egyptian hieroglyphics" of Babel tongues. He calls ascetics selfish Epicureans and a monastery "a house of illfame, where men are seduced from their public duties." Smith supports "the patriotic Whig Government," London University, Jewish Sabbatarians and Charitable "Mahometans" (both examples of Voluntarism), Quakers, patient Catholic tithe payers of Ireland, and English Dissenters on church rates.

Both Ogle and Smith mixed their reforming concerns with their literary endeavors. While men like Smith decried the apocalyptic fanaticism of the Irvingites and prophecies "adapted to the gazettes," the appeal of novels dealing with the destruction of Jerusalem and the destiny of the Jews was based emotionally on the very things Smith sought to reject. Napoleon's "Great Sanhedrin" (1806), interpreted in apocalyptic terms, and the London Society for Promoting Christianity among the Jews (founded in 1809, reorganized in 1815), preparing for the Last Day, are just two instances from many showing the kind of eschatological speculation that accompanied the religious and social upheaval of the times and the prophetic cries for reform.

The catastrophic destruction of Herculaneum and Pompeii (A.D. 79) continued to generate tremors of interest in the nineteenth century, much as in our own day, and inspired a sizable body of literature.[23] The American Thomas Gray's *The Vestal* (Boston, 1830), Lord Lytton's *The Last Days of Pompeii* (1834), and even the translation of Edouard Schure's *The Priestess of Isis* (1807) are some of the more familiar examples. After the serendipitous rediscovery of the remains of Pompeii in 1709, the Bourbon excavations (1748–82), and the Bonapartist continuation sponsored by Princess Murat, the period from 1828 to 1875 marked a new stage in the scientific exploration of the region's archaeology. Capitalizing on this renewed interest was Sir William Gell, whose *Pompeiana* (1817–19), uncritical in its use of sources but a detailed topographical guide, emerged in a new edition in 1835. Contact with Gell, a general interest in the Italian scene, and the eruptions of Vesuvius in 1779 and in 1822 were all factors in Lytton's decision to compose his historical novel while wintering in Naples (1832–33).[24]

Edward Bulwer-Lytton (1803–73) turned from his earlier historical tales to invest this work, part history with notes and appendixes, part guidebook, with an examination of the age's romance. His earlier novels established Lytton as a critical observer of society. *Pelham* (1828), in reality a manual of Regency dandyism, joins his *Rienzi* (1835), *The Last of the Barons* (1843), and *Harold, the Last of the Saxon Kings* (1848) as nineteenth-century propaganda, masking Lytton's aristocratic and occasional Tory Radical stances toward contemporary issues. As the titles indicate, the "last" stages of society in transition and the emergence of new configurations of power fascinated him. Although the author claims it is "the commonplace routine of the classic luxury, which we recall the past to behold,"[25] it has been suggested by Curtis Dahl that *The Last Days of Pompeii* in fact represents the "last Days" of Regency society. It reflects not merely the passing of the silver-fork school of mannerisms and luxury but the upheaval of all values; the wealthy of Pompeii, burdened by their treasure or locked in their elegant homes, perish. This novel was written in the period following the Reform Bill of 1832, which raised political and economic expectations and stiffened resistance by entrenched interests. The novel preserves that moment in time.

Glaucus, a wealthy young socialite in Pompeii, is the object of the unrequited love of Nydia, a blind flower-girl rescued by Glaucus from a cruel and immoral master. But the young man loves the lovely Ione, desired by the malevolent high priest of Isis, Arbaces. Ione's brother Apaecides, a priest of the cult and a sincere believer (like Apuleius), is sickened by the priestcraft and chicanery of his colleagues, and after meeting the Christian leader, Olinthus, resolves to denounce the priests of the temple in public. Arbaces murders him and shifts the blame to Glaucus. The mob is incited against the Christians. After various, rather mechanical, adventures, the eruption of Vesuvius forces Glaucus and Ione to flee, guided out of the smoke- and ash-shrouded city by the blind Nydia, a plot suggestion made to Lytton by Lady Marguerite Blessington. Later, Glaucus writes from Athens to his philosopher-friend Sallust, informing him that after the martyr's death of Olinthus they have all become Christians in the city where Glaucus' father had heard Paul address the Areopagus. This rather sparse romantic plot holds together the archaeological and topographical observations. The reader is shown the Forum, amphitheater and gladiatorial shows, temples, baths, a gambling den called in Regency style a "Flash House," tombs, topiary gardens, the "villa of Diomed" [Diomedes], and the houses of Sallust and Glaucus (actually the "House of the Tragic Poet"), with descriptions of the public functions and domestic activities carried out in each. Lytton even alludes to the "improper pictures," familiar to the worldly-wise tourist. At times he uses antiquarian details for contemporary satire. Julia, the standard of fashion à la mode in Pompeii, declares her disdain for "effeminate" (i.e., cowardly) gladiators: "They are worthy of a mitre." He elaborates in a footnote: "Mitres were worn sometimes by men, and considered a great mark of effeminacy" (P, 254). Men wore mitres in religious cults; the comment and learned note are meant to be an ironic jibe at English bishops.

When Scott visited the excavated city with Gell, he exclaimed, "The City of the Dead!" (P, 136 n. 1). And when the witch of Vesuvius, a withered hag, asks Arbaces, the incarnation of Thrice-Great Hermes, for added years, she says: "It is not life that is sweet, but death that is awful." The longing for immortality turns Apaecides and Glaucus from pagan cults and philosophy to Christianity. That Christianity is summarized in the cross and scroll of Scripture. Christ's "devoted holiness" in his human character outshines the virtues of Socrates. He came to show the form of virtue Plato desired: "This was the true sacrifice that He made for man" (P, 77). By miracles and the fulfillment of prophecies he established the authority of his teaching: the immortality of the soul, the resurrection, and the reunion of the dead. To confirm this for the reader Lytton introduces the resuscitated son of the widow of Nain. He had become a sort of Wandering Jew proclaiming Christ's divinity in remote corners of the earth. But it is the fiery Evangelical Olinthus who bears the gospel message with an inspired tongue: "one of those hardy, vigorous, and enthusiastic men, by whom God in all times had worked the reformation of His own religion" (P, 76). Lytton recognizes that the enthusiast today, whose vigor is necessary to gain a foothold for Christianity, may be the inquisitor tomorrow, imposing creeds and doctrine on his unwilling fellows. Glaucus comes to hold such latitudinarian views of tolerance as marked the men who rejected the damnatory Athanasian Creed: "I can share not the zeal of those who see crime and eternal wrath in men who cannot believe as they. I shudder not at the creed of others. I dare not *curse* them—I pray the Great Father to *convert*. This lukewarmness exposes me to some suspicion amongst the Christians: but I forgive it" (P, 408).

The novel, rather than offering long philosophical debates on "Epicurus, Pythagoras, or Diogenes," portrays an interest in and feeling for a variety of occult subjects: indeed, Lytton's novel will later be a prime source for Madame Blavatsky's Egyptian and Rosicrucian lore.[26] His most dramatic portrait, the Saga (witch) of Vesuvius, while largely drawn from Shakespeare, had a lasting effect on this genre. All the witches in later novels are offspring of Lytton's hag. The cult of Isis, depicted largely from Apuleius' *Golden Ass*, and the person of Arbaces, master of the Egyptian hermetic *arcana*, are sketched, without overindulging Victorian prurience about pagan immorality. But the celibate and largely plebeian priests of Isis are, in fact, "the Roman Catholic Christians who enter the monastic fraternity, less from the impulse of devotion than the suggestions of a calculating poverty" (P, 97). Lytton reverts to a stock image in Gothic fiction—the monk as repressed satyr—when one such priest confesses, "My days have been consumed with feverish and vague desires; my nights with mocking but solemn visions" (P, 169). Their idolatry, the "Graceful Superstition," is still active:

"It pours its crowds, in listening reverence, to oracles at the shrines of St. Januarius or St. Stephen, instead of to those of Isis or Apollo" (*P*, 189). Such gross credulity can only lead to skepticism. Arbaces denounces Christianity as mere plagiarism: "The believers of Galilee are but the unconscious repeaters of one of the superstitions of the Nile" (*P*, 113). The allegories of the Osiris cult—a Trinity, a Son-"Saviour," a cross, an atoning death, and resurrection—are the mythic elements borrowed by Christianity. Arbaces, skeptic and cabalist, rejects myth for magic: "He who could be skeptical as to power of the gods, was credulously superstitious as to the power of man" (*P*, 139). This had particular force addressed to nineteenth-century audiences as captivated by mesmerism and the almost magical effects of magnetism as they were by the legends of Faustus and Apollonius of Tyana.

Lytton gives many instances of both theurgic ("white") and geotic ("black") magic. The novel presents magical incantations and curses, love philters, oracular dreams, and bird omens, familiar in Nordic lore. The Saga and Arbaces are able to predict the future accurately, although their prophecies are not always clear in detail. Something of this transcendence is conveyed by Lytton's Romantic use of nature. The earthquake of A.D. 62 is dramatically described. Violent storms assail the countryside, ominous lightning kills the municipal decurion, and a meteor passes on "THE LAST DAY." Lytton says that it was an erroneous belief of the Early Christians that the Last Day was at hand, but his plot and imagery reinforce that belief, especially when he uses apocalyptic motifs. The Christian and Egyptian priests fight for the body of Apaecides just as "Lucifer and the Archangel contended for the body of the mighty Lawgiver" (*P*, 282).

For the most part, Lytton is earth-bound, and his novel is the first to introduce to the fiction of the age a real feeling for Italian history and geography. He has a northern tendency, however, to reduce Italian artistry to the ropedancers familiar at Vauxhall or the experts with the stiletto. There is a wide interest in the array of nations and peoples. Sallust, a buoyant gourmand, concludes there is some good in Britons after all: "They produce an oyster." In discussing Greece, Lytton voices the despair current among philhellenes just after 1830 over the whole "Eastern Question": "As ashes cannot be rekindled—as love once dead can never revive, so freedom departed from a people is never regained." And as

Fleishman also notes, he rejects the Mazzinian schemes to unify Italy, "the blind policy which would unite all your crested cities, mourning for their republics, into one empire; false, pernicious delusion!"[27] Italy for the chivalrous Lytton is still the land of the Renaissance city-states.

Lytton has had a lasting effect on historical perceptions of Pompeii. His novel canonized the notion that Christians maintained a communal life in the city, a point still debated by scholars. He is also another example of Whig-inspired novelists pleading for religious and political toleration during the period of revolution on the Continent and reform at home. His interest in Italian history, his summary of the Christian creed in philanthropy and immortality of the soul, his mild anti-Catholicism, and his unsensuous presentation of pagan culture all left a mark on this literary genre. And his choice of a catastrophic event, although he refrained from specific religious application, added to the apocalpyticism of the day.

The Decline and Fall of Empire

The sense of nationhood, race, and *Volk* that was part of the Romantic sensibility and that lay behind many of the revolutionary movements of the nineteenth century found ample outlets in the literature and arts of the period. Revolutionaries looked back into the native heritage of their lands to find their heroes, whose deeds were preserved in bardic sagas. Throughout this engagement with the past, the work of historians was enormously important, almost mythic in its application. Augustin Thierry (1795–1856) called the world's attention in his *Récits des temps Merovingiens* (1840) to the "victims of history": Scots, Celts, and ancient Gauls who fought against Roman oppression. Chateaubriand glorified the "savage and terrible" Franks. And the cult of Vercingetorix found strident devotees in the artists Eugène Delacroix (1798–1863) and Paul-Joseph Jamin (1853–1903). The Goths and various "barbarian" nations were equally the object of historiographical and artistic interest, especially against the backdrop of the weakened power of Rome. Gibbon's barbarians and Christians paraded before the Victorian public. A number of visual artists, including British painters of the "Victorian High Renaissance," contributed to depictions of daily life in antiquity that were sometimes sentimental, sometimes sensuous, and always melodramatic.[28]

They mixed archaeological realism with moral themes, piety, and decadence to achieve historical illustrations that were as much erotic fantasies.
Martyrdom and the sack of Rome were favorite subjects.[29] Overall, this
process of depicting the downfall of civilization and the rise of barbarian
forces owed its visual intensity to the tradition of descriptions of the
Apocalypse and Last Judgment and, more immediately, to the revolutionary barricades of 1789–93, 1830, 1848, and 1870. Catastrophe and
apocalypse were artistically fashionable. This dual interest in rising barbarians and declining Romans was expressed by several secular novelists
of the period in England; some, like Wilkie Collins, had direct connections to the other artistic modes used to paint the lost age.

As a boy of seventeen George Payne Rainsford James (1799–1860)
began writing as the result of reading Scott's Waverley novels. Scott
himself approved the later historical novel *Richelieu* (written in 1825,
published in 1829), James's critical success.[30] His writing career encom-
passed seventy-seven works in 198 volumes; between 1847 and 1860 the
Parlour and Railway Libraries carried forty-seven of his titles, twenty-
eight ahead of Lytton, his closest competitor.[31] "George Prince Regent
James," as he was called because of his grandiloquence and old-fashioned
use of language, served for a time as "historiographer royal" to William
IV before assuming various consular posts, including one in Venice,
where he died. Contemporaries, such as Walter Savage Landor, who
wrote his epitaph and who himself was known for historical fiction
through his *Imaginary Conversations* (1824–29), found James's work filled
with noble principles, virtue, and the historical "spirit" of chivalry.[32]
More earnest Victorians found it escapist, self-indulgent (i.e., of little
propaganda value), and entirely dependent on spectacle for its effects.[33]

Theodore, the eighteen-year-old hero of *Attila* (1837), is the son of a
princess of the barbarian Alani and Count Paulinus, an official in the
court of the "effeminate and treacherous" Theodosius II. Theodore and
his sister Eudochia are cared for by Julia Flavia, who lives in Diocletian's
palace at Split with her children, Ammian Flavius and the beautiful
Ildica, Theodore's espoused. An earthquake, vividly described, drives
them out, and at the same time they learn from the tribune Marcian (later
emperor-consort of Pulcheria and probably an Arian) that Paulinus has
been assassinated by the court eunuch Chrysapheus. They seek refuge
with Paulinus' brother, Bishop Eugenius of Margus, who has opened the

way for the Huns to invade the Balkan peninsula and Greece (441–43 and 447). The prophecy of a fanatic hermit links the destinies of Theodore and Attila, who protects the young Roman, incurring the hatred of Bleda, Attila's unmanageable brother. Bleda's daughter, Neva, however, loves the hostage and rescues him. Theodore becomes the Hun's bondsman for seven years and witnesses his military campaigns. No record of any of Attila's battles survives, but James describes in detail the battle of Chalons (451) on the Catalaunian Plains, fought against the Roman Aetius and Theodoric's Visigothic auxiliaries. Against the interpretation of "Jornandes" (Jordanes is meant) and modern military historians, James claims it as a victory for the Huns, who continued their onslaught. Descending into Italy (452), they are met by Pope Leo I. His mission and Attila's recorded dream of Peter and Paul defending Rome are given a rationalized and nonpious reading by James.

On the eve of a new invasion of the Eastern Empire (453), Attila forces Ildica to marry him and is stabbed to death by her on the wedding night, but the cause of his death is disguised by the elder barbarian chieftains. Years later Theodore, a praetorian prefect, visits the grave of Ildica in Illyria, where she and Neva were nuns living under perpetual penance. Various historical figures are introduced: the larger-than-life-size Attila, like "an equestrian statue of Trajan," Pope Leo with his "fire of genius," the weak and rapacious Western emperor Valentinian III (425–55). James omits the Princess Honoria, however, so as not to "dwell upon pruriencies of a degraded state of society."[34] Roman against Hun is really the combat of "vicious luxury, effeminacy, and cowardice" against a not uncivilized nation of strength, courage, and destiny. James, however, preaches a middle path: refinement with virtue.

The Christianity presented sits lightly on individuals, "so that the same man was often a Christian in belief, who was pagan in many of his habits and almost all his familiar expressions" (A, 1:13 n). Bishop Eugenius, who reviles the Monophysite, the "subtle Eutyches," is himself avaricious and crafty; but Christianity itself will "remain unsullied through everlasting ages, notwithstanding the faults, the follies, and the vices of some of its ministers" (A, 1:77). James shows a variety of other Christian types. Mizetus, the lay enthusiast, prophesies the last day, and he, rather than the reported monk in Gaul, dubs Attila "the scourge of God," giving the Huns a niche within the providential unfolding of salvation history. It is Mizetus who brings Neva and Ildica to take up the ascetic life of nuns. He unlocks the scriptural view of Christ as a sacred being "whose birth and whose death were equally miraculous and beneficent, an example, a teacher, a guide, a sacrifice, and atonement" (*A*, 2:150). More practically, they read the Old Testament for heroic examples: Abraham, Ruth, David; and they read it for vindication of the idea that the defense of one's country is a "just and righteous cause for slaying the oppressor." The outraged Ildica finds her "sure guidance" in the biblical tale of Sisera and Jael.

Hermits and asceticism are seen as being the root of such fanaticism. A cave adorned with a large Gothic crucifix is the home of those enthusiasts who follow a mistaken principle of religion: "Some subjected themselves to the most tremendous inflictions, thinking thereby to please God; and the pillar and the chain still find their place in history as illustrations of human fanaticism" (*A*, 1:165). Gothic tales of horror and raving Jesuit regicides lie behind this view. It also represents a rejection of the ideas in Dr. Pusey's Tract 18 (1833), on fasting and asceticism. James makes much of the clerical claim to prophecy, still confirmed by "facts" for those "in that age." In reality he shows the reader how these self-deluded, but harmless, enthusiasts confound shrewd calculations with presages of the future. This demonstration of the dubiousness of prophetic claims prepares the reader for Pope Leo's prediction that anyone who attacks Rome will suffer terrible reverse, death, downfall, or dishonor. The shadow of Napoleon seems to stir at these lines. But immortal Rome is not, after all, sacrosanct, as James sees it, but "the capital of the greatest and most despotic of governments, whether democratic, imperial, or clerical" (*A*, 2:71). Attila concludes that Leo, who can be politically helpful against the Eastern Empire, is "perhaps" inspired by God. A less than infallible pope is seen as a less than inspired prophet.

James does not spend any time unraveling theological or philosophical matters. He is, however, interested in the religious and social habits of the peoples he portrays. The *pagani* of the Italian villages, he finds, "adhered to their old faith, and through nearly a hundred years of persecution and suffering had retained, either openly or secretly, their reverence for the things their fathers had revered before them" (*A*, 2:89). His view of the syncretist rites of May Day not only reflects his modern awareness of country life in the Campagna but is also meant to describe the religious conservatism of English recusants. That tension of past and present is also conveyed when the Huns recognize the power of Roman letters over barbarian arms in establishing the record of history. In the age of von Ranke and the drill team of German historians, Attila's words could be read only ironically. "We Huns write not our own histories" (*A*, 1:174). It is doubly ironic that James and the expatriate novelists, such as Charles Lever, left it to others to bring "Italian religious and political history to bear on the spiritual needs of their own age."[35]

Antonina, published 27 February 1850, began Wilkie Collins's (1824–89) career as a novelist.[36] The story opens in the autumn of 408, just as Alaric, the Visigothic king, is descending again into Italy at the head of a barbarian horde, this time to avenge the massacre of the families of Gothic mercenaries at the orders of the feeble Western emperor Honorius (393–423). The story culminates in the first of Alaric's three sieges of Rome (408–10), whose final fall prompted Augustine's apologetic *De civitate Dei* (413–25). Collins rejects the standard rehearsal of antiquarianism, topography, and classical architecture. The opening scene of the novel, a cave on a storm-lashed heath, like the Hampstead Heath location of *The Woman in White* (1860), renders the impressive scenery and forces of nature in painterly fashion. Collins himself was a painter and the friend of such historical painters as E. M. Ward; his own father, William Collins, R.A., produced historical and religious works, some of which were commissioned by the Whig politician Lord Lansdowne.[37] The first sight of the Gothic army sets the tone of the whole novel. In a Miltonic period Collins presents "in all the majesty of numbers and repose, the vast martial assemblage of the warriors of the North." He goes on to describe them, bestowing a mythic quality: "Silent—menacing—dark—the army looked the fit embodiment of its leader's tremendous purpose—the subjugation of Rome" (*An*, 15). The Goths assume the "face of Nature"; they are destiny embodied, the realization of the "supernatural" will of their leader. Against this pantheon of demigods is arrayed the degenerate Romans, who have been deserted by the debilitated and effeminate Honorius. The emperor, incapable of the "immortal virtues of a Trajan," had fled Rome for the safety and luxury of Ravenna, where in "spiritualized indolence" he sought the infallible oracles of a flock of sacred chickens, described like the famous Lombard gold statue of hen and feeding chicks. This episode about the flight of the ruler of Rome and claims of infallibility may well have been interpreted as a reference to Pope Pius IX's escape from Rome to Gaeta in 1848.

The initial part of the story concerns Goisvintha, whose children were massacred among the hostages at Aquileia. She forces her brother Hermanric, a twenty-year-old Gothic captain in Alaric's guard, to swear vengeance. In Rome the decadent senator Vetranio, a Petronius figure, becomes infatuated with the fourteen-year-old Antonina, the chaste daughter of Numerian (Cleander), an ascetic fanatic and Bible-quoting reformer, actually a cross between an Evangelical and a Puseyite. He made the girl "learn long prayers and attend to interminable sermons" and read the Fathers' anathemas against love. Raised as a virgin of the Ancient Church, she could never know the delights of the theater, poetry, or the arts. The servant Ulpius (Emilius), allegedly converted by patristic reading but secretly a high priest of Serapis hoping for a restoration of the old religion, helps Vetranio enter Antonina's bedchamber. The unfeeling Numerian brands her a harlot and she flees the city, only to be rescued by Hermanric in the besieging army. They are betrayed by Goisvintha; the young Goth is mutilated and killed. Eventually the heroine reenters Rome, saves Vetranio from suicide at an apocalyptic banquet, and rescues her father from starvation, while she herself sickens with fever. The extended portrayal of death and disease in Rome, brought on by Alaric's siege, is highly reminiscent of the description of the plague of Athens at the close of Lucretius' *De rerum natura*. Ulpius is discovered to be the long-lost brother of Numerian, suggesting that Puseyism, Evangelicalism, and modern paganism are all fraternal forms of fanaticism. When the temples are stripped of their treasure to bribe Alaric, who is unwilling to restore paganism, Ulpius becomes mentally unhinged, relives imaginatively the destruction of the Temple of Serapis in Alexandria (391), and barricades himself in a shrine that has a mechanical engine for human sacrifice, a "deus ex machina." The Romans fire the temple while a priest pronounces excommunication, "an anticipation of an auto-da-fé." When the siege lifts, Vetranio, Antonina, and Numerian seek the chaste shelter of the senator's countryhouse.

While there is some sense of a spiritualized faith, practical Christianity is observed with a jaundiced eye. Even as the barbarians gather, the bishop of Ravenna is busy "converting" an Arian lady in his private study. Ulpius believes that by calculating a precise number of further dissensions, controversies, and quarrels he will know when the Christian priesthood will destroy itself. It is the same kind of numerology seriously pursued by Christian Dispensationalists, measuring the days before the end time. Collins takes particular relish in debunking confession and absolution. Two priests in disguise (actually stock images of crafty Jesuit confessors), set to spy on Numerian's conventicle by ecclesiastical authorities, discuss the matter. The one, after first kicking a female slave in anger, says, "I am afraid these incessant absolutions, granted to men who are too careless even to make a show of repentance for their crimes, will prejudice us with the people at large." The second replies, "Of what consequence are the sentiments of the people while we have their rulers on our side? Absolution is the sorcery that binds these libertines of Rome to our will. We know what converted Constantine—politic flattery and ready absolution; the people will tell you it was the sign of the Cross."[38] In a sermon at St. John Lateran, preached to the beleaguered Romans, a priest promises absolution, even canonization, to any who will fight against the Goths. Instead, they file out quickly and bicker over places in the bread line.

The decoration of St. Peter's Basilica allows Collins to contrast further the "Pagan toyshop" of the Roman Church with the pure rule of faith found in the Gospel and with priests who "craved no finer vestment" than holiness. The basilica itself is decried as the work of a man of blood, infamous for his murders and tyrannies; both Constantine and the later Pope Julius II are the culprits. The mob, desiring spectacle in their religion, come to see a chandelier of 2,400 lamps in the "luxurious palace," while the truly pious seek "dimly-lighted aisles" and "soft shadows." The church is filled with second-class relics: the branch of the olive tree on which St. Luke was hanged, the noose (with knot), the Evangelist's painting of the Apotheosis of the Virgin, baskets of controversial pamphlets, "Pagan images regenerated into portraits of saints," pictures of Arians "writhing in damnation," all designed to "tempt" the pious spectators. All are tokens of fraud, Collins concludes: "The priests seized on Christianity as their path to politics and their introduction to power . . . slowly and insensibly, ambitious man heaped the garbage of his mysteries, his doctrines, and his disputes, about the pristine purity of the structure given him by God."[39] The image of the pagan Julian reappears to Collins's Victorian audience as a reproving apparition; this was the Catholic faith, Collins insists, that the last of the pagans died in fighting. Julian becomes a kind of anonymous saint of the opposition to relics, vestments, confession and absolution, and priests with political power (i.e., the bench of bishops as well as the confessors of kings). It is not quite Swinburne, but it is not Pusey or Newman. Collins in *Ramblings beyond Railways* (1851) shows some sensitivity to the abandoned usages of the past in reflecting on the Holy Well of St. Clare, Cornwall, as an emblem of the English Church "whose innocent and reverent custom it was to connect closer together the beauty of nature and the beauty of religion by such means as the consecration of a spring, or the erection of a roadside cross."[40] But England's bucolic and picturesque piety is not the same as Rome's superstitious "garbage."

Collins's novel, a model he never repeated, is memorable for a number of contributions to the genre. Vetranio, the philosopher and "man of Science," comes to faith, that is, belief in the soul, by no doctrinal route, but by the simple (and silent) act of Antonina's kindness. The doctor's cry over the girl at the end—"Saved! Saved!"—is meant to convey further the ironic relationship of health of soul and body. On the other hand, Collins exploits the sensational in dealing with the pagan cult, its "wretched impostures, the loathsome orgies, the hideous incantations, the bloody human sacrifices perpetrated in secret" (*An*, 388). Although he quotes Dean Milman's notes on Gibbon's conception of Rome, the impartial air of the Enlightenment is gone. And even though we find Alaric drinking from a polished skull in his tent, we are asked to applaud the Goths as a personification of virtue. Parallel to the worthy Goths, Collins places the developing "middle class," which will "hold in its just hands the balance of the prosperity of nations; to crush oppression and regulate rule; to soar in its mighty flight above thrones and principalities, and ranks and riches, apparently obedient, but really commanding" (*An*, 59). In Collins's mind the Goths of Alaric have become the English middle class.

For the other side of the picture, historians and novelists turned to the reign of Justinian (527–65), who through his generals Belisarius and Narses overthrew the Vandals in Africa, ended the Ostrogothic kingdom in Italy, and reclaimed part of Spain from the Visigoths.[41] Justinian also achieved fame for the codification of Roman law, the *Corpus iuris civilis*, along with subsequent additions and jurisprudential texts for school use. Equally compelling was the figure of his empress, Theodora (d. 548), the daughter of a *usarius* (bear keeper) in the ampitheater at Constantinople and an actress on the stage.

Besides those general motives for a historical novelist, Sir Henry Pottinger had some more immediate ones in his *Blue and Green* (1879). The Bulgarian atrocities of 1876, amid the rapid succession of Ottoman sultans in "Stamboul" itself, had made the name of Bulgaria "literally a household word" in Britain. In the Victorian era the Bulgarians were "a harmless pastoral race, victims to Turkist misrule"; but his Bulgarians, Pottinger underscores, were the scourges of eastern Europe.[42] The Russo-Turkish War of 1877 reinforced interest in the history of the land and people, an interest that had grown from the time of the Crimean War. A second immediate reason was the publication of the translation of Felix Dahn's *The Struggle for Rome* (1878), which Pottinger accused of having "out-Procopiused Procopius."[43] Procopius of Caesarea, the chief historian of his age, had in his "Secret History" (*Anekdota*) recorded vile things about Theodora's life. Pottinger says that Dahn had not recognized Procopius' obvious hatred or Dahn himself had not been able to believe that a woman could reform her life. The German depicted her, instead, as a "Messalina of the worst type." Theodora "led the profligate life of most women in her profession," Pottinger admits in proper High Victorian scorn toward the stage (an attitude toward the theater that the Anglo-Catholic priest Stewart Headlam was trying to change). But Pottinger accepted her reformation of life as sincere and permanent. As a corrective to Dahn, Pottinger claims, he wrote his novel and included material on the early lives of Belisarius, Ecebolus the Tyrian, and John of Cappadocia, the praetorian prefect, notable figures either passed over in other romances or treated only in late life. The strong, almost masculine, female is a commonplace in many of these novels. Perhaps too the image of a chaste and noble Eastern empress "who found the purple a glorious winding sheet" gained some luster from the declaration of Victoria as Empress of India in 1877.

Pottinger's understanding of such transhistorical comparisons was that human nature remains the same in all ages; the customs and manners of the sixth century resemble those of the nineteenth. He writes: "The fair Byzantines were as careful to be *bien gantées et chaussées* as their nineteenth-century sisters of London and Paris; if I speak of sumptuous carriages and splendid liveries, it must be understood that such things were as fully appreciated in Old Constantinople as in Belgravia" (*BG*, ix).

The story begins in A.D. 512 during the reign of the tolerant emperor Anastasius (491–518), who is engaged in a religious feud with the

Patriarch Macedonius. The ruler was "Eutychian" and Macedonius was "accused of Nestorianism." The point at issue, sketched only briefly by Pottinger, is the inclusion in the "miraculously revealed" Trisagion ("Holy God, Holy Mighty, Holy Immortal, have mercy upon us") of the phrase *crucified for us* ("the triumphant message of Christianity") after *Immortal*, an addition made by the Monophysite Patriarch Peter the Fuller about 460. Chalcedonians rejected this as imputing passion to God, since they interpreted the liturgical formula to refer to the Trinity, not Jesus Christ. What Pottinger does is basically to side with the Monophysite phrase for Nestorian reasons. The Christological basis of this dispute is handled in passing: "The curious reader is at liberty to bewilder himself by the contemplation of the Savior as existing in, by, from, or of two natures (for over these prepositions was the world convulsed), but for the purpose of this tale sufficient has here been said" (*BG*, 5). Edward Gibbon's famous remark about the use of *iota* to mark heresy (see HOMOIOUSIOS, a semi-Arian term) has been expanded into a preposition, but there is the same indignant refusal to see theology as anything more than sheer logomachy. The religious feuding, connected with the rival blue and green factions (the "livery of the universe") of the Hippodrome, is sensationally handled: "During several centuries the annals of the Christian Church in the East are disfigured by a lamentable appendix: a catalogue of inhuman outrages, atrocious crimes, and wholesale massacres, perpetrated under the cloaks of religious zeal, by bigotry and fanaticism . . . hatch-works of minute and vexatious sophisms. . . . the ardour communicated itself to women and even children, and the streets of the Eastern capitals witnessed as horrid sacrifices to the Holy Catholic Faith as ever disgraced the rites of heathen idolatry" (*BG*, 1). Pottinger finds that the Catholic faith and heathen idolatry are, in fact, intimately linked: "Paganism was far from being extinct;—it is not yet extinct in the nineteenth century,—a large proportion of its traditions having been ingeniously dovetailed into and assimilated with the mysteries of Christianity. It would have puzzled a curious investigator to decide whether the old faith or the new predominated in the hybrid creed of a large section of the population" (*BG*, 241).

The riot in St. Sophia over the amended Trisagion is precipitated by two boy choristers, Dulcissimus ("Dul") and Pudens. The fashionable crowd is there, "simpering and ogling, as might have made the boxes of a modern Parisian opera-house ashamed of their comparative solemnity and simplicity." At the intonation (in a eunuch's falsetto) of the offending phrase, the opposing choirs stone one another, "while their companions extemporized weapons out of the legs and rails of benches, stools, hassocks, music-tablets, and prayer-books indiscriminately" (BG, 33, 35). This folly of man fills the house of Eternal Wisdom. Pottinger is, of course, referring to the various ritual riots of his own day, intensified by the "no-popery" agitation after the Vatican Council (1869–70). These demonstrations against the revival by Anglo-Catholics of long neglected Prayer Book rubrics or borrowings from Rome culminated in the Public Worship Regulation Act of 1874/75 and a series of prosecutions of Ritualist priests, at the instigation of the ultra-Protestant Church Association among others.[44]

Pottinger equally opposes monasticism for men and women and the related veneration of martyrs and intercessory prayer to saints. He cites solitaries such as St. Simeon the Younger, who worked miracles but who yielded to "sweet temptation." There is, he says, a veritable pantheon of reputed Simeons, so that it is impossible to separate them or distinguish the historical from the spurious. He also rejects those "who from shame or pride struggled with their temptations in utter loneliness, rejecting all earthly sympathy, and blotting out their glimpses of heaven by the lurid vapours they evoked from hell" (BG, 236). It is this monastic fanaticism that ensnares the emperor-theologian Justinian, powerless to be an iconoclast of this idol of self-mortification. Pottinger tolerantly smiles his post-Enlightenment smile at the polytheism of patron saints and martyrs, mocking these "proxies of Providence." He writes: "If these saintly guardians attended to half the petty requirements of their clients, or performed half the menial work with which they were credited, their celestial hands must have been inconveniently full of, and not a little soiled by, earthly business" (BG, 242).

The religious degeneracy is only a symptom of a wider social corruption. Pottinger dwells on this and observes: "The corruption of morals extended through all ranks of society, not always excepting the clergy, and the depravity of taste through every branch of art and literature, every phase of life, public or domestic, every beauty of the older forms of architecture was replaced by a bastard system abounding in feeble curves and florid ornament, and the elegant simplicity of the earlier writers by pleonastic declamation" (*BG*, 7). Pottinger stands against Art Nouveau in architecture and literature. He rejects the "Byzantine" style as basically un-British; there were no Byzantine remains on the island, therefore, it was a foreign, unacceptable style. This critique predates the erection of the Westminster Roman Catholic Cathedral (1895–1903), designed by J. F. Bentley when Byzantine was the vogue of progressive architects in the 1890s and considered suitably "spiritual." The architectural program of that cathedral was, of course, itself a propagandistic challenge to the English Gothic and Tudor styles of the Established Church.

Society had decayed, Pottinger concludes, because of the loss of hereditary claims of birth, just as the Eastern Empire suffered from a line of rulers from the ranks. The development did not aid democracy but "served only to establish a tyranny of wealth, impudence, and unscrupulousness." The Ballot Act of 1872 was one of a series that undercut landowning interests, for whom Pottinger speaks, against the middle class and new rich. The great general Belisarius ("Belitzar"), the novel stresses, is a young, handsome, Thracian aristocrat. Despite such class distinctions, Pottinger exalts the low-born Theodora; her name, "Gift of God," part of the novel's title, is proof that what man condemns as common and unclean may be the instrument of Omnipotence. He fleshes this out by granting the empress second sight, even enabling her to "see" her sister Anastasia dying of consumption in a nunnery. In a novel that consistently mocks such supernatural gifts in other figures, it is an indication of Pottinger's apotheosis of Theodora.

Second only to the interest in the Fall of Rome was Victorian fascination with the Fall of Jerusalem (A.D. 69) before the forces of Vespasian and the benevolent Titus. Religious motifs and dreams of chivalry and the Crusades combined with the practical matters of the Eastern Question in European politics and the role of the Jews in the political life of the nation (after Jews were admitted to Parliament in 1858) to foster this type of story. George Alfred Henty (1832–1902), whose adventure books for boys set the style for similar literature before 1914, attempted to view the events at Jotapa, Gamala, and Jerusalem from the perspective of Josephus and the besieged Israelites, while maintaining the mythic quality of Titus' clemency in *For the Temple* (1887). On the other hand, Jane Margaret Strickland (1800–1888), the lesser known sister of Agnes Strickland (1797–1874), author of popular royal biographies, produced a "modern-antique" novel in which Jews are instantly converted along the guidelines of the London Society for Promoting Christianity among the Jews.[45] Strickland had the misfortune of being reviewed by George Eliot, who used this occasion to ridicule the whole genre of "silly novels by lady novelists."[46] Eliot herself later explored the contemporary role of the Jew in society and the nature of Zionism in *Daniel Deronda* (1876). As in Strickland's *Adonijah* (1856), most earlier novelists were cautiously concerned to have the Jews baptized, thus resolving any theological or social ambiguities posed for the Victorian age.

George J. Whyte-Melville (1821–78), the eldest son of a Scottish laird, composed *The Gladiators* in 1863.[47] Known as a veteran of the Crimea and an inveterate hunter (he was killed under his horse during a foxhunt in 1878), he was not highly regarded for his costume novels and modish attitudes; one critic, Michael Sadleir, has called him " 'Ouida' in breeches."

The Gladiators opens in Britain, where Esca the noble young British hero is captured by Roman legions during a Druid uprising and taken to Rome in slavery. Esca is described in terms of the physical beauty and strength of a statue of Mercury that readers recognize from the Tom Quad at Christchurch, Oxford. The novelist also lets his audience surmise that Esca is in fact the unacknowledged son of the Roman general Caius Levius Licinius, with whom the youth serves later in the story. Kept as a household slave, Esca excites the love of Valeria, a masculinized noblewoman, but rebuffs her for the pure spiritualized love of the Jewess Mariamne, a figure largely drawn from Scott's Rowena. Mariamne is in Rome with her father, Eleazar, a fanatical Jewish patriot, and her uncle Calchas, secretly a Christian and once a companion to Peter and Paul. They have come to bribe the emperor, Vitellius, to relieve the besieged city of Jerusalem. Vitellius is overthrown (A.D. 69) by Vespasian and reviled by the Roman mob before his death. Whyte-Melville makes oblique references to events in the nineteenth century; Victor Emmanuel had been proclaimed king of Italy in 1861, and the novel's fallen emperor bears a striking resemblance to Pius IX (Pio Nono). The action then shifts to Palestine. Esca joins the Jewish defenders out of love for Mariamne, and the young couple are won over to Christianity by the simple preaching and holy example of Calchas, who is eventually stoned to death by Zealots for proclaiming his conversion and repudiating

Judaism. The story of Stephen in *Acts* is an obvious reference here. During this sequence of events and throughout the novel (e.g., the Jews are served suckling pig at a Roman banquet) there is a strong anti–Semitic current.

The novel closes with a long and detailed portrayal of the final battle and storming of the Temple, announced by a prophet's lamentation. Valeria, who has followed Esca, joins the Roman legions clothed in armor like a "tutelary deity" and is killed. To post–Freudians her sexual transformation and the erotic quality of her ideas about warfare are important symptoms of Victorian attitudes toward women. The titillating use of the vulgar cry "Virgines ad lenones" ("Virgins to the panders") as a couplet with the more familiar "Christianos ad leones" ("Christians to the lions") is another aspect of the range of feelings about female sexuality held by male writers. Eleazar, the "Lion of Judah," is killed by the elephants of "asiatic auxiliaries," but Esca and Mariamne escape and are sheltered by Licinius. The depiction of famine and plague in the city recalls scenes associated with the Fall of Rome. Whyte–Melville has certainly read Horatio Smith's earlier re-creation of a similar scene and also shows his familiarity with the use of elephants in India for warfare. The novel presents vivid, although stylized, portraits of Vespasian, Titus, John of Gischala, and other historical participants.

Although Christianity and Judaism are presented as jumbled together in the vile reports of pagans, Whyte–Melville stresses the discontinuity. The novel repeats again and again that Judaism is flawed by its pride of pedigree and race, both secret and public, and the belief in a destiny "to lord it over the whole earth." This is especially characteristic of the Pharisees: "Their failings seem to have been inordinate religious pride, an undue exaltation of outward forms to the neglect of that which they symbolized, a grasping ambition of priestly power, and an utter want of charity for those who differed in opinion with themselves" (*G*, 295). As is obvious, he is referring to more than a distinct historical group. He is attacking the pharisaical attitude of other religious groups. Whyte–Melville also enumerates the "Epicurean" Sadducees and the Essenes; these last are singularized by their celibacy and communism of goods. They furnished early Christianity with converts and lessened both the "unnatural stage of fanaticism" of the Jewish nation and the lack of sufficient zeal in attracting converts. Chapter 8, on the composition and function of the Sanhedrin, shows the close link between this material and the Bible; it constitutes a footnote to the trial of Jesus before that body. So too, the extended description of the city and Temple precincts functions in much the same way, fleshing out the Gospel accounts.

Christianity is described as a religion of hearty self-sacrifice and compassion for one's neighbor, qualities especially identified with women and feminine virtues. Christianity is basically a conversion experience, but a gradual and slow one. The novel enunciates the particular problem involved in converting members of the "higher religions," certainly reflecting the contemporary experience of missionaries in the Middle East and India. Defining religion in largely deistic terms, he writes: "A religion which accepts the first great principle of truth, the omnipotence and eternity of the Deity, the immortality of souls, and the rewards and punishments of a life to come, stands already upon a solid basis; and, in all ages, the Jew, as in somewhat less degree the Mahometan, has been most unwilling to add to his own stern tenets the mild and loving doctrines of our revealed religion" (G, 117). In the same abstract vein, Whyte-Melville discerns that true religion is always prone to schism and factionalism for some providential purpose, and that while worship of God is part of a natural religion, tolerance and philanthropy needed the authority and example of "a teacher direct from heaven." Whyte-Melville insists on the simplicity and purity of primitive Christianity, apart from doctrinal or ecclesiological disputes. He states:

> There were no dogmas in those early days of the Christian church to distract the minds of its votaries from the simple tenets of their creed. The grain of mustard seed had not yet shot up into that goodly tree which has since borne so many branches, and the pruning-knife, hereafter to lop away so many redundant heresies, was not as yet unsheathed. The Christian of the first century held to a very simple exposition of his faith as handed down to him from his Divine Master. Trust and Love were the fundamental rules of his order. (G, 240)

Like other novelists of the period, he responded to the interest in church building and restoration, at its heyday in the 1850s and 1860s. He is adamantly anti-Ecclesiologist, which he defines in terms of spiritual pride: "In building the church they take note of every stone in the edifice, and lose sight of the purpose for which it was reared" (G, 249). While maintaining this simple gospel of love and philanthropy, he invests Christianity with a martial spirit and rhetoric (an inflated use of the Pauline imagery of armor and sword), a not uncommon choice of metaphor during this period and slightly later with the Salvation Army and Church Army. Sabine Baring-Gould composed "Onward Christian Soldiers" in 1864. Whyte-Melville's own military background in the Coldstream Guards and in the Crimea also contributed to his definition of a soldier's religion. Christianity, unlike the schools of gladiators, teaches one to die well, doing one's duty.

Like other examples of this genre, *The Gladiators* is a romantic tale of adventure and exotic locations. It paints a picture of classical society and religion that stresses the sensational, even erotic, qualities, from the imperial court to the debauches in the cult of Isis. After the turn of the century this attitude swung around, and works such as Dill's *Roman Society from Nero to Marcus Aurelius* (1904) were commonly cited to show that the standard conception of corruption and depraved morals needed radical revision. Whyte-Melville's tale, however, continues to be of service to the social and intellectual historian because it expresses Victorian attitudes, consciously and unconsciously, and maintains a bipolar view of two ages, so that Mutius Scaevola, who charred his hand in the flame, recalls Thomas Cranmer's martyrdom, and the elephants that topple the defenses of first-century Jerusalem recall the Bengal elephants of the Victorian Raj.

THE END OF THE AGE

The years after 1870 constituted a watershed in English thought, as indeed in European thought and political order in general, particularly in a united Germany, a united Italy, and a defeated France. During this decade there occurred a momentous "turning of the balance of educated intelligence from the current creed to unbelief."[48] Whatever the statistical evidence for such an assertion, there was a perceptible shift within the attitudes of all kinds of Christians who became defensive and at times hysterical, while humanist philosophers in Britain appeared confident and aggressive. Mrs. Humphry Ward announced "The New Reformation" triumphantly. The loss of faith and the desperate struggle to recover it were indeed common motifs in literature during several decades. After 1870 a purely human Christ and a purely humanistic "kernel" of Christianity, devoid of dogma, ritual, and one could say history, drew many religious seekers, of whom Ward's hero "Robert Elsmere" was representative. In church circles this concern over "essential" Christianity, reevaluating in particular the role of historic creeds and confessions, emerged in the agitated debate over the continuation of the Athanasian Creed in the revised Anglican Book of Common Prayer and the authoritative status of the three ancient creeds in the "Lambeth Quadrilateral" (1888).

In its way, however, humanist philosophy was a radical attempt to deny that orthodox Christianity could properly interpret its own message. Like the argument used by early Christianity against Judaism, orthodoxy was seen as an outmoded, feeble pedagogue carrying the message of human destiny that only the younger humanistic seers could read. That message was Christianity without a divine Christ. Winwood Reade, in *The Martyrdom of Man*, almost a substitute Bible for secularists, proclaimed: "We who assail the Christian faith are the true successors of the early Christians, above whom we are raised by the progress of eighteen hundred years. As they preached against gods made of stone, so we preach against gods that are made of ideas. As they were called atheists and blasphemers, so are we."[49]

At the other end of the spectrum the American revivalists Dwight L. Moody and Ira D. Sankey capped an enthusiastic reception throughout Britain by a triumphal visit to London in 1875. Although this "Yankee Hanky-Panky" was not welcomed by everyone, it signaled a return in some quarters to the security of fundamentals that persisted unabated down through the tidal wave of revivals in Wales in 1904. In the 1880s a feeling for mystery and intuition marked the critical interest in the philosophy of Henri Bergson and the mystics of the Middle Ages and later Church history. Even Richard W. Church, the Anglo-Catholic dean of St. Paul's, contributed to this fascination with his work on Blaise Pascal. Spiritualism, Theosophy, psychic research, and occultism were disparate manifestations of this mood. When Dean W. R. Inge, the modernist-Platonist, arrived in London in 1905, the ambiguous blends of rationalism and mysticism were already far advanced. He declared: "We cannot preserve Platonism without Christianity nor Christianity without

Platonism, nor civilization without both."[50] *Plato Christianus* shone forth in the mystic gloom. The difference earlier Victorian churchmen had seen between philosophy and Christianity, even when acknowledging the role of the former in the acceptance of the latter by the educated classes, was blurred. Philosophy was now seen as a rival revelation. Nonchurchly authors reflected these enigmatic variations between Christianity and humanism in the novels re-creating the Church's more distant past.

Marius the Epicurean (1885) has elicited a mass of modern critical comment because of its pivotal role in the evolution of the modern novel.[51] Different in particulars from most of the other novels in this study, Walter Horatio Pater's (1839–94) allusive, but detailed and personal, psychological Bildungsroman delineates the hero's elegiac "sensations and ideas" (as indicated by the book's subtitle) through twenty-eight nearly dialogueless chapters. Its treatment of antiquity never devolves into antiquarianism. At the beginning of chapter 16, Pater states, "Let the reader pardon me if here and there I seem to be passing from Marius to his modern representatives—from Rome, to Paris or London." But the topical intrusions are kept general so as not to disrupt the tone of his internal monologue.

Marius, a young provincial living during the reign of Marcus Aurelius (161–80), experiences a spiritual odyssey, moving from the tradition-bound religion of Numa to a hybrid Epicureanism (New Cyrenaicism), a process that "parallels Pater's move from traditional Christianity to Arnoldian 'culture,' from [Matthew] Arnold's 'Hebraism' to his 'Hellenism.'"[52] The second step from New Cyrenaicism to Stoicism takes place when Marius becomes an amanuensis for the emperor. That Stoicism is defined by the *Meditations* of Marcus Aurelius, letters to Marcus Cornelius Fronto, and the discourse "The Nature of Morals" by Fronto. These writings were traditionally taken as a kind of unbaptized Christianity. There is much of the medieval ascetic, "despiser of the body," in this view of Aurelius as "saint." But Pater sees this as the "error of Montanus" pitted against the psalmist's "beauty of holiness" (revised to an arch-Aesthete phrase: "the elegance of sanctity"). Extending the Renaissance back in time, Pater states that it was the bishop of Rome who defined what is called "humanism" by condemning the irrational excess of the Montanists and other "puritans." Marius turns from this radical disjunction of senses and spirit when he witnesses the insensitivity of the emperor at the gladiatorial shows ("Manly Amusement"), the renewal of persecution (described from Eusebius' *Epistle of the Churches of Lyons and Vienne*—a source of Anglo-Catholic devotion), and the limits of that Stoic reserve, tested at the lingering death of the little prince, Annius Verus. This pagan death closes the second stage of Marius' development. The death of children, a common Victorian experience, was a poignant and controverted point in contemporary debate over a legitimate Christian theodicy. Even Dostoevski's *The Brothers Karamazov* (1879–80) grapples with it at a critical point in the plot, in the "Rebellion" chapter prior to the parable of "The Grand Inquisitor." Why does a good God allow the innocent to suffer? Earlier in the century the dispute over baptismal regeneration had centered on children as well.

Marius has been exposed along the stages of life's way to other formative experiences. He bears the cumulative impression of Apuleius' *Golden Ass*, the deep significance of the Cupid and Psyche story, and the lessons in aesthetic Euphuism ("beautiful writing") of the supposed poet of the *Pervigilium Veneris* (in which love is, in fact, a rival religion). The death of this poet, Flavian ("A Pagan End"), punctuates the close of Marius' first phase. He is also exposed to the skepticism and philosophical relativism of Lucian, the author of the *Hermotimus*. There is no "one way," Marius learns from him; the best elements of all the rival philosophies are really the same as they approach transcendence. Everything that rises must converge. Current factions in Victorian England were advancing claims for various philosophical schools as the means for supporting the religion of the day, just as a redefined Thomism was declared in the papal encyclical *Aeterni Patris* (1879) to be the quintessential support of Catholicism, before the constructive pluralism of medieval Scholasticism was fully understood. Joseph Henry Shorthouse, author of the mystical pastiche *John Inglesant* (1880), a novel re-creating the reign of Charles I, had suggested that a renewed Platonism as expressed in previous times was compatible with high Anglicanism.[53] For some, such a philosophical underpinning claimed for theology was blasphemous; for others, philosophy was enough in itself. Marius desires to rise above diverting and exclusive claims of rival philosophies. "There is but one road that leads to Corinth" (chap. 24), Lucian claims. All are pilgrims on that way.

Marius has also been in contact with Christians, seen as a fringe group in antiquity—an important aspect of the novel's historical verisimilitude. He attends a Ritualistic church ("Divine Service") and becomes friends with Cornelius, who materializes in gold helmet and armor (described like the spiritual ideal of Sir Galahad for Charlotte Yonge or St. George for Shorthouse). This figure is actually Christ, the knight of a new age, who is to marry the "temperate beauty" Caecelia (like Anastasia in Lockhart's *Valerius*, neither sensuous nor erotically tempting), who is the Hellenic embodiment of early Christianity. The question of the degree to which Christianity had absorbed Hellenism into its ritual, doctrine, and moral values was a complex one for late Victorian religious writers. Inquirers asked whether Hellenism was a legitimate preparation or vehicle for Christian truth or whether that received truth had to be dehellenized in order to restore the original, pristine message. Pater stands on the side of Christianity's absorptive power but is not concerned with the larger doctrinal dispute. In his symbol set Cornelius and Caecelia are Christ and the Church. Marius, largely ignorant of Christianity, has also experienced a mystic illumination ("The Will as Vision") as one step in his spiritual growth, establishing his belief in a personal creator. The controverted ecclesiastical debate over miracles is far from such an experience. In the hero's final stage, a frenzied mob, panicked by an earthquake (described without the sensationalism of the "Catastrophe School"), apprehends Marius and Cornelius, who has mysteriously reappeared, while they are at the tomb of the Christian martyr Hyacinth (perhaps at Sabino). Marius arranges for his friend's escape and takes his place. On the journey back to Rome he contracts a fever and is cared for by Christians who give him the *viaticum* just before he dies and then venerate him as a martyr.

The argument among critics over Marius' death and its meaning has been prolonged and fervent. Did he have a conversion? Was he a martyr? It seems clear that Marius did die a Christian; Wolff's suggestion concerning the verbal transformation from pagan *animula* to the Christian *anima* (as in Tertullian's *Anima naturaliter Christiana*) in referring to Marius' death is an indication of Pater's intention.[54] T. S. Eliot observed that Marius just "drifts," not undergoing a full conversion, basically because Pater had no direct anchor in contemporary religious developments or institutions.[55] Vogeler argues, on the other hand, that this is the very reason for viewing the talk on primarily psychological rather than theological grounds. Religion, such as the comprehensive "Atmosphere" of ritual, is anthropologically necessary; the dogmatic truth of a particular religion is not ultimately necessary.[56] While leaning toward her understanding, it is necessary to maintain that even the undogmatic, untheological "essence" of Christianity for Marius is still Christianity for Pater, not Buddhism or Theosophy. Another way to ask the crucial question is whether the "test" of Marius' Christianity would christen believers in the 1880s. Is the Christlike sacrifice of one's own life for one's friend sufficient to define a "Christian"? For Pater and for other writers concerned with the metamorphosis of modern Christianity, the answer is yes. This is confirmed further by the illumination (a form of baptism) in the symbol-laden garden of olives. The further questions about immortality, resurrection, and purgation after death are best left to silence, these later writers insisted. Anglo-Catholic theologians of the period, like the *Lux Mundi* group and their kenotic Christology, stressed the Incarnation of Christ. But Pater, and writers like Mrs. Humphry Ward, focused on the Imitation of Christ. This explains the wide Victorian popularity of lives of St. Francis of Assisi, reports of Father Damien the Leper of Molokai, the novel *In His Steps* (1897) by the American Charles M. Sheldon, and the republication of the late-medieval *Imitation of Christ*, which went through over a hundred separate editions in the two decades before the close of the century.[57] The quest for the historical Jesus, the human Christ, was not the quest for the historical Church that characterized one aspect of the early Tractarians.[58]

Contemporary critics recognized the relation of *Marius* to the tradition of the novel of antiquity; the *Edinburgh Review* discussed it jointly with John W. Graham's (1859–1932) melodramatic novel of the age of Tiberius, *Neaera* (1886).[59] This novel re-creates Tiberius' retreat on the island of Capreae (Capri) in the Gulf of Naples around A.D. 32. From that island lair the imperial "tiger" issued edicts of death, orders compassed and executed by the prefect Sejanus and the pander Tigellinus, who appear in the novel. The book alludes to rumors of Tiberius' "vicious habits." The seat of empire is bathed in "Imperial luxury, and, if tradition speak truth, of Imperial vice" (*N*, 132). A centurion of the praetorians ("janissaries") falls in love with the beautiful seventeen-year-old Neaera, the daughter of a potter, an inventor and craftsman, who is called a "leveller." She is discovered (by the possession of an Islamic, but perhaps

Masonic, amulet!) to be the kidnapped heiress of Senator Fabricius, the aged survivor of an old Etrurian family (read pre-Conquest English gentry). A Petronius-like feast is given by the historical Apicius, "most wonderfully like unto the manner of moderns." This jaded spendthrift hosts languid dandies, his youthful Greek favorite ("Erotion" is the youth's name, if there was any doubt in the reader's mind about why he was the favorite), and the vulgar nouveau-riche Zoilius. Apicius insults them and then commits suicide. His sister, Lady Plantia, described as though a Hardy heroine, loves the centurion; she impulsively joins a transport stocking Tiberius' island brothel and connives to have Neaera abducted to Capri. Tiberius, surrounded by Chaldean soothsayers and philosophers, whimsically decides to see justice done in the matter, perhaps out of fear of the senatorial class. He himself plays the sleuth, uncovering the motives and deeds of the several characters. Neaera is restored to her wealth and noble family. It is observed that "none but noble blood could so nobly withstand such a terrible test." But her refinement and bearing already reveal her station from birth. At last she marries the young praetorian, whom Tiberius uses later as a spy on very Victorian cloak-and-dagger assignments to precipitate the downfall of Sejanus.

Christianity, of course, does not appear. There is, however, a sort of proto-Christian concern for the poor and downtrodden. These are not the poorest people but the oppressed artisans, shopkeepers, and middle class. For the first time in these novels we are conducted through the Transtibertine quarter, teaming with "swinkers" (laborers), fishermen, tanners, and Jews. It is like the "bustling images of the Liverpool or London docks." This environment and its hardships take a toll on these honest craftsmen. The potter observes to the court dignitaries, who are discussing abstractly the boom and bust economy: "The life of a poor workman is seldom anything but the dreary history of toil for daily bread. One day resembles another, save when food is scarcer and labour harder" (N, 332). He is then murdered by imperial order. Although it is not fully worked out in the novel, Graham's concern for these questions reflects contemporary discussions of social Darwinism and the class struggle.

The potter and his daughter represent the pure, moral standard; in the depths of moral decay are arrayed both the lowest classes and the aristocracy, connected through their orgies. The person and conduct of the seventy-year-old emperor are focused on. The "self-imposed waste" of his life and its "vicious indulgence" are blamed on bad stock: "He was of the Claudian family, and were they not ever proud and insufferable?" The narrator goes on to say in summation: "Such were the most particular personal characteristics of the tyrant who, for some occult reason, had foresworn the seat of his empire, and had secluded himself in a rocky islet. . . . His continued absence, taken in conjunction with the busy ambition of the Pretor, was fruitful of rumours in no way favourable to the supremacy of Caesar" (N, 147). Contemporary readers would recognize the imperial retreat of Osborne on the Isle of Wight, where the sixty-seven-year-old empress was rumored, even in print after 1867, to have made an unseemly alliance with John Brown, the queen's gillie, either for erotic or occult purposes.[60] Of course, it was remembered, she had sprung from the mad, bad, and overbearing House of Hanover.

By the mid-1880s a novelist could choose to tell a tale of classical antiquity without trying to mention Christians, even obliquely. The anachronism of talking about Christians in A.D. 30 would not have been absolutely determinative. Other novelists made the necessary historical leaps; some even discussed Christianity and Periclean Athens together.[61] Instead, Graham is interested in a romantic tale that is at the same time an expression of late Victorian attitudes on class, station, and the morality of social obligations connecting the levels of society. He seems to side with the expectation of upward mobility for a properly deferential lower and middle class, accompanied by a view of the aristocracy's need for new blood and moral rigor. Religion is replaced by a careful observation of class structures. By making his potter's child a secret heiress, he adopts a familiar literary convention of his times but blunts the point of his social criticism. The sentimentalized story of a poor girl who may in fact be the offspring of the aristocracy, as in "The Princess and the Pea," is romance, not social realism.

The reign of the emperor Domitian (81–96) traditionally stood—as did the reigns of Caligula and again Nero—in sharp contrast to that of his brother Titus (79–81), who preceded him, and of "The Five Good Emperors," who succeeded him. Mary Hoppus's (Mrs. Alfred Marks) three-volume *Masters of the World* (1888) delineates the brutalities of this self-styled "Master and God," culminating in his assassination.[62] The story opens in A.D. 93 and follows the initiation of the plot of Caius Piso against Domitian. Piso, impatient with current Epicurean conduct, draws his moral values from Plato and Socrates, who are the "Masters of all," and chooses other aspects of the age's competing philosophies. The logomachy of Stoics and Epicureans has disgusted him. Furthermore, he believes, a priori, in a judgment to come, despite the scoffers. Piso learns that a young friend, Aulus Atticus, "radiant as the young Apollo" (another "Cornelius" figure), has been converted to Christianity at Ephesus by John, an "old Jew priest." The novel stresses the presence of noble Christians at Caesar's court: Pomponia Graecina, the wife of Plautius, who was a general under Agricola in Britain; the British Claudia Rufina and Pudens; and even Domitilla and her husband, Flavius Clemens, consul in 95, who stood on the step to the throne.[63]

Piso thinks that the Christian superstition is some form of self-mutilating fanaticism, like the priesthood of Cybele, and has difficulty distinguishing circumcision from the "mysterious washing" of the new sect. Celibacy and baptism are the dimly perceived notions. The confusion between circumcision and baptism is meant to link those two rites for the knowledgeable modern reader. Other pagans explain that "Chrestus," an "artificer" (the word is intentionally ambiguous to convey the sense of both craftsman and reputed trickster), founded a religion that was harmless but appeared to have much in common with Cynic philosophy, appealing to the dregs of society. Others indicate that Christians believe in one God, slay no victims, and avoid the Jewish "hatred of the human race." The Jews in the novel are moneylenders, drawn in part from Scott's *Ivanhoe*, and are dressed in Shakespearean "garbardine." The city tolerates them because of "poor little Poppaea." Like the Stoics, they hate the world, save for the soul. But Christians take pleasure in the world because of its divine origin. Of course, this holy pleasure does not degenerate into license. Christians keep as pure as the Pythagoreans; in fact, Christianity is better than the other philosophies: "Are not these doctrines more adapted to the circumstances of men than anything the philosophers have taught us?" a Christian observes. The fundamental belief of Christianity is the Resurrection. Because Christians are sure of that as a "fact," they then believe Christ's words in Scripture. To this belief is added traditional images of Christ. Jesus appears in a dream as the stigmata-marked Good Shepherd. Christ is acclaimed as the culmination of the lineage of the kings of Judah, but is ruler of a heavenly kingdom, postponed until the end of the world. There is, then, no eschatological tension in the novel.

Hoppus uses the Roman Catholic Douai version of Scripture throughout; likewise, the full name *Jesus Christ* is set off from the text in a different typeface (*M*, 3:31). The Sermon on the Mount is worn as a parchment talisman, as though in imitation of Blaise Pascal. (Even with all this solemnity, the subject of death and immortality is treated with one touch of unintentional humor. When asked what death is like, a character responds, "Like going out alone into a cold winter's night,—like those in Britain—away from all I love.") Anacletus, the bishop of Rome, presides at a Eucharist (also called a Sacrifice and Sacrament), a solemn service of prayer and thanksgiving. After psalms, a discourse, oblations of bread and wine, portioning of gifts for the poor, and love feasts, the Christians take the white bread from a golden plate and drink from a golden cup. They stand, kneel, and prostrate themselves, perhaps reflecting the author's distinction of various classes of catechumens and public penitents. At the communion they exclaim, "The Body of Christ! The Blood of Christ!" anachronistically chant the Trisagion as a thanksgiving, and then disperse. Baptism is not treated. The martyrdom of Aristarchus is described, but the narrator cautions that the spectators may have elaborated details to suggest supernatural events. She is not overly credulous but nevertheless includes miraculous details: a flaming halo on the martyr and an unseasonal snow.

The most formidable rival to nascent Christianity is not philosophy, Judaism, or pagan cults but the most renowned celebrity of that period, the wonder-worker Apollonius of Tyana, a pagan Christ. His biography was written by Flavius Philostratus. Various reports described his itinerant preaching, miracles, his message of love for one's neighbor, and the persecution he suffered. Newman himself had written flippantly on Apollonius and miracles for the *Encyclopedia Metropolitana* (1825–26). Apollonius appears in the novel and is described as dignified, self-possessed, upright, and active. An enthusiast declares: "He's the wisest man alive—a second Socrates. He foretold the Plague at Ephesus, and he knows all about a man as soon as he looks at him" (*M*, 1:216–17). Apollonius is arrested, brought before a prosecutor, and charged with having sacrificed a young boy during the waning moon in order to learn the line of imperial succession. The miracle worker suddenly disappears from the basilica. The novel is filled with similar allusions to magic and the occult: a talisman with the Seal of Solomon, ghosts (including Flavius Clemens), incantations, mystic candles made of human fat, walking statues, centaurs and camelopards, a "black dinner" (like Flaubert's), dreams, and visions. Much of this is presided over by the psychic and soothsayer Ascletario ("Star-gazer"), whose "house was a Private Inquiry Office for half Rome." This reflects the large following spiritualism and occult experimentation had in England in the 1880s.

Far more central to the expressed concerns of the novel, and second only to the description of court life, are the two major moral questions Hoppus treats: homosexuality and divorce. Both demonstrate for her the moral decay of the age. She constructs a biting tract for the times about the love whose name she does not hesitate to speak. She describes the "silk-bedizened fops" who ostentatiously parade their vice "and who always seemed just ready to expire with well-bred languor" (M, 1:177– 78). One such "little marmoset" is seen "walking with an elderly man, who had his arm in lover-like fashion round the neck of a very handsome boy. As he walked, he played with the boy's long and beautiful hair" (M, 1:232). This is post-Wildean London with a vengeance. Parallel to this is the indignant appraisal of contemporary attitudes to women. Hoppus opens the novel with the image of Nature as the Great Mother, the Mighty Mother. As a vocal feminist, she finds society of the antique period, reflected in the Victorian scene, wretched. Epicureans preach that the gods did not make woman, and women acquiesced to this lesser status by affecting to be more licentious than they in fact were. A number of negative types—the adulterous empress Domitia, a gladiatrix, and snobblish coquettes—are introduced. Such a skewed view of woman, she feels, promulgated by men and accepted with docility by women, is behind the rising divorce rate: "In that age of corruption and license, all the old hooks were loosened. It had once been the boast of Rome, that for five hundred years no Roman had divorced his wife; but now the law itself permitted eight divorces" (M, 1:315). This question had generated considerable debate in England before the Divorce Bill (1857) and then in the following decades as further refinements in the laws were made.[64] Liberalization of the marriage laws was contested by various religious groups. The question of true divorce a vinculo matrimonii was even a subject investigated in the writings of the Fathers of the Church, whose opposition complicated the legal changes. Hoppus does not look to the Fathers of the Church for her ideal of womanhood or woman's role in society. She portrays Pomponia, Claudia Rufina, and Domitilla for that purpose. These were not "nuns" and virgins but pious and strong Christian mothers and matrons.

Social evils exist, Hoppus insists, while the State claims the right to establish and regulate religion. Piso tells the Christian Aulus, who is preempted by his religious affiliation from a role in government by the classical version of the Test Act, that "religion is at best a matter of opinion and not knowledge, and as the chief use of religion is to promote public morality, and render Government easier by the invocation of divine sanctions and prohibitions, the State has a right to decide on the religion that shall be adopted—adding that it had always exercised this right" (*M*, 3:171). In Victorian terms, the Established Church, as Hoppus understood its nature and function, not only violates freedom of conscience but also fails to maintain the moral quality of the nation, which alone could justify that privileged position. Unlike other authors of her generation, she retains a definite core of necessary doctrine (as a Catholic she stresses the centrality of the Eucharist and the Resurrection) and does not find philosophy a satisfying substitute for Christian belief. She has a highly developed sense of Christianity as a religion, a historical community maintained by cultic activity. Apollonius and magic are therefore seen as serious threats, understood as rival religions. But like her contemporaries, her energies are focused not on theological questions and explanations but on the moral crises of the age. Morality, rather than dogma, is at the heart of the *Masters of the World*.

The reign of Nero (54–68) was a popular theme for nineteenth-century authors; British writers found it particularly appealing, partly because the burning of Rome mirrored the Great Fire of London (1662) and the conflagration of the houses of Parliament in 1836, and partly because the luxury and vice of Nero's aesthetic court, contrasted with the example of the persecuted Christians, yielded a sensational mine of material. Victorians in the 1880s and 1890s had their own aesthetes to ponder. The emphasis in a novel by Hugh Farrie ("Hugh Westbury") is on the cruel and sensual; Nero gives a graphic description of scourging, and a beautiful twelve-year-old boy is hunted down in the palace by romping dandies using bullwhips. This work does not depend on detailed or accurate knowledge of Roman society or antiquarian information; all the Latin quotations, for example, are jumbled or misspelled. The three volumes of Farrie's novel *Acte* (1890), each devoted to a separate female figure—Judith, Poppaea, and Acte—depict graphically the moral corruption of the last of the Julio-Claudians, while at the same time commenting on the effect of religious experiences on the eponymous heroines.[65] Unlike Hoppus, the author has no feminist conscience to ease; it is quite the reverse. The novel is blatantly misogynist and women are seen, as one character states, as the "gender of gestation and jealousy." It is clear that Farrie did not intend, nor was he equipped, to re-create classical attitudes toward women; he thought his own viewpoint sufficed. The age itself, a period of ennui that is destructive of individuality and generative of skepticism, is the main attraction. The narrator observes: "The uncertainty of life, the fading away of old faiths, the doubtful voices of philosophy, and the desperate and jubilant wickedness of the foremost men and women of the Empire, bred, in thoughtful minds, an almost sullen fatalism which left its stamp upon the features."

Christianity and Judaism are portrayed as "like and yet unlike." Judith is the Jewish example of a woman filled with "mystic fervour," unable to assist mankind as she desires because of her "formal faithless faith." The animosity toward the Jews is disguised but present throughout the novel. The Jews are seen as oriental fanatics, cousins of the Carthaginians. They are "stiffbacked," a quality more positively identified in the "Teutonic peoples" as independence. Jews with "harsh semitic features" appear shabbily dressed and grimy, characterized by a "love of shekels" and "Hebrew profit." This is not so much a picture of Jews in Rome but the imagined Jews in the slums and sweatshops of the immigrant East End of Victorian London. Judaism was a fashionable novelty in Nero's circle (as it was in the contemporary prince of Wales's set). The narrator reports that Poppaea had patronized it "without understanding anything of Hebrew theology," having been introduced to it by Babillus the astrologer, an Ephesian Jew. Nero even tells Tigellinus he plans to establish Judaism as the State religion and appoint a Jew as pontifex maximus (AC, 3:30). The hatred of Jews for Christians is absolute, a passion "only possible in Oriental theologies." Through Poppaea they are finally able to vent that fury.

The Greek Acte, Nero's servant and mistress, represents dawning Christianity. She already believes in a god of love active in human affairs; but through "the Preacher" she learns of a "great god" whose qualities are love for the weak and pity for the suffering. That is the core of Christianity. This core, however, has an eschatological thread woven into it. Acte is persuaded by her dreams of the immanent arrival of "armies of angels" bringing the Last Day. The novel views this as pious delusion. The Preacher, a harsh Evangelical enthusiast, convinces her also of the sinfulness of her relations with Nero and the need for repentance attached to the promises of eternal life and forgiveness. The Christian preaches, "He that believeth is saved, but he that believeth not is damned" (Mark 16:16); significantly the Marcan phrase *and is baptized* after "believeth" is omitted. Faith, rather than regenerative baptism, is the converting experience and focus. The narrator makes a distinction between the girl's true and immediate conversion (i.e., resolution to reform) and the distinct process of reformation, a later, gradual transformation. This process in Acte's case is hampered by the Preacher's own dogmatic position: "The subtle-minded Hebrew was an enthusiast in technical theology, and he perplexed her by his expositions of the principle of justification by faith. Just as she was beginning to lay hold of the idea of wrong and repentance, she was plunged into confusion by the suggestion that abstract opinion, and not practical amendment, is the keystone of happiness" (*AC*, 2:80). The identification of the principle of justification by faith with the Hebrew mind is a reflection of the Victorian debate over Pauline Christianity. Here Farrie derides this point of Paul's theology. Theology and doctrine, "abstract opinion," are not, the reader is informed, true Christianity. This contrast is heightened by the confrontation between the Preacher and Seneca, Nero's Stoic mentor. The narrator observes that cultivated Romans recognized the moral poverty of their old creeds and philosophies and perceived that Christianity filled "a hidden want," providing solace for the soul that rationalizing paganism was incapable of giving. Only the Vestal Virgins, a wealthy "religious corporation," escape the cynical humor of the age, "which did not spare the Supreme Pontiff," even as *Punch* did not spare Pio Nono or Leo XIII but was generally respectful of the nuns in nursing sisterhoods. Seneca, on the other hand, is a "Stoic saint" who poses a real threat to the Preacher's new gospel, a gospel demonstrating the fulfillment of prophecies to the Jews and "marvellous narratives" to the Gentiles. Against Seneca, who flatly declared that prophecies are silly legends and miracles simply do not occur, the Preacher "faltered." The Stoic, for whom virtue alone is the summum bonum, sums up some hard questions for the

Christian. Why should a good God let his innocent Son suffer death, when even the immoral Father Zeus would not have allowed such a thing? Where is justice in the Atonement? Seneca also wants to know, as others do, why stories about the dead raised to life always occur in out-of-the-way corners of the world, like Judaea or in primitive societies: "I would gladly know why the gods always choose the earliest days of a religion to manifest themselves" (*AC*, 1:242–43). The Preacher, noted as a finer orator than Seneca, admonishes the philosopher that it is through Jesus alone that mankind can come to God. Seneca's response exhibits Farrie's understanding of the true relationship of the human (half-brute, half-God) to the divine. It is the credo of the liberal, humanistic philosophy of the late Victorian period. He recognizes the limits of that message: Seneca cannot control Nero's vice; but philosophy alone can express a true religion of tolerance and philanthropy. "'God,' answered Seneca sternly, 'is our Father; He is a friend never far off; He has ever been worshipped and loved by the best men of the world, who have sought Him behind the mysteries of our nature; and you say that none may come to Him save through the foolish superstitions of your race'" (*AC*, 1:252–53). During an ecstasy "the Voice" tells the Preacher that Seneca is correct and humbles the persevering enthusiast: "May not Mine come to Me save through thee?" (*AC*, 1:254). The Christian is instructed to oversee only that portion of humankind that gladly adopts the Preacher's message, doctrine, and authority. Hebrew has met Hellene, duty has confronted love, and the Hellene has conquered.

NOVELISTS OF ANCIENT BRITAIN

During the last decades of the age, while some authors probed the culture and social relations of classical Rome to provide a base to articulate concern over the declining morality and competing philosophies of their own day, other novelists sought to find those basic virtues, which seemed to characterize the British spirit, within the history of the nation itself. Churchly writers had exploited this material as the basis for either affirming or rejecting connections between British Christianity and the Roman Church. They either affirmed the Roman mission of Augustine to Kent in the sixth century or emphasized the non-Roman tradition and usages of the earlier independent Celtic Church. This theological debate entered imperceptibly into the romances of nonchurchly authors who were intent on describing British character and topography, based on an exalted patriotism and love of Empire.[66] For the first time novels of antiquity portrayed life and events primarily situated within the British Isles.

The revolt of Britain in A.D. 60, tied to the establishment of emperor worship and the ensuing tax support for that (identified by some later commentators as a "tithe"), had provided native-minded Victorians who had read Tacitus and Dio Cassius with the compelling figure of the warlike British queen and widow Boudicca (mistakenly called "Boadicea" at times), recalling the heroic bronze figure of the East Anglian liberator that was placed near Parliament during the nineteenth century.[67] The loss of imperial control in Britain under Honorius, the gradual Roman withdrawal (385–407), and the coming of the Saxons play important roles in historical fiction. George Alfred Henty (1832–1902) combined in *Beric the Briton* (1893) the story of Boudicca's rebellion, the sack of Colchester (where the cult of the emperor Claudius was imposed), and the climactic burning of Rome, during the period A.D. 60 to 70.[68] Druids, Christians, gladiators, and Calabrian bandits appear alongside Boudicca, Suetonius, the Roman governor of Britain, and Nero. Sir Herbert Eustace Maxwell (1845–1937), the Scottish antiquarian and military historian, portrayed in *A Duke of Britain* (1895) the Roman district of Novantia (Galloway in southwest Scotland), Milan, and Rome during the period A.D. 397–406, managing to mix history with a dose of Charlie-over-the-waterism.[69] The title of earl of Galloway was held in the nineteenth century by a branch of the royal Stewarts. Flavius Stilicho, Honorius' general and effective ruler of the empire (395–408) by his defeat of the Ostrogoths and Visigoths, appointed Cunedda, a Pict tribune, as duke of Britain. Alaric's invasion of Italy and defeat (402) are also treated in the story.

Thorpe Forrest's *Builders of the Waste* (1899) depicts the Saxon conquest of Deira. The story of Pope Gregory the Great's pun about Angles and angels, after viewing the sale as slaves of pretty blond English boys in Rome, is recounted, as in so many of these novels. The late Victorian fascination with this story, traditionally seen as the impetus for the later mission to Kent (597), reflects both the contemporary literary cult of the child (i.e., the pure child who becomes the evangelist of the pure, British Gospel) and the homoerotic boy-love of such figures as Symonds,

Carpenter, Rolfe, and Wilde.[70] Miss H. Elrington's *A Story of Ancient Wales* (1900) brings together the patriotic aspirations of the early Britons with the indigenous religion of the Druids. Their ruins are described, as are their fire-worship rites and sacrifices of criminals, prisoners, and physical defectives for the purposes of propitiation and augury. The turn of the century was also the heyday of this Druid revival mixed with magic, as seen in the career of Aleister Crowley. Florence Gay's *The Druidess* (1908) is another example, using the vividly rendered locale of Devon and the Severn River. In Elrington's tale the Druid defeat at their sanctuary of Mona (the isle of Anglesey) by the Romans in A.D. 50 is treated, along with the exploits of Caractacus both in the region around Chester and in Rome.[71] Unlike the churchly writers who saw these events in terms of the dawn of Christianity in Britain, the Druid sympathizers saw it as a twilight and end of an age. Britain's own imperial colonizing had made people sensitive to the suppression of indigenous cultures and religions. The Druid hill forts are often compared to the African kraals of the Transvaal. The Victorian novelists also conveyed a revisionist view of the pervasive importance of the Druids, especially as teachers and judges, that no ancient writer had understood. Rudyard Kipling's stories of the evacuation of Britain by the British in his *Puck of Pook's Hill* (1906) and A. Conan Doyle's stories in his collection *The Last Galley* (1911) capped the wide interest in similar tales concerning Britain up to the imperial Age of Arthur.

Early Church or classical novels by nonchurchly authors exploited the basic components in such literature. Their romantic tales used historical and geographical material, blending historical figures and events with myth and extracts of classical literature. The day-to-day details of life in antiquity were deemed as important as the philosophical or political highlights of those times. Pater and other observers contributed to a new interest in Italian history and culture linked to a reevaluation of the Renaissance, although the details of such study more often merely confirmed the superiority of northern, Gothicized culture over an indolent south. By the end of the century there are fewer architectural and topographical digressions, replaced by concern for the social institutions and relationships of the early age. Descriptions of the sanitary functions of aqueducts fade and details about class structure or the politics of the principate come forward. It should be remembered that Fox Talbot's first calotype photograph appeared the same year as Lytton's *Last Days of Pompeii*. Photographic collections (many of which were undertaken by clerics) and the boom in Victorian tourism curbed the need for the earlier detailed accounts. The novels continued to slake the thirst for spectacles and circuses. The catastrophic and violent images of gladiator shows, battles, the Fall of Rome, and the sack of Jerusalem mark these novels. These events are described for their pure sensationalism and are not intended as apocalyptic images proving scriptural prophecy. But their use of the traditional images, tone, and eschatological language of the Bible assisted the theological use of this material by churchly novelists. On the other hand, the nonchurchly writers depend on Gibbon and more modern historiography as sources rather than the patristic sources, great monastic collections, or earlier hagiographies.

These novels continue the Gothic tradition in literature. Horror, melodrama, and violent action distinguish them from the more meditative and increasingly psychological studies of much religious fiction of the Victorian era. There are, however, elements of both melodrama and meditation in almost all Romantic literature. Sensational details abound: talismans, violent deaths, daring abductions and hairbreadth escapes, disguised identities, love philters, secret doors, and witches. Shakespeare's weird sisters, Horace's Canidia, and Lytton's Saga of Vesuvius appear transformed in novels throughout the period.

Religion and philosophy play prominent roles. Pagan cult is ridiculed, usually in association with the popular devotions of modern popery. But there is an Enlightenment toleration, even sympathy, for pagan philosophies: Stoic, Epicurean, Cynic, Platonic, and Aristotelian. These are not seen, however, as a mere stage in mankind's preparation for Christianity, as the churchly writers stress. Rather, particular philosophies are either rejected outright as inadequate solutions to moral problems or seen as viable alternatives to Christianity. The philosophies are primarily weighed as ethical systems in the balance of Victorian justice. There is at times an idea of a linear climb from particular schools of philosophy to an all embracing "Truth." That truth is not automatically identified with Christ or the Gospel. On the other hand, there is some disparity in the depiction of classical society generally; it is either sunk in vice and despair or exalted to a proto-Christian perfection. The figures of Titus, Trajan, Hadrian, the Antonines, and Seneca are canonized as pagan saints. There is a more complex understanding of the confrontation of Christianity with classical culture; it is not the simple "darkness and dawn" suggested by churchly writers.

Jews are aligned with early Christianity but condemned for their negative, "manhating" theology. Anti-Semitism and "Teutomania" abound in the novels. There is almost no recognition of a continuing theological role for Judaism in salvation history. The Old Testament prophecies are vaguely recalled, but even in relationship to Christological questions these are seen as having little force. The role of the Jews in Victorian society and the emerging Zionism of the age are the unarticulated questions expressed haphazardly in this literature. The novelists savage the oriental fanaticism of Jewish moneylenders, but at the same time pay courtesy to Baron Rothschild.

Christianity is presented as the expression of a simple message, at times indistinguishable from humanistic philosophy. The cultic and institutional life of the Early Church in priesthood and sacraments all but vanishes. Christians are divided into two basic types: the harsh, intolerant dogmatists and genial, Hellenistic philanthropists. Churchmen are more likely to identify ideal Christianity with historical churchmen, for example, Augustine, Cyprian, or John Chrysostom, or ecclesiastical institutions. If churchmen criticize a particular Father, they invariably offer alternate models. Charles Kingsley criticized Cyril of Alexandria and substituted Augustine of Hippo and Synesius of Cyrene. Christianity for these churchly writers is not just the quest of individual believers or doubters. The Gospel of Christianity is viewed in nonchurchly novels as basically a promise of eternal life and immortality as recompense for poverty, suffering, and death. Biblical miracles still appear, but ecclesiastical miracles are openly questioned or mocked. Just as prominent as these are the magical and prophetic experiences of non-Christians, many of whom are treated with great sympathy. The novels reflect the increasing Victorian fascination with psychic and paranormal phenomena: mesmerism, magnetism, spiritualism, occultism, and dream interpretation. Those experiences often play a role in the conversion of characters. Such conversion is not sudden, as in the case of Paul or Constantine as these were traditionally understood. Conversion is portrayed as a spiritual progress, and education, a development of "wings for the soul," using a highly significant Platonic vocabulary.

The novels are also important records of an ongoing critique of contemporary society, its ideas and sensations. Issues are discussed or mentioned in passing that demonstrate the intellectual topicality of these novels. Early in the period, attitudes about Regency culture and Reform were displayed in fiction. Utilitarianism, imperialism, and feminism also leave their marks. The post-Gibbon reevaluation of the historic "barbarian" roots of the nation, animated by Romantic nostalgia and heroicism, sets the national life apart from the weak and decayed universalism of the Roman Empire, just as it was set apart by its military and economic power from the political universalism of Napoleon or the religious universalism of Roman Catholicism. Late in the century that localized patriotism is reexpressed in tales of Britain rebelling against or being evacuated by the alien legions of Rome. That historical epoch is probed to yield elements of a basic national character and peculiar British virtues. These are seen as an indigenous remedy to the moral crises of the age. Institutional churches and the established religion seem to nonchurchly writers either unable or unwilling to handle effectively this pervasive crisis as the century and the reign ended.

2

"NEW FOES WITH AN OLD FACE"

Historical Novels of Charles Kingsley, Nicholas Wiseman, and John Henry Newman

VICTORIAN ANTI-CATHOLICISM boiled over in the events surrounding the Papal Aggression of 1850, the deferred restoration by Pius IX of the English Catholic hierarchy headed by Nicholas Wiseman as cardinal archbishop of Westminster.[1] Several long-standing issues contributed to the ferocity that greeted the Papal Bull, misread as a usurpation of political power instead of a program for reordering the spiritual government of the Catholic community.[2] Wiseman's own flamboyant pastoral, "From Out the Flaminian Gate"; the paranoid accusations in the "Durham letter" of the prime minister, Lord Russell; the injudicious Mansion House oration of Lord Chancellor Truro; the hue and cry of the *Times* and the popular press, all contributed to and perpetuated the spontaneous combustion of Guy Fawkesism throughout the nation. Taking the cue from Russell, this popular Protestantism also railed against those "unworthy sons" of the Established Church, the Anglo-Catholic Ritualists, who betrayed the "immortal martyrs of the Reformation" with the "mummeries of superstition."[3] Once again apocalyptic imagery was employed: at the Great Exhibition six months later visitors described a colossal statue of St. Michael trampling Satan as "the Queen and the Pope."[4] In the eternal contest between Light and Darkness, free Englishmen, the polemicists urged, needed weapons to counter the agents of papal tyranny. Novels were one such weapon, and the novels of Wiseman, Newman, and Kingsley should be considered against the background of those popular literary efforts.[5]

The 1850 papal rescript, "Universalis ecclesiae," besides affecting the polity of the Roman Catholic Church in England, also influenced profoundly the spirituality and liturgical piety of that community. Polity and piety were intimately linked. Ultramontane circles in England, like those earlier on the Continent, combined reactionary Romeward social and political expectations with more fervid personal piety and public devotional practices. Three major categories of devotions were gradually introduced to England: benediction of the blessed sacrament, more frequent communion, the forty-hours' devotions and exposition of the sacrament, the stations of the cross, Good Friday devotions, devotions to the Sacred Heart of Jesus (identified as a modern French practice instead of an ancient British one), the Marian month, and devotions to the Immaculate Conception of Mary are important examples.[6] This Ultramontane piety was often repellent to the older English Catholic body, the remnants of the Recusants who had endured the penal days and who were raised on the quiet spirituality of Bishop Richard Challoner's (1691–1781) *Meditations* (reprinted 1814). Matters of style and taste sometimes flared into furious theological disputes; A. W. N. Pugin's cantankerous advocacy of Gothic architecture over baroque and neoclassical styles, the battle of "the Goths and the Pagan," is one striking example of the opposite extreme. Reserved and undemonstrative in their religious sentiments, marked in ways with that milder Gallicanism of the Cisalpine Club carried over from the late eighteenth century, and long associated with Ushaw College and Douay, the "old Catholics" rose to protect local usage and privilege against Roman Ultramontanism in advance. Recent converts, however, such as Frederick William Faber (1814–63) found in Italianate piety, expressed with exaggerated sentimentality and extravagant credulity in Faber's own series "The Lives of the Modern Saints," the form and tone of spirituality they had learned by reading such works as Alphonsus Liguori's *Glories of Mary* (1750) or in what Faber called "hot prayers."[7] These Ultramontanist habits of piety stressed faith healing, miracles, both medieval and modern, and the most rigid apologetic grounds. Christianity stood firm or fell on the authenticity of the liquefaction of St. Januarius' vial of blood each year in Naples.

The years between 1840 and 1854 also saw the reestablishment and new foundation of religious orders for both men and women as part of the wider Catholic Revival of the age.[8] This development was met by hysterical reactions, fostered by literature like *The Awful Disclosures of Maria Monk* (1836) and *Six Months in a Convent*, as well as the events surrounding the litigation involving the nuns of Scorton and the legal maneuverings of Pierce Connelly.[9] Debates over celibacy, ascetical practices, and the larger topic of conversion are central to the mid-Victorian mind. A general heating up of religion can also be seen in the system of parish missions and new ways of preaching. The work of Fathers Dominic Barberi, Luigi Gentili, and Ignatius Spencer, Catholic equivalents of circuit riders, should be traced against the backdrop of the larger Revivalist movement.[10] While the uncatechized mass of urban poor were being thus evangelized, the "steady conservative Wesleyans were just then regretting the loud techniques of itinerant American evangelists, [at the same moment] steady conservative Catholics regretted the fervent excess of itinerant Italian missioners."[11]

The historical novels of both Wiseman and Newman draw on these important issues and exhibit stresses appropriate in such "Tales for the Times." As the living symbols of Roman Catholicism in England in the imagination of everyone from *Punch* to the prime minister, both undertook the task, although Newman more than Wiseman, to set the record straight on theological matters in response to Charles Kingsley's anti-Catholic works. At the same time, Newman's novel is a subtle revision of contemporary English Catholic attitudes played off against the extravagances of Wiseman's historical re-creation. The ghost of the earlier English Catholic prelate Challoner was correcting "St. Nicholas of Seville."[12]

The relationship between Newman and Wiseman, beyond the attachments of a priest and his metropolitan, are especially complex. During the 1850s the emotional links forged during the Papal Aggression uproar and the convening of the first Provincial Synod (1852), which cast Newman again in the limelight, were more than offset by the initial frustrations and bitterness caused by Wiseman's handling of the Achilli case (1851–53), the libel suit brought against Newman by a disreputable ex-priest, and the archbishop's embarrassing failure in 1854 to secure episcopal rank for Newman during the latter's tenure at the Catholic University in Dublin (1854–58).[13] The links go much further back, however. Wiseman's popular lecture series in 1835, arguing the role of authority over against private judgment, prompted the Anglican Newman to respond to these "hereditary foes" in his work *The Prophetical Office of the Church Viewed Relatively to Romanism and Popular Protestantism* (1837), while at the same time the Tractarians were involved in the first Hampden affair.[14] But by the Long Vacation of 1839 Newman had become unsettled by his study of the history of Monophysitism. In the events of the fifth century the nineteenth century was reflected. "I saw my face in that mirror, and I was a Monophysite."[15] In July 1839 Wiseman published an article entitled the "Donatist Schism" in the *Dublin Review*. Newman eventually read it and had his earlier doubts recalled as a ghost.[16] Wiseman was the necromancer, and St. Augustine's dictum "Securus judicat orbis terrarum" was the incantation. Newman regrouped his position in his article "Catholicity of the Anglican Church" in the *British Critic* (January 1840), which led to his work on Tract XC, merely letting the doctrine of Athanasius and Augustine, as he put it, speak through the Thirty-Nine Articles. In the summer of 1841, while engaged at Littlemore on his translation of St. Athanasius, Newman "received three blows which broke" him.

The fourth-century Arian controversy proved to him an even more striking historical instance to which Wiseman's controversial stance was applicable; Newman groaned to find himself Arian. The two other events were the response of the Anglican bishops to Tract XC and the government scheme for the creation of a Jerusalem bishopric for Protestants.[17] Wiseman, then, was a continuing external stimulus of a powerful internal reappraisal by Newman of his ecclesiastical position, discerning in historical circumstances "ghosts" and "faces" of the contemporary religious debate. Newman's startling language to describe this transformation of latent historical notions, identifying these events with Augustine's conversion experience and with the heavens opening in "a heavenly vision" and a "sudden visitation," foreshadows both the method and dramatic forms he would employ later in his historical novels of conversion and ultimately in his *Apologia*. It is significant that from the end of 1841 Newman described himself as "on his death-bed" in the Anglican Church. Anglo-Catholics invariably spoke of conversion in terms of security within the Church's authority and surety in its sacraments, using the vocabulary of the Last Things: Death, Judgment, Heaven, Hell.

"Can I die safely in this Church?" they asked. In Newman's case the physician who signed the death certificate was Wiseman.

In much the same way the long relationship between Newman and Kingsley that resulted in the *Apologia* (1864) is as complex as a spiral stair. An observer of the issues that emerged when these two fought hand to hand in the early 1860s could extract from previous writings statements that summarized their adversarial positions. Newman's later stance could be read in the statement: "There is no middle course. Either deism or the highest and most monarchical system of Catholicism." And Kingsley's eventual moral indictment of Newman could be read in the following: "We see its [Rome's] agents, smiling and nodding and ducking to attract attention, as gipsies make up to truant boys, holding out tales for the nursery, and pretty pictures, and gilt gingerbread, and physic concealed in jam, and sugarplums for good children. . . . We Englishmen like manliness, consistency, truth. Rome will never gain on us, till she learns these virtues, and uses them." The problem with these extracts is that the first is from Kingsley, not Newman, and in the second the words are Newman's, not those of the Lion of Eversley.[18] The literary relationship of these two eminent Victorians needs to be more closely traced, at least from 1841; what takes shape is apparently a mutual fascination, even an obsession between these two figures. The controversial literature of the 1850s carries this out: on Kingsley's side the important chapter 14 of *Yeast* (1851), the direct reference to Newman in *Alexandria and Her Schools* (1854), and a short paragraph in *Fraser's Magazine* (January 1859) and on Newman's side the *Lectures on the Present Position of Catholics* (1851) are material evidence.[19] The historical novels of both combatants to be considered here merely extended the temporal limits of that continuing contest between Liberalism and Orthodoxy in which past and present were one.[20]

CHARLES KINGSLEY

Unlike many other historical novels, those of Kingsley, Wiseman, and Newman have elicited a large corpus of critical evaluation and close analysis;[21] the countless biographies and studies of the literary production of these figures leave little to add. But beyond collating the various findings of recent critics, this study attempts to trace more closely the topicality of the novels and to suggest new approaches, placing the works within the wider category of Romantic literature and indicating their role in response to Victorian religious concerns, public and private.

Any consideration of the literary reconstruction of the Early Church is not adequate without attention directed to the most prominent example militantly polemical against the Roman and Anglo-Catholic models. The works of Charles Kingsley (1819–75) provide that material for the 1850s. Although not directly in response to any particular Catholic writing, his novel *Hypatia; or, New Foes with an Old Face* (1853),[22] which elicited Wiseman's and Newman's novels, actively entered the lists against a range of contending principles he found upholding the Catholic side: asceticism, monasticism, celibacy, ecclesiastical authoritarianism, and theocracy. Yet Kingsley was also aggressively engaged in a polemic against skepticism (see his treatment of Edward Gibbon in the preface to *Hypatia*), aristocracy, "spiritualism" and "mesmerism," and the other social, economic, and philosophical positions opposed to his Maurician views of Christian socialism.[23] He held both to the Athanasian Creed and to science. His concerns were wider than the immediate debate over Catholic belief and practice; his constant ethical stress and definition of "muscular Christianity," a term he in fact rejected as "Byronic," introduce social and confessional concerns into each of his works. But the events of the day, in particular the new wave of No Popery sentiments, made this historical work appeal to a wide audience. This popular attitude forcefully shaped his novel of the New World, *Westward Ho!* (1855), motivated in fact by the Crimean War effort but criticized for its jingoistic nationalism and anti-Catholicism, *Two Years Ago* (1857) to a lesser degree, and even his notable *Water-Babies: A Fairy-Tale for a Land-Baby* (1863), which attacked monks and popes as evils like measles and scarlatina.[24]

Hypatia stakes out positions Kingsley had scouted in previous works. The attack upon asceticism had begun with the publication in 1848 of his blank-verse drama of self-sacrifice, *The Saint's Tragedy*, treating the life of St. Elizabeth (d. 1231), daughter of King Andrew II of Hungary, for which Maurice wrote the preface.[25] In 1851 *Yeast*, previously published in series in *Fraser's Magazine* (vol. 38, July to December 1848) under the pseudonym "Parson Lot," was brought out, with changes to make it more topical, under Kingsley's own name. The Tractarian curate featured in it was the foil for a systematic attack on Puseyite errors, or rather an attack on the Roman she-wolf in Puseyite wool. Following publication of the Chartist "autobiography," *Alton Locke, Tailor and Poet* (1850), the next production was *Hypatia*. This novel had been in Kingsley's mind for two years, he wrote in 1851 to Maurice, discussing with him this proposed historical romance: "My idea . . . is to set forth Christianity as the only really democratic creed."[26] He felt the urgency of such a task because of the threats of dissolution of the family and the rule of the people in the nation, "those two divine roots of the Church," as well as an assault on the integrity of private judgment and ethical action occasioned by many forces in England at the time, but especially in the Anglo-Catholic party. Also, it was in 1853 that a Royal Commission recommended a divorce court, and on 1 January 1853 the announcement was made public in England by Mormon missioners that polygamy was revealed as licit.[27] The sacredness of marriage, which Kingsley had learned from Maurice's works, presented to him by his wife, Fanny, appeared to be a real occasion of the cosmic combat between good and evil, a struggle Kingsley had learned from Maurice and Thomas Erskine, whose brand of Platonism was linked to the thought of Francis Newman (John Henry's controversial brother) by the Evangelical *Record*. The novel is, therefore, despite Kingsley's attempts at scholarly research, not so much a historical study as a trumpet blast against the "New Foes"; it draws on relatively few historical sources: Philo Judaeus, Philostratus' life of Apollonius of Tyana, the Alexandrian Fathers, Augustine, selected letters of Synesius and Abbot Isidore of Pelusium, segments of Socrates' *Ecclesiastical History*, John Toland, and Edward Gibbon.[28] Polemical exposition and rebuttal of Puseyism and Roman Catholicism constitute the chief purpose of the novel. Historic Christianity has a quite singular face for Kingsley, a "*wilful* mingling of the quite modern with the ancient colouring," as one prominent Victorian critic, George Henry Lewes, observed.

The action takes place A.D. 413–15 while Alexandria is at its ascendancy and Rome is ravaged. The city is a seething melting pot of many races, cultures, and religions. The topicality of these varied individuals and groups has been traced. The imperial prefect Orestes, who covets the throne, Philammon, a youth fresh from the monastic laura at Scete, and Raphael Aben-Ezra, an aristocratic and morally earnest Hebrew, are all

infatuated with Hypatia, the beautiful but chaste Neoplatonic philosopher, who is a new "Julian the Apostate" (361–63), dreaming of a pagan
revival. This historic figure, the daughter of Theon, who edited Euclid's
Elements, was actually a middle-aged woman who taught mathematics at
the Mouseion in Alexandria and left no records of her philosophical doctrines; her youth and achievements are part of Kingsley's Romance.
Raphael, accompanied by his faithful British mastiff, Bran, distances
himself from his mother, Miriam, a sorceress, and the pogrom against the
Jews in the city but finally learns self-sacrifice and love from Victoria,
daughter of the patriotic general Majoricus. He is eventually converted
to Christianity after encounters with Synesius of Cyrene (ca. 370–ca.
414), bishop of Ptolemais, a "squarson" widower who historically was
once a student of Hypatia's. Raphael is also won over by Augustine,
bishop of Hippo Regius (395–430), who reconciles Judaism and true
Platonism with genuine Christianity, eulogizing marriage in the process.

Against the effeminate Egyptians, the Arian Goths are led by Prince
Wulf and Amal the Amalric (the term for a nobleman), who loves the
dancing girl Pelagia, Philammon's long-lost sister. Cyril, patriarch of Alexandria (412–44), is one face of the hierarchic church, contrasted with
the virtuous Isidore of Pelusium and the Abbot Pambo, a man of Broad
Church sympathies. The *parabolani,* "district visitors," are engaged in
meritorious social work but are also sectarian fanatics, led by Peter the
Reader. These enraged monks seize Hypatia for her connection with
Orestes; she is at the point of accepting Christianity, but they kill her
with shells or tiles at the Caesareum, on whose ruins Athanasius had built
the church dedicated to St. Michael. The Goths, seeking vengeance for
the death of Amal, slaughter the black women and children trapped in
the amphitheater. The disillusioned Philammon and Pelagia retire to the
desert, where they partake communion together, eventually die, and are
buried in one grave. Alexandria, torn for generations by theological and
racial disturbances, eventually falls before the Muslim invaders.

Hypatia is not actually the center of plot, characterization, or motives in this novel; the New Foes are the center. One primary example—
"an Old Evil"—is Cyril; the death of Hypatia is imputed to him, as are
political machinations, "lying for the cause of truth," plotting an
Alexandrian theocracy that ultimately damaged the Christian faith and
the city's security, using doctrinal issues for personal aggrandizement,

jealousy of the Ecumenical See at Constantinople, spiritual manipulation of Councils and those in his See, as well as artificiality and hypocrisy. Cyril is the classic opponent of Nestorius, who allegedly emphasized the humanity of Christ over against his divinity. The humanity of Christ was further subordinated and eclipsed in Monophysitism; Cyril's nephew and successor, Dioscurus, was a Monophysite, deposed by the Council of Chalcedon (451)[29] along with its Anathema on Nestorianism. It was just such denigration or eradication of the humanity of Christ and therefore his contact with mankind's sufferings that Kingsley saw as the fundamental error in a certain type of Christian doctrine; he was pro-Nicaea, but anti-Chalcedon. Cyril's spurious doctrinal Christianity, which Kingsley believed to be totally alien to the simple teaching of Jesus, was parallel to the school of nineteenth-century idealism. If not a seeker for the historical Jesus, Kingsley was a champion of the historic Man-God.

But in this novel characters mean much more than individual selves.[30] Cyril represents the "Church of the Fathers," the focus of so much Anglo-Catholic thought and literature. It was this same Church of the Fathers "whose doctrine nineteenth-century Englishmen had been told to obey without question, though it might condemn Greek philosophy, supplement the teachings of Solomon and Jesus beyond recognition, ignore the wisdom that coming centuries of Christian thought were to develop, disagree with the conclusion of science or scholarship, and defy the democratic hopes of a progressive nation."[31] That list at least sums up the features of Kingsley's caricature of the Anglo-Catholic appeal to the Fathers. In the final analysis, however, the really destructive element in Cyril's history Kingsley isolated was the foundation of a theocracy, manipulating the worst instincts and superstitions of the mob to effect it. History, he thought, had shown this as the real cradle of the papacy:

"Ay, my brothers!" said Cyril, as he passed proudly out in full pontificals, with a gorgeous retinue of priests and deacons,—"the Catholic Church has her organization, her unity, her common cause, her watchwords, such as the tyrants of the earth, in their weakness and their divisions, may envy and tremble at, but cannot imitate. Could Orestes raise, in three hours, thirty thousand men, who would die for him?" "As we will for you!" shouted many voices. "Say for the Kingdom of God." And he passed out.[32]

It is their fanatical violence, unleashed by Cyril and directed against the Jews, that turns young Philammon, the former monk, against the abstract concept of the Catholic Church, the credulous mob of laity and clergy, and makes him doubt that there can be true ministers of the Christian gospel and "fruits of Christ's spirit":

> This was the harmonious strength and unity of that Church Catholic, in which, as he had been taught from boyhood, there was but one Lord, one Faith, one Spirit. This was the invisible body, "without spot or wrinkle, which, fitly joined together and compacted by that which every member supplied, according to the effectual and proportionate working of every part, increased the body, and enabled it to build itself up in Love!" He shuddered as the well-known words passed through his memory, and seemed to mock the bare and chaotic reality around him. (H, 110)

Kingsley's attack on Cyril is much more than an assault on the Church of the Fathers, the theocracy of Alexandria, and the gap between ideal and practice in the Catholic Church. It is an assault on the idea of the communion of saints, intercessory prayer and the mediation of grace, cultic veneration, and the use of the saints, especially in Ultramontanist devotions, as the only proper models for the Christian life. Other aspects of the cultus, including relics, miracle, and images, are also attacked. This, he seems to say, is the side of hagiographics no Anglo-Catholic shows. Kingsley did not wish to obliterate the cult of saints entirely; he praised the devotions and self-sacrifice of St. Francis de Sales, St. Dorothy, and St. Elizabeth of Hungary. But he made it clear in his work *The Hermits* (1869) that he objected to the cult of saints because of the corrupting connection with legends, relics, ascetic practices, "superstitutions and theurgies," like the contemporary fascination with "mesmerism," in which his closest friend, Charles Blachford Mansfield, dabbled, and postbiblical miracles. Two saints venerated at Alexandria were sure to arouse his ire: St. Ammon, who deserted his wife on their wedding night, and St. Anthony, who thought bathing was sinful. The figure of Cyril was triply repellent because he was not only a theocrat but also a "saint" and even a "doctor" of the Roman Church.

Kingsley had launched his critique of the cult of saints years before in *Yeast*. There the main character, Lancelot Smith, informs his converted cousin, a Tractarian:

When your party compare sneeringly Romish Sanctity, and English Civilization, I say, "Take you the Sanctity, and give me the Civilization! . . . Give me the political economist, the sanitary reformer, the engineer; and take your saints and virgins, relics and miracles. The spinning-jenney and the railroad, Cunard's liners and the electric telegraph, are to me, if not to you, the signs that we are, on some point at least, in harmony with the universe; that there is a mighty spirit working among us, who cannot be your anarchic and destroying Devil, and therefore may be the Ordering and Creating God."[33]

In *Hypatia* the canonization of saints is motivated by political reasons; thus, Hypatia could find herself destroyed by fanatical monks who represented the "Catholic and Apostolic Church" and yet declared a saint, if it would serve Cyril's ends against the civil government: "He will be most happy to make the whole story a handle against you, give out that she died a virgin martyr, in defence of the most holy catholic and apostolic faith, get miracles worked at her tomb, and pull your palace about your ears on the strength thereof" (*H*, 58). It is for such political ends that Ammonius the deacon is canonized under the name Thaumasius the Wonderful. Later, in fact, an ironic point is made with Hypatia's actual death. She had come to the point of seeing the truth of Christianity when she was murdered. At that moment "the other long, white arm was stretched upward toward the great still Christ, appealing—and who dare say, in vain?—from man to God." Her end is at least as ambiguous as that of Pater's Marius.

The other approach to the cult of saints is one of complete ridicule. A rich matron who could sniff out the subtlest deviances from orthodoxy in doctrine is pictured in an intricate garment, really a crinoline gown and bustle: "Down her back hung, upon a bright blue shawl, edged with embroidered crosses, Job sitting, potsherd in hand, surrounded by his three friends,—a memorial, the old priest whispered, of a pilgrimage which she had taken a year or two before, to Arabia, to see and kiss the identical dunghill on which the patriarch had sat" (*H*, 108).

The other points of attack Kingsley develops are against asceticism and monasticism. Both, he feels, are perversions of human life and the gospel. In *Yeast* asceticism was scored severely for making "piety a synonym for unmanliness." In *Hypatia* asceticism and monasticism (the systems perpetuating celibacy as an ideal and an institution) are condemned for creating religious illusion and sectarian fanaticism, displacing the simple Christian virtues with speculative doctrines. They are also destructive of individual conscience exercised in willing obedience to the Father and manful self-restraint in one's personal ethic, while in the social sphere they seek to destroy marriage, the "divine root" of the family, which is the nucleus of national life. Philammon, the "young Apollo of the desert," possessed beautiful manhood, labor and endurance, daring, fancy, passion, and thought, which "had no sphere of action in such a place. What did his glorious young humanity alone among the tombs?" Newman stated exactly the opposite in *Loss and Gain*, arguing that the young Charles Reding might use fasting, abstinence, and celibacy as a remedy and recompense for sin, like an "Apostle."[34] Monasticism and involuntary asceticism had left Philammon weakened and unequipped to face the moral decisions and difficulties in the city, so that he succumbed rapidly to temptation, never having formed the habit of personal decision. He is even willing to jump blindly from a window at the patriarch's command. In consequence he can never truly know the love of a woman and the "pure," ethical virtue of marriage. Having once felt a powerful attraction for monasticism himself, Kingsley balances this extreme position elsewhere by observing that "perhaps, in so debased an age, so profligate a world, as that out of which Christianity had arisen, it was impossible to see the true beauty and sanctity of those primary bonds of humanity."[35]

On a national scale, the undervaluing of the binary relationship of marriage led to a quantitative increase in moral evil, in a continuous enervation and diminution of the total population, in contempt for social and political life, and in the brutalizing of the general lay population.[36] This process culminated in the age of Justinian and Theodora, "the two most hideous sovereigns," in an age of "stereotyped effeminacy and imbecility." Some critics suggest that the personal animus in these assaults was due to Kingsley's simple equation of clerical celibacy with the homosexuality of his novelist brother, Henry.[37] Whatever his private motive, Kingsley rejected the concept of *imperium in imperio*, whether in monasticism or sectarianism, because it undercut national life, whatever noble role monk or Methodist had once played. In place of the gathered congregation, he exalts the *Volk*, thus politicizing the issue and introducing another aspect of his philosophy of history, extracted from Augustine and F. D. Maurice.

As this is true of men and monks in the novel, it is even more true of the women presented. Certainly the resuscitation of Roman Catholic and Anglican religious orders for women and the spiritual counseling for women undertaken by Pusey and other Anglo-Catholics provide the contemporary background to Kingsley's argument. But his own cult of true womanliness, seen before in the drawing of "the Triumph of Woman" in *Yeast*, and his rejection of "Mari-idolatry" help delineate his position.[38] Pelagia, a bright, spontaneous creature, is broken down by a long retreat of penance. Miriam, the royal "daughter of Solomon" who tried to be the "bride of God" as a nun, the "spouse of Joshua ben Joseph" who was "Jehovah-Ishi," is broken by that ideal, becoming a bitter and disillusioned hag, more witch than woman. Hypatia too is a virgin, and her Platonic ideal of chastity makes her cold and aloof, lacking the love and selflessness of true Platonism. She has gone astray, Kingsley suggests, because she is a "dialectical daughter," or in other terms, an "emancipated woman."[39]

Kingsley's most solemn and vitriolic statement of this subject is offered in Raphael's reaction to Majoricus' intention to place Victoria, Raphael's love, in a nunnery among "sexless priests." Much of Kingsley's own biography is implied here; he was hypersensitive to the long-standing Tractarian influence upon his wife-to-be, Frances Grenfell, who once considered the conventual life. As Kingsley sees it, the Fathers and the monks thought women were the "mother of all mischief" and "first-fruits of the Devil," which made it necessary to wall women in a nunnery. This runs counter to good English tradition: "There is no trace among the Egyptian celibates of that chivalrous woman-worship which our Gothic forefathers brought with them into the West, which shed a softening and ennobling light round the medieval convent-life, and warded off for centuries the worst effects of monasticism."[40] Drawing on a set of older associations in the national myth and in the Gothic novel, the figure of the monk is also a symbol of excessive and abnormal sexuality, generated to oppose, and therefore confirm, regular marital relations. Englishmen hated monks not because they were saints but because they were suspected of being satyrs. Kingsley argues for the ethical imperative to marry and the pure life of self-restraint that this will foster in each partner. Christianity, after all, had established, he insists, woman's moral and spiritual equality with man, although the Church at times neglected the symbiosis and synergy that relationship denoted.

Kingsley finds that his views on this subject are eminently expressed in clear language in the Bible. Like other members of his generation, he was sensitive to the critical approaches to Scripture; the long discussions of the text and interpretation of Homer are actually disguised comments on the new biblical scholarship. An investigation of this aspect of his thought demonstrates for us not only his views on marriage and conjugal love but also his understanding of Judaism, the shape of the Christian life, and his exegetical methodology in treating Scripture. One text he deals with at length is the *Song of Songs*.[41] Kingsley was setting himself against contemporary conventions thereby, since in the early Victorian era this portion of Scripture often was not bound with other books in the family Bible. Through Raphael, Kingsley shows the text's high moral meaning, underscoring the fact that Jews and some Christians did not understand their own Scriptures. Monogamy is there enshrined. Other portions of Scripture are treated similarly. In reading the *Epistle to the Hebrews*, calling to mind Maurice's work on this text, Raphael discovers that Paul [*sic*] knew more about true Platonism than the Neoplatonists.[42] *Hebrews* was viewed by this Victorian generation as a proof text of the fulfillment of Old Testament prophecies in Christ. The fundamental opposition Kingsley finds is between the literal interpretation of Scripture and the allegorical, practiced by the Jews in the manner of Philo through cabalistic commentaries and by the Catholics. The rabbis, distinct from the old Hebrew seers, were, he asserts, "some of the worst and wickedest men who ever trod this earth." Promoting this scriptural obscurantism, the pope and the Jews were unexpectedly in league. These elements of Kingsley's interpretation come together in Raphael. As a Jew, he is the embodiment of Scripture. And thus it is he, summing up Hebrew morality and Hellenic philosophy, who leads Hypatia to faith, having been converted himself by Augustinian theology. In his conversion the history of Christianity is recapitulated. "Hebrew men," Kingsley observed, "teach us the real meaning of the Old Testament, and its absolute unity with the New."[43] Neoplatonism, too intellectual and aristocratic, provides no real alternative, since it is engaged in the spiritualizing of paganism's books, from Homer to abstract treatments of conic sections.

For Kingsley the test of any true system of metaphysics, anyway, is whether it makes men good. That is why the Bible is of perennial value. Kingsley's principles for interpreting Scripture are geared accordingly, stressing (1) the literal and "reasonable," (2) the ethical, (3) the nondogmatic, and (4) the natural and personal understanding of the Bible without special, institutional guidance. The influences of Higher Criticism and Broad Church tendencies are manifest.

Kingsley presses his attack on the question of dogmatism. It is an attack, however, against Hypatia and her attempt to reinstitute the past, as well as against Catholics. Those "who have no other means for regenerating a corrupted time than dogmatic pedantries concerning the dead and unreturning past"[44] end by using the very evil of the present age they wish to correct, he asserts. For his own age this is especially true in regard to varying conceptions of Christ and the excessive doctrinal concern over the question of "Orthodox or Unorthodox," a question he execrated. The narrator of the novel uses a paragraph to trace fourth-century conceptions of the person of Christ and concludes that the shift in understanding of Christ as personal savior to divine being left the sinner with the feeling of desolation and abandonment. As Kingsley sees the question, the Athanasian Creed taught that in the person of the Incarnate Logos, that which was most divine had been proved to be most human, that which was most human had been proved to be most divine.[45] For him Christianity is preeminently a religion of sinners; it was on this point that Christianity really overcame philosophy. The various schools of philosophy had nothing to say to the harlot. When doctrinal questions replaced the primary identity of Christianity and the Church, a wrong direction had been taken. What is spiritual is not to be equated with intellectual formulations or processes but rather equated with the moral side of the scale, reflecting righteousness and justice. It takes this character because "God is a righteous person"; this divine ontology constitutes for Kingsley the transforming power of belief and the model for human activity: "God's kingdom was not a kingdom of fanatics yelling for a doctrine, but of willing, loving, obedient hearts" (H, 457). That obedience, on the other hand, was not won by threats of hellfire and eternal punishment. Allan Hartley suggests that Pelagia's dilemma over this popular picture of hell, indeed even her name, reflect the position Maurice was unraveling in his Theological Essays (1853). Pelagia was sinful, but she had love and boundless goodwill. Having already been baptized, was she eternally condemned? Kingsley suggests not. On this point too Newman later contrasted his character Callista; whatever her merits, she *could* go to hell, a tenet Newman himself described in his *Apologia* as "Calvinist."

Where then does the hope of the Christian life lie? Kingsley answered:

> The health of a Church depends not merely on the creed which it professes, not even on the wisdom and holiness of a few great ecclesiastics, but on the faith and virtue of its individual members. The *mens sana* must have a *corpus sanum* to inhabit. And even for the Western Church, the lofty future which was in store for it would have been impossible, without some infusion of new and healthier blood into the veins of a world drained and tainted by the influence of Rome. (*H*, xiii)

Fortunately, Providence had ordained just such a people to emerge at the time: the Goths. Kingsley draws close comparisons between the vigorous, spontaneous life of the Gothic warriors and the effete, metaphysical concerns of the native Egyptians and other denizens of the East. The comparison goes to all facets of life, including literature. It also ties in with his understanding of "woman." The Goths were to his mind the source of reverence for women and domesticity. Elsewhere he carried this over into literary theory, since the literary monuments of Old English, such as *Beowulf*, were the offspring of the "female" Anglo-Saxon and the "male" Norse. In a lengthy quotation from Paulus Warnéfridus' *De Gestis Langobardorum* (edited in 1838), an imitation of an early Eddaic saga is introduced. It is treated as equal in literary stature with Homer, especially when Homer is spiritualized and allegorized. Kingsley's inclusion of such pieces reflects part of the nineteenth-century Romantic concern for national history and bardic traditions; the *Ballads* were still popular at this time and the influence of Ossian still felt. A further aspect of Kingsley's concern for the Goths is his association of them with English national life. He mentions that England began its worldwide mission with the landing in Kent of the "mythic Hengst and Horsa." Such statements had strong contemporary associations, since Britain was then in the midst of managing a worldwide empire. This empire was its divine vocation, inaugurated with the defeat of the Armada. The crucial event of 1588 was for the English nation a Red Sea crossing. The continuity Kingsley saw working in history was one of the manly, natural spirit; this emerges while waging war and standing forth as the embodiment of courage and honor. If these are peculiarly English virtues, they are also peculiarly Protestant: "Protestantism in Kingsley usually means reliance on natural instinct (as opposed to the acceptance of a celibate ideal), on the natural man's understanding of the Bible (as opposed to interpretation under guidance of the Church) and on the natural conclusion of human intellect (obedient to no previously accepted doctrine)."[46] It is also based on the primacy of individual conscience, the movement of the individual will, and an instinctive regard for flat honesty. On this last point it is interesting to note that the cunning and prevaricating monks of *Hypatia* are paralleled with Puseyites in *Yeast*. There the Tractarian curate (later a "pervert" to Rome) expressed a lack of sympathy "with that superstitious reverence for mere verbal truth which is so common among Protestants."[47] It was in a later comment concerning the use of just that Gothic and Protestant virtue, as Kingsley claimed them, that the parson of Eversley found himself confronting an old foe with John Henry Newman's face.

NICHOLAS WISEMAN

Haec, sub altari rita sempiterno,
Lapsibus nostris veniam precatur,
Turba, quam servat procerum creatrix purpureorum.

This inscription of Prudentius on the title page of Nicholas, Cardinal Wiseman's (1802–65) *Fabiola; or, The Church of the Catacombs*, first published in 1854, accurately signals the reader that this piece of hagiography is, by its own definition, part of the wider production of literature for spiritual edification appearing in Victorian England. But the work purports to be more than this. The novel attempts to arrange a vast amount of antiquarian data, much of it unavailable to the public. Elsewhere, however, Wiseman contrasts the "dry eye of an antiquarian" with the vision of a world torn by revolution, famine, and urban poor. In 1829 he had undergone a spiritual "conversion" from "desolation," doubts occasioned by his study of biblical criticism, and in 1834 reported having lost his scholarly "coldness." He wrote: "I might almost say that I am leading a life of spiritual epicureanism, opening all my senses to a rich drought of religious sensations."[48] His later taste for Ultramontane devotions and flamboyant gestures should be viewed against this conversion experience. He used "scientific" findings of archaeologists in Rome, being an amateur expert in this field himself, to address this "age of railroads and newspapers," but he sought to touch the heart and imagination primarily. His novel contrasts "impressions," "spirit," "associations," "feeling," and living "in imagination with the Early Christians" to material "examined scientifically and critically for mere antiquarian purposes." Yet Wiseman was the author of the popular lectures "Connexion between Science and Revealed Religion" (1835), which, without using science as a final proof of religion, contended that faith was so far justified by scientific findings themselves. The application of this stance to doctrinal questions and the links to Newman concerning this will be considered later.

The novel attempts to investigate and relate the historical foundations of the Church's rites and ceremonies, something neither Newman nor Kingsley felt compelled to do. Further, as religious, didactic literature it attempts to comment, in the manner of other examples of this genre, on the contemporary situation in England through historical analogy. And last, it attempts to be recreational literature. It is, despite its prolix rhetoric and flights of pious fancy, an intricate meshing of motives, sources, and contemporary analogies: "But once begun, it has proved what it was taken for,—a recreation, and often a solace and a sedative; from the memories it has revived, the associations it has renewed, the scattered and broken remnants of old studies and early readings which it has combined, and by the familiarity which it has cherished with better times and better things than surround us in our age."[49] Drawn by Romantic nostalgia for a cavalier society whose customs and protocols he tried to maintain, Wiseman was superbly adapted for presenting such a réchauffé, as he proved in his Recollections of the Last Four Popes, and of Rome in Their Times (1858).

The novel presents Rome and the "Church of the Catacombs" in A.D. 302 and the years following until the coming of Constantine, during the final imperial persecution of the Christians. The emperor Maximian (Augustus in the West, 285–305) and a number of historic martyrs—

Sebastian, Agnes, Cassianus, for example—appear, and there are long digressions dealing with archaeological and antiquarian material. Fabiola, the daughter of Fabius, learns from her slave, Syra, and several martyrs about Christianity. She eventually obtains instruction in Christian doctrine, followed by baptism and communion, and survives the period of persecution.

The characters are principally props for the motions of the spiritual drama around them. They are a litany of saints (Agnes, Lucy, Caecilia, Sebastian, Pancras, George, and many others) who are little more than incarnations of the breviary and martyrology accounts. Whole sections of their speeches and dialogue have been lifted from their respective "Offices" or Ruinart's *Acta Primorum Martyrium* (1713). Other characters take on metaphoric significance; for example, the three handmaids of Fabiola are Afra, Graia, and Syra, all of whom are Christians by the novel's close. Their conversion to Christianity symbolizes its triumph in those lands. Fabiola herself is really only tangential to the story; the saints and martyrs are the central concern of the narration. Fabiola is, of course, not a martyr, even fictionally. Wiseman hesitated to undercut the historicity of his other figures by mingling such a character in with their sacrosanct sufferings. Fabiola was actually the offspring of a story of Roman life, "Fabius" (later Fabiola's father), written while young Wiseman studied Roman antiquities and topography at Ushaw College.[50] The evil men are thoroughly evil, although one, Fulvius, converts at the end of the novel, thus serving a didactic purpose to affirm the efficacy of a saint's death and the eventual triumph of Christianity over its bitterest foes. Torquatus, the renegade Christian, has been identified by some commentators with Giacinto Achilli, the spoiled priest who sued Newman for libel when Newman published accounts of criminal acts committed; but he could also represent J. Blanco White, an ex-Roman priest who adopted Unitarianism and was known to Wiseman from student days in Spain. There is also a metaphoric quality about two of the villains; Corvinus and Fulvius are treated under the terms *wolf* and *fox*, who descend upon pure Agnes (Latin for "lamb"), a character who recalls Wiseman's frequent "camerata" visits to the catacombs of St. Agnese in Rome.

If individual and prominent characters are treated in such a flat, stereotyped manner, the Roman mob and various nations are treated similarly. Wiseman reserves his severest, categorical censures for Germans and black Africans. The emperor and some of his bodyguards are portrayed as Germanic barbarians, marked by stupidity and violence. This played up the anti-German feeling rising at the time in England. The "negro," however, such as in the character of Hyphax of the imperial guard, displays wild, orgiastic cruelty. This attitude is also shown in the description of Afra (Jubala): "One is black; not of the degraded negro stock, but from one of those races, such as the Abyssinians and Numidians, in whom the features are as regular as in the Asiatic people" (*F*, 1:28). These characterizations reflect the current fascination in England with the life of African chattel slaves. *Uncle Tom's Cabin* (1852) had sold 1.5 million in England and the colonies between April 1852 and April 1853.[51] Children, as well, are shown to be particularly cruel and depraved; a band of students is described as "young bears' cubs with full-grown hyaenas' hearts within them," and their role in the martyrdom of Cassianus is graphically recounted. With general categories of people, as with individuals, the purpose is to contrast the pure, defenseless virtues of Christians against the frenzied cruelties of the pagan world, plummeting toward its dissolution and plagued by Nemesis.

Nature, too, provides a range of intimations and object lessons. In the name of the district surrounding one villa, Ad Palmas, a name used in other historical novels, is an ironic intimation of the palm of martyrdom soon to be conferred upon those in that region. Each locale, each aspect of nature is translucent, often in two distinct ways. In one way nature reveals a solemn, serene, and majestic order, sketched with a Romantic sweep.[52] In the other mode of instruction, the several "layers" of monuments or events that have occurred on one location are presented together. For example, Sebastian addresses Pancratius (Pancras) at one such locale: "I was going to show you, when we stepped out here, the very spot just below our feet, where I have often fancied the triumphal arch, to which I have alluded, would stand" (*F*, 8). Wiseman's narrator adds the note that "the arch of Constantine stands exactly under the spot where this scene is described." The connection between Sebastian and Constantine may be based on Wiseman's knowledge of Roman artifacts. The relic head of Sebastian was buried in Santi Quattro Incoronati near the arch; that church's connecting chapel was decorated with frescoes showing the legend of Constantine and Pope Sylvester I. Usually an archaeological site is described and, as a reference for the reader, the later constructions are mentioned; the hidden purpose is to maintain the physical continuity of identification and veneration of certain holy places. And not only places provide this connection between various epochs in the Church's history, details of landscape and even atmospheric conditions do the same: "It was just such an evening as, years after, Monica and Augustine enjoyed from a window at Ostia, as they discoursed of heavenly things" (F, 89).

The view of the city, with all the archaeological paraphernalia that can be mustered and all the antiquarian detail that can be displayed, is basically one more arena of Christian contrasts to pagan elements. Wiseman, like Pater and Kingsley, chose a major city in which to cast his story, instead of the obscure, provincial center of Newman's novel. The city of Rome is not important in itself, however, as it was presented in the civil religion of *Callista*, but only as the battleground for a conflict that will end in the Constantinian revolution and exaltation of the Church. The "perennial monuments" of the Capitol are weighed against the Christian and found wanting. Two Christian gravediggers (*fossores*) of that early "guild" exchange comments on this subject:

> "And yet a curious thought struck me as I was carving her epitaph."
> "Let me hear it, Majus." "It was, that perhaps some thousand years
> hence or more, Christians might read with reverence my scratches on
> the wall, and hear of poor old Pollecla and her barley-stall with interest,
> while the inscription of not a single emperor, who persecuted the
> Church, would be read or even known." "Well, I can hardly imagine
> that the superb mausoleums of sovereigns will fall into utter ruin, and
> yet the memory of a market-wife descend to distant ages. But what is
> your reason for thinking thus?" "Simply because I would sooner com-
> mit to the keeping of posterity the memory of the pious poor than that
> of the wicked king. And my rude record may possibly be read when
> triumphal arches have been demolished." (F, 213–14)

The contrasts are sharply lined between the imperial palaces, which are transitory (Nero's Golden House had already been demolished) and the centers of Christian worship: the house-churches, the *tituli*, the country villas, and the "sweetest catacombs." These have been preserved,

Wiseman implies, by some divine Providence to be a further support of present faith. The simple gathering place of Christians stands starkly out against the gaudy, imperial structures. With the catacombs the cardinal makes the historical leap to England and Ireland, where "Catholics had just emerged from the Catacombs."[53] Wiseman also draws on the immediate experience of his audience to relate them to the style and use of such houses. He states in a footnote: "The Pompeian Court in the Crystal Palace will have familiarized many readers with the form of an ancient house" (*F*, 4 n). The contrast, though, of pagan city with Christian house or oratory is a central element and appears consistently throughout this genre.

It is the city that provides the stage, Wiseman feels, for the struggle for power between empire and papacy, the latter a fully developed and structured authority throughout the novel, at whose command "To hear was to obey." Maximian Herculeus is presented as most anxious over this authority, independent from his own, existing in Rome. In a footnote Wiseman quotes from an epistle of Cyprian the reputed response of Decius upon the election of St. Cornelius to the Roman See (Ep. 52, *ad Antonianum*), concluding: "Could there be a stronger proof, that under the heathen empire, the papal power was sensible and external, even to the extent of exciting imperial jealousy?" (*F*, 273–74). The city, then, for all the conflation of antiquarian detail, is really only a cyclorama for showing the truth and power of the Church, *semper eadem*, in contrast to a set of opposing principles and structures. This contrast between the power of the State and the independent authority of the Church is part of the polemic addressed to the Anglican Church, agonizing over the Gorham decision and the reopening of wounds in the Denison case. Wiseman rejected any Erastian, or in Roman Catholic terms "Gallican," position, maintaining that spiritual matters could be decided only by the pope, Councils, or the aggregate of Catholic Churches kept intact by communion with Rome.[54] Cyprian is pointedly used as a proof text for papal sovereignty. Referring back to earlier discussions, Wiseman maintains the necessary identity between the See of Rome and the power of the *orbis terrarum*, which judges kings and is not judged by them.

This view of religion, contrasting Christian and pagan belief and practice, is as stereotyped as other aspects of the novel. The principle of selection used and the limitation of facts, details, and imaginative reconstruction rationalized on the grounds of pious edification: "It was necessary to introduce some view of the morals and opinions of the pagan world, as a contrast to those of Christians. But their worst aspect has been carefully suppressed, as nothing could be admitted here which the most sensitive Catholic eye would shrink from contemplating" (*F*, xii–xiii).

There is very little discussion of pagan cultic practice or belief, either on the level of popular piety in ancient Rome or the level of philosophical speculation. Fabiola is portrayed as an "epicurean," but there is little content given to that concept and only vague associations as to how that philosophy guides her life. Christians are seen through pagan eyes, but only the most evil eyes, as worshipers of the head of an ass or as traitors—customary charges historically. The background and significance of these pagan attitudes are not included. Among educated pagans there is a total misunderstanding of Christianity, as shown by the "historian" Calpurnius, who constantly confuses persons, events, and themes from the Old and New Testaments and pagan mythology.

For the most part, however, the pagan view of specific Christians is transformed into respect, awe, and dumb admiration. A glance from a Christian child, beaten to death by a pagan mob, is enough to kindle belief in a watching Roman matron; it is not from his witness to faith but by a supernatural, mystical look: "From that look came the light of faith." Christians walk lightly on this world and are possessed of an uncanny wisdom; they perfectly anticipate the truth, future events, and the development of the Church. Their speech and manners are always informed by the highest virtue:

> She [Fabiola] was surprised, however, to find how her slave, by a
> simple remark, would often confute an apparently solid maxim, bring
> down a grand flight of virtuous declamation, or suggest a higher view
> of moral truth, or a more practical course of action, than authors whom
> she had long admired proposed in their writings. Nor was this done by
> any apparent shrewdness of judgment or pungency of wit; nor did it
> seem to come from much reading, or deep thought, or superiority of
> education. . . . But there seemed to be in her maid's mind some latent
> but infallible standard of truth, some master-key, which opened equally
> every closed deposit of moral knowledge, some well-attuned chord,

which vibrated in unfailing unison with what was just and right, but
jangled in dissonance with whatever was wrong, vicious, or even inac-
curate. What this secret was, she wanted to discover; it was more like
an intuition than anything she had before witnessed. She was not yet in
a condition to learn, that the meanest and least in the Kingdom of
Heaven (and what lower than a slave?) was greater in spiritual wisdom,
intellectual light, and heavenly privileges, than even the Baptist Precursor. (F, 155–56)

If one substitutes for Greek slave the expression *Irish Roman Catholic servant,* "degraded and debased by their cruel superstition" as the Evangelical *Record* would put it, one can understand the contemporary force of
such an analogy. This is a key passage, since it is the model showing that
for Wiseman the individual Christian's appropriation of truth and revelation is analogous to the Church's own appropriation. It is not developed
the way Newman's concept of consultation of the faithful on matters of
doctrine was developed, but it shares a common foundation with
Newman's sense of the *consensus fidelium.* This shapes Wiseman's view of
history, the meaning of historical development, and the internal "grammar" of the Church's life.

For Wiseman the deep feelings and beliefs of early Christians were
embodied in the liturgy; in the words of his biographer, borrowed from
Newman, the liturgy was the "exhibition of great facts."[55] The controls
shaping these depictions are usually one or another of three approaches
to the material: (1) It must be an edifying detail, in line with Victorian interests and sensibilities; (2) it must affirm present belief and practice in the
Roman Church, anticipations traced by direct historical continuities;
and (3) it must be open to the special emphases on doctrines and practices
within Wiseman's scheme. Thus, from the very beginning of Christianity there are fully developed hierarchical structures and liturgical practices: for example, the priests of the *tituli* are presented as "cardinals";
there are elaborate, medieval ceremonies for the veiling of nuns; hymns
sung anticipate the sentiments embodied in later chant; and the early
Christians' underground developed the architectural principles that directed all later ecclesiastical building (ignoring thereby the influences of
the construction of the *tituli* and the existing basilica patterns):

We need not remind our readers, that the office then performed was
essentially, and in many details, the same as they daily witness at the
Catholic altar. Not only was it considered, as now, to be the Sacrifice of
Our Lord's Body and Blood, not only were the oblation, the consecration, the communion alike, but many of the prayers were identical; so
that the Catholic hearing them recited, and still more the priest reciting
them, in the same language as the Roman Church of the catacombs
spoke, may feel himself in active and living communion with the martyrs who celebrated, and the martyrs who assisted, at those sublime
mysteries. (F, 349)

In historical terms Wiseman never clarifies what peculiar efficacy or what
suasive argument for such "re-creation" of the past is constituted, outside
of the incorporation of the present Christian into the continuing worship of the *communio sanctorum*. The saints and martyrs are much more
than mere characters in the book; they are the models of perfection who
edify and provide certain parameters for the range of Christian life. They
are the touchstones of truth and virtue for each doctrine and practice
mentioned; the descriptions of prayers, miracles, personal piety are always in terms of that litany of blessed names. An essential "note," therefore, of the true Church is the holiness and heroic virtue of its members.
The chief expression of this communion of saints is by prayer and intercession: "Had her eyes been opened in that hour and had she been able to
look up above this world, she would have seen a soft cloud like incense,
but tinged with a rich carnation, rising from the bed-side of a kneeling
slave (prayer and willing sacrifice of life breathed upwards together)
which, when it struck the crystal footstool of a mercy-seat in heaven, fell
down again as a dew of gentlest grace upon her arid heart" (F, 72–73).
Ecstasy, rapture, martyrdom, miracles, and sacraments are all grown together, so that even the everyday performances of the sacraments take on
miraculous features, for example, a man afflicted with gout is cured by
baptism. This is accomplished, Wiseman states, through the efficacy of
the lives and prayers of the saints. What transpires, however, is that certain other features of Christian life and practice are almost totally sub-
merged. For example, Scripture has practically no role. One scrap of it is
treated as a mysterious hieroglyph (Vulgate: Matt. 5.44) that helps
Fabiola identify some Christians. At other junctures are heard fragments

from the psalter (Ps. 26; 4.9ff.). Scripture does not have the role in Fabiola's conversion that it does in other novels. In *Fabiola* the maid Syra's sacrifice of her own life effects the conversion. Wiseman does, on the other hand, rigorously maintain the continuity between Old and New Testaments, defending the former from contemporary critics. His scholarly career as an orientalist and arabicist in Rome under Cardinal Mai had prepared him for this debate; and he had made significant contributions in the question of the antiquity of the *Peshito*, as well as of the *Itala* and its African origin.[56] But the novel's focus is upon the communion of saints in the Roman Church, transmitted as a unity through all time and space: "Glorious Church of Christ! great is the . . . combination of thy unity, stretching from heaven to beneath the earth" and in which saints expire in their "first virginal blush" (*F*, 502).

MARTYRS: PAST AND PRESENT

The subject of martyrdom is an important consideration in mapping the contours of the mid-Victorian generation. Religious novels, framed as spiritual biographies of contemporary Catholics, joined historical reconstructions in vividly, graphically portraying the physical and mental agonies of Christians.[57] In Wiseman the subject of persecution and martyrdom is the constant connecting link between the ancient Church of the Catacombs and the modern Age of Revolution. Pius VII (1800–32) was the type of Cornelius, bishop of Rome (251–52), because both underwent exile and persecution, just as the decree on the Immaculate Conception of Mary (1854) was like the decree of Ephesus (431) because the formal object of the pronouncements was the same. There are three foci of such identification between the early Church and martyrs: (1) the history of Catholicism in England and Ireland, (2) Wiseman's personal history, and (3) the experiences of other contemporary Catholics.

Wiseman's tenure as rector of the English College in Rome confirmed earlier tendencies of his to identify the martyrs with contemporary Catholics in England and Ireland. The chapel had a vivid representation of St. Thomas Becket of Canterbury and was filled with relics of members of the English mission who had been greeted by Philip Neri, founder of the Oratory, with the salutation "Salvete flores martyrum" before their fateful departure back to England.[58] An extensive literature, by Challoner, Dodd, Stevens, Dugdale, and Parkinson, contributed to the longevity of that tradition, which Wiseman recalled in his initial pastoral by referring to "all those blessed martyrs of these later ages." He was not unmindful of the literary remains that made the claim for martyrdom for other Englishmen; in the library of the English College was a copy of the Protestant John Foxe's *Book of Martyrs* in which Parsons had made notes for his refutation.[59] The bloody Lord George Gordon Riots ("No Popery") of 1780 were commemorated, under Wiseman's auspices, by the erection of St. George's Cathedral, Southwark, on the very site of the pillage of Catholic houses. In like manner, his novel of martyrs and saints was issued during the silver jubilee of Catholic Emancipation (1829). The No Popery outburst in 1850, raising the specter of Penal Days, was only one in a series of major incidents exhibiting hereditary feeling, to which must be added the Maynooth College disturbances near Dublin in 1845 and the Orange and Green clash in Ireland in 1849.

In Newman's sermon "The Second Spring," preached before the first Provincial Synod of Westminster (13 July 1852), the identification with the martyrs was canonized. Eight out of twenty sections deal fundamentally with this subject, often quite explicit in their catalogue of sufferings: "The long imprisonment, the fetid dungeon, the weary suspense, the tyrannous trial, the barbarous sentence, the savage execution, the rack, the gibbet, the knife, the cauldron, the numberless tortures of those holy victims, O my God, are they to have no reward? Are Thy Martyrs to cry from under Thine altar for their loving vengeance on this guilty people, and to cry in vain?"[60] The most notable reference in the sermon is to "a Prince of the Church, in the royal dye of empire and of martyrdom," at once drawing the line of confrontation between Empire and Church and urging Wiseman as a type of the martyrs. The Anglican Newman had made just such an allusion in Tract 1 (1833); as a Presbyter he could not wish the bishops better "than the spoiling of their goods [by the State], and martyrdom." In his *Certain Difficulties* (1850) he was less sure about the possibility of such an occasion, but by the time of his *Present Position of Catholics in England* (1851) he could say: "This may not be the age of Saints, but all times are the age of Martyrs."[61] In *Grammar of Assent* (chap. 10.2.10) he portrayed the brutal, cruel deaths of the martyrs as proof that they died for no small cause or for an infatuation.

The expectation of and desire for martyrdom were also expressed by F. W. Faber (1814–63) in his strongly Catholic hymn "Faith of Our Fathers," which appeared in his *Jesus and Mary* (1849; 2d ed., 1852) and was popular across confessional lines.[62] Newman also felt that this was a form of personal identification, since he was undergoing the turmoil of the Achilli trial; he was met by one friend in the courtroom with the greeting "Holy Martyr of Christ, pray for us."[63]

Wiseman similarly made personal connections. At his episcopal consecration in 1840 he accepted the title, *in partibus*, Bishop of Melipotamus, because it had belonged to a martyred vicar apostolic of Tonquin, Indochina. *Punch*, as recorded above, styled him "St. Nicholas of Seville . . . a willing and joyful martyr."[64] Last, Wiseman had been involved in litigation and stood under a libel charge in the Boyle affair (1854) while working on his novel; in an "Ode to St. Laurence," composed at that time, he identified his own trial with the trials of the martyr-deacon of Rome (d. 258).[65] Added to this were continuing charges of mismanagement of his diocese and clumsy handling of the restoration of the hierarchy in England. Amid this turbulence, Wiseman sought solace by identifying with the martyrs.

He also saw similar parallels in the situations of other Catholics of the period. In the article "The Persecution of Catholics in Prussia" in the *Dublin Review* (December 1836) he identified Gregory XVI with Leo I, and Frederick Wilhelm IV of Prussia with Attila. The shooting of Archbishop Affre of Paris in June 1848 during the revolution there called to mind similar comparisons with the martyrs made when French émigrés fled to England from the Terror and from subsequent upheavals. Later, in 1862, the solemn canonization in Rome of the Japanese martyrs was the occasion for a comparison between Christ's sufferings and those of Pius IX at the hands of the Garibaldians, as Wiseman's biographer shows (2:443–46).

This stress on martyrdom was a constitutive part of mid-Victorian spirituality, shared by Roman Catholics and Anglo-Catholics, just as the theme of self-sacrifice was constitutive of much popular literature of the period: "Such self-sacrifice is the ultimate source of emotional power because there is no defense against it."[66] For Wiseman, as for Newman and others, the martyrs were the type of the Church's real power. In Kingsley's vocabulary, it was a feminine weapon (see n. 38).

Wiseman draws on a full range of sources, treating each as critically authoritative without making distinctions between historical and devotional works and the essentially different materials with which each deals: Edmond Martenne [Martène], *De antiquis ecclesiae ritibus*; Joseph Bingham, bk. 11, chap. 11, "Clinical Baptism"; Cardinal Caesar Baronius' notes to the *Martyrology*; various *Acts* of the martyrs, in particular those of Sts. Felicitas and Perpetua; Carlo Bartolomeo Piazza's work on the stational churches of Rome; Giovanni Gaetano Bottario [Botari] and his work on subterranean Rome; Alessio Aurelio Pellicia [Pelliccia]; Justin Martyr's *Second Apology*; several epistles of St. Cyprian; Tertullian; Eusebius; Thierry Ruinart's *Acta*; the hymns of Prudentius and Pope Damasus; Macrobius' *Saturnalia*; various pagan Roman poets; the Offices of St. Clement and St. Agnes; Ammianus Marcellinus; Lucien [Lucian], *De morte peregrini*; the life of Honorius from Anastasius; Claude Fleury's *Manners of the Christians*; Giuseppe Marchi's *Architecture of Subterranean Christian Rome* (1844); Giovanni Battista de Rossi's work on the catacombs; Alban Butler's hagiographical collections; and Bartolini's work on the wooden altar in the Lateran.

The "modern antiquarians" Wiseman chiefly relies upon are "the Accurate Marchi" and "the learned and sagacious Cavalier De Rossi." He does not hesitate to correct citations occasionally (as he does with Marchi), but on the whole he appropriates their work uncritically. The recent archaeological excavations in Rome reported in these sources are obviously a large factor in generating Wiseman's interest in writing such a historical reconstruction, which presented these findings to the British reading public long before they were collected and translated by J. S. Northcote and W. R. Brownlow (1874). Wiseman wishes to "speak scientifically," introducing straight historical exposition as "digressive" elements in the fiction. He tries to maintain that in various aspects he is not "misguided by national or personal prepossessions," but there are principles of authority introduced that belie the detached, objective approach of just any antiquarian. Quite clearly for Wiseman the history of the Church is the Church's history, and it exercises the final authority in validation and interpretation of its own past. In introducing material from various hagiographies, he states this principle cogently:

> What writer that introduced the person would venture to alter the character? Who would presume to attempt one at variance with it? Or

who would hope to draw a portrait more life-like and more exquisite than the Church has done? For, putting aside all inquiry as to the genuineness of the acts by which these passages are suggested; and still more waiving the inquiry whether the hard critical spirit of a former age too lightly rejected such ecclesiastical documents, as Gueranger thinks; it is clear that the Church, in her office, intends to place before us a certain type of high virtue embodied in the character of that saint. The writer of the following pages considered himself therefore bound to adhere to this view. (F, xi)

If the Church's reflexive action is the principle of authority introduced into the study of history, Providence is the generating and inspiriting factor behind the course of history. Here Wiseman is drawing on his understanding of Hegel, derived through the work of Moehler, Schlegel, and the Romanticist historians with whom he was acquainted on the Continent. He does not, of course, present a fully articulated philosophy of history. In a discussion of discoveries in the catacombs, a further historical element is introduced: "The place was unknown at the peace of the Church, till discovered by Divine manifestation" (F, 240). Providence even allots the times and seasons when historical evidence will best be discovered and utilized.

This view and use of history Wiseman feels is justified because of two controlling factors: (1) as an "artist of fiction" he may adopt whatever viewpoint and presuppositions for reading history he wishes, and (2) since the novel is for edification, the elements tending toward that end must obtain. For Wiseman the Christian view of history is not only objectively true, it is also subjectively the most uplifting and beneficial to the individual. In a discussion contrasting the lives of the saints to contemporary French literature, he states this belief that Christian literature is more humane and insightful:

If the reader would compare the morbid sensibility, and the overstrained excitement, endeavored to be produced by a modern French writer, in the imaginary journal of a culprit condemned to death, down to the immediate approach of executions with the unaffected pathos and charming truthfulness which pervades the corresponding narrative of Vivia Perpetua, a delicate lady of twenty-one years of age, he would not hesitate in concluding, how much more natural, graceful, and

interesting are the simple recitals of Christianity, than the boldest fictions of romance. And when our minds are sad, or the petty persecutions of our times incline our feeble hearts to murmur, we cannot do
better than turn to that really golden, because truthful legend, or to the
history of the noble martyrs of Vienne, or Lyons, or to the many similar, still extant records, to nerve our courage, by the contemplation of
what children and women, catechumens and slaves, suffered,
unmurmuring, for Christ. (*F*, 414)

What he has done is to define the moral limits of fictional literature and
show more clearly why he has included such extensive fragments from
hagiographical works.

Yet if edification is the goal of the novel, the audience being addressed is most specifically the English nation. Time after time Wiseman
makes passing allusions to England and to England's history within the
Roman fold; the novel, then, takes on a mildly irenic as well as didactic
character. The conversion of the English king Lucius (mythical second-
century ruler and martyr used by the English reformers as a precedent of
the royal "Vicar of Christ") is mentioned, as is the martyrdom of St.
George. The net of the *communio sanctorium* is drawn tighter. One of the
chief characters of the novel, Pancratius, emerges as the St. Pancras long
revered in England. There was "no anticipation of a church in his
honour to rise in faithful ages on the banks of the distant Thames, which,
even after desecration, should be loved and eagerly sought as their last
resting-place, by hearts faithful still to his dear Rome" (*F*, 17). Wiseman
adds in a footnote that this was "Old St. Pancras's, the favourite burial-
place of Catholics, till they had cemeteries of their own." Pancras is also
used to recall the outrages of revolution; the relics of St. Pancratius in
Rome were scattered by the French in 1798, and his church was
wrecked by the Garibaldians in 1849.[67] Wiseman develops this theme of
nostalgia for the days when England enjoyed visible unity with the communion of saints through the Roman Church. It is the task of such literature of edification to urge the readers to unite themselves once more to
that visible and invisible body. One could also posit that Wiseman's pastoral "From Out the Flaminian Gate" was intended, besides observing
appropriate Roman protocol, to make a similar connection. It was at the
Milvian Bridge, out the Flaminian Gate, that Constantine, whose father

had ruled from his capital at York, was victorious over Maxentius in 312. Rome and England were forever linked by that fateful portal.

Wiseman's didacticism, using the historical example of the martyrs, is the sharp edge of the novel, urging the present readers to turn to the source of such models of virtue: "The example of our Lord has made the martyrs; and the example of the martyrs leads us upwards to Him. Their blood softens our hearts; His alone cleanses our souls. Theirs pleads for mercy; His bestows it. May the Church, in her days of peace and of victories, never forget what she owes to the age of her martyrs. As for us . . . we are indebted to it for our spiritual lives. May many, who will only read of it, draw from it the same mercy and grace" (*F*, 615–16). It is an appropriation of history using the master key to history—the Church's understanding of itself and its saints—whose purpose is, by didactic and irenic means, to edify the contemporary reader and instill a sense of contemporaneity with the models of virtue of a given historical epoch through a metahistorical modality. That purpose and methodology most strikingly delineate both the chief contrasts between this novel and other historical reconstructions of the nineteenth century and its chief links to classic forms of hagiography.

The acceptance of the novel not only by the general reading public but also by ecclesiastical authorities, including the pope, thrilled Wiseman. He wrote, "I consider this a perfect revolution, a great triumph of the 'spirit of the age' or 'progress' over forms and etiquettes."[68] The vocabulary he chose may indicate to the close observer a partial cause of the distance between him and Newman, not in terms of the acceptability of novels, but rather in terms of the relationship of the Church to the present age, to use Kierkegaard's terminology. Pitted against the Church before the nineteenth century, in Wiseman's mind, was the "world," composed of two antagonists: heathenism and Judaism. The evil in the former was due to its viciousness, sensualism, and decadent refinement; in the latter it was its pride, self-conceit, and carnality. In the nineteenth century the Church's adversary had become the practical/mechanical genius of the age corrupted by being "*in league with* [italics mine] materialism, expediency, and fear of too much faith" (Ward, 2:23). That genius was not itself corrupt or under the burden of sin but only by virtue of being in league with corrupting attitudes, whereas Newman had a deeper distrust of that modern, liberal genius in and of

itself. Citing a sermon (12 October 1839), Ward, his biographer, maintains that Wiseman sketched a theory of doctrinal development: each age
has its characteristic thought, and the Church's dogma represents her attitude face to face with that thought creatively, not just nihilistically
through prohibitions (1:314–17). Ward is at pains to harmonize
Wiseman's position with Newman's; that effort can be historically maintained, since Wiseman approved the *Essay on the Development of Doctrine*
submitted to him by Newman and did not require revisions. But
Wiseman's idea of doctrinal development, never fully elaborated, is that
the Church should always reflect what is the best in the spirit of each age
(1:301). For Newman that kind of rhetoric could easily mask the liberal
face of men like Charles Kingsley.

John Henry Newman

Callista: A Tale of the Third Century appeared anonymously late in 1855;
but as John Henry Newman (1801–90) himself noted in the postscript of
the next edition, dated 8 February 1856, the identity of the "Author"
had become such public knowledge that he could include a significant
dedication to Henry William Wilberforce (1807–73).[69] It was a work
that collated various preliminary sketches and versions antedating the final draft of 1855, when Newman was distracted by troubles with both
the Catholic University of Dublin and F. W. Faber's London Oratory.[70]
Significant sections of chapters 1, 4, and 5 and the characterization of
Juba, the antagonist, were already shaped by 1848, shortly after the publication of *Loss and Gain*.[71] And although it was not composed, as some
have romantically suggested, upon the backs of envelopes while the author traveled in railway carriages, this allegedly impromptu work generated considerable comment and prompt comparison to contemporary
examples of this genre.[72] Wiseman's *Fabiola* was the primary historical reconstruction thus compared: "Kindred as they are in subject, they are
nevertheless entirely dissimilar both in the treatment and in the plan.
Callista avowedly is but a sketch. Fabiola is an elaborate and highly artistic story."[73] This off-handed attitude in treating the novel as a "trifle,"
the word Newman himself used in the dedication, may have moved him
to substitute in later editions the designation "Tale" for "Sketch." It was
to be expected, though, that *Callista* would be weighed against
Wiseman's novel, since it was Wiseman who suggested that Newman

compose a companion piece to *Fabiola* entitled "The Church of the Basilicas." When J. M. Capes, J. S. Northcote, and E. H. Thompson attempted to organize Burns's and Lambert's Catholic Popular Library late in 1853, Wiseman proposed a series of four works: the Church of the Catacombs, the Church of the Basilicas, the Church of the Cloister, and the Church of the Schools.[74] Wiseman's historical project, in line with similar apologetic articles in the *Dublin Review*, failed; but the publication of *Fabiola* and its popular success stirred Newman to complete his own. He wished, however, to make it clear that the work was more than his deprecatory "trifle" suggested and was in fact a serious artistic piece of historical fiction with an imaginative and complex structure of sources,[75] incident, and characterization. A more detailed comparison with Wiseman's *Fabiola* will follow the close analysis of *Callista*.

In significant ways such an analysis demonstrates the intensely personal psychology of the piece, the crafted interweaving of various secular and religious themes that point to contemporary issues, and, finally, a treatment of biography and history in a polished literary form that is decidedly superior in comparison to Wiseman's didactic work and manifestly not "amateurish" in comparison to Newman's other prose. Because it stressed the roles of a lay martyr and Bishop Cyprian with little or no treatment of a centralized papacy, the novel was read in some quarters as implied criticism of papal power. Newman later answered this publicly through a new postscript in the 1881 edition. Much has also been said about considering this work within the fabric of both Newman's life and literature. The happenstance of Agellius' typhoid symptoms and the occurrence of Torres Vedras in both *Callista* and the *Apologia*, to quote just two examples, may be only happy equivalences.[76] But the contribution of *Parochial and Plain Sermons*, first published 1834–43, providing circumstances and substantial dialogue, as well as the intriguing, though unhistorical, relation of *An Essay in Aid of a Grammar of Assent* (1870) to the central motive of the novel, points to subtle links between the author's life and this work. The bases of this are his understanding of historical analogy, his personalist theory of literature, and his imaginative ability to re-create the past dramatically: principles that informed all his writings, but particularly the various autobiographical essays.

Set in Sicca in North Africa in A.D. 250 during the Decian persecution, the novel traces the religious development of the pagan girl Callista, introduced to Christianity by the lapsed youth Agellius and the rigoristic, fugitive bishop Cyprian (Caecilius). Various characters represent certain mental temperaments: her brother Aristo; Juba, Agellius' brother; Jocundus, uncle of the boys; Gurta the witch, their mother. There is also a cavalcade of contemporary religious faiths, much as in *Loss and Gain* (chaps. 7–9): devotees of Astarte, Isis, and Mithras, the civic religion of Rome, agnosticism, Epicureanism, Neoplatonism, witchcraft, Gnosticism, and Marcionism. These characters and groups can be identified with parallels in Victorian England such as Evangelicals, Liberals, Irvingites, and high-and-dry Churchmen.[77] Callista, mistaken for a Christian by a frenzied mob, moves slowly in prison from rejection of paganism through an agonizing period of uncertainty to Christian belief and baptism. She recognizes in Christianity the absolute correlative of the reality of her own consciousness and conscience, identifying her thus with Newman's personal process of conversion.

The two central and developed characterizations in the novel are those of Agellius and Callista, but it is no tautology to assert that Callista is the focus of *Callista*. In Kingsley's *Hypatia* the figure of that name surrenders the focus to the "new foes with an old face" of the subtitle. And the title character in *Fabiola* is eclipsed by the mass of antiquarian detail and the saintly pantheon. (The anachronistic introduction of Arnobius and Lactantius together, noted by Newman in the advertisement to the novel, is at best tangential to the story. They are not pivotal characters. Arnobius, for example, is used to deflate the philosophical posturing of Polemo, a disciple of Plotinus.) Callista is the center because her process of conversion is the core of the story; the conceptual study of conversion and the character of Callista are as intimately bound together as form and matter. The character of Agellius is also highly developed because of his role in Callista's approach to faith and his own return to the discipline of Christianity. He provides important occasions for Callista's "knowledge" of the faith. He supplies her the opportunity to declare her inner turmoil; it is at his farmhouse, to which she fled to warn him of anti-Christian mobs, that she chances upon Caecilius (Thascius Caecilius Cyprianus) and receives the Gospel of Luke; his is one of three examples (Chione and Caecilius being the other two) of the Christian life that haunts her deepest imagination. Yet his own belief is tinged with remorse and a recognition of the failure of nerve; it is just such depth and ambiguity in characterization, and such complex motivation, however, that save these creations from being one-dimensional. The actual process of conversion she undergoes and the intense psychological stages in that process will be discussed later.

The only other Christian to be considered in depth is Cyprian, bishop of Carthage (248–58); indeed, this Father of the North African Church was a distinguished figure, but he is presented disguised, fleeing the imperial proscription of Decius. Unlike the Anglo-Catholic novels, where he is portrayed as a charismatic bishop in full possession of his episcopal office prior to a glorious martyrdom, Newman's work shows him hunted and confused. He does not present a forceful or compelling figure, brilliant in argument, naturally attractive in personality, or otherworldly in aspect. He is unable to bring Juba to baptism (only the direct intervention of the supernatural at the end of the novel does that, although he is able to keep the demoniac calm), and he only alienates Callista in their first interview (although his argument unsettles her confident self-possession). He is even less the stereotyped saint because of his free admission of guilt and sin before this girl; he does this to show her that a naive approach to holiness is not the proper way. He will not present himself to her as a sinless statue. Just as she has "a past," so does he. Newman wants him to be more than the breviary sketch, a dictionary of virtues, that Wiseman provided in each of his saints. Yet there is an element of the otherworldly about Cyprian, because the bishop is made to bear symbolic functions as well. In the interchange with Juba the discussion and its participants take on cosmic shape: "The priest stopped awhile; there was no emotion on either side. It was strange to see them so passionless, so antagonistic, like St. Michael and his adversary" (C, 164). And the dominical imitation is clear when the mob sets the bishop upon an ass with the cry "He shall go back in triumph to the city which he loves."

But if Cyprian at times sums up in his person the principle of good, Juba sums up that of evil. His is the true face of "liberal" thought and the logical end of private judgment. "What you slaves call pride . . . I call dignity," he says. It is with such Promethean pride and stubbornness that he refuses baptism and compares himself to God: "'I am as free,' he said, 'in my place, as He in His.'" The irony used for this character becomes clear when his subsequent possession by a demon and idiocy are juxtaposed to his assertion "I will be lord and master in my own soul. Every faculty shall be mine; there shall be no divided allegiance" (C, 165). His punishment by madness is standard in such religious novels, and his eventual exorcism takes as its model a modern exorcism in England.[78] Religion based on feeling is also exemplified by Juba, since private judgment is the very mode by which an individual evaluates religious sentiments: "Religion was a fashion with me, which is now gone by. It was the complexion of a particular stage of my life . . . I acted according to the feeling, while it lasted; but I can no more recall it than my first teeth, or the down on my chin. It's among the things that were" (C, 36). But here too there is some ambiguity in characterization. It is Juba who engineers Cyprian's escape from the mob: "He then turned to Caecilius and whispered, 'You see, old father, that others, besides Christians, can forgive and forget. Henceforth call me generous Juba.' And he tossed his head" (C, 36). His generosity, though, is egotistical, capricious, whimsical, and inconsistent; it is not based upon solid first principles but on a general anarchistic urge. Juba, however, functions at another level in the novel; it is part of Newman's irony that this proud catechumen provides one of the most telling critiques of undisciplined Christians. The failure of so-called Christians to undergo the rigors of their faith, living lives little better than baptized pagans, is an important theme in Newman's stories, especially in *Loss and Gain*. It is part of his critique of culture and the Church's loss of nerve in that period and what he considered the national apostasy of his own century. Through the contrast of rigorism and laxism in the third century, he found a suitable counterpart for his own. This stress emphasizes the continuing importance of "holiness" and asceticism for Newman from his Anglican days:

"I despise you," said Juba; "you have not the pluck to be a Christian. Be consistent, and fizz upon a stake. . . . I despise you, and the whole kit of you. What's the difference between you and another? Your people say, 'Earth's a vanity, life's a dream, riches a deceit, pleasure a snare. Fratres charissimi, the time is short;' but who love earth and life and riches and pleasure better than they? You are all of you as fond of the world, as set upon gain, as chary of reputation, as ambitious of power, as the jolly old heathen, who, you say, is going the way of the pit." (C, 35)

The satire is even more pointed if the reader notes that "Charissimi, the time is short" was a favorite locution of Newman himself.

The "lesson" of Juba, though, is clearly drawn after his possession by a demon, inflicted on him by his mother, Gurta the witch, with whom he made love; the reality of infernal forces is shown active and alive in him, possessing him, so that after a scene of Romantic frenzy and horror he stands "like Satan looking upon Paradise" and laps the blood on sacrifices at the rural festival of Pan, causing panic among the rustics.

The other pagan characters, notably Jucundus, the wealthy uncle of Agellius and Juba, and Polemo of Rhodes, the philosopher, are eminently sensible men with various civic virtues. In Jucundus is the figure of a man of position who "was a zealous imperialist, and a lover of tranquility, a despiser of the natives and a hater of the Christians." He was one with strong family ties toward his nephews, but who found Agellius' refusal to sacrifice to the genius of Rome incomprehensible. He was a rather crude follower of Epicureanism, the "established" philosophy, yet not without saving characteristics and a mediating attitude toward the persecution of Christians—he thought that only the leaders should be tried. For both Jucundus (like Mr. Malcolm in *Loss and Gain*) and Polemo (cf. his panegyric on Rome) the one reality was the political and cultural status quo in which the government rightly limited and structured the religious beliefs of its citizens. For Newman that attitude was just another reflection of the nineteenth-century crisis. These characters owe much of their portrayal to the working out dramatically of the concept of the relation of Church and State, especially in the Erastian principle at work in the Anglican Church in the Gorham decision (1848–50) and Denison case (1853–58) and in the Roman Church in the Austrian Concordat (1855). This same temperament is drawn out in the civil servant Cornelius (comparable to the college head in *Loss and Gain*); in fact, he may be a portrait of Kingsley.[79] The religious claims of the State collapse, however, not so much because it is distinguished from the Church but because the State cannot be, for Callista just as for Newman, the image of the "inward friend," "the Monitor" who will judge the soul. This is a connection of character and concept that Newman consistently used. The genuinely evil people in the novel, those who have surrendered themselves for power, worldly or occult, are the most stereotyped, as is seen in the character of Gurta. But the way the wicked flesh out the concept of evil provides the novel with startling images and symbols. For example, the concept of incestuous lust is presented by the image of a child's crucifixion.[80] This demonstrates that the fleshing out of concepts in actions and characters is not intellectually abstract and does not impoverish narrative fiction.

But Newman's full view of man is not adequately seen by concentrating merely on the major characters. There is one character, one personality, that elicits his most uncompromising criticism—the mob. It is a collection of "villain ratcatchers and offal-eaters," a parade of humanity at once barbaric and bestial. The locust plague sent upon them as a providential judgment is the reflexive image of their own scavenging, destructive fury. This is an image closely drawn from portions of the prophecies of Joel, Paulus Orosius, and Robert Southey's *Thalaba the Destroyer*. The mob's decimation by the military after the riot is part of the vivid, historic reconstruction designed to draw out its character.[81] That character is developed in other ways. Confronting the visible presence of grace in Callista at her execution and afterward in her incorruptible body, the attitude of the crowd progresses from curiosity, through amazement, to awe. The identity of the mob is, as well, linked closely to Newman's conception of nature (cf. the peasants at Pan's festival) and the city. However, the mob draws as much for its character from the popular risings of Newman's own day, especially in the experience of the 1850 No Popery riots[82] and the earlier Chartist disturbances in the 1830s and 1840s, as from the reconstruction of ancient incidents.

Another dimension of Romantic imagery is conveyed in the periodic and meticulous delineations of nature. Newman's avoidance of important historical figures and locales is carried out in his choice of Sicca as the site of this story, although Gustave Flaubert made it the setting for the early chapters of his pre-Christian and highly sensual novel *Salammbô* (1862). Wolff suggests that Sicca is the coded embodiment of the critical "high-and-dry" metaphor for the Anglican Church itself.[83] Yet Newman's wider attitude toward nature is evidently ambivalent. The serene, sensible, and respectable life on a modest farm is affirmed; the farm cottage itself recalls Newman's interest in the holy house of Loreto.[84] Simple, rural domesticity is thus linked with the earthly, hidden life of Jesus. The description of the flora of the region is meticulously precise about botanical types. Indeed, Newman had asked his publisher, James Burns, for assistance in gathering information about such aspects of North Africa.[85] His attention to the fauna of the district is equally detailed. The meticulous Romantic attention to and preoccupation with nature is behind this precision. Newman's other prose demonstrates a mind highly conversant with the imagery of nature and organic growth, an imagery he does not disdain to use for the concept of doctrinal development. Significantly, the hidden, persecuted Church is identified with natural symbols: the rock, mountain, and cave, which are also traditional religious symbols. A man of letters so impressed by Wordsworth, Southey, and the school of Lakeland poets as Newman was would find such Romantic images of creation natural to use. The precision and detail also seem part of the influence of scientific observation traditional at Oxford, the revival of interest in medieval tapestries and stained glass, and the lush pre-Raphaelite exteriors. This is the side of nature that has order, the world cultivated into a garden. But he indicates another side of nature: the impenetrable mystery eliciting awe and fear, which Newman always found in his own apprehension of the cosmos. So, too, over nature is a thin veil of iniquity; creation is fallen and dominated by evil. *Deus absconditus* is a recurrent theme in his sermons, a theme that draws him back from any easy identification between creator and creation. Newman does not use this as the grounds for neglecting nature, however. The principles that safeguard him from extremes in either direction are his developed conceptions of the Fall and the Incarnation. The latter mystery is indirectly touched upon by the image of Callista's *corpo santo* lying impervious to decay.

Another major theme is the attitude toward the city. This concept is closely aligned, as noted above, both with the character of the mob and with nature. The single, simple Christian and his life in retirement are contrasted with the city and its toils: "'I am a quiet being,' answered Agellius, 'I like the country, which you think so tame, and care little for the flaunting town. Tastes differ'" (*C*, 10). This line is spoken by Agellius before his return to a more rigorist Christian life, but the mention of taste shows the immediate nature of the Christian aversion to the city. Augustine's two cities are certainly the theological background implied here, but Newman relies on his own concrete images. The indirect contrast of city and rock-Church informs the entire novel. Simply put:

"Those who are shut up in crowded cities see but the work of man, which is evil." Newman reiterates the solemn quality of his rejection of man's city: "And yet, as Agellius ascended the long flight of marble steps which led the foot-passages up into that fair city . . . , did he not know full well that iniquity was written on its very walls, and spoke a solemn warning to a Christian heart to go out of it, to flee it, not to take up a home in it. . . . You will understand the great Apostle's anguish at seeing a noble and beautiful city given up to idolatry . . . , but now a Christian enters it with a Christian's heart and a Christian's hopes" (C, 113). It lies as far from the City of God as Birmingham's mills were from the looms of Blake's Jerusalem, yet the missioner of Newman's day is called into those Brummagem sinks and cockpits.

But it is not the physical city alone that is tainted with evil; it exercises an influence and spreads a miasma over the populace and the surrounding countryside. As Agellius muses: "'The very air breathes sin to-day,' he cried, 'oh that I did not find the taint of the city in these works of God! Alas! sweet Nature, the child of the Almighty is made to do the fiend's work, and does it better than the town. O ye beautiful trees and fair flowers, O bright sun and balmy air, what a bondage ye are in, and how do ye groan till you are redeemed from it! Ye are bond slaves, but not willingly, as man is; but how will you ever be turned to nobler purpose?'" (C, 11). It is part of the activity of Providence that the city of Sicca eventually disappears; as Christianity waxes in history, so does Sicca wane. The same Christian calculus is used to measure the religious development of the characters. Callista is initially rich in the things of this world, but poor in heavenly gifts. It is part of the novel's irony and theology that the beauty of the city is seen through the Christian eyes of Agellius and the beauty of Callista through the eyes of Cyprian, while the visible beauty of nature is torturous to the possessed Juba.

A fourth area of concern is the experience of religion. The external part of this historical reconstruction let Newman partially portray Christianity's reflection upon itself, the popular, non-Christian understanding of Christianity, pagan and natural religion, and the various philosophies that functioned as religion. Each section of this representation lends itself, in Newman's hands, to a plastic reconstruction of the past and comment on the present. Each section of this representation is also intimately bound to the character in whom the model is made particular.

There is much said about Christianity's reflection upon itself, especially in Cyprian's Christian community; also, the narrator of the story is himself Christian, suggesting, hinting at a Christian understanding and solution behind the narration. It is in the character of Agellius, however, that the simple apprehension of faith of a third-century Christian is most poignantly expressed. It is a faith built on scant knowledge, no community support, and little Scripture, yet the unity and destiny of the faith are clear: "'Christians boast, I believe,' answered Agellius, 'that they are of no one race or country, but are members of a large unpatriotic family, whose home is in the sky'" (C, 203–4). He deals with many of the problems and drawbacks that a convert to Rome faced in Victorian England. It is important to note that not merely orthodox Christianity is presented but various heresies as well, although these are presented as naively confused in the pagan mind. Gnostics and Montanists ("Tertullianists") are presented as fanatics all too eager to suffer martyrdom.

The popular mind tended to regard Christianity in superstitious categories: magic, ass worship, devouring asses and little boys, and witchcraft. Newman points to the parallel between this ignorance and the Victorian ignorance concerning "papism." Catholics in England were accused of the most absurd and horrendous beliefs and acts. Although the lower classes acted out their violence, this antipapist attitude cut across all classes. It is the narrator, though, who sums up the contemporary view of Christianity shared by both educated and illiterate pagans:

> In that day there were many rites and worships which kept to themselves—many forms of moroseness or misanthropy, as they were considered, which withdrew their votaries from the public ceremonial. The Catholic faith seemed to the multitude to be one of these; it was only in critical times, when some idolatrous act was insisted on by the magistrate, that the specific nature of Christianity was tested and detected. There at length it was seen to differ from all other religious varieties by that irrational and disgusting obstinacy, as it was felt to be, which had rather suffer torments and lose life than submit to some graceful, or touching, or at least trifling observance which the tradition of ages had sanctioned. (C, 24)

Popular paganism is shown in its panoply of magic, witchcraft, cultic variety (e.g., Pan, Astarte, Isis, Mithras, Cybele), and civil religion. There is a strong sexual element involved in this depiction, whether promiscuity in the cults or the pagan conception of marriage. The worship of Astarte is really a syncretic cult of Urania, Juno, and Aphrodite, or Woman as goddess, wife/mother, and lover. Gurta the witch, set alongside Callista's mottled past, completes the spectrum. During the mob rampage the baptized children of the Christian Duumvir's widow are taken, the girls sent to the shrine of Astarte and the boys to the "wild Votaries of Cybele" for "execrable" rites. The stress here is on the sexual horror, once again involving children. Callista's celibacy, then, stands out more starkly against this lurid panorama. The two extremes of paganism are typified by Gurta and Jucundus. While Jucundus, like Aristo, maintains an official show of hedonistic Epicureanism (Newman's portrayal of that philosophy lacks the depth and detail of Pater's), his is basically no more than the civil religion: "He knew his own position perfectly well, and, though the words 'belief' or 'knowledge' did not come into his religious vocabulary, he could at once, without hesitation, state what he professed and maintained. He stood upon the established order of things, on the tradition of Rome, and the laws of the empire; but as to Greek sophists and declaimers, he thought very much as Old Cato did about them" (C, 80).

A more philosophical approach to religion is portrayed by Polemo of Rhodes and Callista herself. The former is a "friend of Plotinus" who comes to lead the girl back from slipping too close to Christianity. Newman's MS notes contain material on Plotinus that was not used or developed.[86] It is significant and no small part of her conversion process that his philosophy is no longer convincing to her, just as Polemo's presentation of Platonism proves untrue and ineffective. At another level it is through the character of Callista that Newman is able to make observations concerning natural religion. She attempts in this philosophical vein to locate Christianity among other religions:

> . . . but a new religion begins by appealing to what is peculiar in the minds of a few. The doctrine, floating on the winds, finds its own; it takes possession of their minds; they answer its calls; they are brought together by that common influence; they are strong in each other's sympathy; they create and throw around them an external form, and thus they found a religion. The sons are brought up in their father's faith; and what was the idea of a few becomes at length the profession of a race. Such as Judaism; such the religion of Zoroaster or the Egyptians. (C, 215)

And it is the narrator who posits principles of natural religion, while considering Callista's Greek background, which on the purely natural level are a kind of *praeparatio evangelica*:

> There are certain most delicate instincts and perceptions in us which act as first principles, and which, once effaced, can never, except from some supernatural source, be restored to the mind. When men are in a state of nature, these are sinned against, and vanish very soon, at so early a date in the history of the individual that perhaps he does not recollect that he ever possessed them; and since, like other first principles, they are but very partially capable of proof, a general skepticism prevails both as to their existence and their truth. The Greeks, partly from the vivacity of their intellect, partly from their passion for the beautiful, lost these celestial adumbrations sooner than other nations. (*C*, 98)

Newman's approach to atheism and to non-Catholic religions has come in for some exposition; basically he felt that Christianity, adapted to differing ages and places, gathers and fulfills scattered religious truths that were gradually being communicated to humankind. There is an affinity here to the general theories found in *An Essay in Aid of a Grammar of Assent*, but there is also a particularity, grounded in the person and history of Callista. In natural religion and the philosophical approach to truth, shadowy adumbrations appear, probabilities emerge, leading back to Christianity, the need for supernatural intervention into this life, and the slow mills of conversion, *ex umbris* into light and "reality."[87]

A last group of images of note consists of the author's views of art. There is none of the detailed and functionally integral incorporation of parts of literary masterpieces and the author's evaluation of them in this story as in Kingsley's or Pater's tales. There is little stress upon the plastic arts, outside of random references to pagan cultic objects and the ornamentation of Christian homes and oratories. One ironic feature of the story, however, is that Callista and Aristo manufacture idols and graven images; the profession is not seen as a high or respectable one, and no comment is made in this connection concerning art or craft. But Callista is also described as accomplished in improvising poetry and acting Greek drama; she is the aesthetic principle personified. Image making does provide some further links to the nineteenth century, when Newman states that the "modern arts which enable an English town in this day to be so fertile in the production of ware of this description for the markets of the pagan East, were then unknown" (*C*, 21). Wolff, on the other hand, suggests that this is part of an extended metaphor and identifies Callista's image making with the Evangelicals and their missions. The figure, often repeated in contemporary paintings and prints of the era, of the itinerant sculptor and caster must have been familiar to Newman.

In line with such antiquarian interest, he mentions an alto-relievo from the reign of Constantius found in a Roman basilica at El Kaf (modern Sicca). This artistic device is used to give a vivid interpretation of court procedure as seen on a bas-relief; like the procession on Keats's well-wrought urn, the proceedings are suddenly alive. There is, however, none of the visible mass of antiquarian detail to be found in Wiseman, Kingsley, and Pater. In a real sense there is such a lack of emphasis on great works of art because, as in Pater, the greatest work of art is the single life of the convert, and it is this that occupies the author's and the reader's attention. The theological basis is a consistent rejection of aesthetic categories for religious ones. But the verbal care and uniformity of diction, the control of incident, character, and suspense, are the concern of the author and the immanent form of the novel's view on great art.[88]

It is in the realm of the experience of religion that the novel is most detailed, possessing an internal as well as external dimension of views on piety, belief, and morals. It is external because it portrays the outward, physical features of persons, events, relationships, and ceremonials. It is internal because it delves into the psychological and spiritual processes and motivations of these same persons and events, as well as suggesting the hidden, invisible movements of grace and Providence.

The primary reality permeating the novel is one of divine presence, but it is portrayed in a way significantly different from the constant supernatural intervention in *Fabiola* or the real absence of the supernatural in *Hypatia*. The image of God and the attitude of believers are delineated in complex fashion: in statements of personal piety, in prayers, in the interpretation of Scripture, in sacraments, in rites and ceremonies, in reflections on the Church, and especially in the concept of the *communio sanctorum*. These points and others unmentioned here reflect concerns of the author. It is part of Newman's own sense of reverence, for example, that the name *Jesus* is never used in the novel. And the narrator provides a fundamental picture that governs the sense of the divine presence throughout the story. Early in the novel, a prayer by the narrator, interesting not only for its statements about God but also in its articulation of a Victorian piety impressed upon the third century, stresses the image of the movement of grace and the protection of Providence:

> Be of good cheer, solitary one, though thou are not a hero yet! There is
> One that cares for thee, and loves thee, more than thou canst feel, love,
> or care for thyself. Cast all thy care upon Him. He sees thee, and is
> watching thee; He is hanging over thee, and smiles in compassion at
> thy troubles. His angel, who is thine, is whispering good thoughts to
> thee. He knows thy weakness; He foresees thy errors; but He holds
> thee by thy right hand, and thou shalt not, canst not escape Him. By
> thy faith, which thou hast so simply, resolutely retained in the midst of
> idolatry; by thy purity, which, like some fair flower, thou hast cherished in the midst of pollution. He will remember thee in thy evil hour,
> and thine enemy shall not prevail against thee. (*C*, 21)

For Agellius the relationship to God is one of child to loving parent. But, as will be touched upon later, it is the identification of God with love that is central to Callista's movement in grace. Newman's early insistence on fear of God has undergone a metamorphosis to love. It must also be noted that the acknowledgment of God's existence and presence, for Newman, directly implies the existence and working of the "enemy" from whom Christians will be protected by God's care; there is no heaven without hell. And Cyprian specifically insists that Callista acknowledge the reality of hell and eternal punishment.

A second fundamental feature in this piety is the dependence on familial piety and the support of a community of faith. Here as elsewhere in Newman's work the *communio sanctorum*, living and dead, is a necessary and critical modality of the Christian life. Being cut off from this living body is the chief reason Agellius experiences so much difficulty: "Am I for ever to have the knowledge, without the consolation, of the truth? Am I for ever to belong to a great divine society, yet never see the face of any of its members?" (*C*, 28). Growth in the faith demands this living community with its sacraments and habitual knowledge of the faith against which to measure itself. But contact with other Christians provides two vitally important features: spiritual counsel and sacramental confession, things the solitary Christian needs:

There was no repose out of doors, and no relief within. He was lonely
at home, lonely in the crowd. . . . A very great trial certainly this, in
which the soul is flung back upon itself; and that especially in the case of
the young, for whom memory and experience do so little, and way-
ward and excited feelings do so much. Great gain had it been for
Agellius, even in its natural effect, putting aside higher benefits to have
been able to recur to sacramental confession; but to confession he had
never been. (C, 27–78)

The place of prayer is also extremely important, whether it is the pa-
ternoster, the psalms, the formal prayers of the liturgy, or the private
prayers of individuals. It is in form penitential, intercessory, and eucharistic, mentioning specific concerns of the one praying and collecting the
prayers of all the faithful. Prayer is efficacious only after the person has
been turned to Christ: "I have been saying many prayers for you, while
my prayers were of no good, for then He was not mine. But now I have
espoused Him, and am going to be married to-day, and He will hear me"
(C, 357). It is just this pious language of spiritual espousals and a celestial
bridegroom, traditional images in mystical prayer, that infuriated
Kingsley. There is also intercessory prayer to saints, although one may
note the reserve in this in the offertory chant used at Callista's commemoration; the name of God is the focus of intercession, but her name
and her relics have power: "We use her name, we touch her bier. We
know her God is nigh." This is demonstrated by the final exorcism of
Juba, and such stresses are clearer in that context; once again the presence
of a demon is the occasion for exhibiting divine power. Prayer is the language of the *communio sanctorum*; the whole nexus of prayers, saints, sacraments (especially the Eucharist) is tightly woven. But it is also the
exultation and devotion of the individual; in a loose paraphrase of the
Magnificat Callista shows this side of prayer: "He has done great things for
me; I am wonderfully changed; I am not what I was, He will do more
still" (C, 346).

It is logical next to introduce Newman's treatment of sacraments,
since they (baptism and the Eucharist are presented as the central ones
and most discussed) are intimately connected. The Eucharist, however,
takes precedence over baptism as the first presented. *Callista* provides a
very clear expression of Newman's eucharistic piety; two citations are
notable in this regard:

This was the course of thought which occupied him [Caecilius] for many hours, after (as we have said) he had closed the door upon him, and knelt down before the cross. Not merely before the symbol of redemption did he kneel; for he opened his tunic at the neck, and drew thence a small golden pyx which was there suspended. In that carefully fastened case he possessed the Holiest, his Lord and his God. That Everlasting Presence was his stay and guide amid his weary wanderings, his joy and consolation amid his overpowering anxieties. Behold the secret of his sweet serenity, and his clear unclouded determination. He had placed it upon the small table at which he knelt, and was soon absorbed in meditation and intercession.[89]

And again:

Caecilius ought to have taken flight without a moment's delay, but a last sacred duty detained him. He knelt down and took the pyx from his bosom. He had eaten nothing that day; but even if otherwise, it was a crisis which allowed him to consume the sacred species without fasting. He hastily opened the golden case, adored the blessed sacrament, and consumed it, purifying its receptacle, and restoring it to its hiding place. (C, 348)

Perhaps Cyprian is used in this instance because of his position on the Eucharist, which underscored the sacrificial aspect and the sacerdotal character of the ministry. Newman had worked extensively on Cyprian, including the *Treatises*, for which he wrote a preface and over which he disputed with Pusey on the latter's doctrinal notes.[90]

With Callista the doctrine of the real presence is drawn out further: "It was her first and last communion; in a few days she renewed it, or rather completed it, under the very Face and Form of Him whom she now believed without seeing" (C, 348).

If Newman's views on the Eucharist mark part of his most Catholic stance, then his views on baptism mark what would ordinarily be categorized as a Protestant stance; such labels are, in Newman's own case and in this historical reconstruction, generally unilluminating. Such observations are as relatively worthless as those made by some critics that *Callista* defines Newman's Catholic understanding of the Fathers to balance his earlier Protestant understanding in various essays and biographies. It is curious, however, to see such a strong emphasis on adult believer's baptism. Christianity is not something transferred "with one's mother's milk," as Callista assumes and Caecilius corrects: the adult must make a decision and request baptism, as do both Callista and Juba. This may be derived from Newman's stress on and use of the Gospel of Luke. There is even a surprising denigration of anything other than believer's baptism: "'You will find,' said the priest [Cyprian], 'that the greater number of African Christians at this moment, for of them I speak confidently, are converts in manhood, not the sons of Christians. On the other hand, if there be those who have left the faith, and gone up to the capitol to sacrifice, these were Christians by hereditary profession. Such is my experience, and I think the case is the same elsewhere'" (C, 215). The historical Cyprian took a very different view on infant baptism.[91] This should alert us that this quotation must be read as a comment on the situation in England. Newman, as a recent convert, felt the disdain of many "old Catholics." In this historical parallel he implies that such cradle Catholics might apostatize the way the duke of Norfolk and his son did in 1850. But it is in a discussion of postbaptismal sin and whether baptism might be delayed that further thought on the act is drawn out. The stress on baptismal regeneration naturally increased the gravity with which postbaptismal sin was considered and subsequently raised the importance of the penitential system. Baptism is a sacrament to be conferred only once; when it is conferred, sins are remitted, "laved away," and the believer enters a new relationship to God. "In baptism God becomes your Father; your own God; your worship; your love—can you give up this great gift all through your life? Would you live 'without God in this world'?" (C, 154).

Besides baptismal regeneration and grace, at least in Callista's case, other qualities or immanent expressions of grace seem to accompany the sacramental act: "It was a sight for angels to look down upon, and they did; when the poor child, rich in this world's gifts, but poor in those of eternity, knelt down to receive that sacred stream upon her brow, which feel upon her with almost sensible sweetness, and suddenly produced a serenity different in kind from anything she had ever before even had the power of conceiving" (C, 347–48). Confirmation and penance ("a new grace") are other sacraments mentioned. Marriage is never spoken of in terms of the sacramental order; only chastity and divine espousals—total consecration to God—are clearly presented as the avenues of grace. Holy Orders are not discussed, although some sort of sacramental character in ordination is implied; ecclesiastics are deferred to and reverenced, but so are confessors in prison and other "holy men." Extreme unction, anointing of the sick and dying, and viaticum are similarly disregarded. When Cyprian stops on his journey to care for Agellius, it is spoken of as a "duty" to "restore" the sick man and "attend to his spiritual needs"; but this is more in line with simple works of mercy rather than sacramental functions. It must be remembered as well that the novel does not claim to be a "sacramentary," or *ordo ritualis*; Newman felt himself under no special compulsion to reconcile this picture of the Early Church with the full-blown Tridentine system.

It is with the treatment of Scripture that more of the theological basis of the novel is disclosed. *Fabiola* contains almost no substantial treatment of Scripture; the difference, one of some significance, with the treatment in *Hypatia* will be commented upon later. Actually the Scripture dealt with in Newman's novel constitutes a canon within the canon: the psalter of David, the Gospel of Luke, and Paul's Epistle to the Romans. This has elicited some critical attention: "The choice of the books found in Agellius' cottage—the Psalms, the Gospel of St. Luke, and St. Paul's Epistle to the Romans—is controlled by this same personalizing spirit. They are the great documents of the incarnation. They are the touchstones by which one separates Caecilius from Polemo, and what Callista became from what she was."[92] It is true that much of Newman's personal spirit is exemplified in this choice of books, and the incarnational effect of Scripture upon the reader is its central function in the novel. But the psalms are never discussed in their prophetical role, pointing to Jesus as Messiah or to a foreshadowing of the Incarnation. In addition, it is not just Scripture but the whole apprehension of life's meaning and of moral action that separates Caecilius from Polemo. Finally, Callista reads only the Gospel of Luke, not the other documents. Newman's treatment of Scripture is important to note, however. Scripture delineates the picture of a "real individual," showing Callista, as Cyprian has stated, "who it is we love." It opens for her "a new state of things" and ushers her "into the presence of One" who surpasses her imagination for perfection. In Scripture she finds the "Voice" and "Person" who spoke in her own conscience and who inspired the Christians she knows best. She is at once stricken by the conviction of her own sin and guilt and comforted from self-abasement by its words of assurance. All of this is impressed upon her by the vivid images of Scripture, and it impresses as a reality. "This is no poet's dream," she concludes. Although Scripture is not the central or sole basis of Christian faith and belief, it is still the most vivid presentation of the saving message, having an influence and efficacious pull upon the neophyte. It is also the basis of statements of identity: in its pages Callista can see herself as the forgiven wanton anointing the Lord's feet, and Chione, Agellius, and Cyprian as faithful representatives of the gospel's model of self-sacrificing love and perfection. This is, of course, a simplified application of meditation techniques embodied in the Ignatian *Exercises*. Scripture not only provides information about Christ but makes a vivid impression upon the imagination and offers a call to the heart, all based on "fact," "a reality," in which moral and intellectual components are bound up.

As has been seen in the reference to "saints" in the midst of the discussion of Scripture, the fabric of the example given in Scripture and the example given in the lives of the saints is closely interwoven. Mary, the angels, and saints are each given special attention. The image of Mary as the *Advocata* is presented in the decoration of a Christian home and an oratory and in several "visions." These visions, parallels to which appear in Pater's novel, are part of Newman's own perception of religious experience but may also derive from the vivid examples in Charlotte Brontë's *Jane Eyre* (1847).[93] Yet the last vision of Mary and the saints is forcefully christological; as Callista peers closely into the face of the "Maid and Mother," it becomes translucent and she beholds the features of Christ. Then, upon Mary, the saints, and herself, she beholds the imprint of the stigmata. Mary and the cross are never separated: "The ever-blessed immaculate Mother of God is exercising her office as the Advocate of sinners, standing by the sacrifice as she stood at the cross itself, and offering up and applying its infinite merits and incommunicable virtue in union with priests and people."[94] Other saints, such as Sts. Perpetua and Felicitas, are mentioned, and material from their *Passio* is used for illustrative purposes. Indeed, much of *Callista* must be seen as part of the hagiographical tradition, including, as the novel does, the "words" of the saint, the *passio*, trial sequences, as well as cultic and sacramental embellishments, for example, the offertory verses mentioned above. Nevertheless, it is a hagiography and an edifying literature basically different from Wiseman's. Here there is more reserve in the discussion of the miraculous, and there is a range of characterization wider than Wiseman's meticulous paraphrase of the breviary offices and legends of the saints. Newman saves them from being pallid mannequins; they grapple with the faith, flee persecution, fail in strength, and confess sinfulness. Yet they are in touch with more than the natural order; by their holiness they possess charisms and a prophetical power in the form of "intimations" of people's needs and future events.

As with saints, so are there specific functions for angels and the other angelic orders. They are part of the instrumental cause of Providence working itself out in the world and stand as protectors over Christians: "We must suppose that angels held those heathen eyes that they should not recognize them [the Christian group]" (C, 376). But just as real as the angelic realm is the demonic; Agellius begs Cyprian's blessing "that evil may not touch [him]." The demonic also confers charismatic gifts, such as speaking in tongues as the Irvingites and Mormons did in Victorian England. And the whole panoply of relics (for both good and evil use), miracles (e.g., Juba's cure, the preservation of Callista's body, the reliance on a miracle to supply the Christians with water), the use of images, passwords, symbols (as ornaments, as instruction, and as apotropaic signs), and the accepted occurrence of visions are all treated in close connection with one another as legitimate manifestations of the Christian life.

All these aspects of that life are meshed together even by simple gestures within the life of the Church, its liturgy, and the penitential piety it produced: "They beat their breasts." For Newman the concrete problems of ecclesiology or the question of the sacramental life are founded on a strong and developed concept of the Church:

> By this time they had gained the end of the long gallery, and had passed through a second apartment, when suddenly the sounds of the ecclesiastical chant burst on the ear of Agellius. How strange, how transporting to him! He was almost for the first time coming home to his father's house, though he had been a Christian from a child, and never, as he trusted, to leave it, now that it was found. He did not know how to behave himself, nor indeed where to go. Aspar conducted him into the seats set apart for the faithful; he knelt down and burst into tears.[95]

The piety and identity of the Church have as much relation to the Victorian era as they do to that earlier epoch. The image of the Church as hidden and rocklike is central and of grave consequence in Newman's thought. Characters talk again and again of being strengthened by the "solidity of the See of Peter in Rome." It is a complex of fundamental images, pointing to the doctrinal stability the Church provides and Newman required. It also connotes the future mission when, after political pressures had been relaxed, the preserved structure of the Church would emerge from under the mountain—a sort of play upon Arthurian metaphors becoming familiar to Victorian audiences—and expand over the world. The position of the Church in this respect was, Newman felt, the same in both eras. His approach to progress and the changed world situation was, however, more complicated than this, as his essay *The Tamworth Reading Room* (1841) shows.

The Church emergent in this dream scenario would then illumine the world by its given message of truth in the form of authority, both doctrinal and moral. The secular, the sophisticated, the philosophical mind sees Christian dogma as "too dismal, too shocking, too odious to be believed." It is a secular world of private judgment, as seen in Juba, who bears in this respect the likeness of the liberal, free-thinking Francis William Newman (1805–97), John Henry's younger brother. The dogmas of the creed, in contrast, are similarly undeniable facts of nature, not opinions about the shape of things but facts, revealed more cogently than by the profoundest intellect or the purest human affection. The individual may reject these facts, but there is a consequence to such an act: "Assuming then, first, that the soul always needs external objects to rest upon; next, that it has no prospect of any such when it leaves this visible scene; and thirdly, that the hunger and thirst, the gnawing of the heart, where it occurs, is as keen and piercing as a flame; it will follow there is nothing irrational in the notion of an eternal Tartarus" (*C*, 220). Heresy, on the other hand, was a workable example of "untrue speculations." Gnostics and Montanists, for example, attacked the historical integrity of the Incarnation and the apostolic order, also under assault in the nineteenth century.

This attempt to present the Church's doctrinal life and its maintenance of authority is still another edge of the "map" of conversion, the central motif of the novel. The movement of Callista from unbelief to belief is one of the most closely mapped out psychological studies in nineteenth-century fiction; this feature marks the effectual boundary between this novel, along with *Marius*, and works like *Fabiola* and *Hypatia*, although Kingsley does attempt to unfold the conversion of Raphael before the reader. There are subtle gradations and shifts in tone as Newman's heroine moves from questions, to intimations, to probabilities, to certainties, to belief, to faith; as has been noted, *An Essay in Aid of a Grammar of Assent* could function as a gloss upon the novel.[96] The transformation is not based upon any clear incident, person, relationship, or qualification; it is a movement of mystery, for all the detail in the process. It is notable too that it is experienced before the reader, not undergone and then narrated; it is re-created in the dialogue and events of the fiction. Further, the change is elicited in the course of the heroine's experience: her meeting with Christians, her reading of Luke's Gospel, her chance apprehension by the mob. Not one of these factors is shown as unique or critical, but each contributes something to the process, so that the end result is stronger than the logical sum of the various probabilities.

Callista begins that process already possessing the intimations of what she should believe; like Charles Reding in *Loss and Gain* she has an openness and capacity for faith before knowledge or belief is opened to her. It is on this basis that she berates Agellius during his proposal of marriage; as a Christian, she instructs him, he should have been first concerned with her salvation, besides the obstacles such mixed union would prove because of radically different orientations and the problem of religious education of the children. Agellius himself was the confused offspring of such a union. In the 1850s marriage and religious education were topical problems vexing the nation. But Agellius too has noted some incipient movement of grace, perhaps, or some undefined openness before grace in her: "Could not a clever girl throw herself into the part of Alcestis, or chant the majestic verses of Cleanthes, or extemporize a hymn upon the spring, or hold an argument on the *pulchrum* and *utile*, without having any leaning towards Christianity? A calm, sweet voice, a noble air, an expressive countenance, refined and decorous manners, even these specific indications of heavenly grace?" (*C*, 108). No. Agellius is suffering from a "fascination." Christianity is different in kind, not only degree, from Callista's state at that moment. Callista has still the blankness of "Greek sculpture" upon her rather than the calm of the portal figures of Chartres.

Yet a process of change is initiated; suggestions have been made to her intellect and the processes of the mind contain their own necessity. Associations are made, apprehensions are confirmed; the necessity based on some initial principles—the desire for happiness and love—leads her to accept part of what is presented; logical necessity, events, and decisive acts of the will lead her to accept the whole. What is a "most beautiful imagination" is perceived finally as reality. The examples of Chione, her former servant, Agellius, and Cyprian, intermingled with her visions, contribute to her development. She sees that faith is a reality for them. She sees that what she wants to affirm they already affirm in their lives; questions such as these lead her to ask "Am I a Christian?"

> Yet, had she been asked, at the time of which we speak, where was her
> principle and her consistency, what was her logic, or whether she acted
> on reason, or on impulse, or on feeling, or in fancy, or in passion, she
> would have been reduced to silence. What did she know about herself,
> but that, to her surprise, the more she thought over what she heard of
> Christianity, the more she was drawn to it, and the more it approved
> itself to her whole soul, and the more it seemed to respond to all her
> needs and aspirations, and the more intimate was her presentiment that
> it was true? The longer it remained on her mind as an object, the more
> it seemed (unlike the mythology or the philosophy of her country, or
> the political religion of Rome) to have an external reality and sub-
> stance, which deprived objections to it of their power, and showed
> them to be at best but difficulties and perplexities. (C, 291–92)

It was Newman's position, in passing, that a thousand difficulties do not make one doubt. Callista's accidental capture and trial provide further impetus to focus all her life and thought on this question. She has little definite knowledge or understanding of Christianity, yet she feels that her visions were from heaven and that God is dictating what to do in her heart. She must remain honest; she does not believe any longer in Jupiter, she cannot sacrifice to the emperor's *genius*, yet she is not a Christian. Two processes are involved: to see that paganism is false and to see that Christianity is true. It is in her reading of the Gospel of Luke that the reality is confirmed in her and the assent made; she is divested of natural pride, self-regard, and beauty and takes on humility, simplicity, and meekness. There has been a reckoning, deliberate movement of the will, and power has been transmitted to her by Christ to accomplish that which He has instigated. Upon reception in prison (the shadow of which still hung over Newman himself) of baptism, confirmation, and the Eucharist (Newman asked advice from friends concerning the verisimilitude of such a rapid conferral of sacraments in a third-century setting), which she has requested, and after a short catechesis, her conversion is complete—she has entered that "higher reality" which she had longed for: "Callista was beyond reflecting on anything around her, except as in a sort of dream. As common men think and speak of heaven, so she now thought and spoke of earth" (C, 358). And she has entered that state with an assurance of perseverance in it until the end. What had been prophesied in her vision, that the lost sheep was found, is now a fact. The novel itself, ending with a quotation from the Catholic poet Aubrey de Vere's verse "Reality," underscores this ontological thrust.

If there can be said to be a view of morals given in the novel, it is clear that the purely moral has been collapsed into religious categories. There is much discussion of love and the unfolding and perfection of the person in love, but it is of a religious character. The ethical side of marriage, for example, has been merged into the religious side of a celestial espousal. This is characteristic of Newman's writing and was one factor he himself stated that led him to an appreciation of Southey, whose poems generally end, not with a marriage, but with death and future glory.[97] It is basically an ascetical application of the phrase "Amor meus crucifixus est" (C, 222), wherein the love of God (both as a subjective and an objective genitive) is the primary goal of life. Yet this is intimately connected with the character of Callista and her conversion, since "her instinctive notion of religion was the soul's response to a God who had taken notice of the soul" (C, 293). The imagery and vocabulary of love are a logical embellishment of that intense dialogue. It shows, as well, that this central theme—"myself and my Creator"—in Newman's personal devotional life was one that, while transformed by a different doctrinal approach, remained his primary concern, emerging even in his fictional characters.[98] Apart from this internal model of the novel, the question of celibacy is the chief one pointed out by critics comparing this work with Kingsley's.[99] Newman's answer to Kingsley is much more specific than is usually indicated, however. At the center of *Hypatia*, Raphael the Jew gives a literal paraphrase and interpretation of the Song of Songs, identifying it as a revelation that divine and human love are the same. At Callista's trial, the procurator comments on her faded beauty and coloring, and she responds, "I am beautiful when I am black" (chap. 32). And again, on the rack she cries out, "Accept me, O my Love, upon this *bed* [italics mine] of pain! . . . and come to me, O my Love, make haste and come!" (chap. 33). Callista is, of course, using the phrases of the Song of Songs (1:5, 2:10), charged with the double meaning of *bed*. In responding to Kingsley's position on marriage and celibacy, Newman has reinterpreted the same fundamental passage of Scripture and met him head on.

The historical reconstructions of Kingsley, Wiseman, and Newman share several perceptions. Whether describing the persecuting pagan empire, the State on the eve of the Constantinian revolution, or the Christian empire, the picture of "Rome" (or the idea of empire) is one of decay and sensuality, a picture consistent with other artistic expressions of the Victorian epoch. For Wiseman the Constantinian embrace of Christianity transforms and transfigures that "Rome," Church and State governing in concord the Christian commonwealth. Newman sees an oppressed Church eventually transforming individuals, but the persecuting State is historically always a possibility. In Kingsley the whole nation—the people—has a messianic role in bringing about the "Kingdom"; elsewhere Kingsley made it clear that the Church had departed from the Kingdom at the time of the earliest followers of Jesus. The depictions of raw sensuality place these reconstructions squarely in the context of Victorian thought. The writhing tortures of the martyrs, usually naked and female, are explicitly and lengthily described, especially by Wiseman. Although they are drawn as spiritual models, intent only on the next world, their beauty and physicality undercut that. Celibacy is shown as a corrective for the lubricious pagan (or Christian) society by Newman; but his descriptions include incest, child rape, and a Pan figure, connoting the priapic "herm" at a rustic fertility rite. Kingsley also suggests a corrective in monogamy, or perhaps a palliative, since marriage is so highly eroticized in his work. This dimension of their critique of culture, blending sensationalism and moralizing, tells the reader much about the deeper conflicts behind mid-Victorian taste.

In the depiction of the Jews there is some divergence. In the two

Catholics' works, the Jews are all but invisible. This may mirror the theological reflection on the role of the Jews in salvation history following the Council of Trent: there are two covenants and the Church had become the "new" Israel, displacing the "old." Kingsley condemns the "cabbalistic" and "magic-mongering" rabbis, while defending the "old Hebrew seers." His character Raphael recapitulates the course of Christian history. On the other hand, the writers elsewhere maintain the fundamental unity of Old and New Testaments, defending all of Scripture against radical biblical criticism and thereby affirming the historic role of the Jews.

Two faces of the institutional Church are shown, sometimes by the same author. In Wiseman a powerful, hierarchical Church is sketched; its liturgy and doctrine are elaborately and ahistorically defined. In Kingsley there are two competing "churches," the one dogmatic and theurgic, the germ of the medieval papacy, and the other gathered in simple devotion to the Father's will, which Kingsley defines as "the Kingdom." Cyril's pontifical spectacles are contrasted with the scholarly homiletics and stark English "Evensong" service of Augustine, whose *City of God* encapsulates the image of the true Church. In Newman the hierarchical Church and its ceremonies are affirmed and described, but as by an outsider. The martyr-heroine is a recent convert, and the lapsed Agellius observes only the hidden liturgy. Newman's mystical binary unit, the soul and its creator, could ultimately undercut any institutional form, although his sense of history prevents this.

Neoplatonism and Epicureanism, the two philosophies most fully presented in the novels and the two most appealing to a Victorian audience, elicit varied responses. In Wiseman a truncated Epicureanism appears, without substance or allure for the characters or reader. Newman presents Neoplatonism and a character to embody it, Polemo of Rhodes, although he suppressed MS notes on Plotinus that might have been used. The convert moves away from this philosophy to Christianity, as in Kingsley, because a correlative is found there consistent with the inner experience of the seeker. Philosophy had exercised the intellect but not the conscience. Kingsley, on the other hand, presented a varied and alluring profile of Neoplatonism, contrasting it with the "true Platonism" of love and self-sacrifice, righteousness and justice found in Paul and

Augustine. For Kingsley this reconciliation of Hebraic morality and Hellenistic philosophy, evidenced in the Alexandrian Fathers, is the key to the Augustinian view of history, as interpreted by F. D. Maurice.

The authors are also similar in that they posit necessary, connecting links between history, personal and public, and literature. In their characters, united to structure and theme, the reader traces the meaning of history in terms of personal change or development. Each in turn is marked by Romantic images, themes, and concepts. They share a fundamental vocabulary and "grammar" of Victorian sentiment, values, and conventions. But that is only to say they were men of their times. Talismans, timely recognitions of filial relationships, and the props of Gothic mystery and horror form part of the literary tradition they hold in common. Yet Newman and Pater are far from the types of Romanticism of spiritual power in Wiseman or the democratic nationalism in Kingsley. Wiseman, in fact, stresses the reading of history in exemplars and models of order, the eternal lessons learned in the rise and fall of Empire, and yet the absence of any real change. In his characters there are no distinctive mannerisms; individuality is suppressed. They submit their natures to rules supplied by models of classical literature, whether Greek "character" lists or Christian hagiographies. His saints are virtues without flesh, in spite of all their fleshiness. Kingsley has a built-in confidence in the modernity of the age and the superiority of the world in which the Victorians ruled in contrast to any other age, thus undercutting any Romantic nostalgia. Unlike other authors, including the Anglo-Catholics, he does not preserve, rediscover, or trace developments from antiquity. The past re-created is used to display the progress made or prophesied; it is used to understand the future, to see the finitude of future possibilities, and in this some glimmer of Romantic historicism is to be found. That Romanticism blooms in his apotheosis of individualism and private judgment, his mannerist theatricality, his sovereign naturalism, and the Romantic literary models of bardic ode and folk epic he returned to as sources. In the union of Raphael/Victoria, East/West and Jew/Gentile are reconciled. And in the mingling of Goth and Latin, "reverence for woman and domesticity" were born. These reconciliations at the heart of history are the Maurician understanding of Augustine's philosophy of history, sketched briefly by Kingsley in "The Author to his Readers." So too the Catechetical School of Alexandria, led by Clement and Origen, reconciled Greek philosophy and Hebrew morality with Roman polity in a Christian metaphysic that was a "true world philosophy."[100]

In Newman, Hebraic love of nature, soberness, and chastened feelings combine with a painfully incisive psychology and probing of personality; the literary models here can only be the "confession," the diary, or the autobiography. Newman's believing unbeliever and Pater's picaresque saint, both sensitive characters moved upon a quest of faith by intense self-knowledge, provide directions for future literature justly termed "modern."

The movement of inquiry with Newman is twofold; if his other writings help unlock *Callista*, the novel serves to define better for the reader the personality and methods of Newman in his other prose. It provides its own gloss on such statements as "The Fathers made me a Catholic."[101] His apprehension of the past throughout his literature shows how he consistently tried to read the present through the past by the same process of analogy he outlined in his *Development of Doctrine* and *Apologia*. So, too, the devotional side of *Callista* better illumines for us how the logic of piety pushed Newman to a decision. Finally, the whole imaginative endeavor of creating fiction, the dramatic representation of biography, polished later in the *Apologia*, and the skilled use of historical and contemporary sources mark Newman's ability to construct an imaginative world of experience and a mode of arranging experience. Because past informs present, as the present does the past, he is able to refer to the historical tradition vis-à-vis the present problem with a minimum of polemic and rhetorical flourish. His most intense interest, finally, is in the psychological mapping of an individual's progress from doubt to faith. The words he used to sketch the personality of St. John Chrysostom in another essay could be applied to him as well, since he was "a writer who delights to ponder human nature and human affairs, to analyze the workings of the mind, and to contemplate what is subjective to it."[102]

3

"ANGLICANISM IN THE CATACOMBS"

Anglo-Catholic Authors of Early Church Novels

"NEWMANIA," THE SYNDROME that critics of the Tractarians identified as an epidemic among undergraduate admirers of John Henry Newman, could be used to describe the obsession of generations of historians of the Oxford Movement with that central figure of Newman to the exclusion of other important contributors. R. W. Church, himself a highly significant but often ignored participant, helped perpetuate this concentration on Newman in his history of the movement from 1833 to 1845. Recent historians, however, have begun to redress that imbalance, investigating a host of fellow travelers of the movement and the routes by which "Catholic consciousness" infused the Victorian Church.

In the years between the winter of 1841, following the hostile reaction to Tract XC, and the death of Cardinal Newman in 1890, succeeding Anglo-Catholics cultivated and pruned that high, "apostolical" sense of the Church initially forced in the theological hothouse of Oxford. The "Second Spring" of the Roman Catholic Church in England owes much to the seed broadcast from the city of "dreaming spires" and "impossible loyalties." But Anglo-Catholics regrouping after Newman's departure were not merely maintaining a nursery for eventual transplants to Rome. They attempted to create and propagate an "advanced" understanding of the English Church as a legitimate and fruitful branch of the Catholic (i.e., Orthodox) and Apostolic Church that would lay out a via media between the Roman system and popular Protestantism. Whether

142

through the sacramental synthesis of Robert Isaac Wilberforce, or the ascetic devotionalism of Henry Manning, or the liturgical revival of the Ritualists, or the schemes for Church reunion by early ecumenists, the underlying purpose was the revivification of specific doctrines and a spiritual ethos in the Church of England, amid the thorny theological and social issues that threatened to encircle Christianity in general and the High Church Party in particular during Victoria's reign. That ethos could be seen in the parochial evangelism of Keble at Hursley, Hook at Leeds, and Butler at Wantage: moving out from the university common rooms, that spiritual discipline shaped a new style in the parish ministry. In the general religious unsettlement over Genesis and geology, for instance, someone had to remind the Church that she was "older than the rocks she sits upon." At critical moments Anglo-Catholics appeared to carry on that task as theologians, biblical critics, historians, orators, popularizers, pamphleteers, and even novelists. Their novels were often tendentious, heavy, dogmatic expositions, but they were heavy with "the burden of modern experience."

This chapter treats the various works of six representative Anglo-Catholics engaged in using their fictional craft to address theological questions. The extent to which they grapple with specific topics debated by religious parties within and without the Church of England varies according to the interests, temper, and resources of the respective authors. The guise of historical fiction masks for the modern reader much of the sharpness of purpose with which these authors waded into the fray. Such disparate prophets as Thomas Carlyle and A. W. N. Pugin used medievalism as a critical lever against the society of the Industrial Revolution. These Anglican novelists, in turn, used their re-creations of the Middle Ages, the Civil War period, and the Early Church to the same end. It is, then, precisely by examining such secondary literature, designed for didactic, even propagandistic, purposes, that the reader can isolate the subtle shifts in nuance and focus that characterized the ever-changing battle line of the Victorian religious debate. Major intellectual projects comprised theological treatises, the highly complex Victorian "essay," and the various "libraries" of Anglo-Catholic thought. These do not provide more than a general map. This lesser literature furnishes dimension, color, crude formulations that at times unconsciously reveal significant social and psychological substructures.

The works gathered here span the age, from 1841 to 1898. Four clergymen and two laywomen are represented. Among that number are an influential Tractarian theologian, a major novelist and disciple of the movement's "founder," a diverse set of Ritualists, and two who eventually became Roman Catholics. While not every Anglo-Catholic novel of this genre is treated here, a broadly representative selection is given. In the case of one novelist who wrote many of this type, one typical example is discussed. Where the author composed only one or two specimens, all those are treated. Whether the novels were primarily written for juveniles or adults, they demonstrate a wide acquaintance with the contemporary study of patrology, hagiography, archaeology, and historical theology. This chapter ends with an appraisal of a High Church manual written by one of the novelists. It is included to show how other types of literature treated similar topics. Like this Prayer Book companion and commentary, the various novels present an ecclesial model of the Early Church that may be examined for its distinctiveness from Roman Catholic models, with which it shares many common components, and the models produced by other Church parties.

ROBERT ISAAC WILBERFORCE

In 1841, following the critical uproar over Tract XC, Newman retired to the ten acres and cottages he had purchased close to St. Marie's chapel-of-ease, Littlemore. Hard on the heels of that controversy, which left the Tractarians stunned, in disarray, and momentarily leaderless, the British government and King Frederick William IV of Prussia sanctioned the creation of a joint Anglican-Lutheran, Protestant bishopric in Jerusalem. Political and commercial considerations for such a presence in the Levant joined more religious ones, not the least of which was an apocalyptic interest by Evangelicals who looked for the conversion of the Jews to usher in the latter days.[1] That same year Robert Isaac Wilberforce (1802–57), sometime Fellow of Oriel and son of the Great Emancipator, succeeded Francis W. Wrangham as archdeacon of the East Riding, Yorkshire.[2] His two closest spiritual guides, his brother Samuel and Henry Manning, who was related to the Wilberforces by marriage, were already the archdeacons of Surrey and Chichester, respectively. These two were destined to become preeminent ecclesiastical statesmen. But in the early 1840s

Robert Isaac was the one looked to as "a scholar and a theologian" and "the Athanasius or Augustine of his generation."[3] Although neglected until this century, he produced a great doctrinal synthesis on the model of the Tübingen school, to whose works his may creditably be compared.[4] He was, in fact, the greatest theologian of the early Tractarians, more renowned by far as a theologian than Newman. His theological writings, massive syntheses of Anglo-Catholic doctrine, were the intellectual underpinning of that movement until its temporary collapse after the Gorham judgment and his own conversion in 1854.

Between 1840 and 1842, long before his more systematic studies, Wilberforce published three works: *The Five Empires: An Outline of Ancient History* (1840), *Rutilius and Lucius; or, Stories of the Third Age* (1842), and *Church Courts and Church Discipline* (1843). The first was a short work on ancient history, from Creation to the fall of the Roman Empire in the West. The second consisted of two independent tales of the final persecution under Diocletian and Galerius on the eve of the Constantinian triumph. The third work treated the jurisdiction of the Church in cases of spiritual discipline. The Church needed to recover from Parliament her legislative power and the right, enjoyed by all voluntary associations recognized by the State, to bind its members by specific rules. In fact, Wilberforce argued, the Established Church was at present disabled by its status. He based his argument on scriptural injunction (1 Cor. 5:1–5) and the traditional practice of the Early Church and the Reformers.[5] He was, as it turned out, rehearsing the role he would play in the later battle concerning the revival of Convocation.

In a short span Wilberforce had touched on the vast and providential movements of peoples and nations. The rise and fall of empires, couched in the images of apocalypse and prophecy, were preparation for a new world order in the Constantinian revolution, and the claims of the Christian Church as a spiritual *imperium in imperio*. The dimension of this vision is made clearer if one considers events in general history at that moment. Between 1840 and 1843 the first of three major epidemics, affecting primarily the laboring poor, swept over the British Isles. The last phase of the first Opium War had ended with the annexation of Hong Kong; India, a center of that trade, was drawn closer under British sway. Livingstone had sailed for Africa, bringing the Gospel and raising European interest in colonial expansion over the peoples and nations of the "dark continent." Sir Robert Peel was prime minister, and his ministry promised a renewed wave of reform in ecclesiastical affairs, as he had begun in the mid-1830s with the creation of the Ecclesiastical Commission. Millenarian predictions of the end of the world had reached fever pitch; agents of the Latter Day Saints pointed to the signs of the times, beginning in 1840 in England, and the Millerites predicted the second Advent in 1843–44. Indigenous bouts of religious hysteria fired the countryside, in South Wales, for example, from 1839 to 1842. It was a time of religious awakening, unsettlement, rancorous secession, and a rise in the number and strength of sects; the most famous example was the Great Disruption of the Church of Scotland (1843). For industrial Britain the period 1839–42 played out the economic drama of boom and collapse amid the "dark, Satanic mills." Agitation for the *People's Charter* overflowed into the spontaneous hunger riots of 1842, ushering in the revolutionary unrest of the "Hungry Forties." Against that backdrop we must consider Wilberforce's literary work.

In *Rutilius and Lucius*,[6] published in the same year as Thomas B. Macaulay's *Lays of Ancient Rome*, Wilberforce used the literary device of a double tale as a didactic vehicle for sketching the doctrines of the pre-Constantinian Church. That catechesis (much of the writing is in the form of query and response) is in part proleptic, demonstrating doctrines elaborated later in the General Councils. The message is clearly addressed to the nineteenth century. These are the doctrines handed on by the apostles, proven by Scripture, exhibited in tradition, proclaimed by Councils, taught and guarded by the episcopate, believed and practiced by Christians throughout the succeeding ages. Such a declaration of Tractarian belief was not unique in the framework of a novel by this time; it had already been accomplished by the Reverend William Gresley (1801–76) and the Reverend Francis Edward Paget (1806–82), who were the "acknowledged fathers" of such early Tractarian tales.[7] Wilberforce, however, was the first Tractarian to make the subgenre of the Primitive Church novel his own.

Rutilius, the first and longer of the tales, relates the story of the young hero of the title, born at Antioch, who reaches young manhood and seeks the patronage of his uncle Marcellus, a distinguished veteran in the imperial guard. The story unfolds in the eastern provinces of the empire, especially Jerusalem and Armenia (the area served in the nineteenth century by the Church Missionary Society, founded by the Claphamites). It begins in A.D. 297–98 during the rule of Diocletian and Galerius. The opening sections of the work are a brisk and exciting adventure story, played out against the backdrop of desert tribes and marauding warrior bands. It is classic melodrama of peril and rescue, also employing many of the props of the Gothic tale. Rutilius, brave but foolhardy, rescues the young damsel Flavia from slavery (pace William Wilberforce); he rises like a ghost before her through a secret door leading to caverns known only in legends in order to free her from her prison, the windswept, impregnable tower of Semiramis. He thinks he is saving his uncle's future bride, although he himself is in love with her. He is in rapture when the true relationship is revealed near the end of the tale—Flavia is actually Marcellus' daughter. The veteran is martyred in the initial phase of the Diocletian persecution. Rutilius and Flavia escape to Gaul and the benign rule of Constantius; there they are at last able to wed—a rather ironic end to a tale with a singular emphasis on Christian celibacy.[8]

In the second story, Lucius is a Briton, a non-Christian, come to seek service at the court of Diocletian in the years 303–5. The public incidents are drawn, Wilberforce relates, principally from Lactantius' *De morte persecutorum* (ca. 318). The young Briton bears a letter of introduction from the bishop of York to his colleague in Nicomedia; Wilberforce thus demonstrates the unity of the Church, underlying his contemporary concern for the unity of his sacramental ministry in the East Riding of York with that of the Eastern branch of the Church. Through the influence of prominent Christians who hope for his conversion, Lucius is housed in the palace and witnesses the private intrigues and public acts of the reign as Diocletian transfers power to Galerius. Lucius helps the young Constantine, an imperial hostage, kill a lion during an assassination attempt. After the accession of Galerius and Daia (Maximin), the Briton helps Constantine escape, using a secret passageway to steal a safe-conduct pass from the bedchamber of the sleeping emperor. This "last flight of Constantine" to meet Constantius at Boulogne, followed by the elevation to the imperial throne at York, is the narrative cap of the tale. Sandwiched between these melodramatic incidents is a lengthy summary of Christian doctrine and practice, rendered in long catechetical dialogues. Within that discussion of pre-Nicene belief Wilberforce presents a developed, structured picture of the Christian Church as "a kingdom," existing within the empire but independent of it.

Pagan culture appears before the reader in the garb of philosophy and in the person of Porphyry (or Malchus), the Neoplatonist. Various schools of thought are discussed with Rutilius, who finds each one wanting: the Platonists of the Academy, the Peripatetics of the Lyceum, the Stoics of the Porch, and the Epicureans. The thought of Plotinus is advanced as the latest development in the reworking of Plato and linked to the rise of Christianity.[9] "Thus he [Plotinus] looked for a perpetual revelation, but without that miraculous sanction which had proved the reality of the Christian" (R, 64). Christianity is the "something substantial" that explains the "empty theories" of earlier speculation. Philosophy is part of the "providential preparation" for the Church of Christ: "Philosophy had sounded the depths, and discovered the chill desolation of the world of waters, at the very moment when the ark drew near, in which was to be found safety, certainty, and contentment."[10] Pamphilus, the Christian priest, future martyr, and catechist, contrasts the model believer with the philosophic pagan, represented by Rutilius: "You are for the present state,—we fear for that which is to come. Sense, therefore, is your guide,—faith is ours. You measure the useful, the beautiful, and the grand, by the rule of nature,—but we by the principles of grace. Your poets, therefore, and your artists, exhibit in its utmost perfection the present loveliness of the visible creation; but what is ideal, immaterial, impalpable, they do not attempt" (R, 171). Those words were better spoken to the sons of Locke, the Deists, or the children of the Enlightenment than to a recent inquirer about Plotinus.

Philosophy is clearly not evil in itself, however; Christianity does not require an intellectual change or a denial of human nature. In fact, one chapter is entitled "The Christian Philosopher," and Pamphilus is intent on demonstrating the compatibility of Christianity with man's nature, his reason and will. God's providential "ancient system" for fulfilling the religious impulse can be discerned, despite subsequent impurities, through better realization of our natural longings. Using the image of two languages with a common origin, he maintains a single cause in the religious usages of nations. "The corrupted traditions of the heathen flowed from a source which originally was clear and uncontaminate" (R, 164). Literary culture and tradition are his references. The pure portions of that culture can be extracted by conscientious reason and identified as an impulse toward Christianity. That natural discernment is complicated, however, by the wild speculations of the Gnostics, mixing Scripture and popular fiction and confusing the pious pagan seeker.[11]

Philosophy falls short, not on the intellectual level, but on the moral level. It fails as a way of life. No intellectual system had been able to satisfy the entire social spectrum or to harbor the weak, the poor, the hopeless, or those without the money or leisure to cultivate the meditative life. Pamphilus points out the "honor guard" of the Christian "palace"— the blind, the lame, and the orphan. Christianity is the one means for settling a lasting improvement in man's condition:

> I see not how either rich or poor are to be improved, except by something which will give all men greater dignity and self-respect. This is certainly done by the system of the Christians: the opinion that every one possesses an immortal soul, for which he must give account hereafter, which Plato could never induce the generality to believe, is by them universally admitted; and their doctrine of the resurrection of men's bodies enables the vulgar to enter more completely into its meaning. Then their union into one Church gives them such a close interest in each other, that their baptism is like the introduction of a new principle of life into the world. (R, 64)

That social dimension, observed by Rutilius, is the area that Wilberforce pinpoints as the undoing of philosophy and the triumph of Christianity. That analysis is weighted with the previous associations of this carefully observant child of William Wilberforce; Claphamite insistence on benevolent works for social improvement surfaces here. It takes in Robert Isaac's hands a basically conservative shape; change of the heart— through the gradual "habit" of Christian belief and discipline—is the only assurance of external, social change.

Wilberforce's theology has been compared unfavorably to that of F. D. Maurice. Their thought on social issues might also be contrasted. But it is well to remember David Newsome's warning in his study of Wilberforce.[12] Historians of theology tend to concentrate on futuristic thinkers who address problems that might prove valuable to current theological debate; conservative theologians, those who sum up the work of previous generations, often languish in obscurity. It is in retrospect that we see the inadequacy of Wilberforce's approach to the pressing social dilemma of the Hungry Forties and compare it unfavorably to the efforts by more "muscular Christians." Wilberforce and other Tractarians were not unaware of or insensitive to the outcry of the laboring poor, as is often charged by critics who see the Oxford Movement only as an involuted turn of bookish dons. One should remember that the harvest of Henry Manning's work for laborers and strikers later in the century was sown in the 1830s and 1840s. Instead of basing programs for social improvement on political or economic pillars, the Tractarians sought to reiterate the preaching of Scripture and the early Fathers for social justice, using the language of self-denial and the imagery of the *Magnificat*.

In *Rutilius* Wilberforce calls for rather spectacular evidence of that self-denial by the Christian. Christianity is "exactly fitted to the nature of man," but something must be voluntarily abandoned in order to "startle" the world. That remarkable challenge to the "refined and noble spirits" of the heathen world is voluntary poverty and celibacy. No ordinary specimen of religion would "affect their hearts": "But when they see persons of rank and fortune cast away all that they hold so valuable, and with a willing mind embrace poverty and an abstracted life for the sake of God's service, they cannot but recognize the reality of that Gospel which is proclaimed among them" (*R*, 173–74). Persons of rank are singled out, since they possess things of value in the eyes of the world, so their renunciation is all the more effectual. And this conversion appears as a proof of the reality of the Gospel, much the same way that martyrdom was a proof of the Resurrection in Athanasius' *On the Incarnation*. Although married men could equally function on these principles, "yet our Scriptures tell us that a single life affords peculiar advantages for their display: and therefore, though not in itself more meritorious,—for no act of ours in reality merits anything,—yet we consider that a single life, when entered upon with a view to God's service tends most to the display of that angelic nature of which it is our object to afford an example to mankind."[13]

One focus of the Church of England's contemporary criticisms of the Tractarian fascination with the second evangelical counsel, celibacy, was the exaggerated, even inflammatory, language of its proponents and the statements of the Fathers they extracted in support of it. Wilberforce recognizes that the contrast of self-denial with the gross selfishness of the world may have led some in the Primitive Church to use highly colored language to describe their conduct. On the other hand, sometimes that contrast demanded boldness and a heightened rhetoric. He is ready to defend even the extremes found in the Thebaid, Charles Kingsley's target in 1853. "Our Egyptian solitaries may outrage nature by shutting themselves up in caverns from the very sight of heaven, and denying their appetite its needful aliment; but how much fouler an outrage is this to the best feelings of the heart—to worship Venus on the Hill of the Passion! You have here . . . the secret of Christian asceticism."[14] This attitude is conditioned by time and circumstance: "What men may do in some future state of the world, when the pollutions of the heathen are no longer so apparent, I know not" (R, 196). This historical recognition of progress might argue against flight to the "desert" in Victorian England, if it were not said with such an ironic tone. Is there really that much difference between those pollutions of that "green hill far away" and "in England's green and pleasant land"? Are not rigorous exemplars of Christian life always needed? Yes, he insists, "we have ever found that the Church has flourished most when its discipline has been most rigid. It is like those trees which shoot the stronger, the more they feel the pruning-knife. For its strength does not lie in the soft and careless, but in serious and self-denying spirits" (R, 264). In Robert Isaac Wilberforce we are in touch with a spirit nourished by the early Tractarian understanding of a serious call to "holiness" and "purity," who, like Manning, stated in the terms of ascetic theology a discipline as "muscular" as that of any party within the Church of England.

The Jews are presented under two different lights: as an important part of the *praeparatio evangelica* and as the center of contemporary resistance to Christianity. Pamphilus instructs a Jewish convert:

Your covenant was understood from the first to be only a preparatory one. . . . Your covenant was not to be done away, but to be fulfilled. . . . It is somewhat curious that we have no express order in our Scriptures that the sacrifices and usages of the Jewish law should be left off. We are told, indeed, that they were necessary, but the Apostles declared they were lawful, and their own practice shewed that they thought them expedient. They seemed to be waiting for some decisive declaration that the Jewish system was ended. (R, 142–44)

That decisive sign came with the Fall of Jerusalem: "The law was given amidst the smoke of Sinai; and the flames of Jerusalem declared it to be fulfilled" (R, 145). The Roman destruction of Jerusalem and the subjugation of Israel, the Diaspora from the Promised Land, the cessation of the Temple service, and the impossibility of full observance of the Law showed that the "prophecies of Moses" were completed and the Jews had ceased being a nation.

Scripture is really the basis for the continuing animosity between the Christians and Jews: the text of the Old Testament and its prophecies are the points examined by Wilberforce. The Jews are tendentiously accused of tampering with certain critical passages or of treating the text in such a way that the Christian interpretation is excluded: "Look, for instance, at this Psalm. In it, according to the Greek version, the object of the Psalm exclaims, 'They pierced My hands and My feet.' But the Jews have altered the words, rendering them, 'as a lion my hands and my feet.' Their interpretation robs the passage of signification; yet they are willing thus to alter it, rather than admit so clear a statement of our Lord's sufferings upon the cross" (R, 176). Prophecies also pose a problem. How can one understand the foretelling of the restoration of Israel by the early prophets? One must see that the birthright of the Israelites has passed to the Christians, first through those Jews who, in the days of St. Paul, joined the Church of Christ, and then clearly to all Christians after the Fall of Jerusalem. The apostles had anticipated this by the reception of Cornelius; under the teaching of the Holy Spirit they understood that the Church would not consist only of enlightened Jews, but that the Church was to be a kingdom encompassing all nations. The Jews, on the other hand, did not accept "the further doctrines of our Lord and His Apostles" and ceased to be a nation in A.D. 70. The prophecies, then, must be understood in a new symbolic sense: "Jerusalem means the Church of God." Jews, however, persist in expecting a restoration of their nation: "The error is very injurious; for the opinion that the prophecies will still be fulfilled to their nation as a separate body, and that by holding together they will share in the promised grandeur of their people, is what, more than aught besides, retains the Jews in their impenitence" (R, 202–3).

In raising the question of the conversion of the Jews, an important consideration for the proposed Anglican–Lutheran bishopric in Jerusalem, Wilberforce has linked his rather negative understanding of Judaism together with important questions about the text of Scripture and the problems of interpretation, prompted by various discordant translations, as well as questions over the fulfillment of prophecy and the use of allegory in the Christian understanding of those prophecies. These were, in fact, some of the pressing questions that vexed biblical critics and traditionalists investigating the Old Testament during the mid-Victorian period. Wilberforce's re-creation of ancient Judaism treated those theological issues at a time when Jews were entering more fully into the political and social life of the nation, at least when their role in the life of the nation was the subject of public debate. The period 1847–58 marked the high point of that political discussion.

The image at the heart of the novel is the Church as a kingdom, deriving its authority from beyond the "boasted" earthly empire and antedating the Constantinian, Erastian state:

> For, as some philosophers tell us, that, in all these seas the water stands at the same level, so our widely scattered brethren, by being united into one body, retain the same rules, and continue members one of another. Perhaps you are not aware that our being thus a kingdom within a kingdom, a separate people, having our own government—an empire, in truth, though not offering any disloyalty to our earthly rulers,—is exactly one of those things which were long ago predicted, and to the complete fulfillment of which we look with confidence. (R, 74)

Through such oracles as the prophecies of Daniel, Christians are able to understand the true meaning of empire. The Roman Empire had been in its own way a preparation for Christianity, but with Diocletian and the Thracian soldier-emperors the very concept of Rome's principle of power had disappeared, just as the Jews no longer understood their own heritage. "The unity of Roman domination, its especial connexion with that city which had so long swayed the earth, the fated superiority of the eternal name,—all these were henceforth forgotten. Thus did God's providence prepare the way for bringing forth that new principle of unity which was already leavening the earth" (R, 41). Christianity had usurped the place of Rome as the unifying principle of the world. Since Christ's Church is a kingdom, it must have officers in all lands; but being a kingdom "not of this world," it did not interfere with worldly powers.[15] Its offices or deputies are the bishops, whose office, function, and various relationships Wilberforce carefully delineates. "'Each bishop is the deputy of Christ,' answered the Christian apologist, 'and represents our Master's immediate presence. This is a primary law of our system, which we have received from the Apostles. The subordination of ranks among bishops is a rule of the Church, which has been introduced by ourselves, for the sake of greater order'" (R, 87). Pamphilus explains this ordering of ranks by an immediate example to Rutilius: "'In this diocese, Methodius is Christ's deputy, though he owes obedience to Cyril, the bishop of Antioch, who occupies what we call the apostolical see, because thither all bishops of the province go for ordination to their apostolic office.' 'And to whom does Cyril owe obedience?' Pamphilus pointed upwards. 'Christ has set His holy Apostles or chief bishops "last of all"; and to Him only do they owe obedience'" (R, 86–87). Wilberforce stresses that Christ alone is the ruler of his spiritual empire, ruling for eternity from his capital "in the heavens." Bishops rule *de jure divino* by apostolic succession, traced back through history to Christ and the apostles and maintained by an "immediate presence." The relationship is both horizontal through history and vertical between earth and heaven, without the mediation of the emperor or any other human agent.

Wilberforce also understands that in the five ancient apostolic sees (the Pentarchy), to which are subordinated the other bishops of their provinces, no single see takes precedence. "There is no place which has such an undisputed lead that its bishop is likely to prevail over others" (R, 87). Jerusalem alone, because it was the place of Christ's "immediate presence," might have made such a claim. But since the precedence of one apostolic see over the others could only produce discord, Wilberforce repeatedly suggests that the providential destruction of that city was to prevent such a claim or any superstitious veneration. This whole argument is, of course, a thinly veiled attack on Romanist claims of supremacy, which might rightly be compared with Henry Manning's anti-Roman sermon, preached on 5 November 1843 from Newman's own pulpit. Rutilius, the Roman citizen born at Antioch, is told: "'You naturally think of Rome,' said the other, 'and, if we were to judge by a worldly standard, its wealth and power, and the notion which you Romans have so long possessed, that your city was fated to an eternal dominion, would go near to introduce division among us. But it is not thus that we Christians decide. We have already a country and a city, whose builder and maker is God'" (R, 88). The Christian catechist states that the Church of Rome does not at that time make claims for supremacy, while he recognizes its great influence in the West, with rich and liberal (i.e., generous) members and numerous clergy. Wilberforce, in an insightful and concise piece of polemic, shows that the Roman claims are an accretion after the time of the Primitive Church and then lists those aspects of its corporate life that would lead eventually to those claims.

If bishops are part of the *esse* of the Church as a kingdom, they are essentially linked as well to Scripture and the sacraments. The interpretation of the former and the efficacy of the latter depend on the unbroken succession from the apostles. But what guarantees that this succession is initially linked to the person of Christ and continues to be efficacious? That guarantee is found in apostolic miracles:

> And this is why I spoke of miracles as a confirmation to the faithful. The holy Apostles, who have left us various rules in the sacred writings, proved, by the miracles they wrought, that God was truly with them in the utterance of their words. If any one was to arise in this day, and undertake to teach or exercise Church-offices, without having received an authority which came from them, we should require that he also should work miracles, and so prove that his claim to teach was derived not from his own fancy, but from the command of God.[16]

Bishops are, therefore, an essential part in the chain by which the blessings of the Church are imparted to humankind. Miracles are the "proof" of that. The general stress among early Tractarians on "holiness" and "sanctity," advanced by some like Newman as equal to antiquity in guaranteeing the legitimacy of the Church, has been used here in an amended form. These "signs of an apostle" are external, objective, and visible. This stress is also used as a challenge to those outside the apostolic succession who claim authority to minister. Wilberforce, however, limits what could be a very extreme position. Do Anglican bishops, for instance, have to perform miracles to prove they possess the charism of apostolic succession? No, he states flatly. "If the Divine presence had on one occasion given a distinct mark by which such intercourse might be known, would not it suffice for future guidance?" (R, 82). Certainly, he responds through Rutilius. The clearest mark or sign of this Divine presence is in the Holy Communion:

> It is part of the bishop's office, that none but he, or those whom he commissions, can administer this holy communion. Such has been the rule since the days of Apostles. I see you are ready to ask, what there is in it which others cannot do? We know not. But since the object is to bring man into communion with Christ, and one proof that we hold communion with Him is the promise which He has given,—we cannot be assured that we use this ordinance with effect, unless we use it in the very manner which He has ordained. What the order was, may be best known from what was done by His Apostles; and they allowed none to minister the sacrament in the Church save those who had received ordination at the hands of bishops. (R, 83–84)

Thus, the Eucharist and the office of bishop make up the core of a system of mutually validating guarantees of the presence of Christ. But what is the nature of the communion in itself? Wilberforce presents a dual understanding:

> —Communion with Christ is not among us sought for vaguely and at random, and referred to the test of our private feelings;—He has appointed a means by which it may be obtained, and all the supernatural blessings which follow from it. This means we call THE HOLY COMMUNION, because in it we communicate with Him; or the eucharist, because it is the sacrifice of our thanks. And just as Gentile worshippers are bound together by sacrificing to the same idol, and feeding together on what has been offered; so do Christians, in the sacrifice of remembrance which this eucharist affords, enter into communion with one another and with Christ. (R, 82–83)

At the Eucharist, the "main service" of the Christians, celebrated in their native language, believers pray at this "mystic feast" and partake this "holy sacrament" when the "Lord Himself is mystically lying upon the altar," to whom they draw near as "members of His body": "We first present before Him ourselves, our souls and bodies, and with them this simple and unostentatious offering [i.e., bread and wine]. Out of it is

then taken what to the worthy receiver becomes the means of being engrafted in the mystic body of Christ. The consecrated elements thus be-
stowed, are the medium by which each man becomes a sharer in that
great sacrifice which, once for all, was offered for us upon the cross" (R,
150). Wilberforce acknowledged the centrality of the Eucharist as sacrament in Christian worship and displayed extensive research into the liturgical celebration of the Eucharist, a slight example of the scholarly
apparatus half-hidden within these stories.[17] The sacrament is celebrated
in the vernacular and administered to the "worthy receiver," both part of
the reformed theological understanding of the Eucharist. The identification of the eucharistic oblation, besides the offering of bread and wine,
with "ourselves, our souls and bodies" shows how closely Wilberforce is
following the Prayer Book formula and the old High Church phraseology. These elements in themselves would not be adequate or even truly a
sacrifice; they become such because this oblation is a reminder of the sacrifice of the death of Christ. The forceful language and imagery of the Fathers—for example, the references to the "mystic feast" and "being
engrafted in the mystic body of Christ"—emerged in the course of
Wilberforce's reticent and guarded exposition of eucharistic theology.
Like early Tractarians in general, he maintains a "real" presence of Christ
in the Holy Communion without elaborating exactly what that means.
The vocabulary he employs stresses "mystical" or "spiritual" presence.
The Church as the mystical body, an image given special weight by Augustine, assumed into Christ's manhood and sanctified, is, then, a basic
element in the one, only, perfect sacrifice of Christ.

The critical point is reached, in fact, in this discussion of the eucharistic sacrifice. For the Tractarians, by 1838 the crucial problem concerning the sacrificial character of the Eucharist was how to maintain the
unique sufficiency of Christ's sacrifice on the cross while maintaining the
unity of Christ's sacrifice with that of the Church. Pamphilus explains to
Rutilius that the Eucharist is a sacrifice. "'But not sacrifice of atonement,' he replied to the other. 'Our eucharist is but a sacrifice of remembrance. In the strictest sense of the words, it is no sacrifice at all; for, like
the offerings of the Jews, it does not make expiation for sin; it only carries
on as they anticipated, the true and sufficient sacrifice;—but it is a
shewing Christ's death—a recalling His sacrifice; and it bears the name of
that of which it is an exhibition'" (R, 83). We see Wilberforce here at an

early stage in the development of his eucharistic thought. He still exhibits
the early Tractarian teaching of the Eucharist, its stress during the 1830s
on the sacramental idea, on the Eucharist as a means of imparting "blessings," on the "commemorative sacrifice" of the Primitive Church, and
on the "prayers of the people." The one element in the present work that
clearly supplies the bridge to his more developed doctrine of sacrifice in
his work on the Incarnation and its controversial sequel, his volume on
the Holy Eucharist, is the perdurance of Christ's mediation: "[Our]
Lord's is the only sacrifice which can make an atonement for sin, and He
Himself is the only High-priest."[18] This doctrine of a perpetual sacrifice
of the God-Man as High Priest is in its developed form the "principal
concern of his Christology and ecclesiology."[19] The idea of the threefold
office of Christ (prophet, priest, and king) can be traced back to the
Laudian divines and through them back further to Socinian sources.[20] In
Wilberforce's work on the Incarnation it became a forceful argument,
answering the concerns of the early Tractarians and supporting the necessity of the sacerdotal system.[21] In this earlier discussion of the Eucharist
as sacrament and sacrifice we are able to catch a glimpse of a theologian
working through a central question of doctrine before his more elaborate
and final position was taken. That can be an invaluable insight into the
theological method and development of such eminent Victorians, leaving the shelter of the High Church position and yet avoiding, at least for
a time, the pull of Rome.[22]

Baptism and penance are also treated as part of the Christian system
but with none of the elaboration afforded the Eucharist. In referring to
the lustral waters of a fountain Pamphilus asserts, "Such outward washing
is doubtless useless, if unaccompanied by inward preparation" (R, 154–
55). Baptism is reserved for "either the day before our Lord's resurrection, in token that by baptism men rise to a new life" or the day after
Pentecost, "because in baptism are continually poured forth the gifts of
the Holy Spirit."[23] Likewise, the Church's penitential system is mentioned in passing, but this should not be construed as a reference to sacramental confession and absolution. Although Manning had theoretically
treated it by 1835 and begun its practice in 1839, and while George
Dudley Ryder and T. W. Allies had adopted it in the early 1840s,
Wilberforce, more than other Tractarians, was personally averse to its

practice and finally agreed on only an occasional use.[24] The others mentioned, however, saw it as a means of maintaining spiritual discipline by its frequency.

Besides the sacraments, the bishops are also placed as guardians and interpreters of Scripture, which in its turn may be used to judge those bishops who stray from the belief of the apostles: "That some should prove rebels, we are prepared to expect; and we have holy Scripture in our hands, by which we can at once discern if it should happen. But this will never be the case with all the successors of the apostles among us" (R, 157). Wilberforce obviously considered this an extreme example of the safeguard of Scripture (the second Hampden affair and the Colenso case were still in the future). The more immediate adversary was the "god" of private judgment: "Now we Christians know but one rule which cannot deceive—I mean the holy Scriptures; and we know but of one true meaning of the holy Scriptures—that which they have borne from the first."[25] The words of Christ have "one certain and appropriate meaning," which the Christian is at pains to discover and obey. All Christians agree on the signification of those words because all should use the same rule of interpretation: the understanding of antiquity. What proof is there, however, that the meaning proclaimed in antiquity is the correct one? There are "many proofs: first, the natural one . . . we have the writings of Christians who lived for years in habits of intercourse with the Apostles, who so likely as these persons to understand their meaning? Besides, we know that the order and course of the Church was appointed by the Apostles; and their judgment God was pleased to approve, by giving them the power of working miracles" (R, 182). This is the classic Tractarian argument, based on the ethos of the early Christians but with a more than usual emphasis on miracles. If the Primitive Church departed from the apostolic model, it was the apostles themselves who sanctioned it. And since Christ confirmed their fidelity by the power to perform miracles, we know, Wilberforce asserts, that they did not depart from the Gospel.

Could the practice of the Primitive Church in its "discipline of secrecy" (*disciplina arcani*) complicate this issue? If some knowledge is "reserved," can we be sure that it has been transmitted to succeeding generations? Wilberforce, through Pamphilus, maintains that the

"commendable discipline" was designed to promote and protect reverence for the "awful sense of God's presence" as a means of forming the
proper "temper of mind": "[We] make no sort of reserve about what we
teach; it is plainly declared, as well in our sacred writings as in the works
of our apologists. What we teach respecting our Lord,—His nature, His
sacrifice for us, the sacraments, by which we participate in the blessings
He bestows,—these things are declared in the plainest words in our
Scriptures" (R, 165). More precisely, Christ's divinity is publicly proclaimed to the heathen, as is "redemption through His blood"; but the
doctrines of his divine nature, contained in the creeds, are reserved for
the instruction of catechumens.

It is in the principle of the proper interpretation of Scripture, then,
that Wilberforce presents the due use of antiquity:

> [To] a Christian, history is not a mere entertainment. It is the ear
> through which God's voice speaks to man. In one respect we are like
> the Pythagoreans,—we profess not to discover the truth by our own
> wit, but think that the right system has been laid down once for all. For
> this we search the Scriptures; but since they contain difficult passages,
> and since they speak of persons and institutions which no longer exist,
> we need the help of history to teach us what interpretation was put
> upon doubtful passages by those who were best able to comprehend
> them. (R, 139)

For men in general the creed, required by all to profess at baptism, and
the church services provide a sufficient commentary to understand
Scripture fully. There are also other writings left by the early Fathers
demonstrating what they thought.[26] By these several ways one can enter
into the meaning of the apostles. Wilberforce has the catechist Pamphilus
observe: "There can be no reasonable man in aftertimes, who will not
feel how much less fitted he is to form a true judgment of the Apostle's
meaning than those who had waited on his steps and listened to his
word" (R, 140). This view of truth is, he asserts, "the real mind of the
Spirit." A classic formulation of the early Tractarians, it underlies much
of the Catholic system they hoped to revivify in the Church of England.
It is a modified "argument from silence," using the ethos of one age to
imply the beliefs, practices, and attitudes of the age directly preceding it.

This method of argument appealed to a strong sense of history, and yet it is not a dynamic view; "the right system has been laid down once for all." That dynamic view of growth and the development of doctrine only began to be unfolded by Newman, under the influence of Frederick Oakeley and W. G. Ward, when the battered leader retired to Littlemore.

In his two short tales, Robert Isaac Wilberforce presented a compendium of doctrines and attitudes held by the early Tractarians. In treating the sacraments he demonstrated the catholicity of Anglican doctrines, buttressed by both Scripture and the Fathers; he also treated contrary doctrines present in the Primitive Church, such as Gnosticism, and implied their recrudescence in his own day in the antisacramental faction. If the sacraments are the extension of the Incarnation, as he maintained, then those who deny the real presence or baptismal regeneration are true successors of the Gnostics.[27] In his treatment of the eucharistic sacrifice and the mediatorship of Christ we see him at work developing themes that emerge transformed in his later *summae* on the Incarnation, on baptism, and on the Eucharist. His discussion of sacrifice must also be seen against the backdrop of the major controversy over justification during the late 1830s and early 1840s, a controversy in which Newman's formidable *Lectures on Justification* (1838) played a significant role. From this time on, among the Tractarians the doctrine of a forensic Atonement is subordinated to that of the Incarnation; the incarnational theology of the *Lux Mundi* group was foreshadowed at this time. And it was at this time of the creation of the Jerusalem bishopric—the Erastian adventure which troubled the Tractarians so terribly and which Newman described as "kicking a man when he was down"—that Wilberforce restated the concept of the Church as a kingdom with its own government and rules. The joint Anglican-Lutheran venture, supported by the principles and power of parliamentary Erastianism, was an assault on the spiritual independence of the Church. It was also corrosive to the branch theory of Catholicism, since the High Churchmen were afraid, and justifiably so, that the new bishop would not only minister to the Protestant nationals in Palestine or evangelize Jews and Muslims but would also proselytize among Eastern and Uniate Christians. That is why Wilberforce takes such pains in the first tale to re-create the liturgy of the Ancient Church of Jerusalem: as a warning against tampering with that Catholic body.

This incident in the history of the Established Church of England, coupled with the intervention by the secular arm in the Gorham case from 1848 to 1851, decided Wilberforce's personal course. His two works *The Practical Effects of the Gorham Case* (1850) and *A Sketch of the History of Erastianism* (1851) summed up the negative side of the argument concerning State control of the Church. *An Inquiry into the Principles of Church-Authority; or, Reasons for Recalling My Subscription to the Royal Supremacy* (1854) functioned somewhat like Newman's *Essay on the Development of Doctrine* (1854), as a valediction to the Anglican Church. With great reluctance Wilberforce submitted to the Roman Church in Paris on All Hallows Eve, 1854, the last major casualty of the Gorham decision. It is significant that shortly after this date attitudes among those in authority in the Church of England and slight signs of the success of Catholic principles had raised the hopes of other Tractarians enough that further defections from this quarter became scarce.

JOHN MASON NEALE

The decade from 1850 to 1860 presented a series of challenges to members of the Anglo-Catholic Movement. It began with the imbroglio over the Erastian side of the Gorham case and the Guy Fawkes-like conflagration of popular hostility over Papal Aggression, and ended with controversies over Darwin's *Origin of Species* (1859) and the unsettling theological and scriptural perspectives of *Essays and Reviews* (1860). In the midst of that decade the first serious rumblings over ritual questions and ceremonial practices started, culminating finally in the Public Worship Regulation Act (1874). In the general historical context it should not be forgotten that the Crimean War (1853–56) enlisted Christian England on the side of the Ottoman Turk against the forces of Holy Russia to preserve the crescent banner over Constantinople/Istanbul. Although publicly committed to the British role, many Anglo-Catholics and churchmen of other parties privately found the war a source of grief; that attitude increased as the conflict lengthened.[28]

John Mason Neale (1818–66), the warden of Sackville College (1846–66) and the cofounder of the Cambridge Camden Society (1839; later the London Ecclesiological Society), was an important figure of this era, as well as a prodigious author. Using him as a touchstone, we see in his work a veritable encyclopedia of Anglo-Catholic doctrines and attitudes and may discern that marked sensibility, formed by Catholic principles, that is vital for understanding the religious temper of the times. Studying his fictional works, then, one can sum up Anglo-Catholic positions in the early 1850s and also give structure to the diverse ecclesiastical and personal concerns of him and his associates, the first generation of ecclesiologists, before various shifts in the years 1855–57 changed the perspectives of persons and parties.

Beginning his writing career in 1841, Neale produced a monumental corpus, even by Victorian standards, treating a large number of diverse interests. Through the work of the Camden Society and its publication, *The Ecclesiologist* (1841–67), he formulated key aspects of the understanding of liturgy, architecture, and church furnishings, thus conditioning the taste of succeeding generations. Similarly, his translation of the medieval *Rationale* of Bishop Durandus provided the theological and symbolic foundation for the ascendant Gothic Revival. It was for the decoration of the chapel at Sackville College, East Grinstead, Sussex, that Neale suffered episcopal censure and inhibition from 1848 to 1863.[29] His second major area of concern was the revival of religious communities for women in the Church of England; he himself founded the Society of St. Margaret (1855). Hymnology, the translation and compilation especially of Latin and Greek material, was his third area of interest; in the early 1850s he published several important collections. Another interest, Christian union, was expressed in various works on the Eastern Church and the Jansenist/Old Catholic Church of Holland.[30]

By the mid-1850s Neale had published several collections of church stories and legends, mostly but not exclusively for children.[31] These sketches culled material from many different epochs and regions. Before 1854 the six novels or tales he had completed portrayed various incidents in England and France from the twelfth century to the present day.[32] In 1845 he had published his *English History for Children*; this remarkable little book demonstrates Neale's literary and propagandistic purposes and his "catholick" understanding of certain crucial historical periods. His object is "to give children a churchman's view of history" and, thus, "to secure a correct first impression."[33]

The history begins with the conjecture that St. Paul and St. Joseph of Arimathea preached the Gospel in England, and ends with a genealogical table of English monarchs from Egbert (of Kent) to Queen Victoria (daughter of the duke of Kent), the secular succession from pre-Reformation times of guardians (not governors) of the Church. His description of the Reformation is a key place to observe Neale's state of mind in 1845, the momentous year of Newman's long-awaited defection to Rome. Luther disrupted Christendom, Neale instructed his young readers, because that Augustinian friar "was enraged that the sale of indulgences was taken away from his own order, because they were thought to have kept back part of the money arising from it" (*EH*, 150). Evaluating the Reformation he concludes that it was "wrong and unjustified." In their use of Scripture the Reformers only advanced the cause of private judgment, whereas "churchmen believe that everyman is bound to obey the Bible *according to the Church's interpretation of it*" (*EH*, 154, italics his).

Its placement of the ecclesial interpretation of Scripture over private judgment cleared the Church of England from the label "Protestant." This was discerned by the Continental Reformers themselves, especially Calvin, Bucer, and their followers, who attempted to "protestantize" the English Church through the second Book of Common Prayer (1551). The Reformers "could not bear that it should still be a true and living branch of the Holy Catholick Church." That status as a branch of the Church Catholick (the spelling demonstrates how much this work is a document of the antiquarian interests and Prayer Book literalism of the ecclesiologists in the 1840s) is maintained by the episcopate. "You know, that, where there is no succession of bishops from the Apostles, there can be no Church" (*EH*, 172). Neale calls Henry VIII "a hypocrite," "the worst prince that ever filled the English throne, and was the Scourge of God for the sins of our country" (*EH*, 158). Henry is singled out for a number of reasons, but the most criminal, Neale felt, was the suppression of the monasteries, "one of the most wicked schemes that ever entered into the heart of man." He goes on to say that the revenues from this "horrid Sacrilege" brought a curse with them. Neale was personally obsessed by this idea. In 1846 he and the Reverend J. Haskoll published *Spelman's History*, a seventeenth-century work tracing the dire fates of those who had acquired alienated church property: most died immediately or their family lines soon disappeared.[34] In 1843 Neale had treated the contemporary application in his novel *Ayton Priory; or, The*

Restored Monastery. A property holder, made sensitive to advanced Catholic principles, attempts to deed the title over for church purposes, in fact, to refound a monastery. This is an important aspect of the religious values of the early ecclesiologists; "church restoration" did not mean only architectural rearranging but the return of "holy things" to the "holy." This was not the primary attitude of the Tractarians, either historically or in terms of the suppressed Irish bishoprics, and was generally viewed as mere superstitious antiquarianism. The republication of Spelman's oracular history, however, was a trumpet blast, calling attention to the quieter melody of those concerned for greater reverence, beauty, and order in church: to use one frequent example, the altar was not to be treated as a convenient hat rack during services or a stepladder to open windows—it was the sacramental center of God's house, "the pillar and ground of truth."

Next after Henry VIII, Parliament drew Neale's fire: "Such a feeble, wretched, reed for the Church to lean on has parliament always been" (*EH*, 173). On the other hand, he defends Mary Stuart and Mary Tudor; of the latter he said, "Her goodness was her own; her faults, those of her advisors." It is a remarkable evaluation in view of the uproar concomitant with the Martyrs' Memorial to Latimer, Ridley, and Cranmer in Oxford (1838) and the general rallying to the standard of the Reformation in the early 1840s against incipient "popery." It was just such a Protestant animus that forced *The Ecclesiologist* to suspend publication and move its base of operation from Cambridge University in 1843, only to reappear in London in 1845 under the aegis of the Ecclesiological Society. In his little book *The Farm of Aptonga*, written for children, Neale, ever a controversialist, threw down the gauntlet yet again. Bishop Ashurst Turner Gilbert of Chichester (1842–70), where Manning was archdeacon, belatedly took up that challenge in 1848 and inhibited Neale from priestly function, apparently because of the "advanced" Catholic decoration of the chapel at Sackville College.[35]

Neale's books, even those intended for children, cannot, evidently, be isolated from the controversies of the day and his own role in those affairs. This is abundantly clear in those novels and tales in the 1850s in which he portrayed the life of Christians in antiquity, with "the minutest details in the description of houses, furniture, dress, and the like, which are so necessary to stories of this kind."[36] The greater economic prosperity of the 1850s, of which the Crystal Palace Exhibition was the exemplar, created more interest in tales that supplied exactly those domestic details, instead of the long, dry, theological discussions in previous novels. Neale's works are a good example of basically entertaining romances and adventure stories written primarily for didactic purposes. The scholarly theological apparatus and footnotes have become invisible, worked into the fabric of the text; the works are not merely tracts for the times. This, of course, makes the task of the investigator interested in those theological points more difficult. Instead of lengthy treatises on some aspect of controverted doctrine or advanced ritual practice, there may be only a sentence, a phrase, a precise word, or the choice of a character to serve as a clue. The ordinary reader will see only a diverting tale with occasional obscure references, while a close reading will reveal specific issues, events, and controversies that exercised the best theological wits of churchmen during that decade. The novels of J. M. Neale are just such a palimpsest; his book *The Farm of Aptonga* is a demonstration of that (on which, see below).

In 1854 the Crystal Palace was removed to Sydenham; the battles of Alma, Inkermann, and Balaclava entered the honor roll of military exploits; Milman published his history of Latin Christianity; and J. M. Neale brought out his novel of the times of St. Cyprian.[37] The choice of Cyprian is significant in itself. To the early Anglo–Catholics this Father of the African Church was important as a controversialist for his severe, even rigid, position on church discipline and order. Unlike other church parties, High Churchmen like Neale tended to emphasize, instead of the open disputes, a basic unity with Rome, although they saw in Cyprian an example of a strong and independent episcopate, instructing and judging Rome on doctrine and practice. Neale joined the contemporary stream of interest in this figure, an interest generated largely by the publication of Cyprian's works.[38] It was not just the person of that beleaguered bishop, however, that fascinated Neale. He was also concerned with the separate histories and interconnection of Christian churches within the Roman Empire. Likewise, the fate of those indigenous ancient sees in his own day, eclipsed by other religions, vexed Neale during the years that Britain marched toward empire, pitting British Christianity against the religions of the Near and Far East. The fascination with this second point reveals a great deal about the unarticulated fears of certain Anglo-Catholics. Before the publication of Darwin's work, there was a vague perception that once vigorous, apparently fit, and widespread branches of the Catholic Church could disappear. Permanence was a critical issue. The concept of extinction of a species appeared like a death's head to those who worried over the continuing Catholicity of the Church of England.[39]

The setting of his novel is the hill farm Ad Fines, in the little town of Aptonga, and Carthage, sixty miles south, during the reign of Valerian (253–60). The simple story concerns the outbreak of persecution and the varying responses of "Chrestians" in the family of the widow Quintilla, her daughters Lucia (the heroine) and Secunda (who temporarily apostasizes), their servant Vivia and their priest Crescens (both martyrs), and their non-Christian relative Acilius Glabro. The action culminates in the execution of Cyprian on 14 September 258 and the escape of the survivors of the family to Spain. Some of the events and persons mentioned were treated in "The Martyrdom of S. Laurence," the third chapter of Neale's *Victories of the Saints* (1850).[40]

The attitude of the characters toward the State and the second edict of persecution under Valerian during the summer of 258 is a significant indication of Neale's research into the North African Church and the case of Cyprian. The author puts into the mouth of a pagan notable one of the reasons, phrased ironically for the Christian hearer, for the recurrence of proceedings against the Christians: "'It's my opinion,' said Acatius, 'that whether people turn Christians or not, our religion won't go on much longer. Do you think there are ten people in Carthage . . . who believe a single word about the gods?—Not they.'" There are not ten believers (one might say ten good men) to save the empire. The edicts were motivated by a sense of peril to the empire as a whole and by the desire to have all inhabitants help regain the celestial favor. The Anglo-Catholic novelists categorized the Christian refusal to sacrifice basically as a crime of lèse-majesté, without seriously allowing for the religious dimensions of the State. In much the same way it was held that Elizabethan recusants and Jesuit missionaries were executed for treason, as distinct from religious motives.

One may suggest in the earlier example that such an attitude reflects the traditional Western sense of dualism between Church and State, as well as the polemical demands of these High Church opponents of the

Erastian principle. Neale, on the other hand, had read deeply enough in the Greek Fathers and the history of the Eastern Church to recognize the religious dimensions of the State, while still being moderately critical of the present parliamentary Erastianism. It is important to remember that Neale did not follow those who felt themselves "unchurched" by the Gorham case. For him, having accurately read the sources, the crime against the imperial cult was only secondary to the major charges of atheism, sacrilege, and irreverence to the gods. The martyrs' judge, Aufidius Bassus, legate of the 29th Legion, declares in passing sentence: "[Neither] will the reverence of the gods, nor the majesty of the Caesars, whom I, however unworthy, represent, permit that their worship should thus be spoken of. . . . But the honour due to the immortal and most blessed gods must be vindicated by one way or the other" (*Ap*, 37). Vivia asserts an important point during her interrogation: Christians do pray for the emperor "morning and evening." Again, reverence paid to the gods, not honor to the emperor, is the issue. Her assertion is historically based on Cyprian's reported reply to a request for formal acknowledgment of the gods: "Christianus sum et episcopus. Nullos alios deos novi, nisi unum verum Deum: . . . huic Deo nos Christiani deservimus; hunc deprecamur diebus et noctibus . . . et pro incolumitate ipsorum imperatorum."[41] This does not preclude a haughty attitude toward those judges and persecutors; Neale records with a note of both triumph and disdain the death of the proconsul of Africa, Galerius Maximus, after sentence is passed on Cyprian and the later death of Aufidius Bassus ("skinned alive with Valerian by Sapor, king of Persia"). Neale also mentions one instance of physical force by Christians against Roman agents of the persecution, the only example of such behavior cited by Anglo-Catholic novelists during the century. The principle of passive resistance to the State, an attitude grounded solidly in the theological work of the Caroline and Non-Juring clergy, was so strongly entrenched in the nineteenth century (especially in light of the social unrest and risings earlier in the period) that Neale's novelistic reference to the use of force, "neither too much, nor too little," stands out sharply.

A standard list of charges leveled by the State against Christians, the "nefaria conspiratio," is provided: infanticide and cannibalism, witchcraft, sacrilege, and worshiping "the Head of an Ass," a list little varied in these novels.[42] On the other hand, the reader sees a wide variety of

Christians. But primary is Cyprian, "no ordinary man," bishop of Carthage and "Primate of 670 bishops," resolute in the face of death with his simple followers, some of whom stand the test and others who vacillate and capitulate but are finally restored to the Church through the intercession of the confessors (when it is allowed by the bishop) and through the penitential system. Cyprian observes: "I hear that there [Rome], as once here, the confessors have been indiscrete in reconciling shoals of apostates to the Church, without any penance and without any satisfaction. There will be an end of all discipline if this is allowed to go on; and I would fain strengthen the hands of my brethren, the Cardinal priests, who are somewhat overpowered by the licence" (*Ap*, 42). In a short space Neale covered a major controversy, dating from 251 and the Decian Persecution, affecting the life of the African Church, and Cyprian's relations with other churches, especially Rome, concerning this issue. At first glance in the novel, Cyprian appears as a rigorist, against the laxist Roman example. But near the end of the story, when Cyprian reduces Secunda's term among the penitents as a *libellatica*, although maintaining the importance of strict adherence to the Canons in such cases, his application of the penitential system and insistence that the Church can forgive even apostasy place him slightly left of center in relation to the Novatianists. Cyprian, then, is a model of the Anglican via media.

The Christian system is similarly sketched on other points. The Church is pictured as tightly organized and rigorously disciplined; trial and examination, for instance, are necessary for Communion, even for the baptized. Neale has touched on distinguishing marks of the African Church without elaborating or reflecting on them as such. The church building described contains the altar tomb of St. Felicitas, martyred fifty years before with her companion, St. Perpetua.[43] A liturgy there is reenacted: diptychs provide prayers for living and dead, martyrs, apostles, and the Virgin Mary. The inclusion of this point, especially prayers for the dead and a later description of a funeral service read by a priest and a deacon, transports us to religious controversies in the Church of England and to Neale's own concerns. The former theological point—prayers for the dead—had disrupted an already tense situation for Pusey and the Tractarians at the consecration of St. Saviour's, Leeds, in 1845.[44] In the 1850s Neale was engaged with the more practical liturgical side of the question, reforming the funeral liturgy and eliminating many secular customs attached over decades. A similar reference to Commodian's *Instructions* and the development of later Latin lyrics that culminated in the great hymns "Stabat Mater" and "Vexilla Regis" and the Victorine sequence "Dies Irae" leads us to Neale's own work in hymnography during this decade. He had criticized Edward Caswall and W. T. Irons for their translations of exactly these hymns. Commodian (or Commodianus) is generally seen today as a poetic transmitter of the basically millenarian view of the kingdom; eschatological language and apocalyptic imagery abound.

There is a certain preoccupation with the figure of Antichrist as an apocalyptic sign and a tendency to employ this sign to express in a religious mode the political conflict with Rome: Commodian's oracle predicted that Nero would rise from hell and proclaim, "I am Christ, to whom you always pray." The later Latin prose and hymns Neale associates with Commodian's style are outstanding examples of millenarian sentiments and were used in various periods marked by apocalyptic tensions over the coming "day of wrath." The mid-1850s were just such a time: the exponents of prophecy claimed to find described in the Book of Daniel and Revelation impending developments in Europe.[45] The Crimean War provided them with a convenient sign of the conflict over the holy places of Palestine, and Papal Aggression raised the image of Antichrist anew. Neale, like many of his contemporaries, unconsciously reflected these deep spiritual concerns of the age.

Baptism and Eucharist are both summarily treated in *The Farm of Aptonga*. Preparatory to the death of Vivia in the ampitheater there is a scene of confession followed by baptism and the kiss of peace. That last ritual gesture is another clue to Anglo-Catholic social sentiments, since Christians of all ranks—masters and slaves—exchanged it. To pagan observers it was a scandal. Neale does not reflect on such a relationship in the Christian community beyond offering this sign of social solidarity; without mentioning Paul's position in Philemon 12–16, Neale accepts the social and class divisions without question. Baptism, which can be by desire, water, or blood, does not affect that social structure. It does, however, transform or regenerate the soul. Once baptized with the "Seal of the Lord," Vivia (as her name suggests "living") can face bodily death and yet be "alive," even when her corpse is dragged by mules out of town and torn by jackals. She appears in a vision, more than a mere dream, to the pagan Acilius; she has fulfilled her promise to come before him again and does so wearing a crown and offering him a crown. Acilius is miraculously converted on the spot.

The treatment of the Eucharist is also brief. Quintilla the widow, a "true child" of the early Church, practices reserve in reference to churchly matters: "[She] preferred that any suspicion should attach itself to her religion, rather than that the mystery of the Holy Eucharist should be made a laughing-stock to the heathen" (*Ap*, 23). That is all the doctrinal side of the Eucharist provided, a singular kind of silence, especially since the years 1852–54 were shaken by the Denison case and its ominous import for the "Catholic" doctrine of the Eucharist in the Church of England.[46] It is likely that Neale wished to diffuse further difficulties in this matter and practice some "reserve" before a final judgment was reached in the courts. Although the Anglo-Catholics supported Denison's doctrine, they thought his behavior in the case was silly; he had opened the discussion of sacred things once again to secular controversialists and Low Church adversaries, making the sacraments objects of ridicule. Neale, Keble, Pusey, and others did publicly support Denison when the legal decision went against him, appealing to a synod of the Anglican communion, and did produce a substantial body of doctrinal and devotional works in this precursor of later troubles over eucharistic worship.[47] In his novel Neale described only some antiquarian details— the use of a silver tube (*fibula*) and chalice for the service—and points concerning the shape of the liturgy. The introduction to the preface prayers, "Lift up your hearts," is used to show the roots of the Anglican forms, "much as we have them to this day." Although the Anglican liturgy had dropped the *epiklesis* (in accordance with the Western usage), he says it is a prayer "which we have not, but which the Scotch Church has retained" (*Ap*, 45). In that allusion Neale demonstrates his concern for the deficiencies of Western forms, the liturgical usages of the Eastern Church, and the persistence of ancient usages in the Scottish Church (basically through the work of the Non-Jurors, who are not mentioned). In the uproar over the Gorham case, Neale had remained firm in his fidelity to the Church of England, but he acknowledged that if he ever left that body he would go to Scotland, not Rome.[48] The example of the Non-Jurors was strong (strong enough for Pusey and others to reject a non-juring scheme when the decision went against Denison). A similar recourse to this historical example was introduced in the controversy over eucharistic doctrine involving the writings of Alexander Forbes, the High Church bishop of Brechin, in 1858. Although one does not find in Neale's novel lengthy transcriptions of liturgies or expositions of ritual questions, things one naturally assumes will be found in a writer with such documented ritual interests, one does find allusions to the important controversial events and documents of the period. This fact should warn us about one limiting perspective brought to the study of the Victorian church: Ritualists did not write only about ritual.

Ritual questions simply are not the core of the novel. The martyrs and their sufferings are the focus of attention. Even Cyprian's major role is not that of Primate and "pope" of Africa but as martyr par excellence, after many instances of escape. *The Farm of Aptonga*, then, is rightly examined as part of the hagiographical concern of Neale and the Anglo-Catholic party during this decade. What this concern produced in the way of literature, what were the sources drawn upon, what picture of martyrs and claims for a martyrology were made, and how all this was applied to current theological debate are questions we turn to now.

Neale had already used the stories of saints and martyrs in his various collections of tales; he also collected them in his *Annals of Virgin Saints* (1846). Like all English hagiographers of the period, he drew his inspiration for such collections from the series edited by J. H. Newman, The Lives of English Saints (1844–45). The work of various ancient ecclesiastical historians, for example, Sozomen and Socrates, supplemented volumes of Fleury, Gibbon, Mosheim, Ruinart, and Tillemont. Neale's work was also part of a wider interest by High Church adherents in the lives and writings of the early Fathers: besides the monumental Library of the Fathers, clergymen like W. J. E. Bennett, John James Blunt, and Bishop Christopher Wordsworth were engaged in this task. Neale considered that there were in Ruinart's *Acta sincera* "documents as authentic as the Law Reports of our own day."[49] Thus he considered his sources not as romantic embellishments by ecclesiastical hagiographers but as testimony as authentic and verifiable as courtroom transcripts, an important insight into how he used that material.

Several groups of martyrs are mentioned: those in Rome, Lyons, and Carthage under the persecutions of Decius and Valerian and the Tenth

Persecution under Diocletian. Martyrs have a special, exalted status; the announcement of martyrdom is "glorious news." In listing the recent executions in Rome, Cyprian concludes: "'. . . and now, blessed Sixtus. And Carthage has not one martyr among its bishops!' 'It has had saints enough,' replied the deacon Flavian. 'But not the highest'" (*Ap*, 13). Martyrs possess extraordinary gifts and charisms. Sixtus prophesies the execution of Laurence, and Cyprian predicts his own death and the eventual martyrdoms of others. The prayers of martyrs and confessors are especially efficacious. Confessors, as noted above, could remit the sentences of penance of others. One would-be martyr is told: "When you are before the throne of God, bear us in mind, for we know that He has great regard to the supplications of His martyrs" (*Ap*, 33–34). Here are not merely prayers for the dead but a belief in the invocation of martyrs and intercessory prayer by the dead. Vivia, dying from her torture, is also omniscient; she knows that Secunda has apostasized in the distant interrogation chamber: "But fear nothing; I have been praying for her; and I know that I am heard" (*Ap*, 58). This extraordinary assurance is only part of the manifestation of graces poured out on the martyrs. The supernatural encounter with Vivia at the conversion of Acilius has been mentioned. Neale is aware, however, that some claims may elicit a negative response from skeptical readers in his day. "How can I, living in an age like this, pretend to describe to you the grace which God put into the heart of His martyrs?" (*Ap*, 36). In relating the story of a miraculous signal that saved two of the characters from capture, Neale plays with "logical" explanations of such events. A spark, one spark, struck by the hoof of the villain's mount, just happens to fall on dry tinder and accidentally flames out and catches on other brush, creating a signal alerting the hunted Christians. The extreme irony Neale employs to show the rational, natural cause demonstrates how his argument works. Miracles are not disproved by natural causality; only a subtler agency of Providence is hinted. As for that dramatically and nervously described spark, he concludes "the god of the Christians" ordered things in that way.

The sufferings of the martyrs also intrigued the author. The application of that suffering to the Church's penitential system has already been shown. He carefully narrates the strictures against turning oneself in (pointedly referring to Cyprian's previous history), although he recounts that Cyprian only smiled when the mob chanted "Cyprian to the lions."

Neale occasionally raises a bizarre theological point in discussing these sufferings: "There was a curious question, which the Christian philosophers of the middle ages used to discuss; whether, when a martyr was slain at once in the act of prayer, his last supplication, or his soul, were first before the throne of God."[50] Neale observes that writers of this period, even Christians, were not as shocked by a wide range of acts of cruelty: he mentioned the burning of a live fox at the feast of Ceres: "It would not be true to say that those early Christians had such softened feelings as we now have. That was the work of the Church in a long course of ages. It could not have been so at first;—and perhaps in a time when men were called on to suffer so much, it was as well that things should be as they were" (Ap, 19). In terms of the actual martyrdoms he concludes: "Nevertheless, as I have told you before, it does not necessarily prove our want of courage, but only the softening influence of the hundreds of years during which the Church has been working upon Christian nations, that it is so powerful to us to hear the details of a martyrdom. I do not believe that it is any diminution of God's grace" (Ap, 39).

Thus, Neale concludes, it was not necessary for Christians of his own day to seek out martyrdom; the witness has already been given in the physical travail of the roll of martyrs. The Church, sprung from the blood of the martyrs, does not need constant transfusion of new blood. On this point some contemporary Roman Catholic apologists and polemicists would disagree with Neale: Rome was still the Mother of saints and martyrs, exemplified in the lives and deaths of nineteenth-century contemplatives and missionaries. Neale's descriptions of physical sufferings at times verge unintentionally on bathos: Crescens the priest speaks to a wavering Christian when they are attacked by wild beasts in the amphitheater: "'Be of good cheer, my brother,' said he to Marcellinus, whose face was becoming purple from suffocation, and whose cheeks the bear was already licking with his rough tongue, previously to devouring his prey" (Ap, 107). The witnesses of these events are presented in a way that shows both their pious devotion and the emotional surge unleashed by the heroic deaths. Names of the holy dead are entered into the diptychs and altar tombs constructed, other apostolic churches are notified; but the mob of spectators hastens with handkerchiefs, towels, linen rolls, and the victim's vestments to soak up the blood (a customary English practice—the executions of the Recusants or King Charles I are examples), while others on a rampage ransack the former episcopal residence, breaking up a chair for relics. Staying close to the sources provided him in Ruinart, Neale has described more than he intended about martyrdom and its psychological and social effects within a formidable, popular movement: the gathered, persecuted Church of North Africa, encouraged by the example of the martyrs in its hope of millennial triumph.

Why should the martyrs take on such importance to a clergyman of the Church of England in the 1850s? And why should Cyprian figure so prominently? It is safe to suggest that the stance of the Anglo-Catholics vis-à-vis Rome and the attempts to clarify that relationship are the cause. It must be seen against the background of Papal Aggression and defections to Rome after the Gorham and Denison cases. Neale was not a no popery agitator. His work on the history of the Eastern Church is no mere anti-Romanism tract; in compiling the "History of Alexandria" he disavowed such propaganda, since both churches were allies "as it were."[51] On the other hand, he was not moved by papal claims. He based his objections on the belief, shared by other Anglo-Catholics and derived from their interpretation of Vincent of Lerins's Canon, "quod semper, quod ubique, et quod omnibus," that Rome had made later additions to the traditional doctrines of the Church, thus violating the first clause, since there were times in history when Rome's jurisdiction did not function in various places. Similarly, the image of the "Rock of Peter" was not a powerful claim for Rome, since Neale identifies that "Rock" in terms of the three apostolic sees that witnessed Peter's presence: Antioch, Alexandria (by way of Mark), and Rome. One must appeal to the unbroken and unaltered tradition of the first eleven centuries. This canonization of more than the first century or the first six centuries is another mark of Neale's Anglo-Catholicism. He insisted that it was by studying the history of the Eastern Church especially that Western theories of the Church could be corrected. In the opening of volume 1 of his two-volume *History of the Holy Eastern Church: General Introduction* (1850), Neale observed enthusiastically: "Roman developments will be tested by the unbroken traditions of sister communions; Roman arguments strengthened or disproved by a reference to Oriental facts. . . . I shall write of Prelates not less faithful, of Martyrs not less constant, of Confessors not less generous, than those of Europe; shall show every article of the Creed guarded with as much scrupulous jealousy; shall adduce a fresh crowd of witnesses to the Faith once for all delivered to the Saints."[52] The reason Cyprian longed for martyrs for the rolls of Carthage when informed of recent executions at Rome is identified here. A numerous roster of martyrs was further evidence of the vigorous, independent life of indigenous churches outside the control of Rome. It is a restatement of the Tractarian debate of the 1840s between the older High Churchmen and the younger Romanizing enthusiasts: saints and martyrs are signs of a chronic virtue and holiness necessary to a true church and equivalent to the argument of antiquity. Neale borrowed part of that argument from the Romanizers (the martyrs of the Early Church and the seventeenth century are his proofs) but remained loyal to the High Church party. By analogy he applied the model of the North African Church to the matter of England.

Why, though, would one choose Cyprian? The answer is clear from the general theological literature and anti-Roman polemic of the period. Cyprian was the classic example cited by Protestants of the rejection in antiquity of papal supremacy. In a letter (11 December 1853) Newman wrote to R. I. Wilberforce, who had been reading the *Essay on Development* again, about the latter's special attention to the opening passages on the inconsistencies in patristic writings. This was in response to the question, Could papal supremacy be reconciled with the testimony of the Primitive Church? In this very long and important letter Newman touches on Cyprian in this regard. "In matters of thought it is a very difficult thing indeed, not to be inconsistent in our words, especially when party feeling (as in the case of St. Cyprian) comes in. . . . St. Cyprian is claimed by Protestants as denying the Pope's Supremacy. . . . I think if any one had asked St. Cyprian in a cooler moment, he would have acknowledged he had spoken to [*sic*] strongly—."[53] In the introduction to the *Essay on Development*, Newman had appealed to other disciples of the school of Bishop Joseph Butler (1692–1752), since he had spoken as one himself, using the peculiarly English interpretation of the *dictum* of Vincent of Lerins. This rule of historical interpretation, so congenial to the English temper, takes up a middle position, neither denying the Fathers or submitting to the pope. Newman's critical analysis of the consensus of primitive Fathers, especially the ante-Nicene bishops and saints among whom Cyprian is numbered, is made, he maintains, to clarify the *unfair* [italics are Newman's] interpretation of Vincent that makes him part of the anti-Roman polemic. By relaxing that historical rule in order to admit doctrines maintained by the English Church, one can no longer reject as doctrinal innovations certain articles held by Rome but denied by Anglicans.[54] If one accepts Athanasius, one is bound to accept Thomas Aquinas. In the religious controversies of the 1850s, when troubled churchmen were examining the evidence of the Fathers once again and rereading the controversial works of the previous decade to determine whether to accept papal supremacy, if and when they rejected royal supremacy, Neale provided a restatement of the traditional High Church understanding of the historical study of the Fathers. The new element was a more serious understanding of and appeal to the example of the contemporary Eastern Church and the Churches of antiquity that could be compared by analogy to the Church of England. Rather than Newman's philosophic application of the concepts of organic growth and development, Neale maintained the older appeal to strict historical continuity and the unaugmented transmission of the original deposit of faith through apostolic succession. He placed that polemical statement in the context of a novel; and in line with the needs of piety and preaching in a decade marked by emotional and religious unsettlement, interpreted by some in millenarian terms, he appealed to the imagination by depicting the suffering Church of the martyrs.

THOMAS WIMBERLEY MOSSMAN

In his *English Constitution* Walter Bagehot announced that a new world had come into existence by 1872. Although the Reform Act of 1867 could be described as the partial cause of that, the great constitutionalist felt that other forces were at work precipitating a momentous change in English politics. Bagehot, of course, discerned those new alignments of forces within the neo-Gothic chambers of Westminster, and did not always mention even significant changes there. Recent commentators have remarked that the most significant fact about the election of 1868 that followed the Reform Act was the number of members prepared to disestablish the Church. In broad political terms the years from 1870 to 1872 marked a low point in the popularity of the monarchy as well and the rise of republican sentiments, prompted by the events in France;

Gladstone in 1870 expressed honest doubts about the survival of the monarchy.[55] The Franco-Prussian War and the cataclysmic history of the Paris commune combined with events—especially in relation to the Vatican—in Italy and Germany to unsettle basic political and religious arrangements on the Continent. Island Britannia felt, or was made to feel, very much a part of the Main in these events, but it was embroiled in its own internal difficulties. The period 1867–74 witnessed the outbreak of the worst passions over ritual questions and was punctuated by the Public Worship Regulation Act (1874). Debate also erupted, as it had in 1848, over whether to retain or abolish the Prayer Book order concerning the Athanasian Creed; many churchmen were startled to find the Ritual Commission of 1869 and Archbishop Tait of Canterbury in the vanguard of those desiring a change. Similarly, agitation over the Irish question led to the disestablishment of the Church of Ireland in 1869. High Churchmen, in fact, seriously considered disestablishment as a means to extricate the English Church from the strangling Erastianism of Parliament but questioned whether that would unravel even more the loosened fabric of society. Tied closely to these developments was the bitter controversy over the relationship of the Established Church to the national education system; the first school board elections (1870) became the arena for that confessional battle. The Vatican Council (1869–70) and its decrees on papal infallibility and immediate jurisdiction precipitated another wave of no popery fervor throughout England, inflamed even by such an unlikely character as the High Churchman William Gladstone in 1874 and 1875.[56] The effects of this unrest, linked inextricably to theological questions, were felt throughout British society:

> All things at the present day seem to betoken as rapidly approaching, one of those great modifications of external Christianity of which there have been only two, or three at the most in the long course of 1,800 years. A deluge it will be: and he would be more than prophet who should be able to foretell all that will emerge when the waters subside. But though this is far beyond all human ken, of one thing we may feel assured, that Christianity as it is, in its own true vital essence, will come forth all the fairer, all the purer.[57]

The author of that apocalyptic prediction was Thomas Wimberley Mossman, D.D. (1826–85). Matriculated at St. Edmund Hall, Oxford, he graduated in 1849 and was ordered as priest in 1850, having become an adherent of the Oxford Movement. After presentation to several successive livings he became rector of East Torrington and vicar of West Torrington in 1859. He was, by the time of his death, a prominent leader of the extreme Ritualist party. His *History of the Catholic Church* (1873), quoted above, presents a picture of an irenicist with open views—for example, on the episcopate and the ordained ministry—who is difficult to group with the older generation of Tractarians or Ritualists. One may suggest that Mossman's extreme position developed after 1874; before that time he was developing into the eclectic kind of Anglo-Catholic one would later meet in Charles Gore and his circle.

In the introduction to his *History*, Mossman desired to retire ecclesiastical history and especially the history of the Early Church from partisan exploitation. The only way to gain a balanced view, to "learn the truth," about the Primitive Church up to his time, he concluded, had been to compare Cardinal Baronius's *Annals* with the Magdeburg *Centuries* and strike a balance. It was, he admitted, an almost impossible task for the ordinary reader. Mossman thus became the first voice among Anglo-Catholics to press for the production of new histories of the church beyond party motives and to move away from dependence on the older printed sources and controversial commentaries. This shift had effects late in the century on the types of books used by interested laity and in theological education. Mossman's argument is based on what he sensed to be widespread sympathy, in effect, to relate to the Primitive Church on its own terms and not as a proof text of sorts for Anglicanism or Anglicanism's mode of ecclesiastical government. He identified his sympathizers as the "interior," that is, lower, clergy of the Church of England. (One should remember that it was only in the very late 1860s and early 1870s that Tractarians were given preferment to higher ecclesiastical positions.) Speaking through this persona of the presbyterate, he concluded:

> "We have all been brought up to look upon the Anglican Church as a
> kind of continuation of the Primitive Church in modern times, and,
> therefore, the Primitive Church itself as Anglicanism upon an extended
> scale. We have all our lives been reading works and histories written
> by those who have looked at the Early Church through Roman Catho-
> lic, Anglican, or protestant spectacles. What we now desire is, that

someone, with fairly competent learning, would look at it, not through any spectacles at all, but with his own natural eyesight, and give us the result of his experience." . . . I am not surprised that under the former system, I always, or nearly always found Anglicanism in the Fathers: nor that I have since discovered comparatively little of it, but a very great deal of what is not Anglicanism. (*HC*, xi)

That does not mean that, although one does not find Anglicanism in the catacombs, one may expect to find any other ism there:

And though I do not say you will find a reproduction there of your own peculiar denomination, or ecclesiastical organization, yet of this I am quite sure, you will not find a close, or absolute reproduction of any other modern system whatsoever. If you do not find Calvinism, or Lutheranism, or Independency in the Primitive Church, neither also will you find any exclusive Anglicanism, or exclusive Romanism. But you will find a very great deal of what is infinitely better—the love and the spirit of Jesus Christ.[58]

In those terms he is willing to confess the misuse of historical data in previous historiography; either collections were made so as to exclude material that would militate against the central hypothesis or falsifications were made. He mentions examples of the latter fabricated in the interests of episcopacy.[59] The use of one type of external organization of Christianity over another "cannot be accepted as the measure of men's love for a personal Christ. St. John's test [1 John 4:2–3] of heresy and orthodoxy must be the only one *in these the latter days* [italics mine], as it certainly was in the first ages" (*HC*, ix). This polemical device, applying the records of the Early Church to contemporary cases as a means of external judgment, is traced by Mossman to St. Cyprian. For Mossman that is not an acceptable method in this "end time." The only test can be identification with "the love and the Spirit of Jesus Christ," acknowledged by belief in the Incarnation (St. John's test). The centrality of the Incarnation is typically Tractarian, but the framework of its presentation had been by 1873 substantially reworked through critical scholarship: "[There] is but one only thing, which comes forth from the fierce crucible of modern criticism, absolutely intact, as gold purified seven times in the fire—and that is, the true, and perfect, and external Divinity of Jesus Christ" (*HC*, xvii). That affirmation is the "one thing needful," cutting across all boundaries between ecclesiastical bodies; it is as true for Anglicans toward Dissenters as for Romanists toward Anglicans:

> Surely, if the salt have not wholly lost its savour, some one in authority, some bishop, or prelate will at length arise, and be large-hearted enough to say to his separated brethren of the Family of God—"There has been enough of strife, enough of division. Henceforth let us be one in Christ. We do not ask for your submission, as we have done in the weary ages of controversy that are past. We ask for nothing, we wish for nothing save your unfeigned love. Your Ministers, we regard as Ministers of Christ in accordance with their work for Him, though you may not call them by our names; and in you we gladly recognize the work and the fruits of the Spirit of grace, in just as full measure as we behold them amongst ourselves." (*HC*, xvii–xviii)

He obviously hoped that the Church, structured and governed as he knew it to be, could respond, perhaps in signal instances, to that challenge. With that end in mind he offered his ecclesiastical history as a picture of "the church as she was, before the era of Constantine made her less, so to say, a Catholic Church, and more a grand ecclesiastical system" (*HC*, xiv). Mossman presented this "Eirenicon" to his fellow Christians throughout the world: "Securus *judicet* orbis terrarum" (italics mine). Besides a reference to recent theological exchanges on reunion, the work is called an Eirenicon because Mossman held that study of the Early Church taught unity and charity; he changed the mood of the Latin verb, revising Newman's quotation of Augustine, to appeal to a future condition.[60] When the Church achieves unity and charity again she will be the whole world judging securely, as during the ante-Nicene period. This is a subtle reiteration of the branch theory; the branches are good in themselves only because they demonstrate that there is one trunk. This preface is all the more remarkable because of the Tractarian affiliation of its author. It takes its place beside the other irenic literature pressing for church reunion in the late 1860s and early 1870s. While maintaining certain fundamental doctrines, it treated as open questions several traditional doctrines and disciplines, demonstrating a sensitivity to critical scholarship of the kind found among Anglo-Catholics in the 1880s and 1890s. The startling reason advanced for that reevaluation of traditional questions was presented by the author through an apocalyptic motif: unity is necessary because the latter days have arrived.

Mossman's novel, following a year later, can be viewed as an attempt to put the irenic principles of his *History* (although concerned here with a later epoch) into effect, while satisfying "the great and ever-increasing interest" of readers in all facets of the Early Church.[61] The story narrates the boyhood and young adulthood, up to age twenty-five, of Epiphanius (ca. 315–403), who as bishop of Salamis (Famagusta) in Cyprus (from 367) and in his "Medicine chest for the cure of all heresies" (ca. 375) launched a devastating assault on Origen's heterodoxy. The novel, presented as an autobiography being composed in 400, does not mention this activity or the role Epiphanius played as an agent of Theophilus (385–412), bishop of Alexandria, in the latter's campaign against John Chrysostom, patriarch of Constantinople (398–404), and against the "Origenists" he sheltered. Nor is he shown as the champion of Rome's doctrinal purity. The later Epiphanius is a much more controversial figure than young man Epiphanius, although enough elements of continuity are present; the later bishop and heresy hunter does not fit the model of Christianity given in Mossman's *History*, except in Epiphanius' resolute, if historically ineffective, assault on the local Gnostics and defense of the doctrine of the Incarnation.[62]

The novel treats the early history and adventures of Epiphanius ("Phaniah" in Syriac) and his younger sister Callitrope, born at Besandouk near Eleutheropolis, when the "British Helena" was beginning the Constantinian renovation of Jerusalem. Born to Canaanite worshipers of Jehovah, "Epiphanie" (as his mother calls him) is adopted by Tryphon, a wealthy rabbi, scribe, doctor of the Law, and member of the Aaronic priesthood, and betrothed to his only child, Salome (or "Irene"). The study of the Jewish Scriptures and chance encounters with Christian clerics are factors in the decision of the brother and sister to be baptized. Using their wealth, they found a convent in which Callitrope eventually becomes abbess. Epiphanius also joins a cenobitic community, eventually being ordained a priest, after surviving a kidnapping by "Saracens." Tiring of his abbatial office, he makes a pilgrimage to the holy sites throughout Palestine and into Egypt. There he inadvertently resides with a Gnostic community but finally escapes to inform the "Catholic" authorities. The narration ends there.

Beyond presenting to the English reader "one aspect of early Christian manners and customs, and habits of thought and express"—the ethos of the period, in short—Mossman believes he has presented important material on two aspects of the Primitive Church: "It will be found, it is believed, to break up what may be called, to some extent, new ground—the contact between Judaism and Christianity at the commencement of the Fourth Century, and the desire of solitude, and bidding adieu to the world, which were among the original elements out of which the more perfectly organized monasticism of later ages was developed" (*Es*, v). Questions about Jewish-Christian relations, the Scriptures, monasticism, and celibacy take pride of place. One line at the end of the novel, "Constantine . . . had given large powers of jurisdiction to the Catholic Church," is the only mention of the political realignment caused by the Christianization of the empire. We also hear about Constantine at Nicaea, but only in terms of the homage he gives to the maimed and mutilated Confessors present. Whereas most Anglo-Catholic authors chose periods before the Constantinian era, Mossman chooses a time and place that would naturally have allowed reflections on the relationship of Church and State, but he does not consider this topic himself. The tension in England in the early 1870s between those two forces provides a partial explanation for this omission. Mossman is interested in the "Catholic Church," not the post-Constantinian "ecclesiastical system." His silence about the empire proclaims a firm belief in the independence and otherworldliness of the kingdom of Christ, alongside the earthly rule of the British Constantine or Britain's Victoria.

His depiction of the Jews in the fourth century has a threefold purpose: to create the impression of friendly, personal relationships between Jews and Christians, especially during the Tenth Persecution (writers referred to the Diocletianic Persecution as a parallel to the ten plagues in Exodus); to examine points of scriptural interpretation; and to discuss certain correspondences in ritual. In treating the first point, one would do well to remember that Disraeli was again prime minister, while at the same time Freeman's historical work, including his massive *Norman Conquest* (1867–79), was enlivening the Teutonic myth of England. Mossman's statement is really an irenic one: "I should mention that the Jews and Christians in our part of the country lived together in a very friendly and neighbourly way. I never heard of such a thing as a Jew refusing to do a good turn to a Christian, or a Christian to a Jew" (*Es*, 43).

In treating Scripture, Tryphon the Rabbi (calling to mind Justin Martyr's *Dialogue with Trypho*) plays a symbolic role as the type of allegorical interpreter. This is clear in the discussion of messianic prophecies:

> Tryphon belonged to what may be called the elder school of Hebrew expositors of the Sacred Scriptures: that school which . . . is almost, if not entirely, extinct among the Jews themselves, but whose traditionary expositions of the Messianic prophecies have become the priceless heritage of the Catholic Church. The Jews, as it is unnecessary to remind those who are acquainted with their literary history for the last two or three centuries, have abandoned those interpretations of the prophecies which influenced the seventy Elders who translated the Hebrew Scriptures into Greek. And this modern school, as I may call it, prefers the versions of Symmachus and Aquila and Theodotion, to that most venerable Septuagint, which our and their forefathers were accustomed to regard as inspired. How true are those words of the holy Paul: "Blindness hath happened unto Israel." (*Es*, 60)

The important points alluded to here are the application of the messianic prophecies to Jesus and the difficulties presented by the several versions of the Old Testament, difficulties that ultimately affect its continued authority as divinely inspired material. Tryphon's daughter, Salome, who was like Miriam, Jepthah's daughter, or Judith, the very image of the courageous martyr (although the old Epiphanius insists that title is meaningful only for "those who believe in the Christ," she anticipates that belief), is the first to make the connection between the prophecies and the person of Jesus. Examining Isaiah together with her father, she observes to him that "it is only since the time of Jesus of Nazareth that our chief doctors and scribes have said that such prophecies must be interpreted of the sufferings of our people Israel" (*Es*, 61). Tryphon suggests that the original intention was not a reference to a personal Messiah. Salome, who "knew the Jewish scriptures by heart," rejected that, while maintaining that the "later Rabbin . . . not being inspired men like the prophets themselves, . . . were, in that point, in error" (*Es*, 44). The rabbinical misreading, alleged by other Anglo-Catholic authors, of the messianic prophecies has wider repercussions. Epiphanius states that "the history of Jesus of Nazareth" was not an infrequent subject of conversation among Jews, "so that they exercised caution in a personal understanding of a Messiah." But the Jews "in rejecting the true and only Messiah are compelled likewise to reject very many of their own traditions" (*Es*, 64–65). He suggests that one difficulty Jews had in applying the prophecies to Jesus was the difference in perspective between victory and being vanquished, between the perspective of heaven and that of earth. The Jews expected a triumphant king to restore Israel, not a suffering servant, despite the imagery of Deutero-Isaiah. Epiphanius explains that it is part of the mystery of the divine will that Jesus chose the path of tribulation and anguish, when he might have chosen the path of power and renown.

The multiplicity of versions or translations of the Old Testament created another set of problems, as noted above. Salome reads a roll of Ezekiel written in old Hebrew characters called the Samaritan letters, used by that people to transcribe the Torah, while Jews used square, Chaldaic letters. Textual variations between the LXX and other versions sometimes rob a passage of Christian signification. Generally, though, Epiphanius in the novel prefers the Hebrew text, since in the very utterance of Hebrew words he feels something awful and terrible is being described. The very language has become a sacrament. The character reflects on this as he composes his own translation of Exodus:

> As I read the Hebrew, I could not help feeling how tame in comparison
> was the Septuagint Version, or indeed any other translation I had ever
> seen. . . . And though it would, perhaps, be too much to argue that such
> vividness of description, such living fire of language, implies that the
> writer of the Book of Exodus must have himself been an eye-witness of
> the plague he so majestically describes, yet it is at least fair to say that he
> must have witnessed a storm which it is given to but few to behold,
> even in a lifetime. (*Es*, 80)

The philosophical argument has a weak ending, but the reader can see an attempt to raise points of biblical criticism concerning text and form that places Mossman in line with those advocates of the newer biblical scholarship in England, even if that apparatus is used in Mossman's case to support a traditional position. Another source the character Epiphanius mentions is the "Prophecy of Enoch," used by Tryphon and others as a veritable supplement to Scripture. Epiphanius observes in passing that they had "often heard of what the Christians were beginning about this time to call the writings of the New Covenant, and to reverence with the Scriptures of the Old Testament" (*Es*, 47–48). That quest for canonicity was applied to the prophecy just mentioned. "I incline myself, as those who care to read my works will know, to the belief that these writings [e.g., Enoch] are a part of the inspired Word of God. But what the Church shall finally determine, that, we know, will be the truth about the matter" (*Es*, 190). In a short space he has affirmed several major doctrines relating to Scripture. The Testaments cannot be separated. The Canon of Scripture is a sure and infallible judgment of the Church, which can reject works reverenced for their antiquity. Personal judgment must defer to this authority in determination of the "truth." Inspiration, however, was not entirely closed by the Canon; inspired works can exist outside it, such as Enoch. These points make up a robust defense by Mossman of traditional doctrines of Scripture, while he is willing to encourage some biblical criticism, much in the manner of the *Lux Mundi* group.

Ritual is another set of concerns. The reader is presented with a range of comparative materials, from the Canaanite worshipers of Jehovah, the Jews, Catholic Christians, and Gnostic sectaries. At the funeral of Epiphanius' father the family intones Psalm 137, "By the waters of Babylon," which "both the Jews and the Catholic church call the 'Peregrine Tone,' or 'Song of the Stranger.'" This service was, Epiphanius says, something "I have since sometimes seen equalled, but never surpassed, even in the solemn and glorious ritual of the Catholic Church" (*Es*, 15). He describes other ritual activity: the "Holy Sacrifice of the Eucharist" on the Lord's Day or the "weekly festival of the Resurrection" (in Egypt this is in addition to a Eucharist on the Sabbath) and ordination to the offices of subdeacon, deacon, and priest in the manner and form "handed down from the Apostles."[63]

It is for baptism, however, that the longest ritual and doctrinal descriptions are reserved; even baptism by desire is illustrated. For children, "instructed in the doctrines and precepts of the Holy Catholic Church," baptism is the "laver of Regeneration." For Epiphanius it is "the Sacrament of our New Birth," validly administered only with the knowledge and consent of the bishop, who in this case conducts the ceremony. The instruction in "all the necessary doctrines of the Christian Faith" is tersely recorded. It is a reception into "the Holy Ark": Epiphanius "puts off" the world and changes into baptismal garments. The loss of his sandals on the steps of the basilica is taken as an augur of this casting off of the world and as a mark of his monastic vocation. Conversion, baptism, and monasticism are thus inextricably linked. The rite itself is explained in minute detail: the various ranks of clergy and two baptismal sponsors are present, the four-foot-deep bath, exhortations by the bishop, baptismal questions while turned to the west instead of in the direction of the destroyed temple in Jerusalem, the blessing of oil and water and his anointing, his triple immersion and second anointing, the Lord's Prayer and further exhortations, prayers while facing east, a reading from 2 Chronicles, the collect proper after the Lord's Prayer, and the final procession while Psalm 112 is intoned. The time is the fourth century, but the ritual questions raised—for example, use of sponsors, exorcists, anointing, and eastward stance—were all topics under review by the Ritual Commissions and other circles from 1867 to 1874.

The questions of baptismal regeneration and the linking of the rite as a sacrament to the office of the bishop had a long history, as we have seen, in Anglo-Catholic discussions. The important stress throughout is on historical continuity, first with the rituals of the Jews, then through succeeding Christian generations. The ceremonies were at least as old as those performed by the immediate successors of the apostles:

And so comparing all the dates among themselves, I could see plainly that I, young as I was, could, as far as time was concerned, have conversed with those who had themselves been baptized by disciples of one who had, himself, been taught the Catholic Faith by the Disciple whom Jesus loved, and whose head had been wont to rest upon the Bosom of Incarnate God. . . . This is what we, to whom God has given grace to hold the Orthodox Faith, call the living voice of the tradition of the Catholic Church. Oh! that all heretics and schismatics, who reject this living voice, would see that in rejecting, they are also rebels against the voice of reason, and fight against the truth of incontestable facts. (Es, 106–7)

Continuity as ritual, a basic claim among Anglo-Catholics by this date, is seen as a further defense of the linkage of the two dispensations, Old and New, under one covenant and, in its historical mode, as a further defense of the Incarnation. Mossman presents a powerful defense of ritual by maintaining the basic unity of Scripture (Ephiphanius was the special foe of the Marcionites on Cyprus) and the applicability of incarnational theology (apostolic succession was a "proof" of the Incarnation against the Gnostics). On the other hand, Roman Ultramontanists, who sought to identify the "living voice" of the Church with an infallible papacy able to create doctrine or tradition *ex sese*, are instructed by the "voice of reason" that this historical, apostolic succession is the authentic "living voice" of tradition.

Monasticism is the second field of "new ground" Mossman has hoed. The first new order for men in the Church of England, the Society of St. John the Evangelist, his readers would have been sure to know, had been founded by Father R. M. Benson at Cowley in 1866. Under the influence of the monk Lucian, the fictional Epiphanius determines to sell all he has and give it to the poor. Some of the money (his inheritance from Tryphon) and property are reserved to endow a convent, and Epiphanius keeps fifty pieces of silver "without any violation of monastic poverty." Veronica, Callitrope's baptismal sponsor, is appointed the first abbess, eventually succeeded by Callitrope herself. The decision to enter such a conventual life is permanent—although monks are able to leave the *cenobium* on pilgrimage or business. Breaking the natural bonds of affection, brother and sister never meet again. This kind of permanent separation of family members or lovers is a constant element in these novels.

The solitary nature of the life is stressed: Elijah is called the "forerunner" of Christian monastic life. The monks' daily existence is devoted to eighteen hours in prayer, study, and work in a garden. Epiphanius eventually becomes abbot over forty to fifty monks but desires to see the monasteries and solitaries in the deserts of Scete, Nitria, Pentapolis, and Nubia. Celibacy, of course, is the basis of his monastic vocation. He had been betrothed to Salome; but even before her death and his decision to withdraw from the world, we see the character transcending natural relationships. Thoughts of Salome's beauty lead him to thoughts on the beauty of the angels and the archangels and saints; furthering that motif, he asserts she was the image of the Virgin Mother of God with light blue eyes and blond hair! Separation by death from her, he concludes, "became an unconscious training, as it were, for my future monastic state" (Es, 71). Her burial place, the Valley of Baca ("weeping"), becomes for him a valley of Berachah ("blessing").

The character's later violent response to the Gnostic community in Egypt must be viewed as primarily a temptation to his vow of celibacy. The porteress at the hospice there is introduced as a consecrated virgin, but she is veiled. Epiphanius observes to the reader that Catholics did not veil virgins, as a protest against Cataphrygian heretics who did. He treats the De Velandis Virginibus by "Tertullianus" as a Montanist treatise proving this. The porteress's name is another clue—Barbelio, one of the Gnostic aeons. She tests the visitor by a secret hand sign (the nail of the middle finger is used to scratch the guest's offered palm). He is drugged with what he calls the "οἶνος δαιμονων" and has a heightened perception of the strange devices, birds, creeping things, pagan myths, Old Testament symbols, mathematical and astronomical diagrams intertwined in designs on the wall—an allusion to the historic Epiphanius' denigration of art in Christian buildings.[64] This incident provides an etiological explanation of that later attitude. The unnamed feeling raging through him during this sojourn is, of course, lust. He treats as pornography the library of Gnostic titles in his room: the Gospel of Eve ("Gospel of the Serpent"), the Gospel of Andrew and Thomas, the Revelations of Adam, and the Questions of Mary to Jesus (Es, 152–65). It is this inducement to sexual license that reveals to Epiphanius the true nature of the hospice, and reveals to us something of the reasons governing the author's portrayal of the character's heresy phobia.

The novel also contains an extended discussion of miracles, moving back and forth between credulity and rationalistic explanation. Cleobus, a Christian priest, blesses the wounded thigh of the young Epiphanius and the pain leaves; he curses the truculent ass that inflicted the wound and the beast immediately dies. Epiphanius observes:

> I have no wish to assert that these, and some other things which happened to me in my childhood, were miracles in the strict and proper sense of the word: but that they were all ordered by the Providence of God, and that they came about through God's governance of the world

and human affairs, and in answer to prayer, I have no more doubt than I
have of my own existence, or of the miracles which happened in olden
times. And I do not say this because I have the slightest doubt myself of
the perpetual continuance of miracles, technically so-called, in the
Catholic Church. Not of course as a normal condition of things, but as
happening now and again. (*Es*, 34)

He maintains the occasional occurrences, at least, of valid miracles and
lists, besides certain scriptural miracles—exorcism of devils, glossolalia,
taking up serpents, drinking poison—the luminous cross that appeared to
Constantine and the heavenly signs and subterranean fire when Julian
tried to rebuild Jerusalem. This is a fair indication of Mossman's method.
He has Epiphanius give a rather guarded, sometimes even rationalistic,
explanation, then recounts events or examples that explode the careful
statement just made. There are two extreme illustrations of this. The
monastery is afflicted at one point by wild animals consuming the garden.
The monk Laetus (his name means "Joyful") preaches an admonitory
homily to the animals, and they leave the monastery garden henceforth
undisturbed. It should be remembered that Mrs. Oliphant's *Life* of St.
Francis of Assisi had appeared in 1870 and met enthusiastic response.[65]
The character of Epiphanius, presented with this Franciscanesque *fabula*,
states: "Whether or not they understood what our brother Laetus said, I
dare not take upon me to affirm, for I do not know. I only narrate that of
which I was myself, with many others a witness" (*Es*, 123). He offers,
though, several rational arguments why the animals left: the power of the
human voice, the growing human population, and so on. Another time,
when he is about to be killed by a Saracen raider, Epiphanius touches the
man's blind eye: "The Saracen's closed eye opened at that very instant,
whether from excitement, or some natural cause, I know not" (*Es*, 128).
He concludes, however, that it was what Christians call a miracle.

On the other hand, visions and miracles associated with scriptural
prophecies are readily accepted. Epiphanius has an ecstatic vision of the
Jordan River; and before her death Salome has a "waking vision" in
which something like the Rod of Moses appears to her in the crossing of
the Red Sea and again as the fourth figure that joins the Three Children
in the furnace. "It is like the Christian cross," she finally decides. Visions
and dreams, linked to prophecy and inspiration, were perennially fasci-

nating to the Tractarians. At Migdol near Gaza, the site of the Flight into Egypt (although Pelusium or Heliopolis are suggested as alternatives), the cross towering over the town is seen as a fulfillment of the prophecy by Isaiah. Associated with this is the legend that here a vine bowed down with grapes to the Virgin Mother sitting beneath—"they say," Mossman quickly adds. Legends of this kind he traces to the Gospel of the Nativity, the Protoevangelium, ascribed to the apostle James. The writer creates distance between himself and such occurrences, except in one instance. "There is however one tradition, which, if I be any judge in such matters, I should say must be true, because it fulfills a prophecy of the holy Esaias" (*Es*, 150). Surprisingly, that tradition is the one in which the pagan idols shattered as Jesus, Mary, and Joseph passed by.

When Newman composed his first essay on scriptural miracles in 1826 and followed it in 1842 with a defense of ecclesiastical miracles, his points became part of the theological arsenal. When the Anglo-Catholic J. B. Mozley published his Bampton lectures (1865; 5th ed. 1880) *On Miracles*, it was the last attempt by a major Anglican theologian to use miracles as proof of the truth of revelation. Later theologians, even Anglo-Catholics, pressing incarnational and immanentist theology further, "did not wish to base revelation upon miracle, but saw the miraculous as part of, a consequence of, the revelation."[66] Mossman is an example of that shift. Miracles are maintained, at least their possibility, however ambiguously; but those that are part of Scripture constitute a canon that he defends against all other combatants.

In 1880 a "historical sketch" by the Reverend Frederick George Lee appeared, dedicated to the "promoters of Corporate Reunion" and offered to the world "in the hope, with a blessing from on high, of restored peace and visible unity, under the paternal rule of the Primate of Christendom."[67] The book is an extended and virulent attack upon the Elizabethan settlement and the subsequent government of the Church of England, looking to the papacy as the only possible center of unity and spiritual authority. For the frontispiece and throughout the work, Lee used a sermon by Mossman as supporting evidence.[68] In the wake of renewed no popery sentiment following the Vatican decrees and the controversial literature that ensued, this work recalls the bitterest attacks against the Reformation by R. Hurrell Froude in his posthumously printed *Remains* (1838). The reader is struck by the change in Mossman from the conciliatory stance of his work in 1873. The quotation from his sermon used as the frontispiece does harken back to Neale's conservative, even superstitious, position on alienated church property: "I believe that the chief and most important work which was done at the Reformation was to render the things of God unto Caesar. I shall always strive, to the best of my humble ability, to give back to God the things of God."[69] But he goes beyond this to decry the entire settlement and its subsequent effects:

> The position taken up by the English Church at the time of the reformation was that a national, or local, or particular Church has a right to sit in judgment upon the Church Universal . . . a right to decide whether or not the Canons of the Church Universal are in accordance with the laws of Christ and His Apostles, and abrogate them, or establish them accordingly; a right to decide for herself, as against the rest of Christendom, which Sacraments were ordained by Christ, and which were not; and a right to decide finally what ritual and ceremonies of the Church are lawful and edifying, and so to be retained; and what, on the other hand, are unlawful and unedifying, and so to be rejected, as tending to superstition and idolatry to be abhorred of all faithful Christians.[70]

That position, he concludes, is "in direct and irreconcilable antagonism to the revealed Word of God, and a bold and daring contradiction to the express will of the Incarnate Son of God."

It was in the prospectus of the Order of Corporate Reunion, founded in 1877, that these protests were organized and given contemporary application. Mossman was a "prelate" of the Order, styled the "Bishop of Selby." The spokesmen for the society explained the need to associate together in this fashion before the corporate reception of the Church of England by Rome and while still hold their livings in the Established Church:

> But a new crisis has arisen with which these Societies; English Church Union, Home Reunion Society, SPG, etc. are powerless to deal; for now it is found, to the sorrow and shame of many, that the Spiritual freedom of the episcopate, is practically extinct. And, having been forced by the invasion and active power of these evils, to investigate

more closely the whole history and condition of the Established
Church since the Tudor changes, certain other defects and abuses have
become evident to the Founders of this Order, which urgently call for
remedy.[71]

They list general conditions in the Church of England that had prompted
the widespread activity of this organization, although the Order held a
more extreme position than similar societies: the Association for the Promoting of the Unity of Christendom (1857), the Home Reunion Society (for Dissenters and the Established Church), and the Association of
Prayers for the Return of the Separated Portions of Christendom to
Catholic Unity (1877). The list of current evils includes the following:
"1. Extreme confusion in organization and discipline. 2. Grave diversity
of doctrinal teaching. 3. Lapse of spiritual jurisdiction. 4. Loss of the
spiritual freedom of the Church. 5. Uncertainty of sacramental status,
arising from the long continued prevalence of shameful neglect and care-
lessness in the administration of Baptism, contrary to the directions contained in the Book of Common Prayer. 6. Want of an unquestioned
Episcopal Succession."
     What had caused Mossman's change of heart from 1873? First of all,
there had been an observable shift in religious attitudes from 1870 to
1879. Benjamin Disraeli, Lord Beaconsfield, wrote to the queen in 1879,
following the elevation of Joseph Barber Lightfoot to the bishopric of
Durham, about "the deleterious designs of Canon Lyddon [sic] and the
Dean of St. Paul's [R. W. Church], who wish to terminate the connexion between the Crown and the Church, and ultimately unite with
the Greek Church. The Church Union is entirely under their control."[72]
Disraeli is incorrect about Liddon and Church and their connection with
the English Church Union, but his communiqué demonstrates the
popular misapprehension of the Anglo-Catholic attitude toward the
State at the end of the decade. Anglo-Catholics sensed with everyone
else the possibility of a momentous change in the relation of Church and
State in the early 1870s and the need to reassert spiritual principles.
Dwight L. Moody and Ira D. Sankey appealed to this general religious
uneasiness in their revival meetings (1874–75), which had a continuing
effect inside and outside evangelical groups. For Anglo-Catholics this
sense of religious and ecclesiastical unsettlement was, as already noted,

sometimes articulated in apocalyptic imagery, so intense and palpable were the crises of the early 1870s, and not just over disestablishment.

The attack in Convocation on the Athanasian Creed (1872) and the subsequent Public Worship Regulation Act (1874), enacted by Parliament with little consultation with the Houses of Convocation, undermined Anglo-Catholic confidence. They trembled to hear the archbishop of Canterbury, A. C. Tait, argue against taking the clauses of the Athanasian Creed in their plain and literal sense (pace Tract XC). While the Act was in reality only a reform of legal procedures for handling aggravated ritual cases, it was especially detested by Anglo-Catholics, both because it was purely a parliamentary invention and because its first administrative head was Lord Penzance, an ex-judge of the Divorce Court, an appointment felt by many to be needlessly provocative. In 1877 the practice of sacramental confession and absolution came under zealous attack after the publication of *The Priest in Absolution*, an anonymous Anglo-Catholic confessor's manual. From queen to commoner, an uproar was heard against this practice, which had been growing since 1840 as part of the parochial evangelism of the Anglo-Catholics. The same year Father Arthur Tooth of Hatcham joined the ranks of "martyrs of ritualism" and served a short term in jail for contempt of court in a case related to advanced ceremonial usages; he was the first of several priests to be jailed on similar charges. Further ritual disputes from 1877 to 1882 reemerged with the Ecclesiastical Courts Commission of 1881 to 1883. Disappointed in earlier expectations, harassed, they felt, by legal proceedings, lacking confidence in the hierarchy, some Anglo-Catholics, like Mossman, looked for a visible source of authority which stood firm against the "Latitudinarianism, False Science, Erastianism, and blank Infidelity" of the day and spoke with one dogmatic voice, judging the world. They looked toward Rome. By 1879 a new pontiff and the cardinalate for Newman offered grounds for hope of a scheme like Corporate Reunion. Except for a very small number, the English clergy remained in place and Rome remained cool to plans for reunion, finally dashing all hopes as "utterly null and totally void" in the bull *Apostolicae curae* (1892). Mossman himself recognized the impossibility of Corporate Reunion. Shortly before his death, he was received into the Church of Rome, alone, by his friend Cardinal Manning.

CHARLOTTE YONGE

Charlotte Mary Yonge published in 1868 *The Pupils of St. John*, a theological and historical survey of the writings of St. John the Divine and his immediate followers: Ignatius, Quadratus, Polycarp, and Papias. She then rehearsed the apostolic succession from this initial group through later disciples—Melito of Sardis, Theophilus of Antioch, Aristo of Pella, and Irenaeus of Lyons—and the churches they served in Gaul and Parthia, in Smyrna and Antioch, bringing the survey down to her own day. England, while not the center of attention, appears in this narrative. Yonge refers to Claudia Rufina, the daughter of the "British king of Chichester," identifying this figure with the woman addressed in 2 Timothy 4:21. In similar fashion, she relates the traditional story that Bran, father of Caractacus, captured during the emperor Claudius' campaign in Britain, took Aristobulus, the disciple of Paul, back to Britain to serve an enduring Christian community there.[73] The English Church, therefore, had a double foundation, once in apostolic times and once during the pontificate of Gregory the Great. Although Yonge has her eyes reverently fixed on the ancient witnesses of the apostolic faith, her real concern is for her own day and the churches that are part of the Johannine legacy. These concerns unite her interests in apostolic succession and the authority of Scripture, especially as these are combined in the evangelical work of the Church. Her range of interests and associations can be tracked by asking two questions initially. Who are the contemporary followers of the apostles? In particular, who are the pupils of St. John?

In 1868 Yonge had been accepted as an exterior sister of the Community of St. Mary's, an Anglican sisterhood, located at Wantage and linked with the Community of St. John the Evangelist at Cowley, just outside Oxford. Writing a self-deprecating acknowledgment to W. J. Butler, the famous Tractarian vicar of Wantage (later dean of Lincoln) who had been offered the missionary bishopric of Natal in the continuing turmoil over the Colenso affair, Yonge, while confirming her devotional duties as an associate of the order, wishes she "felt more worthy" and insists she is "very nearly useless in anything practical."[74] Throughout her life she had profound respect for those who under the tutelage of the Church in faith and discipline gave their lives in Christian witness that was both selfless and practical: "I have been a companion of the Saints, whatever I am myself." It was with this understanding that she identified the apostles and their disciples as primarily missionaries; correspondingly, for her the missionaries of her own day were worthy successors to the first evangelists and witnesses of the lively apostolic faith.

George Augustus Selwyn (1804–78), the first Anglican bishop of New Zealand, was one such churchman. Meeting in 1867 in Torquay, then a center of "the Church movement," the "Primate" and Miss Yonge discussed his missionary activities at the consecration of All Saints Church, Babbacombe, chiefly built by Frances and Joan Patteson.[75] Some of the proceeds from *The Heir of Redclyffe* (1853) and *The Daisy Chain* (1856) had been donated by Yonge to his various ventures, including the construction and outfitting of the steamship *Southern Cross* for use in the Melanesian mission. Selwyn had attracted as a coworker John Coleridge Patteson (1827–71), consecrated as the first bishop of Melanesia in 1861. The Pattesons, Coleridges, and Yonges were relatives, and Charlotte had a special affection for her cousin John, "dear Coley." She saw him as a leader in a holy crusade to win subjects to Christendom and souls to Christ. In discussing such missionary activity, she and her intimate friends habitually used the language of a Romantic quest, not the hard talk of colonial expansion. Her cousin was another candidate for the seven-league boots of Guy Morville/Sir Galahad. When Bishop Patteson was murdered by natives in 1871 in circumstances heavy with christological symbolism, the enthusiasm for the missionary work of the Church of England in the South Seas increased in response.[76] Part of that enthusiasm was nourished by the *Life of Patteson* that Charlotte Yonge wrote at the urging of the bishop's sisters, Frances and Joan. Her literary talents had long been at the service of the missions, but it was her personal devotion to John Patteson and his work, tragically cut short, that swayed her to undertake this commission, producing one of the best of Victorian biographies.[77]

Another candidate for the contemporary role of a biblical and apostolic figure was central not only to the Catholic Revival in the Church of England, especially in defending the apostolic succession, but also to Yonge's own religious development: John Keble, sometime Fellow of Oriel and vicar of Hursley. Preparing her privately for confirmation in

1838, Keble caught her imagination with the Tractarian idea of the Church and Catholic principles, an imagination already receptive, reverent, and obedient. "For 30 years the famous novelist was to be his pupil and friend, in almost constant touch with him, and her books are the best reflection we have of what he himself would have called his *ethos*."[78] Keble died on Maundy Thursday (29 March) in 1866, followed on 11 May of the same year by his wife, Charlotte. While a century later Keble is memorialized in the calendar of saints in some branches of the Anglican communion, more immediate memorials were undertaken by his friends. Work on Keble College, Oxford, was completed in 1869–70. In Yonge's parish at Otterbourne, Hampshire, yoked to Hursley until 1875, a granite cross paid tribute to her "Master and Inspirer." Yonge also undertook to highlight the work she considered the finest literary monument of her spiritual guide, his enormously popular volume of verse *The Christian Year*, which from 1827 to 1873 (the year its copyright expired) sold 379,000 copies, and the less popular *Lyra Innocentium* (1846).[79] Her *Musings* became in time the "official" gloss on the religious poetry of Keble, just as her later work on Hursley and Otterbourne canonized them as models of the Tractarian parish and places of pilgrimage.[80] The former work recorded at one point her sentiments at Keble's burial service, concluding with her hope that "he would not blame us for irreverence for thinking of him in words applied to the first Saint who bore his name [John the Baptist]—'He was a burning and a shining light, and ye were willing for a season to rejoice in that light.'"[81] That characteristic scruple over identifying Keble with St. John the Baptist, while using a quotation from the Gospel of John, was not enough to prevent a similar remark in 1869. While on holiday in France, Charlotte was shown some of the photographic work of Ary Scheffer, most likely genre photographs with a religious motif. She was unmoved by his portraits of men, except for a "magnificent" photograph of "St. John writing the Apocalypse," a work that she "longed to show Mrs. Keble, it gives one a perfect thrill of awe."[82] Without overstepping Yonge's own scruple by making a simple identification between Keble and the last of the apostles, one can still suggest an allusive reference was being made. It is appropriate that a book which enshrines a very tangible sense of apostolic succession should play a part in the developing hagiography of that Tractarian who in 1833 publicly launched the Anglo-Catholic defense of that succession.

These associations in Yonge between figures in her own history and in the history of the Church show the allusive quality of her references, a quality resonant throughout her authorship. On the other hand, she did not depend entirely on such self-effacing, reserved, allusive indirection in making her point. She could be just as direct and declarative. Who are those in line with the apostles? Who are the pupils of St. John? They are those who accept the "spiritual" Gospel, the three Johannine Epistles, and the Apocalypse. That is her formal, external criterion in regard to Scripture. Implicit in this acceptance, it should be noted, is an affirmation of the apostolic succession that guarded, canonized (Article VI), and handed on those writings from age to age. Yonge was responding to the serious, contemporary questions of New Testament criticism, especially German criticism made public in *Essays and Reviews* (1860), defending both the authentic authorship of the Johannine material and the authority of the episcopal tradition linked with it. She had already indicated her distaste for much of the Higher Criticism or "rationalism/Germanism" in her novel *The Two Guardians; or, Home in This World* (1852). Yonge retained this attitude throughout her life. Characteristic is a letter to Miss Elizabeth Barnett: "I wish some one (not a woman) would put it with authority that it is frightful that we, 'whose souls are lighted' by the in-spired tradition of thousands of years, should listen to the German critics who have no Church, even if they believe at all, and who talk as if He-brew was their mother tongue. It seems to me letting the devil in."[83]

The Pupils of St. John also demonstrated various other attitudes about Scripture which were part of her understanding of the Catholic faith and apostolic succession. In the introduction, after listing several instances of heresy, she wrote: "Some of the classes here mentioned professed to be pupils of St. John, to the exclusion of his fellow-labourers. Such gained a one-sided view of the truth, and soon became perverted. For as in an-cient times narrow Judaism, so in modern days wild fancies of apocalyp-tic interpretation, have shown the evil of only studying in one line, without the balance" (p. xx). She decried the construction of a canon within the canon of Scripture, whether Johannine or, more to the point in the late 1860s and early 1870s, Pauline. Her stress on the balance of voices in Scripture is also meant to show the importance of the various ecclesiastical traditions, Johannine, Pauline, Petrine, Synoptic. Harmo-nization, not expurgation, is the method for handling any differences between those witnesses. The British adherents of F. C. Baur, for example (a generation behind those on the Continent), traced a link between the Judaizers of the Early Church and their classic document, the *Apocalypse*. In Yonge's day other forces had isolated the Apocalypse and used it to interpret the present age, as millennial groups such as the Irvingites and the English branch of the Mormons had done in the 1830s and 1840s. The *Christian Observer*, the foremost Evangelical periodical, had announced in January 1860 that Garibaldi's assault on the crumbling papacy was a sign of the Second Coming.[84] Apocalypticism and a theology of crisis were not compatible with Yonge's training or temperament. Prophecy and vision were compatible perhaps, but not apocalypticism and the sectarian, factional spirit of which it seemed part. In the late 1860s she expressed broader toleration in religious matters and placed more stress on the mediating, comprehensive role of the Church. One example of this was in *The Chaplet of Pearls* (1868), in which the via media of the English Church is favorably compared to religious factionalism in the France of Catherine de Médici.

Yonge used another subject—liturgy—to ring a double bob of changes on the themes of apostolic succession and respect for various vital strains of ancient tradition. Like scriptural tradition, liturgy was, she maintained, intimately linked to the Apostles and to the apostolic churches. Liturgy was catholic as well as apostolic. The presence of a liturgical system was a chronic sign of a truly Catholic Church, corresponding to an apostolic and Catholic system of faith. Despite what many observers of the Tractarian Movement have written, the early Tractarians "had definite notions about the meaning of liturgical worship and the principle underlying it."[85] While "slow" in comparison with the "advanced" Ritualists in implementing changes in ceremonial or mastering the technicalities of liturgiology, the liturgical system for the Tractarians, Newman insisted, was a tangible example of apostolic origins, as well as "religious principles and doctrines" (Tract 34).

In preparing for confirmation as Keble's catechumen, Yonge had studied William Palmer's *Origines Liturgicae; or, Antiquities of the English Ritual* (1832). Palmer, a Fellow of Worcester College, acknowledged a debt to Dr. Charles Lloyd (d. 1829), Regius Professor and later bishop of Oxford, for the latter's course of lectures on the liturgy in the old High Church tradition, a course that Newman, Pusey, Froude, R. I.

Wilberforce, and many others avidly attended. How much Palmer was in fact indebted to Lloyd is debated, but Lloyd's lectures attracted widespread attention to the history of the Prayer Book rite and its sources.[86] Keble's *The Christian Year* and Lloyd's investigations were judged by contemporaries to induce a new regard for the Prayer Book. Palmer, in particular, strove to demonstrate the equality of the English rite with the Roman, making a historical as well as a theological argument on that basis. Belief in the apostolic origin of the Prayer Book liturgy was a note of High Churchmanship, as the republication of works by Bishop George Bull in Tract 64 showed. Yet that belief, even in those familiar with the changes the Prayer Book had undergone, was often expressed in a literal and uncritical sense by the early Tractarians, such as Isaac Williams. Palmer sometimes speaks of the English rite as a mere translation of primitive texts, at other times describing its identity with the liturgies of antiquity as one of "order and substance." With such a background Yonge was able to write, concerning the liturgy of St. John the Divine:

> Among all these the Western form of the liturgy of Ephesus has passed away. Rome insisted on uniformity, and superseded it in France, in Spain, and in those Irish Churches that own her dominion. The Reformers of France dispensed with all forms of prayer, but the English have only translated, not disused, their ancient devotions; and thus it is that, while other places may show closer connexion with St. John and his pupils, it is the English communion at home, in her colonies, and in America, that tunes her prayer and praise to the echoes from Polycarp's canopy of flame, and, it may be, from St. John's vision at Patmos.[87]

In Yonge the liturgy has been introduced into the continuing polemic with Rome and in defense of the branch theory of Catholicism. Her argument has a theological rather than historical purpose; as history it is simply inadequate. However, the passage quoted is a rich storehouse of Anglo-Catholic sentiments. Like Palmer, she sees the English rite as merely a translation of ancient liturgies without any sense of indigenous change in that rite. Also following Palmer, she ignores the influence and contribution of the Reformers. Indeed, acknowledgment of liturgical development or the debts to the Reformation, if she were aware of them, would have seriously undermined her apologia directed against

Rome. Other traditions had been suppressed by monolithic Rome in the name of uniformity; but the English rite remained an echo, albeit an English-speaking echo, of the apostolic rite. Yonge has taken Wiseman's earlier claim that the contemporary Roman liturgy was identical with the liturgy of the catacombs and made it her claim for the Prayer Book liturgy, pushing its origin back to the person of St. John.

Two attitudes expressed above need in the case of Yonge to be qualified. The liturgy was not in itself for her a conclusive argument. It was an important aspect of the ethos of the Primitive Church that the Tractarians recognized and hoped to revitalize in the English Church. It was part of what Yonge would call the "livingness" of Catholic principles and doctrines, which were properly internal and "spiritual." But liturgy was subsidiary to theological statements, such as the branch theory of Catholicism. From the first, Yonge had learned from Keble to be self-critical in exalting liturgy over other concerns; he warned her, as she writes in *Musings*, against "loving these things for the sake merely of their beauty and poetry"; holiness should be her concern, not ceremonial. In *The Pillars of the House* (1873) and *Heartsease* (1854, 1862) she candidly portrayed the weak side of High Churchmanship in its externalism, spiritual pride, and narrowness. This self-critical awareness is also manifest in her anti-Romanist feeling. Rome was an interloper on the British scene, a church with a mottled history, but a branch of the Catholic Church nonetheless. She wrote to a friend: "If only you would not snap your fingers at Rome! I don't want to give her more than her due, but I do love and honour S. Gregory to be so treated."[88] The English Church is for Yonge a living continuity with the Church of Augustine (of Canterbury) and Anselm, sufficient unto itself in the present day while historically indebted to Rome for its second foundation. Tractarians professed various attitudes toward the Church of Rome, some like the early Newman quite hostile;[89] in this work Yonge contrasts English usages to the Romanist system based on a sense of parity with and not superiority to Rome. It is that attitude, without any developed theological understanding, that fills her last pamphlet: *Reasons Why I Am a Catholic and Not a Roman Catholic* (1901).

The elements that marked her historical and theological writing in the late 1860s—a rejection of biblical criticism, a partiality for the regular devotional life of the English Prayer Book, an irenic attitude toward

Romanism as part of the branch theory, an earnestness for the disciplined formation of character through the sacramental offices of the church—in sum, the very issues of religious controversy that shook the English Church in this period—also marked her novels, where conscious references to these matters are made with studied verbal precision. She had transformed the "Church novel" from a fictionalized platform for catechesis, often no more than crude propaganda, into a particular subgenre of the domestic novel of manners in which the Church of England (or, as in a later example, its antiquely garbed progenitor) structures the lives and destinies of the actors. She "showed in fiction, as Keble showed in his incumbency, what the Oxford Movement could do in Anglican life without causing violent upheavals or controverting its own doctrine of reserve."[90] That note of reserve, the second part of Keble's primary charge to her, derived from the discipline of the Primitive Church (*disciplina arcani*) and exalted by the early Tractarians, sometimes appears to remove Yonge's fiction from the arena of controversy. In fact, for the careful reader the novels draw a battleline of religious matters that are distinctively Tractarian; *Heir of Redclyffe* (1853), *The Daisy Chain* (1856), *The Young Stepmother* (1861), and *The Pillars of the House* (1873) are only the most explicit examples. But Yonge's innate sense of reserve, her aversion to changing or "developing" the original deposit of doctrine handed on to her by Keble, and her antipathy to later theological trends, even within the Tractarian camp, have helped to foster the idea that following publication of *The Pillars of the House*, her last really strong novel, she lost contact entirely with the changed world around her. While not in sympathy with what she saw, she was nevertheless keenly aware of theological trends well into the 1890s, even if she was not able to analyze them acutely or attack them successfully.

In 1890 Yonge published *The Slaves of Sabinus*.[91] The story takes its title from Caius Julius Sabinus, allegedly descended from Julius Caesar, who joined with Claudius Civilis after the death of Nero to found a separate empire of Gaul. Sabinus has been defeated by Cerealis, who was sent from Rome by the new emperor, Vespasian, when the story begins around A.D. 71. With Sabinus are his wife, Eponina; their two sons, Caius and Sylvius; and two slaves, Esdras the young Jew and Telamon the Gentile, later a freedman, hiding from the imperial troops in a cave near the River Lesse in present-day Luxembourg. Under the guidance of

Eponina's uncle, Cumnorix, a veteran and Gallic chieftain with senatorial rank, they all journey to Rome to plead for pardon. Along the route leading through Lyons, Arles, Nîmes, Marseilles, and the capital, they pass through several Christian households, including that of Flavius Clemens, nephew of Vespasian. Despite the good offices of Clemens and Titus, pardon is denied and the party returns by the same route, although Telamon has by now become a Christian and Esdras has met his long lost sister, also a Christian. The two young sons inadvertently reveal, through an act of disobedience, the presence of their hunted father; the slaves are tortured for information—the Christian resists unto death, but the haughty young Jew breaks down. Returned to Rome, both Sabinus and Eponina are executed, having become Christians in the meantime; Esdras and their guard are also converted. One son becomes a priest of Apollo; the other, Sylvius, becomes a Christian priest, and Esdras, his guardian, serves by his side as a deacon.

This entertaining historical tale is a typical example of Yonge's ability to weave a number of characteristic elements—historical, doctrinal, and moral—into one seamless fabric. The novel does not read like a history text, catechism, or tract on morals; the narrator does not, as is common in these works, step back and give the reader occasional gallery lectures. The historical incidents and personages, points of church discipline and doctrine, and her personal emphases are blended in such a way that they are decisive in providing internal motive and external motion, having real effects on the characters of the participants visible to the reader. We see the psychological construction of conscience, the growing effect of the Christian religious system on the individual personality, as well as the differences in those personalities, especially in her keen portrayal of children. All this is set in the framework of first-century domestic life.

In the preface she tells the reader that the "main facts of the story of Sabinus and Eponina, as well as the fate of one of their sons" rests upon Plutarch and observes that the "history and fate" of Flavius Clemens "are recorded among those of the martyrs of the Church." Indeed, one would expect a good dose of history or transcription of historical sources from someone like Yonge, who had been steeped so long in classical historiography, especially that dealing with Rome. Early in life she had made a serious study of Oliver Goldsmith's *History of Rome* (1769) and was known and highly regarded as a historian (primarily but not exclusively for children) of this later epoch. Her *History of France* was part of the Historical Course for Schools, edited by E. A. Freeman and reissued in 1879 under the editorship of J. R. Green. Although she maintains that "All is true . . . ," one can quickly see that the story's purpose is not to teach the historical "facts" but to illuminate the "effect upon their characters" of Christianity, as she connects the individual stories of fictional actors and factual saints.

Her choice of locale is especially revealing. The major part of the story takes place in those Christian centers clustered along the Rhone River: Lyons, Arles, Nîmes, and Marseilles; the cave in Belgica Prima and the imperial household in Rome, in contrast, are places of hiding, trial, contemplation, and endurance. The French locales and persons connected with them are familiar to readers of her earlier volume, *The Pupils of St. John the Divine.*[92] Trophimus the Ephesian at Arles and the church in the house of Pudens at Rome appear in both works, as does St. John, a chapter of whose newly delivered writings "Father Trophimus" expounds at a liturgy. The history of the Gallic Church is a subject particularly close to Yonge. In the earlier treatise she noted the battle between good and evil taking place in France in her own day and associated that battle with the early Christian martyrs and their Huguenot descendants. The area around Arles and Nîmes had special significance, since Nîmes was the birthplace of F. P. G. Guizot. Historian and prime minister under the July Monarchy of Louis Philippe (1840–48), he was in the summer of 1869 Yonge's host at Val Richer near Lisieux, France, during her only tour abroad.

The struggle with evil in contemporary France and the presence of Christians such as Guizot showed Yonge that "the living power of the faith is as strong in our day as when it nerved men to be the prey of beasts within those arcades of the oval theatre." That passing observation sums up a great deal of Yonge's ecclesiology. Christians today are directly united to those of the Primitive Church by a "living power" of faith, one of whose external symbols is the local colosseum. The pagan monument, like the pagan engine of execution—the cross—is a symbol of Christian victory. That faith gives strength, "nerves" men to face death. Yonge also homogenizes differences between various Christian groups. She af-

firms a branch theory of Catholicism and emphasizes independent traditions of local (national) churches, but any real distinctions are eclipsed by
a deeper unity. The Christian Church, portrayed ideally in *Sabinus*,
stretches from Antioch to Arles in one closely coordinated whole. Unity
with that Church seems to go beyond even Catholicity. The highly
praised Guizot had Huguenot ancestry, from which roots certainly notable members of the Church of England had flowered, and was known
as a Liberal—a mild one, but a Liberal nonetheless. Yonge seems to adopt
a pneumatological ecclesiology at this point in order to stress the
"livingness" of faith and to include Guizot within the Church descended
from Ephesus. This is understandable, since Guizot was recognized in
High Church circles for his spiritual understanding of the Church's entrance into the world as an idea rather than merely as an institution.[93]
Like the Oxford thinkers, Guizot provided a deeper and broader sense of
history.

In *The Slaves of Sabinus* Telamon functions as the topos for the conversion of a Gentile. He has already been prepared for the Gospel by his
"faithfulness and obedience" as a slave and dependent freedman, trained
"in a standard of conscientiousness," and by his tour as guard, chained to
the Apostle to the Gentiles. "Paul the prisoner spoke words that were
strange, and I have never forgotten" (*S*, 93). This preparation, emphasized by Yonge, is strengthened by his contact with various Christians.
Scripture plays a part, but only in a fragmentary way; he hears bits of the
Old Testament from Esdras, some psalms, the "history" of Elisha reviv-
ing the dead and the raising of Lazarus, a chapter from St. John the Divine, and sections of Paul's Epistles. Later he is examined rigorously by
the bishop, Pope Clement, concerning the commandments, psalms, and
Scripture, "the Word itself, not the comments and glosses of men."[94] But
his conversion has long since been effected by his contact with other
Christians. What attracts him to that community is its belief that "there
was a life to come in which there should be perfect compensation."
Yonge sees the appeal of life after death as being a powerful attraction for
Gentiles to the Early Church; the beliefs of the Pharisees concerning resurrection had already prepared many Jews. But that future hope is linked
to an exacting and disciplined moral regimen. In presenting himself as a
candidate for baptism, the Gentile makes that clear:

"This faith opens to me the hope of everlasting life, free from all the
sorrow, toil and oppression here," was the freedman's answer, his eyes
glancing with the thought. "Is that all? That is but the hope of a
brighter Elysian field," said the father. ". . . even in this world, there is a
release from evil and foulness, and men go about pure, happy, and
faithful." ". . . Why should they be thus freed from evil?" "Sir, by the
Sacrifice of the Immortal God becoming Man, that He might be mortal
and die for men." "Thou hast the point there, my son." (S, 121)

The Christian convert looked for holiness, as well as hope. The Incarnation was the guarantee of both. But an intimate part of that teaching of
the Christian's standard of morality was to know "what evil really
meant" and how far short of perfection the suppliant stood. The Incarnation, God becoming Man, was described in terms of "Sacrifice," along
with Christ's death. Here was the soteriological view of the nature of
evil. "He had been faithful, obedient, kindly, and was only beginning to
know how much more so the truly devout Christian might be, and to
understand the sin of numerous habits that had come to him as matters of
course; and it was needful that he should have all this laid before him so
that his conscience might be awakened, and he might know to what a life
his Baptism would bind him" (S, 122).

In the chapter entitled "The Freedman Free," Telamon asks that he
be "first washed from my sins and taste the heavenly food of the faithful."
In the public scrutiny of his doctrine and morals by the bishop, he acknowledges repentance, proclaims his faith, and promises to strive
against sin. The baptismal rite is meticulously catalogued: the oil, lamps,
the sunken pool with steps, the removal of his clothes, the triple total immersion, the white robe, the softly chanted "alleluia," the brow
anointed, the imposition of hands that was "the gift of the Holy Ghost,"
all followed by the Prayer of the Faithful, the Lord's Prayer, "the Feast,"
and finally the Kiss of Peace. Telamon had become "the Lord's freedman" through that "glorious liberty won for all mankind by One who
took on Him the form of a servant," as Paul once told his guards. Here as
elsewhere Yonge stressed the christological aspect of salvation: "Only a
perfect sacrifice could deliver us and all mankind." It was Christ, the
Messiah, the Son of God, who became "the one willing Atonement for
all!" In agreement with other Tractarians in response to the Gorham case
(1847–50), Yonge insists on baptismal regeneration and an infusion of

the Holy Spirit to give the faithful recipient supernatural strength against sin, in the case of Telamon treated quite literally as physical fortitude to help him undergo torture. "'Not I, but He who is in me,' said Telamon . . . 'He the Blessed Spirit . . . Who giveth strength.'" Likewise, the normal form of baptism is adult believers' baptism, although some children under certain circumstances may be baptized "before their understandings reach so far as to know its privileges" in times of persecution. The possibility of repentance for postbaptismal sin is also implied, although not detailed or linked to confession; God, however, can prompt "generous sorrow for a moment's weakness."

In contrast to her treatment of baptism, Yonge exercises a marked reserve in describing the Communion Rite, the "Feast of Sacrifice and remembrance." Telamon, attracted by hope for the world to come, the *saecula saeculorum*, completes his conversion by repentance, affirmation of the creed ("the Symbol"), resolution of his conscience under grace, and the reception of the sacrament. The sacraments of baptism and Eucharist are a perpetual call to duty and a source of strength against temptation. The preparation provided by obedience is, however, all important. Sabinus' child Sylvius, later to be a Christian priest, acknowledges, "I love Telamon's God the best . . . and He says we must obey our father whether he sees us or not" (*S*, 154). The child's voice is authentically Yonge's, with her personal stress on filial duty and obedience, uniting them to the religious impulse. She saw it as a true mark of Christianity for a Catholic of the nineteenth century as for one of the first century.

The Christian Church stood in the shadow of the empire. Yonge and other writers depicted that empire in its role as an administrative and military system. But underlying that purely institutional sketch is a theological understanding of empire that had particular relevance in the England of Victoria Imperatrix. The Roman model is seen in theological terms by its own religious oracles, the Sibylline books, and by the Christian Scriptures, the *Book of Daniel* and the *Apocalypse*. That theological understanding is not highly developed in Yonge, a subject we shall turn to later. She does, however, delineate the dual religious response that supported and was supported by that empire: philosophy and polytheistic superstition. The types for these in *Slaves of Sabinus* are, respectively, Sabinus himself, the sometime Caesar turned criminal by fate, and Eponina, his wife.

Sabinus "had studied in Latin and Greek schools all the systems of philosophy," so that he despised the myths of the gods. He did not treat them, like the stories of Homer, euhemeristically or as allegory for a rational philosophy. The effect of the declining classical philosophy on his mind, much like its rising effect on notable examples in the universities of Yonge's day, was skepticism: "[The] tone of his mind was to think all faiths alike void, and playthings for women and slaves, and perhaps a happy delusion for them, while wise men knew better than to look for truth anywhere" (S, 148). He despised the cultic side of religion, epitomized by Eponina, except where it overlapped the cultus of the State: "He troubled himself very little about such observances as were not connected with state occasions or family celebrations" (S, 148). Two things prepare him for the reception of Christianity. The first was his natural revulsion from idolatry and a philosophic inclination toward "the best," the summum bonum, even if truth was doubtful. Bishop Cletus later observed: "Philosophy overthrows idolatry, and seeks the best. So it prepares the way" (S, 222). Second, the example of heroic, manly figures disposes him to the Christian message. The stories he hears from Esdras, who has "no idea of teaching or conversion," concerning David and Jonathan, "the Pylades of this Jewish Orestes," are one early source. The most telling models are Pudens, "a man of rank and wealth," "the brave Caractacus," and Telamon, dying confident of the truth of eternal life. The example of others, such as Flavius Clemens, and the expectancy of his own death decide him. Yonge presents a complex picture of this conversion process, based on a rudimentary sociology and psychology of religion. Without developing a consistent method, she examines the questions of temperament, the concern for social rank, the bearing of the male seeking peer models, and the prejudices of a literary, educated class as an example of how such a mind would confront the Christian system. Through her characteristic emphasis on preparation—a kind of protoevangelium—for the actual Christian message, she personalizes the process of conversion.

Yonge also presents a theory in flesh of how this higher, literate side of the Roman State was "married" to the wider, semi- or illiterate culture. Yonge had rigid standards concerning the role of women in Church and Society, whether a wife and mother or, like herself, a dedicated spinster, a "Mother Goose" to her circle of little goslings. Her antipathy to the emancipated woman is well known. Eponina lives only as an extension of Sabinus. "Poor thing, she was an intensely devoted wife, and her whole soul was set upon her husband, with scarcely room for other devotion or thoughts of abstract truth; she only cared for what would serve him or make her one with him—this being the true model Roman wife" (S, 223). It is through Sabinus alone that she can work out her salvation, although she voluntarily accepted death before sentence was passed. "Sabinus thought of perfection and of Paradise; she thought of never being separated from him" (S, 233).

This is not the final word on pagan worship. There is a darker side, represented by Bito, the haruspex from Delphi who wins the child Caius as a prospective priest of Apollo to supplement falling recruitments. Yonge develops her sociology of paganism further. Bito is eager to have the child, since "the worship of the god was on the decline in Greece, not from Christianity, which had as yet made little progress, but from weariness and indifference, and the old gods were far more popular among the younger and more vigorous Western nations, to whom they were more recently known" (S, 214). Caius had been prepared for this role by the confusion created by his mother's contradictory tales of the gods, while Telamon tried to tell the children about God. Esdras reproaches himself later that this selfish silence concerning the Hebrew Scriptures had deprived Caius of a defense against the blandishments of Bito. Yonge pictures the lack of proper preparation and religious education as a recurrent danger for youth. In terms of the nineteenth century, Yonge believed that "some recent secessions to Rome were those of persons who had never been taught what the Church of England really holds."[95] Secessions to the infallible oracles of Delphi or the Vatican are quickened by such ignorance of true doctrine. But Yonge also discerned a psychological tendency within the adolescent himself. Caius, who had engineered the disobedient act that resulted in his father's capture, is attracted by the glories and beauties of the pagan rites and his own advancement as a priest of Apollo; but he is also intrigued "partly with the strange fascination that horror and terror have for some young natures." Yonge has a keen, quite unsentimental, understanding, often overlooked by critics, of the makeup and turmoils of the adolescent personality, as shown in her novel *The Heir of Redclyffe* (1853). However, this is often translated into a truism: it is easy to go wrong, difficult to recover. Yonge displays no little psychological insight in documenting the drawing awe that horror, terror, and sin can have for children. In an age that tended to sentimentalize upper-class children, she applies no small touch of reality.

Having seen some aspects of the sociology of religion that Yonge suggested and the personalism she used to identify the philosophic and cultic sides of religious practice, grounded in attempts to construct some psychological view of the effects of the Christian religious system on the mind, we can turn to her one reference to the theology of empire. She presents that reference in the subjunctive mood and frames it in terms of the personality of Flavius Clemens, who was the heir of the Flavii when executed under Domitian (r. 81–96). She observes, "A Christian Emperor—what hopes did not that possibility give?" The ambiguous attitude she and other Tractarians had to the Erastian principle, the concept of a national church, and the problems of Establishment constitutes the background to their understanding of the Constantinian Church. That attitude was also evidently translated back into the time of Clemens and personalized (what would be the effect on Clemens?) rather than theoretically treated in terms of Church or State. Yonge raises the issue and drops it: "Clemens was to be spared the trial of carrying his faith to the Imperial Chair, a trial that after two centuries more proved too great for Philip [the Arab]." It is possible that Yonge would advance the proposition that the accession of Clemens as a Christian emperor would have been premature, since the empire had not been adequately prepared. She had consistently insisted on that preparation in the lives of the individual characters treated thus far; it is reasonable to assume she would insist on it for the collective. The judgment of the whole world was not yet secure.

That preparation of the empire had been significantly advanced by the Jews. Yonge understands the role of Judaism in a complex analysis of Providence, showing the continuity of that role before and after the Fall of Jerusalem. Before the Fall, really the result of their rejection of the Messiah, "Jerusalem might have fulfilled the most glorious prophecies, as a centre to all the world." Now the role was indirect. The Arch of Titus stood as a monument of that defeat but also preserved as "the great record" the "symbolic forms of the Temple." And the Jews of the Diaspora permeated the Roman Empire, paving the way for Christian communities closely linked to the Jewish centers. Esdras Bar Joachim of Edrei, of the tribe of Zebulon, the slave of Sabinus, is Yonge's type for the Jewish convert and the focal point of her analysis of character. He is, in fact, the immediate instrument of preparation for Christianity for each of the later converts, despite his own hostility to those "craven-hearted recusants." While preparing others, he himself was being prepared: "In fact, Judaism so entirely prepared the way by its Divine morality and the absolute truths, that, when once self-righteousness was laid aside and the true Messiah was owned as the atoning Redeemer, a Jew was ready for baptism" (*S*, 210–11). Christianity did not mean the abolition of the Old Law but the fulfillment "of all that the Law and the Prophets wrote of the Anointed Who was ever promised." This fulfillment is seen as a natural, organic development, one of the few metaphors of growth Yonge uses, recalling Newman's similar language in the *Development of Doctrine* without sharing his sense of doctrinal growth: "even as the plant grows out of the seed, and that the ruin of our beloved country was but as the husk bursts asunder when the plant grows up and spreads" (*S*, 90).

Christianity is shown as the only way to comprehend the prophecies that were "too perfectly accomplished" and to bear the burden of the Law. Esdras, who had studied Hebrew in the synagogue and Temple under Rabbi Hillel and was conversant with the Septuagint and other material, "happily without the later exaggerations of the Rabbis," is instructed that the prophecies of the Old Testament point to a suffering Christ. It is the example of "supernatural strength" in suffering by Telamon, suffering that had physically broken Esdras, that breaks the pride and self-righteousness of the young Jew. He identifies Christianity with the source of strength to keep the perfection of the Law. "Trust and pray, and the Holy Comforter will make thee strong," he is assured. He lives out his life as a deacon, a life of "devotion, uprightness and knowledge of Scripture," serving the ministry of the priest Sylvius, "last of the race that claimed to spring from the pious Aeneas," and the almsgiving of Domitilla, wife of Flavius Clemens. Esdras the Jew, who had been part of the providential preparation of the Gentiles, continues in an ancillary role to the gentile Christians. This is also due to his own scrupulosity; although solicited to become a priest, he declines because of the remembrance of his fall. Yonge pinpoints once again the psychological motive; the sense of regret and continued repentance as an impediment to the priesthood is also subtly blended with some sense of Esdras' pride and alienation. The connection between Christians and Jews is treated in diverse ways by Yonge. In *The Pupils of St. John* she portrayed St. John in the dress of a

priest of the old sanctuary, with a mitre and on the brow a gold plate in-
scribed "Holiness unto the Lord." Church architecture also provides a
link. Commenting on the use by Christians of basilicas or "halls of justice" for liturgical gatherings, she makes the astonishing claim that "such
places were the origin and model of our churches, so far modified as to
agree with the pattern shown in the Mount to Moses for the tabernacle,
or to David for the Temple" (S, 95). She was, undoubtedly, making a
claim for the symbolic unity of the one atoning sacrifice, bridging
Temple and Church.

Esdras, the learned young Jew, whose name is taken from the
postexilic prophecies of the Apocrypha, an orphan in the new Exile, is, as
I stated above, the keystone of Yonge's novel. He is the one who prepares, albeit unknowingly but providentially, all the others for conversion. His collapse under torture results in the death of his master and his
own difficult conversion. And we see in his character, however flawed,
the real attempts by a struggling Christian to lead a life of devotion and
repentance amid the cares and temptations of the non-Christian world.
Yonge has selected Esdras, we may suggest, for other reasons, however,
reasons that illuminate her own concern for theological trends late in the
century.

The years 1889 to 1892 saw in the Church of England and the Free
Churches a new crest in the arguments over the inspiration of the Old
Testament: "Hitherto the criticism of the Old Testament was generally
associated with extremists, with *a priori* assumptions against the miraculous and probably against revelation, and therefore did not divide the
Church."[96] But in November 1889 *Lux Mundi* appeared. Edited by the
principal of Pusey House, Charles Gore, the book was taken by many
old-line Tractarians as a betrayal of their cause. Liddon attacked it at St.
Paul's, London, on 8 December 1889 in a sermon entitled "The Worth
of the Old Testament." The basis of Liddon's argument was that the infallibility of the Old Testament rested on the infallibility of Christ, a line
of argument quickly taken up, but one that would eventually cause more
problems than it would solve. In September 1890 Liddon died. S. R.
Driver, professor of Hebrew at Oxford (1882–1914), came out for the
critics in a sermon delivered at Christ Church, Oxford, on 31 August
1890. Many shuddered at the spectacle of the occupant of Pusey's chair
attacking, as they saw it, Pusey's principles. Driver, one of the moderat-

ing churchmen who enlivened theological thought late in the century, followed his sermon in 1891 with his *Introduction to the Literature of the Old Testament*, presenting Julius Wellhausen's theory about biblical literary forms without the latter's jarring tone. Charles Gore, in the meantime, tried to clarify his position in a new preface to the tenth edition of *Lux Mundi* (13 August 1890).[97] In 1891 his Bampton lectures on the Incarnation further developed his radical kenotic theory.

By the end of 1890 Liddon, Church, and Newman, names from the Tractarian pantheon, had all died. Yonge's touch with the younger literary audience was enough in question that Christabel Coleridge, as associate editor, undertook the work of the *Monthly Packet* until its demise in 1895. Seeing so much of the old order passing, Yonge felt out of sympathy with the new age. She was more specific in a conversation in 1890 with Ethel Romanes: "As we went she began to talk of Church matters, of the *Lux Mundi* school of thought, of the Christian Social Union. She could not, she said, feel in sympathy with much of these newer phases of thought." I would suggest, then, that *The Slaves of Sabinus* is part of the controversial response to *Lux Mundi*. In the person of the Jewish convert Esdras, Yonge makes two fundamental points. First, the infallibility of the Old Testament and that of Christ are intimately linked through the modality of prophecy and its literal fulfillment. The unity of one covenant with two dispensations is maintained. Second, Christianity was spread by missionaries, by the contact of person with person under grace, not by the critical examination of texts: "The Christian does not first fetch his faith by applying his reason to the critical study of the Bible but by apprehending the truth from other Christians and thereafter being led by them to find the evidence and proof of these truths in the Scriptures."[98] Both arguments are grounded in Yonge's personalism: the authority of the person of Christ is joined by grace, the work of the Holy Spirit, to the person of the Christian, who experiences repentance, resistance to temptation, and the strengthening of the sacraments.

Yonge had never had the theological background or the sympathy to follow the trends of the latter-day Anglo-Catholics attempting their own new and synthetic apologetical approach to biblical, doctrinal, and social questions at the end of Victoria's reign. She was no longer in the mainstream of that Anglo-Catholic movement but passionately defended with the tools she had the deposit of faith once delivered to her, however dull or wrongheaded that defense seemed to the new generation. Yonge died in 1901, the same year as her monarch, on the eve of the Annunciation (March 25), and was buried at the foot of John Keble's memorial cross in the Otterbourne churchyard on the thirty-fifth anniversary of Keble's death.

SABINE BARING-GOULD

By 1897, the year of Victoria's Diamond Jubilee, the character of the Anglo-Catholic movement had changed; the story of its founding had become the stuff of history books, and its early heroes had become material for the hagiographers. Whereas Newman, Pusey, Keble, Manning, and the other central figures had studied history intently—from the history of the primitive church through the Reformation period—using mostly collections and commentaries from the eighteenth century and earlier, the later generation hardly looked at history. In church history, the study of the movement itself took pride of place. R. W. Church's self-effacing work *The Oxford Movement*, published posthumously (1891); Anne Mozley's edition of the letters and correspondence of Newman during his life in the English Church (1891); R. H. Hutton's *Cardinal Newman* (1891); E. S. Purcell's *Cardinal Manning* (1895); Tom Mozley's often misleading *Reminiscences Chiefly of Oriel College and the Oxford Movement* (1882); William Palmer's defensively sharp work *A Narrative of Events Connected with the Publication of the Tracts for the Times* (1883); and the lives and letters of J. B. Mozley, Bishop Christopher Wordsworth, Walter F. Hook, W. G. Ward, and Isaac Williams, among others, supplied ample reading matter. Anglo-Catholics were also composing popular works of church history covering other periods. Study of these latter-day saints of the Oxford Movement went hand-in-hand with study of the lives of earlier saints, a type of reading infrequently utilized in the earlier period. The collection used for this purpose was invariably that made by Sabine Baring-Gould, notable as a hagiographer, hymnographer, Ritualist, folklorist, antiquarian, Anglo-Catholic squarson, and novelist.[99]

Baring-Gould (1834–1924), born at Exeter to an old Devonshire family, was educated at Clare College, Cambridge (B.A. 1854; M.A.

1856). While there he joined a "Holy Club," which he defined as "a Society of the Holy Cross, for mutual edification, prayer, theological study, and alms giving. We had prayers together, read papers, and passed resolutions." The group was known for its enthusiasm and piety, much like the group of Cambridge Apostles Alfred Tennyson found when he matriculated in 1828, but with the theological interests that J. M. Neale and his associates introduced a decade later. Among the early members of the society was William Dalrymple Mclagan, eventually archbishop of York (1891–1908); such groups of serious undergraduates obviously drew members from various theological backgrounds and sentiments. Although Baring-Gould served, against his family's wishes, as assistant master in the choir school of St. Barnabas, Pimlico, for a few months in 1847—St. Barnabas was a showcase of ritual practice at that time, attracting the devout, the curious, and the hostile—it was not until 1870 that he became established in extreme Catholic views. He also taught at Hurstpierpoint College before he was ordained deacon (1864) and priest (1865), despite the family's larger plans for their eldest son. Having been called to several parishes in Yorkshire and Essex, where he supplemented these meager livings with his writing talents in order to support his wife and fifteen children, he presented himself to the family living at Lew Trenchard in 1881, following the death of his father. He remained there until his own death, fulfilling in every way the country life of a squarson.

Perpetua (1897) was his first attempt to deal with the Church of the third century in Nîmes, Arles, Narbonne, and the outlying regions. During an ancient rite, the virgin Perpetua is selected as a human sacrifice at the Holy Fountain, sacred to the androgynous god Nemausos. She is rescued by Aemilius Lentulus Varro, a young, cynical pagan who despises the gods, with the help of his clients, the Utriculars (the guild of boatmen from the river tributaries). His friends spirit Perpetua to a country residence, Ad Fines (cf. Neale's Farm of Aptonga), while the high priestess unleashes the cultores Nemausi, the religious guild of the shrine, in an anti-Christian riot, precipitated by the desecration of the cultic statue by the deacon Marcianus (who apostasizes before his death in the amphitheater). The focus shifts to Cneius Baudillas Macer, another deacon, who undergoes doubts about whether to renounce the faith or suffer martyrdom. Perpetua returns to Nîmes to find her mother, Quinta. The

example of Perpetua and Baudillas as martyrs, as well as the instruction he
receives from Bishop Castor, effects the conversion of Aemilius, already
unsettled in his beliefs.

The antagonists of the novel are the high priestess, the college of attendant priests, and the *cultores Nemausi*, remnants of the older Druidic
culture and religion. Baring-Gould demonstrates how by the third century this older religious establishment had paled before the influx of later
socioeconomic groups and their religions, the higher philosophical culture, and the much less important Christian Church. The sacred fountain, a manifestation of the god Nemausios (a synthesis of the older Gallic
feminine Nemet and the later effeminate male Neumausios), is the scene
of human sacrifice once every seven years, when forty-nine girls, aged
seven to seventeen, participate in the chance selection, using a silver image of the god, a golden pippin, and a Gallic "gingle" (of which the
children's incantatory "One, two, buckle my shoe" is a late variant). Baring-Gould's etiological explanation, given a further reinterpretation by
Aemilius to prevent the sacrifice, draws together the author's interests in
antiquarian subjects, folklore, and country ballads. The worshipers of
"Madam Isis and the White Ladies" (the Faeries) are mentioned, but the
cruel, ignorant, and socially inferior *cultores Nemausi* are the focus. They
repeat the typical list of charges against the Christians, who worship an
ass's head, devour children, hold debauches, and preach atheism; these
pagans lead the riot in the city, settling social as well as religious scores, as
their victims are either killed instantly or dragged off to prison and the
amphitheater to be devoured by beasts or dispatched by soldiers.

Baring-Gould gives a fuller explanation of these guilds, which are
"much like our benefit clubs." At the lowest social level he indicates a
significant comparison between pagans and Christians, showing how the
Christians of this time formed themselves into the *cultores dei* along the
lines of the older models in order to procure a modicum of legal standing; the Christian *agape* is also conceived by many in terms of the guild
supper. Baring-Gould, then, has shown, amid the hostility of the pagan
world, part of the religious response of a certain class of Christian converts, borrowing from recognized pagan models. That depiction goes a
long way to provide the background and explanation for the ferocity of
the pagan reaction to the rising Christian group. He also probes the psychological connections of this confrontation. Popular paganism was not
constituted as a religion affecting the lives of its adherents by the exercise

of moral control. "It was devoid of any ethic code. . . . It was their fear for themselves and their substance that rendered them cruel." Paganism at this level, he states, was a code of external ritual behavior, without an isomorphic pattern of internal moral doctrine or discipline.

He has, in this short space, given an explicit definition of mass-culture paganism and an implicit definition of Christianity, based on this psychological disjunction of inner and outer religion. This is linked to the sociological question he raised earlier: fear for their social standing and material well-being is aggravated by confrontation with persons rejecting the status quo of social arrangements—masters and slaves mingle, whether as equals or not—and the heretofore unquestioned benefit of material acquisition. We will see later, in discussing the author's view of third-century Christians, that this contrast with paganism serves a dual purpose: identifying popular paganism and the roots of its reaction to the new religion, as well as ironically identifying true Christianity by that contrast. Christians, in fact, do not always and everywhere exercise mature moral control or internalize a reasonable ethical code. What was true in the primitive epoch is true in the Victorian era. There is some evidence that Baring-Gould modified this argument—some Christians rely only on external directions to fulfill religious duties—to make a subtle point against the Church of Rome. In chapter 10, entitled "Locutus Est!" the narrator observes: "The god Nemausus, the Archegos, the divine founder and ancestor had spoken. His voice was rarely heard. . . . That had been in ages past; of late he had been sparing in the exercise of his voice." The college of priests, harried by the free-thinking Aemilius and feeling their ancient control over the masses slipping, issue a clarion call through some trickery in the cultic shrine, summoning devotees of the god back to their primal obedience, to reject the religion and the new order of priests of the Christians. This is the first time the syncretist god (blending old deity and newer cult) is called "Archegos": the "divine founder and ancestor" but also "leader," "first father," "prince," the Latin *auctor*. The *auctor*, the one who has spoken (*locutus est*) with the notes of finality and absolute authority, may be a complex reference to the pope of Rome; when he speaks the case is closed ("Roma locuta, causa finita"). Not as powerful or as bold as in times past, even as recently as 1870, the Archegos of Rome was not entirely silent. The year before this novel he had declared in the papal brief *Apostolicae curae* (13 September 1896) that Anglican clerical orders were "totally null and utterly void." Baring-Gould is capable of such an oblique criticism of the papacy and the Roman system, played off of a view of paganism; there is a similar point in his later novel *Domitia* (1898). Anglo-Catholicism, through the end of the century, continued to define itself over against Rome. Vaticanism is the ghost that sits upon the grave of the Roman Empire and popular paganism.

The initial opponent of the entrenched pagan system is the higher philosophical culture, represented by Aemilius, a rich young man with legal training. After his dramatic rescue of the drowning Perpetua, he reinterprets the basic myth of the shrine, although cynical of any veneration given to such gods. He even relates how the priests apply drops of oil or water in the ears of oxen brought to the altars, so that they appear to nod in consent to their own sacrifice. It was his father, he says, who shrewdly ascertained that the ignorant created their own gods out of heroes or the forces of nature. The mob accuses him of being a Christian or an atheist. Baring-Gould makes the point later that Aemilius' philosophy had prepared him and is part of a providential preparation of the world for Christianity; the connection is underscored in advance by having the mob hurl the vulgar accusations at him they later use against Christians. In legal fashion Aemilius, however, tries to sway the crowd by pretending to extend his rearticulation of the shrine's myth (the fountain and apple are symbols of life, not death) by a euhemeristic appeal to the higher Olympian deities and an apostrophized faculty: "Make room on Olympus, O ye gods, and prepare a throne for Common Sense, and let her have dominion over the minds of men" (*Pp*, 38). Paganism had, as mentioned above, lost all hold on the thoughtful and cultivated. Something new to appeal to the rational mind was needed. On one side, consciences "agonised by remorse, sought expiation in secret mysteries, only to find that they afforded no relief at all" (*Pp*, 46).

One senses behind this apprehension of the anxiety of the third century a statement about the nineteenth-century fascination with supernaturalism, occultism, and Eastern mysticism. Annie Besant and Madame Blavatsky, spiritism, and theosophy are emblems of the late Victorian religious unsettlement. Besant toyed with Anglo-Catholicism for a short span. At a time of widespread despair, Baring-Gould remarks about the primitive age, "Christianity flashed forth," rapidly spreading among all social and intellectual strata. But it did not meet with instant success with the Roman merchants, "round-headed, matter-of-fact looking men, destitute of imagination, but full of practical sense," or with the youth. "The youth of Rome and of the Romanised provinces, was, at the time of the Empire, very blasé. . . . It became sceptical as to virtue, and looked on the world of men with cynical contempt. It was selfish, sensual, cruel" (*Pp*, 63). The characterization of those two poles, fathers and sons, could just as easily have been a miniaturist's portrait of the marquis of Queensbury and Lord Alfred Douglas. Notice the careful selection of vocabulary in the descriptions. "Round-headed" is a term that could be applied to the portrait heads of the later Roman Empire, but it had a special denotation in England: the Cromwellian burgher. The rest of the portrait has a Dickensian barb in it: devoid of imagination but full of practical sense. In the description of youth we are placed in context by the phrase "at the time of the Empire," Victoria's empire. Two other words are placed to catch the reader's eye. The sophisticated, foreign, and symptomatic word "blasé" puts us squarely in the last decade of Victoria's reign and the society of the Cafe Royále, as does the even more emblematic word "sensual." One could further point out the contrast between "sceptical" and "cynical," on one hand, and "virtue" and "the world of men," on the other. That last phrase, "the world of men," is a potent charge against effeminate aesthetes of the third century, as it was in England after Oscar Wilde's notorious trial and conviction. *The Ballad of Reading Gaol* appeared only the year following this novel, in 1898. The characterization of culture and the social milieu is a major concern for Baring-Gould in this novel and in *Domitia* (1898).[100] He undertakes that social criticism with careful attention to historical parallels; but the vocabulary and imagery he employs help the careful reader to pinpoint the target he kept ever in his sights.

The higher philosophical culture is a preparation, individual and corporate, for Christianity, working at times subconsciously. It works mysteriously on Aemilius—as Baring-Gould stresses again and again, without the organization and subtle nuance of Newman's *Essay in Aid of a Grammar of Assent* (1890) but with a similar sense of the independent growth of a true "idea" within man which has coalesced in Christianity:

> In the heart of Aemilius there was, though he knew it not, something
> of that same spirit which pervaded the best of men and the deepest
> thinkers in that decaying corrupt cold world. All had acquired a disbe-
> lief in virtue, because they nowhere encountered it, and yet all were

animated with a passionate longing for it as the ideal, perhaps the unat-
tainable, but that which alone could make life really happy. It was this
which disturbed the dainty epicureanism of Horace . . . the craving
after this better life . . . filled the pastoral mind of Virgil. And now this
dim groping after what was better than he had seen, this inarticulate
yearning after something higher than the sordid round of pleasure, this
innate assurance that to man there is an ideal of spiritual loveliness and
perfection to which he can attain if shown the way . . . (*Pp*, 64–65)

The question that activates Aemilius' interest in Christianity is one
he finds unsatisfactorily handled by natural reason alone: the problem of
mortality. What happens after death? Was there any continuance of existence? This question, concerning the immortality of the individual self-
conscious ego, raised by Yonge and other Anglo-Catholic writers more
and more late in the century, plays a dominant role in late Victorian religion and is isolated as a major component in Christian apologetics for this
period. Baring-Gould conveys the pervasiveness of this complex of questions about mortality and immortality, fear and yearning, death, dying,
and life after death, so that the questions posed and answers offered take
on a centrality known only too vividly a century later: "There was no
shaking off the oppressive burden, no escape from the gathering
shadow." To that characterization of ancient paganism as dark, doomed,
and depressing—images often used by writers in the late Victorian and
Edwardian periods, including G. K. Chesterton—Baring-Gould juxta-
poses Christianity, which "flashed forth." Aemilius had been impressed
with the serenity with which Perpetua, never wavering, had faced death.
But it is with an old woman, dying in a timber merchant's cottage, that
he learns about the Christian understanding of death. The dying woman
desires only one thing: "to be dissolved, and to be with Christ." She informs her pagan visitor, "I have passed from death unto life." Aemilius,
of course, is not convinced by this "delusion and mere talk." He asks
himself: "Where is the evidence that it is other? Where the foundation
for all this that is said?" Baring-Gould answered the pagan youth's question in the structure of the novel; the page following his question begins
a description of the Christian Church. The author does not mean that
the Church is itself the answer or foundation sought; it is, however, the
community in which the convert can find models and support to make

his personal profession of faith and credo. The "president" of that community, Bishop Castor, instructs Aemilius on the Christian position on various topics: the use of material goods, care for animals, death sentences, and war. The proselyte, prepared by his own craving for a reality that corresponds and that will give him repose, comments that he finds the Christian philosophy humane. Castor replies, "It is not a philosophy. It is a revelation." To underscore this point, a vivid image is used: a child on a pedestal being catechized. The bishop thus demonstrates that the wisdom of Christianity "is revealed unto babes. Where your philosophy ends, there our religion begins." But the "humane" aspect, the correspondence of Christianity to human nature and its deepest faculties, is stressed several times. Aemilius' philosophy is part of a providential arrangement, orienting him ever toward truth because of the presence in him of his own conscience and reason.

The theological argument here stretches back, at least in the Anglican context, to Richard Hooker, but beyond him to the philosophical synthesis of Thomas Aquinas. This theological anthropology is the base from which Christianity makes its exclusive claim: "[No] other religion professes to have been revealed to man as the law of his being by Him who made him" (*Pp*, 200). It was the Creator himself who put in man's head the aspiration to know the law of his own being. That has prepared man to receive the final revelation from his Creator: Christ is the power of God. For Baring-Gould's godly pagan Aemilius, then, the evidence and foundation for belief in immortality and power over death are christological. The Church is not the end, but the means by which the convert recognizes that. At the novel's conclusion Aemilius does, with the simple admission "Credo" and the statement "He [Christ] is a power." That apparently strange christological formulation may be Baring-Gould's attempt to avoid an anachronistic use of later credal terminology; it could be suggested that he is expressing Origen's explanation that the Father and the Son are one in power and will while being two distinct realities, distinguishable in hypostasis. Highly technical language or theological concepts, however, are not usually employed in the novels, in contrast to the expert use of precise terminology for ritual or ceremonial points.

Those ritual notes occur throughout the novel. The "sacred sign" of the cross is gestured on the brow by the believer. The physical and

architectural arrangements of a Christian church are also briefly outlined.
The altar—not a block of marble—is a slab of wood or stone on three or
four bronze legs. Curtains screen the sacred area, a use continued, the author says, in the oriental churches of Greece, Armenia, and Syria. "In like
manner the *tablinum*, with its conch-shape termination, gave the type to
the apsidal chancel, so general everywhere except in England" (*Pp*, 83).
The English reader is thus instructed in the architecture and decoration
of ancient house-churches, given a historical lesson on the domestic origins of such things as altar and altar curtains, and directed to contrast
present or past English usage (medieval English churches also employed
riddle-posts and altar curtains) with the continued usages of the Eastern
Catholic Church. Some of the architectural detail is based on archaeological evidence that is also in the contemporary English mind; a footnote, a rarity in Baring-Gould's works and in other novels of this type in
the 1890s, describes the "recently exhumed" house of Sts. John and Paul,
that extremely important fourth-century private palace on the Coelian
Hill.[101] A third-century *agape* and dawn Eucharist are re-created, although it is mentioned that by the end of the fourth century the love
feasts had ceased. This custom of the Subapostolic Church referred to the
narrative in 1 Corinthians: the foods for the love feast are quoted from a
list of St. Clement of Alexandria, who complained about the "dainties"
provided. No children are present. The "president" of the assembly is the
bishop, although the presbyter dispenses a blessing in his absence, and
two deacons assist at the rather free-form, extemporaneously improvised
liturgy. Members of the laity, for example, are permitted to add prayers,
poems, and songs to the service.

Baring-Gould is equally intrigued by the language employed for
worship. The password and response, admitting members to the Christian assembly, are given in Greek; the Scriptures are read in Greek, the
prayers in Latin and Greek, and preaching is in the vernacular. Evening
prayers are also given in Greek, following the model of the *Apostolic Constitutions* (viii.37).[102] For an extreme Ritualist this spare outline of liturgical practice should not escape notice. The details given demonstrate the
author's interests and expertise, but they rest on the fuller depiction of
the liturgical usages of the Subapostolic Church given in other sources
over the last half century. Baring-Gould is not fighting the same battles as
his predecessors; the public debate and litigation of the previous decades
had already educated his readers.

There is also in this Anglo-Catholic author a tendency toward concentration on interior attitudes, for which ritual details are only the visible signs, a tendency that especially characterized the movement late in the reign. It is to that complex overlapping of opinion, viewpoint, attitude, and sentiment that we must turn our attention.

The first viewpoint to be considered is that of the intellectual, civic-minded pagans and their compatriots in the lower classes. Baring-Gould uses them as types in order to depict, not only third-century paganism, but also the contemporary Christian reaction. The references are, one could say, triangular: pagan and Christian are held in tension by a third angle, sometimes invisible, which is Baring-Gould's critique of Victorian society. In relating the pagan social view of Christians he observes, "A Christian gave great offence by refusing to comply with the generally received customs, and his disregard on this point of etiquette was held to be as indicative of boorishness and lack of graceful courtesy as would be the conduct nowadays of a man who walked into a drawing room wearing his hat" (*Pp*, 81). One often has the sense of seeing his characters, like Kingsley's earlier creations, walking about with toga and derby. These pagans also have their contemporary counterparts in conservative Broad Churchmen. The Roman official Fuscianus remonstrates, "I hate all meddlers with usages that are customary. I hate them as I do a bit of grit in my salad" (*Pp*, 301). Worship for them is merely a formality, but a necessary formality of civil allegiance. Christians are discredited because they refuse to venerate images of Augustus, swear by the emperor, or sacrifice for the welfare of the empire; the Christians, on the other hand, insist that they do pray for Caesar, while refusing to offer incense. Pagans, however philosophical in outlook, could not match the moral revolution of the newer group. "They were unable to supply a child with any moral principle, to give it any law for the government of life which would plant the best guardian of virtue within, in the heart. . . . Public opinion was an unstable guide. It did worse than fluctuate—it sank" (*Pp*, 163–64). The Christian withdrawal from society is explained in part by this pessimistic, sinister portrait of general corruption. "Christian parents could not expose their children to contamination of mind by allowing them the wide freedom given at this day to an English or American girl" (*Pp*, 165).

This moral revolution takes place in the forefront of a larger social revolution that has upset tradition, old alignments, and social classes: "[A] great social change had taken place in the provinces, and . . . the freedman had stepped into power and influence, to the displacement of their power of control . . . their patrician places filled by a new nobility of army factors and money-lenders" (*Pp*, 281–82). The social upheavals and extension of the franchise in the nineteenth century to "freedman," Irish Catholics, Dissenters, and Jews, as well as to lower social ranks of nominal churchmen, are clearly half of Baring-Gould's double reference. He sees those political and sociological developments as being at the root of the spiritual unsettlement of the age. His mind is such that we should see the appeal to the "wide freedom" of Victorian English or American girls ironically. But he is less ambiguous at other times. One pagan magistrate condemns Christianity because of its exclusivity, worshiping "Christos" alone. "He must reign alone. That I call illiberal, narrow-minded, against the spirit of the age and the principle of Roman policy" (*Pp*, 258). Liberalism, the bête noire of Newman, the mark of the beast on the Victorian age, is seen as a fundamental, eternal antagonist to Christianity—especially Christology. Baring-Gould sees this liberal, philosophical spirit, free and undogmatic, as the undoing of the moral principle in Roman and Victorian society. All that is left to the liberal religious sentiment is a form of civil piety; but virtue, even civic virtue, needs stronger foundations. Philosophy used as a substitute for Christianity is inadequate, however much believers may in fact derive support from the philosophical systems of such thinkers as T. H. Green and other contemporary philosophers who wished to cut Christianity loose from its troubling historical base. Christianity conquered the world of antiquity not as a philosophy, Baring-Gould reiterates, but as a revelation.

That revelation was conditioned by the historical context and, in lesser degree, by social, political, even geographical considerations. To speak of historical Christianity is to speak of historical Christians. Baring-Gould portrays Christians in general, making careful and illuminating distinctions between the rich and poor and, in particular, uncovering some basic motives for Christian behavior and allegiance. His task is especially difficult, since the mantle of sanctity had been spread so copiously over all sorts and conditions of men and women who belonged to the Christian community. In the piety of the Victorian era, it was enough to have been a Christian in those historic times and climes to be classified as a saint. Cardinal Wiseman was not alone among modern hagiographers in imputing to all early Christians (except an occasional scapegoat, Judas figure) unearthly qualities: they were prophetic, impeccable, omniscient—in short, perfect. They were everything except historical participants in a historical setting. Baring-Gould's own hagiographical work often ran to the anecdotal because he believed one would remember the homely detail long after genealogical or theological points were forgotten. But these details provided a clue, amid the recrudescence of later hagiographical embellishment, to the personality of the real historical "saints" as they were, not as a later age expected they should be. Baring-Gould is in some sense a realist, investigating *pia fabula* for the historic artifact: an authentic sounding phrase, a quirk of character, a certain manner. In that context we can understand his attempts to clear the hagiographical fog surrounding the Early Church:

> We are prone to imagine that the first ages to the Church saw only saints within the fold, and sinners without. But we have only to read the writings of the early Fathers to see that this was not the case. If we consider our mission stations at the present day, and consult our evangelists among the heathen, we shall discover that the newly converted, on entering the Church bring with them much of their past: their prejudices, their superstitions, their ignorance, and their passions. The most vigilant care has to be exercised in watching against relapse in the individual, and deterioration of the general tone. The converts in the first ages were not made of other flesh and blood than those now introduced into the sheepfold, and the difficulties now encountered by missionaries beset the first pastors of Christ fifteen and sixteen hundred years ago. (*Pp*, 96–97)

The three assumptions he makes in this paragraph are revealing. The basic one is that we may imply the character of converts and the nature of the Early Church from the contemporary experience of the Church. This use of historical analogy, derived from Joseph Butler, modified and refined by succeeding Anglo-Catholic interpreters, is a basic tenet of the historical consciousness of the late nineteenth century in England. It is a benchmark of Anglo-Catholic historiography and historical theology. The second assumption is the total identification of the ministry of the Early Church as missionaries, evangelists, "apostles," linked now to that important sense of mission in colony-ruling England. We have seen this identification made by C. M. Yonge, among others. The third assumption is that the knowledge on which the first two assumptions are based is derived from, must be derived from, reading the early Fathers, a constant Anglo-Catholic emphasis. The Fathers provide, then, not only a "factual" theological resource but a "factual" historical resource.

The motives of many early Christians, he underscored, were questionable. The higher classes disbelieved in heathenism rather than truly believing in the Gospel, while the poor, "the almoners of Christ," were attracted by the flow of charity. During the third century the wealthy gradually withdrew from the communal *agape*, using the admonition of Scripture as their excuse; in reality their distaste for the lower orders prompted the withdrawal. And although the Church was not a respecter of persons, the upper clerical echelons were for the most part selected from the cultured and noble classes, since the influence of the upper strata of society would seep down more readily to the lower classes; the reverse situation, however, was not unknown. Christians, for the most part, seem unperturbed by the critique made by pagan culture. Philosophy seems no real threat and the popular accusations—Baring-Gould is especially fixated on the charge of the cannibalism of children—are ignored.[103] The only threat is an occasional outburst of mob violence, which is met passively by the Christians. Sometimes, according to Baring-Gould, it was met with duplicity and no little show of worldly wisdom: a Christian seeing the mob approach set before his door a statue of the Good Shepherd and a votive lamp. The mob was fooled into believing it was Mercury and left the household unmolested.

Christians, then and in the nineteenth century, the author observes, can be woefully ignorant of much of Christian belief. In a delightful, almost comic touch, Baring-Gould as narrator mentions a recent trip to Nîmes to see the present-day churches of St. Baudille and Ste. Perpetue. He asked the attendant sacristan at one church for information about the martyrs. The attendant could only reply: "Mais, monsieur, qui sait?" Christians, however, are generally characterized by a certain plain and simple form of discourse and address; the character Callipodius is identified as a nonbeliever because of his exaggeration and flattery in address. There are also differing attitudes among Christians concerning persecution. The rich for their part try to avoid confrontation with the pagans, since a general persecution would "break up families, arouse . . . passions, and, above all, disturb business." The deacon Baudillas tries to avoid the persecution. He is the kind of personality who is "thrown into helpless incapacity when undirected by a superior mind or not controlled by a dominant will." He is, in fact, in the author's view, representative of the vast assortment of the common crowd. But the author, in examining the doubts and hesitation, frailty and indecision of this reluctant martyr, underlines the basic dignity and integrity of common humanity. Baudillas reflects, "If I were to fall [apostasize] it would be a shame to the Church of God in this town." Baring-Gould is not Georges Bernanos and Baudillas is not the country priest, but the Victorian sense of duty (or negatively phrased, pride and ego) rising above personal doubt is here skillfully and subtly introduced.

Contrasted to this simple sense of office and integrity is the other deacon, Marcianus (the name may be meant to recall the bold heretic Marcion), who decollates the cult image on his own initiative, thus unleashing the popular persecution of the Christians. In the amphitheater, after an initial show of boasting, his courage collapses, and he makes himself a laughingstock as he hastens to offer incense rather than *festinat ad martyrum*. He is devoured by a "monster wolf" just as he denies Christ. Marcianus is the exemplar of the Christian moved by private judgment, pride, and contempt for his fellow Christians, despite the proscription of Scripture ("When they persecute you in one city—fly to another!") and the instructions of the bishop. Baring-Gould is directing the attention of his Victorian readership to their own affinity for private judgment over Scripture and the episcopate in an age when other wolves were waiting.

The novel concentrates on martyrdom and conversion. One would expect, given some precedents in this genre, something other than the very careful and circumspect treatment of saints, martyrs, religious language, and miracles that one does find. But that very shift in attitude gives us some sense of the particular viewpoint of Sabine Baring-Gould and members of the Anglo-Catholic party late in Victoria's long reign. Various canonized saints and eminent ecclesiastics are used as references: Clement of Alexandria (d. ca. 215), the great Christian Platonist and apologist to cultivated society; Ferreolus of Vienne (d. 304), a tribune (his escape from prison and eventual beheading parallel events in the story of Baudillas); Sidonius Apollinaris, the Gallo-Roman aristocrat and bishop of Clermont (ca. 469); Venantius Fortunatus (540–600), sometime bishop of Poitiers and the great hymnographer; Gregory the Illuminator (ca. 240–332); Theodoret (d. 466), bishop of Cyprus, the Syrian theologian and historian; Eulalia of Merida (d. 303), whose story was used for Perpetua; and Prudentius (ca. 348–ca. 405), hymnographer and cultist of saints and martyrs. They are a limited choir of authorities but form a list reflecting Baring-Gould's various interests. The author finds no problem mixing historical and fictional characters. But he is especially circumspect in handling religious language. Christian poetry and hymnody, as well as preaching, were often marked by "extreme" language, highly colored and provocative, at least to nineteenth-century Anglican sensibilities. Often in the course of the century Anglo-Catholic clergy were criticized or ecclesiastically disciplined for nothing more than repeating the language or imagery of the early Fathers: St. Cyril of Alexandria's rhapsodic vocabulary, used to describe the real presence in the Eucharist, did not sit well with most churchgoers. Anglo-Catholics were, with a few radical exceptions, careful to avoid such usages, while still agreeing with the doctrine or sentiments expressed. This "reserve" was necessary because the English Church did not yet possess to the full that ethos which enlivened primitive Christianity. The High Church party was particularly afraid that "advanced" language, borrowed from the Fathers, would provoke rejection of or hostility toward specific doctrines or practices thus described; its rejection of the language would mean a denial of the apostolic doctrine and the authority of the Fathers. Baring-Gould illustrates this in an exchange during a eucharistic service. A Christian had composed a poem in honor of St. Andeolus, the subdeacon martyred under Septimus Serverus at Vivarais. Bishop Castor admonishes the poet and the congregation: "[A] poet in treating such subjects should restrain his too exuberant fancy, and not assert as facts matters of mere conjecture, nor should he use expressions that, though perhaps endurable in poetry, cannot be addressed to the martyrs in sober praise. The ignorant are too ready to employ words without considering their meaning with nicety, and to quote poets as licensing them to do that which their pastors would forbid" (*Pp*, 100–101). This is also, of course, part of the Anglican case against Roman Catholicism, especially the Italianate form of piety associated with F. W. Faber and some other Anglican converts.

Miracles are discussed with precisely that same discretion. The escape of Baudillas from the Roman prison (*robur*) is explained, not by a miracle, but by a "rational explanation." The records of early martyrdoms are examined objectively to reinforce this point. "The simplicity of the Acts of the Martyrs, the stiffness of style, the absence of all miraculous incident, did not suit the taste of medieval compilers, and they systematically interpolated the earlier Acts with harrowing details and records of marvels" (*Pp*, 303). It is not difficult, Baring-Gould further states, to distinguish the genuine from the fictitious in such records. The Acts, then, are accepted as authentic documents, which are established by modern critical methods, focusing on style, form, and philology. The position expressed here is overtly rationalistic: the authenticity of the Acts is proved by the absence of miraculous incidents. Comparing various third- and fourth-century Acts, such as the *Acta Scillitanorum,* the *Acta Perpetuae,* or the *Acta Crispinae,* whose texts were more and more assessed and catalogued by various scholars, the author accepted the absence of miracles as normative for this particular literary genre and constitutive of the belief of the Early Church. This ties in closely with his earlier discussions of the simplicity and plain style of early Christian discourse. It also reveals a sensitivity to the argument of historicism. Early Christians, in taste as well as conviction, were significantly different from the medieval compilers who doctored the earlier records. Baring-Gould does not push this point further in order to characterize the religiosity of the Middle Ages; it is enough for him to point out the dramatic divergence of the two periods. The problems of evidence and rational assessment of these documents is not as easily solved as he implies; detailed study still occupies scholars.

Having constructed, in his estimate, a case for the Early Church's strict controls over the credulity of the pious masses, and at the same time establishing his own credentials as a critical, scientific investigator, Baring-Gould rounds off his martyr's tale with a miracle. When Perpetua is executed in the amphitheater, a snowstorm, a "mighty wonder," covers the arena with a veil of innocent white. He uses as his historical references the incidents surrounding the later martyrdom of the child St. Eulalia of Merida, Spain, under the Illyrian Maximian, Diocletian's colleague, in the general persecution, beginning 23 February 303, and material in a hymn by Prudentius. He is not repudiating his earlier position or even demonstrating the kind of ambiguity about miracles demonstrated in other Anglo-Catholic authors. The storm is treated as circumstantial evidence: a natural event that by its timing and location, as well as the faith of the assembled observers, points to the understated working out of providence in human events. The "mighty wonder" is not so much the physical element, although this is a necessary anchor in history, as the internal impression on the faith of the believer. Anglo-Catholics by the end of the nineteenth century had interiorized their religion; the "evidences" of Christianity were not less certain or sure by making them preeminently internal evidences. The pillar of fire by night and the cloud by day still kindly lead the believer's unsure steps.

In his novel *Domitia* (1898), completed the year following *Perpetua*, many of the same themes recur; the references or allusions to Victorian taste and civilization are, however, less oblique. The story concerns Domitia Longina, the daughter of Anaeus Domitius Corbulo and Longa Diulia, enamored of Lucius Aelius Lamia and served by Eboracus the Briton. Corbulo, whose sister was wife of Caligula, a virtuous Roman general much concerned with the formation of conscience, is ordered to die by Nero for jealous motives. Domitia, living only for vengeance, meets the Stoic philosopher Claudius Senecio (Spernologos), the Chaldean magus Elymas (Ascletarion), and the physician of Troas, Luke, her introduction to Christianity. After Nero's death she is forced to marry Titus Flavius Domitianus, about whom she has been warned in a vision and who abducts her. The emperor causes the death of Lucius, driving Domitia insane. She recovers enough before her death to embrace Christianity, "the Daylight of the Soul," encouraged by the example of Domitian's cousins, Clemens and his wife Flavia Domitilla, and her own maid Glyceria.

The pagan Corbulo, who believes that a woman is never bad unless shown the way by a man, is concerned for conscience and its formation in his daughter. That is the "light" he commands her to follow wherever she finds it. It is only in following that light that she can find happiness: *ubi lux—ibi felicitas*. Domitia, on the other hand, is concerned with the foundation and sanctions of morality: "Of what avail is a good life? What motive have we to induce us to lead it?" (*D*, 48). Philosophical or cultic responses to the problem of mortality (immortality is seen as a necessary precondition of any moral system) are inadequate. The solutions "at which the minds of the great thinkers of the East have arrived" were, in fact, "no more than a guess." The assurance that her father will have a kind of immortality "on the page of history" prompts Domitia to retort: "First assure me that the page will be written, and that impartially." Devoid of the knowledge of life's purpose, its obligations, and its destiny, "like matter uninformed by Life," she follows an "unaccountable impulse" to address Luke. The physician tells her: "No certainty can be attained, in all these things man desires to know, the basis of hope, the foundation of morality, that cannot be brought out of man. It can only be known by revelation of God" (D, 50). Christianity is not foreign to man's true nature; the impulse of man's internal conscience, discerning truth from falsehood, is already divinely formed in humanity. Revelation brings "light" to that conscience, "the eyes" of the soul. Simply put (and it is significant that one can phrase it so succinctly), Christianity means trust in God, His revelation, and the goodness of mankind. That tripartite creed defines and constitutes the summum bonum, in the author's words. Domitia sees this creed in action in the lives of Glyceria and Flavia Domitilla, who are directed in this unwritten, unarticulated "rule of faith" by "the Spirit that is within." They are instructed by Scripture (the rolls of the Law and the prophets, like the psalms and an epistle of John, are read in Church, emphasizing the origins of the service in the synagogue) and directed at times by visions (Glyceria in rapture beholds the stigmata of Christ), but the primary note struck is the metaphorical one of light, by which the believer beholds the divine face to face. For the Anglo-Catholic of the late Victorian age, Christianity had been interiorized; moreover, in developing an apologetic stance, opposing various philosophical schools and cultic eccentricities, the Christian creed has been focused on fundamental truths ("Trust God, His revelation, and the goodness in mankind"), interpreted optimistically (see the stress on "trust" and "goodness") against the fatalism or pessimistic determinism of the age, against which writers such as Chesterton also later reacted.

There are many other points of correspondence between the two novels, but we should consider the various ways in which *Domitia* is addressed specifically to a Victorian audience. The vocabulary and references used are a good indication: "cheap and nasty," "fops," "crackers" meaning insane, "tarry soldiers," "Jew rag-and-bone men," "jobbers," "push" meaning ambition, the importance of the "discharging of duty," a comparison of Wagner's operas, all place the novel squarely in the late

Victorian period. The initial inspiration for the novel itself is a product of a visit to Italy made by the author; in the Chiaramonte Gallery of the Vatican Museum he saw an "exquisite" bust of Domitia Longa as a girl and a second in Florence showing the same subject aged and hardened after her marriage to Domitian. This use of classical artifacts, parallel to the use of archaeological discoveries and surveys, is characteristic of novels of this subgenre in Victorian literature. Another feature of this literature late in the reign is frequent reference to Britain and its culture during classical times: belief by Britons in a "death ship," British oysters, a necklace of pearls from the River Severn, British war chariots, British ballads in Celtic, as well as British characters. In some novels, especially juvenilia, the British Isles become the center of the action; this is a later development of the novel, attuned to the growing power and historical significance of the British imperium.

The Victorian fascination with spiritualists, occultists, and astrologers is depicted by Baring-Gould with the characters of the Roman dame Longa Diulia, whose almost mechanical epigrammatic, decadent wit indicates she is the direct offspring of Oscar Wilde's Lady Bracknell, and of the magus Elymas and his clairvoyant Helena. "It was now fashionable to dabble in sorcery, and a distinguished lady liked to be able to talk of her Magus, to seek his advice, and, at table, air a superficial familiarity with the stars, and the Powers and Aeons, the endless genealogies of emanations from the primieval and eternal light" (D, 96). Being familiar with the "wonderful vision" of a "christian seer," Elymas uses his crystal ball to forecast the future for Domitia in terms of the beast with seven heads. The images of the first half of the novel, thus, focus on Nero. The historical figure is seen as the archaesthete, surrounded by an "Augustal band of 5000 youths with flowing locks and gold bangles on their wrists," and as the apocalyptic figure of Revelation, Antichrist, the "new Nero" resurrected in Domitian. This reintroduction of apocalyptic imagery, introduced at one level in terms of Domitia's future and her dabbling in the occult, may suggest at a deeper level a reappearance of tension and concern for the end time that infected the Victorian psyche after the Diamond Jubilee and before the momentous turn of the century, intensified by the unsettlement of the numerous crippling workers' strikes and later by the draining Boer War (1899–1902).

Christian artifacts—a lamp, a fish medallion, a statuette of the Good

Shepherd—are the instruments for instruction in Christian belief. The statuette of the Good Shepherd is described from a second-century model in the Lateran Museum. The narrator, striking a familiar note, concludes, "It is an error to suppose in early Christians a complete emancipation from old usages and modes of thought" (D, 165). But even this usage, vindicated by that historical awareness, is purged of any taint of idolatry. Baring-Gould is especially concerned with the use of cult images; in this novel a pagan statue is beheaded by lightning, calling to mind the incident in *Perpetua*. Glyceria the Christian declares, "Oh Lady! it is only so much His image as the words Good Shepherd written in characters are such, they call up a notion and so does that figure. But in our worship we have no images, no sacrifices."[104] This attitude also explains the satire employed in relation to relics. Simon Peter's former jailor runs a profitable market in relics: "I have the chain whereby he was bound, and I sell the links, to the followers of the Nazarene. . . . But any bit of old iron will serve, and they are not particular" (D, 324). At the same time, Baring-Gould has shown the veneration of images and collection of relics to be present at the earliest age in the Church, while decrying the pagan background of the one activity and the credulity exposed in the other. He develops the argument further for use in the continuing polemic against the Church of Rome:

> Nothing so completely differentiates Christian worship from that of Pagan Rome as the congregational character of the former contrasted with the uncongregational nature of the latter. At the present day in Papal Rome the priests may be seen behind glass doors in little chapels annexed to S. Peter's and S. Maria Maggiore saying their offices, indifferent to there being no laity present, indeed, with no provision made that they should assist. This is a legacy of Pagan Rome. (D, 125–26)

Not all pagan religious culture or Christian borrowing is condemned. The college of Vestal Virgins, who had for 1,150 years, from 753 B.C. to A.D. 394, played an important religious and social role in Roman society from their cloister in the Forum, are seen as the prototype of the religious communities in convents, abbeys, and collegiate buildings of Christendom. Theirs, however, was a paganism purified, chastened, and locked inextricably into the cult of the State and the maintenance of civic virtue and morality. His laudatory mention of the lady abbess, Cornelia, may be a reference to the famous case of Cornelia Connelly, which fifty years before had rocked England.[105] All in all, however, Baring-Gould held that the apologetic needs of Christianity demanded elimination of credulity and superstitious customs in order to extract Christianity from association in the popular mind with other forms of religious enthusiasm. This had been a problem for intelligent converts in the first age. "There were old prejudices to be overcome, there was the consciousness that the promises so largely made by the votaries of the many cults from East and South who came to Rome were unfulfilled, and this made her [Domitia] unable to place confidence in the new religion held by slaves and ignorant people, however alluring it might seem" (D, 332–33). The "brotherhood of Poverty" could also prove an obstacle in the conversion of the upper classes, but the fundamental need was to show that Christianity was reasonable, attuned to human nature and the best instincts of conscience, virtue, and duty. It was distinguished from philosophy and Eastern mysticism by its historical guarantees, its promise of immortality, and the self-authenticating power of its revelation.

Baring-Gould's novels, besides highlighting his own antiquarian and artistic interests, are representative of several shifts that mark Anglo-Catholic thought late in Victoria's reign. While acknowledging Catholic faith and tradition as the "scarlet thread" uniting every historical period, he is interested in using his picture of the Early Church as part of a larger apologia for Christianity to his late Victorian readers. The distinguishing note he extracts from his study of antiquity is that Christianity is *contra mundum*, opposed to the standards and values and powers of the age and opposed by them in turn, in what is sometimes depicted as an apocalyptic tension. Christianity itself, however, was, as Richard Hooker taught, attuned to the basic nature of man: philosophy and the higher religions evolved by man's noblest instincts are rightly considered providential preparation for the coming of the Christian revelation. Finally, Christianity has been interiorized, nurtured by a community but supported internally by visions and the working of the Holy Spirit. Rationalism and mysticism coalesce. Although Baring-Gould is easily distinguished as a Ritualist by the precision of his technical references to liturgical and ecclesiastical matters, the basic creed he presents—belief in God, immortality as the basis of morality, the unique efficacy of Christian revelation, and the optimistic estimation of human nature—cannot be distinguished from the presentation of Christianity by the Broad Church party. At the turn of the century Christianity itself, not the Anglo-Catholic party, was in the dock.

MRS. JEROME MERCIER

Anglo-Catholic novels were closely linked to other types of religious literature produced by that party. Pamphlets, prayer-book commentaries, and confirmation-class manuals used many of the same historical sources as the novels, and they contained similar arguments about issues that had vexed the novelists.

Borrowing George Herbert's maternal imagery from "The British Church" in *The Temple*, Mrs. Jerome Mercier provided in *Our Mother Church* an annotated commentary on the Prayer Book and services that was also a key to church history, ancient and modern.[106] Written in the form of a fictional dialogue between the Anglo-Catholic Mrs. Askell (modeled on Charlotte Yonge) and Joan Leslie, her niece, Mrs. Mercier addressed those girls who like Joan "knew nothing about her own Church, its history or principles, and in this was like nine-tenths of all English school-girls." Recognizing that ignorance, Mrs. Askell advises her niece to "look back at the Church of the first three centuries as to a model of tried and perfect faith." Although the Church "lost her first purity" under Constantine, her virtue spread. Like other Anglo-Catholic authors, Mrs. Mercier is concerned with the history of the undivided Church up to the eleventh century and the era of Hildebrand.[107]

One consideration in this historical schema is the Anglican acceptance of the General Councils of the Church, extended by Anglo-Catholics to recognition of the first six. That recognition of conciliarism, albeit ambiguously worded to avoid conflict with Article XXI, is used to underscore recent "errors" of Rome: "The first four of these Councils are recognized by the English Church, and the last two are also generally reckoned with them, as having uttered wise decrees led by the Spirit of Christ. . . . The effort made by the Pope to summon such a Council in 1869 was futile, as only the Roman branch of the Church was properly represented there."[108] Skirting the issue of the authority or infallibility of such a General Council (only the approved Councils "uttered wise decrees"), the authority of the Vatican Council is undercut by the important Anglo-Catholic understanding of the branch theory. Mrs. Askell explains that

> "separation came, and we have now three great branches, Greek, Roman, English or Anglican. But remember, there are not three Churches, a Greek, a Roman, and an English. . . . They are three branches of one great tree—or tree of life." "But our forms of worship are so different from theirs." "They are different, but the differences consist chiefly in errors which crept into the Roman branch, and which still do not prevent its being a true branch of the Church; and partly in omissions of our own which it would be well to remedy. . . . You will see that our English Church goes straight back to the Apostles' time; and as they derived their laws, their forms, their prayers, in many instances, from the Jewish Church, so we pass back into the patriarchal days. The Patriarchs and all the Jewish Church had a saving faith in Christ as the Messiah who was to come, and thus in some sense were of the one great Catholic Church to which we belong." (*O*, 5–6)

Several familiar Anglo-Catholic themes are struck here. Rome had fallen into error by the accumulation of certain doctrines and practices evident in its liturgy, errors which are not sufficient, however, to unchurch that body. No similar evaluation, one must note, is made of the Greek Church. Second, several Anglican "omissions" need to be remedied in order that its full status as a branch of the Catholic Church might be evident. Third, the prophecies, types, and symbols of the Jews are fulfilled and explained in the Christian Church. This connection is explicitly made in discerning liturgical practices; the author includes a comparative list of usages of the Church under the one covenant with two dispensations. Attention to such Jewish roots and the historical forms of the other branches of the Catholic Church is a typical Anglo-Catholic point, differentiating that party from the isolationism of the old-style High Church wing. For Mrs. Mercier, "such considerations help to enlarge our views, to free us from the cold, lifeless way of thinking that we English people owe all, even our Church, to ourselves, and are able to stand by ourselves. Never was a more fatal idea" (*O*, 21). On the other hand, she is careful to maintain a via media, neither approving nor disapproving too much differing usages. Anglican "omissions" are insufficient grounds for secession. "To some these differences seem so important, and our forms so excellent beyond parallel, that they despise the other branches of the Church; some find our ways so unsatisfactory when they differ from the rest that they must needs join another communion, in order to remedy our defects. Both are wrong" (O, 39). Implicit in this rejection of secession is the belief in the need for the Anglican Church to restore ancient doctrines and practices that are both emblems of and aids to a spiritual ethos. It is this very ethos, this "sense" quite different from subjectivity concerning Catholic truth in its beauty, order, discipline, doctrine, objectivity, and devotion, that brings Joan a clearer vision of the Mother Church: "She had begun to feel her ignorance. The mere beauty of the Church constantly before her eyes (so different from the base classical manner of those she had seen before) had worked its way into her heart like a poem, making her feel that in the very lines of its building there must be a meaning deeper than she understood. Her aunt's devotion had had the same effect: its freedom from self-assertion, its manner of clinging to some strong support without herself."[109]

By the late 1870s such manuals of instruction, written in part as guides for confirmands and Sunday School teachers, had become commonplace. These companions and commentaries, both for the preparation of the clergy and for the instruction of the laity, provided handy tools for the study of theology, church history, and Scripture especially, although frequently not representative of up-to-date scholarship. This genre of ephemera has gone unnoticed because of its rank below the first-class theological works of the age and its rank above the more intriguing and colorful tracts and pamphlets (although it could compete with such productions in tendentiousness, fissiparousness, and party spirit). Examining the list of suggested readings provided in Mrs. Mercier's key, the student of this literature learns what a widely read Anglo-Catholic laywoman of this period judged essential topics for her readers' attention and what sources informed her work. Various histories of Christianity are included, covering the period from the Early Church and the Fathers through the Reformation. This typical Anglo-Catholic stress on history is extended to a parallel enterprise, the lives of the saints. Besides the Anglo-Catholic R. W. Church's *Life of St. Anselm*, one finds the tremendously popular *Life* of Francis of Assisi (1870) by Mrs. M. W.

Oliphant, a work that signaled the immense interest of Victorian Protestants in a saint so much in contrast with their age.[110] There are suggested
readings also on the Prayer Book, the Holy Bible, church architecture,
art and music, devotional works, and readings "For the Poor," mostly
sermons and extracts to be used by parish visitors ministering to the sick
poor. The authors cited make up an important list of Anglo-Catholic
clergy who produced historical popularizations and intended scholarly
works addressed to an eager audience.

Mrs. Mercier's little list, however, is significant beyond providing
that information. First, Anglo-Catholics are not represented alone there
or in her text. For example, the Broad Church dean of Westminster, A.
P. Stanley, is one source quoted. The Low Church clergyman W. H. B.
Proby is another. Party affiliations and platforms were not as rigidly conceived in the decade of the 1870s. Disputes between parties were very
much ad hoc. In fact throughout the reign there was more cooperation
between persons of divergent labels than is usually recognized. Second,
the works listed, distinct from the works cited in the text, were for the
most part produced after 1850. This is understandable, since a distinct
Anglo-Catholic position on the range of topics mentioned had not really
coalesced until after that date and had not spun out from clerical circles
into programs of parochial evangelism. This manual also presents a strong
claim of being very much "up to date." It is remarkable, however, that in
the area of Church history the often cited works of Tillemont, Fleury,
Ruinart, even Gibbon, which had been the staples of earlier Tractarians,
are neglected here, perhaps because of the audience addressed. But there
are not even recommendations to consult the sources provided in the Library of the Fathers, nearing its completion during this decade. Only secondary works, commentaries, and lives are recommended. Mrs. Mercier
herself had used older sources—especially Joseph Bingham, whom she
terms a "dear old big fellow" (Bingham's work was available, however,
in a nineteenth-century edition), and collections of liturgical material,
such as Thomas Brett's collection (1720). Third, with the possible exception of Bingham and Henry H. Milman, dean of St. Paul's, the historians she includes, like the writers on Scripture, are far from the first rank
of native or foreign scholars whose works would have been available
to an English audience by the 1870s. Like Milman, those included are
basically Church of England clergy, some of eminent station (Edward

Burton, Regius Professor of Divinity at Oxford, is one example), who wrote historical studies of primitive Christianity and its texts. The names of Baur, Lightfoot, Hort, Westcott, Freeman, Stubbs, Driver, and any number of other eminent scholars are missing. Again, one could explain this absence by the audience at whom Mrs. Mercier aimed or by the reticence of church groups generally to accept biblical or historical criticism until the late 1880s and early 1890s. It could be that Mrs. Mercier herself was of such a conservative temper that the absence of such "scientific" works by professional historical and biblical scholars is explained. Indeed, her use of conservatives such as Dean Burgon indicates this. What is significant, however, is that in a generation that increasingly insisted on such professional and scientific expertise, Mrs. Mercier, along with other Anglo-Catholics, was satisfied with the literature produced by "nonprofessional" clergy and laity.

An examination of such popular, at least accessible, histories might tell us much about the historical interests and methods of churchly writers in the middle and late Victorian periods. It is clear from the evidence that the distinction between professional and amateur was not very strong, nor would those who can be termed amateur parson-authors admit engaging in anything less than "scientific" history. Indeed, Mrs. Mercier places herself in the tradition of scholarly historiographers. Straight historical narratives dealing with early Christianity, sometimes penned by novelists, had gradually become the vogue. The call for scientific history, more distinct from imaginative reconstructions, was one cause. The development of the novel itself, aiming more at the need for entertainment or psychological interests sought by the reading public and therefore turning away from the footnoted, doctrinally packed examples of an earlier day, is another cause. The distinctions between history/historiography and imaginative reconstructions—that is, fiction—continued for some time to be vague.

Mrs. Mercier's guide to doctrines and practices, it should be remembered, appeared in a fictional framework. As a literary device, such a blending had had a long history, and Mrs. Mercier's career as a novelist was a further factor in this interchange. It may be suggested, however, that a theological point, rather than a purely literary one, lies at the basis of this blend of fact and fiction. The young girl in the story is attracted to church principles not only by the physical fabric of her parish church but most importantly by the example of the devotion, discipline, obedience, knowledge, and personal subordination of her aunt. She is drawn by the holy place and the spiritual ethos nurtured there. This viewpoint, drawn from Johan Adam Möhler's works *Die Einheit in der Kirche* and *Symbolik*, which W. G. Ward and Frederick Oakeley had impressed on J. H. Newman—the Church cannot be evaluated from outside but only by those corporately experiencing its doctrine and discipline within—passed down to a later generation of Anglo-Catholics. Mrs. Mercier's manual of Church principles is not presented as a flat textbook of rules and regulations but in terms of the lives of Church members and the personal, spiritual relationships of two in particular. She is carrying out in this example the basic purpose that prompted her elsewhere, along with other authors, to depict the Early Church at once both in a history and in a novel.

While each novel considered above is readily distinguished from other examples of the genre, even other Anglo-Catholic examples, a certain general position emerges. A great deal of the interest of this ephemeral, often second-rate, literature is due to the occasional character of its creation. As we have seen, the novels, more than just a general program of using history for dogmatic exposition, addressed or reflected very specific issues and events in the institutional and intellectual life of the Victorian Church. The peculiar interests and attitudes of the various authors determined the subject matter of the novel and the points at which the connection with contemporary, disputed questions emerged. On the other hand, there was enough agreement on certain issues, or certain motifs were generated consistently enough, to argue that a definable Anglo-Catholic position is presented in the novels. Underlying this was a generally accepted attitude, shared by more than just Anglo-Catholics, that these novels were not merely antiquarian exercises. In their temper and purpose they shared much with the state-of-England genre of literature that arose about the same time. They had something to tell the British nation, whether sitting in Parliament or kneeling in the parish "pue."

A basic point of agreement was that the Church of England needed to rediscover its roots as a "divine society" and to assert its status as one of the three existing branches of the Catholic Church. The note of apostolicity and the Anglican understanding of the Vincentian Canon express this assertion. Rome grew on one side of this trunk of the undivided

Church of the first eleven centuries. The authors are sympathetic to the Roman Church, recognizing their connection through Anselm and Augustine of Canterbury, but they are careful to express reserve toward, if not condemnation of, popular Roman practices and the Tridentine system. Much of that system is seen as a residual accumulation of pagan cultic practices or superstitions. In distinction, then, to Roman Catholics, Anglicans are "Holy" Catholics. The Eastern Church was a recognized "tag" of Anglo-Catholicism, as shown above. Anglo-Catholics were often suspected Russophiles in the period of the Crimean War.

The Fathers of the Early Church are present in the novels as characters or sources demonstrating the ethos of the primitive Christian community. They and their teaching are used, not as a source of authority in themselves of specific doctrines or practices, but rather as proof that those doctrines and practices existed at the earliest stages of the history of the Church. One would be right to claim that the Anglo-Catholic novelists did not intend to re-create the church and ethos of the Fathers but rather the church and ethos of the apostles, from whom the earliest Fathers derived their doctrine and usages. This at least is how Victorian Anglo-Catholics applied Butlerian analogy to argue from an early age to the earliest. It is interesting to note that a certain "canon" of Fathers appears recurrently in these novels: Cyprian, Augustine, Cyril of Alexandria, Clement of Rome, Ignatius of Antioch, and Irenaeus are the most commonly cited. This could be due to the identification individual Fathers had with important doctrinal or ecclesiastical questions that vexed the Victorians (such is certainly the case with Cyprian and Ignatius) or because of the limited number of works available beyond this stellar ring of ancient authors. That limitation, especially in terms of Greek Fathers, affected the novelistic enterprise at just the time when English theologians were decrying the unavailability of a broader range of patristic sources. The nineteenth century witnessed a growing interest in the subtle, high voice of Origen, beyond the deep, familiar admonitions of Augustine. The Anglo-Catholic novelists used the collections and commentaries compiled in previous centuries, especially by the Maurists, but their children turned more and more to histories and translations produced during the historiographical flowering of their own time.

The ethos that the Anglo-Catholics wanted to suggest and not impose found expression in various ways. The liturgical and sacramental systems were dominant concerns. The ancient roots of the English liturgy were traced in detail. Ritual and ceremonial were connected intimately to the historical defense of the Incarnation, linked to the office of the bishop, the observance of the Lord's Day, and the sacramental channels of grace. The special character of the Eucharist emerged. The Eucharist was presented as the real presence of Christ, distinct from transubstantiation, consubstantiation, or the Zwinglian commemorative rite. Christ is portrayed as the eternal high priest, making a perpetual offering of himself as victim on the spiritual altar in heaven. This idea, adapted from the Caroline Divines and Non-Jurors and traceable back to Socinian sources, was a central element in the synthesis of sacramental theology worked out by R. I. Wilberforce and preserved by other Anglo-Catholic writers. The link to the Incarnation and the power of the Holy Spirit are other elements treated.

Similarly, the penitential system of the Early Church, if not sacramental confession and absolution, is depicted. It is carefully distinguished from the "mechanical" system of penance in the Middle Ages. The authors unanimously maintain the doctrine of baptismal regeneration, supporting this with the formularies and tradition of the English Prayer Book. Although most of the novels deal with Christianity antedating the major credal formulations, references in those works underline the importance of the creeds and early "rules of faith." The defense of the creeds, especially the Athanasian Creed and its role in the Prayer Book, was an emblem of the Tractarians. It is a distinguishing point, separating them from Evangelicals and Broad Churchmen, who either stressed Scripture alone as regulative of faith or who pushed for a more "poetic" understanding of creeds. The attack on the Athanasian Creed, from Lord Russell's suggestion in 1848 that it be dropped altogether to Archbishop Tait's suggestion in Convocation that it be interpreted outside its "natural sense," rallied the disparate groups of Anglo-Catholics and conservative churchmen of other parties. Since the novelists treated the period before the establishment of the canon of Scripture, the reader finds mention only of parts of the Old and New Testaments. Rarely is a text apart from those in the canon treated as revelatory; the Book of Enoch is one such exception. In line with general Anglo-Catholic principles, the Fathers and creeds teach and interpret, but Scripture proves. Revelation is in that sense primary, although the fragmentary corpus available to early Christians restricts the role it plays. The novelists defend the linkage of

Old and New Testaments, most significantly, by the modality of prophecy. There is only one covenant. The types, symbols, and prophecies of the old dispensation are fulfilled and explained in the new dispensation. Even pagan prophecy is accepted, although it is clearly held to be providential and not evidential.

Despite the credulous predilection of many Anglo-Catholics for fantastic or picturesque legends of the saints, the attitude of the novels toward saints and martyrs, both historical and fictional characters, is strictly governed within the context of the Prayer Book. The questions of the invocation of saints and intercessory prayer are more problematic and not treated sufficiently to make a general characterization. Holiness, purity, and perseverance through tribulation, major Tractarian motifs of moral certainty, provide iconographical tone to the portraits of the "saints." Miracles too are treated with some hesitancy and ambiguity. Authors may enumerate definite guidelines, sometimes approaching a purely rationalistic stance, as the basis of their evaluation of ecclesiastical miracles, while at the same time reproducing traditional tales that seem to eclipse those rules. Scriptural miracles in particular are not questioned, because of their intimate link with the person and work of Christ and the fulfillment of prophecy. To discard the Old Testament, or any part of it, they felt, would shake the foundations of Christology.

The relation of Christian Church and Roman State is an important, if not always developed, focus of attention. Christianity is an *imperium in imperio*. Most Anglo-Catholic novelists treat only the period before the accession of Constantine (313) and the establishment of Christianity (381). They look to the transformation of Christianity from persecuted minority to favored majority as a disadvantage, although there is no direct argument for disestablishment. The civil government of the pre-Constantinian State ranges from a neutral stance toward Christianity to one of active persecution. The Church is portrayed as a sacred society having its own rulers (the episcopate) and a tightly and elaborately developed organization that is part of its strength against the worldly power.[111] Following the model of the Non-Jurors, the Anglo-Catholics described their understanding of the interiorized nature of the primitive church. It was a shadow society of the State, conformed by absolutely passive obedience to that State in all civil questions. Time and again the private and corporate prayers of Christians for the emperor and the State are sworn, despite the general Christian refusal to offer incense in the formalistic imperial cult. The Anglo-Catholic novelists as a whole neglect to draw any far-ranging conclusions from those instances of the social accommodation of Christianity to the pre-Constantinian State which their narratives document: service in the military, policing the provinces, holding public office, familial and social connections with the imperial family. Emperors are judged by their attitude toward Christianity: Titus, Philip the Arab, and Antoninus Pius receive the accolade of "godly" magistrates. The persecutors—Valerian, Decius, and Diocletian, for example—are stereotyped villains. Nero emerges late in the century, the decade of the Wildean decadents, as the arch aesthete, while earlier he is pictured in terms derived from apocalyptic literature.

If we consider the State from the religious side, early Christianity is opposed by the philosophical, intellectual culture on one level and the mass, popular, cultic paganism on another, just as it was confronted by all levels of material culture in late antiquity: customs, recreations (particularly the gladiatorial games), manners, and social relations. Christianity appears *contra mundum*, against the highest and lowest standards and values of classical civilization. Romanticism has frequently been termed an extended reaction to the French Revolution, which identified itself at several points with classical antiquity, especially Roman Republican culture. These novels present the reader with a further, obsessive reaction to that antique culture. That response is conditioned by complex factors, not the least of which is the hidden agenda of the novelist intent on preaching to his or her own age. Various schools of pagan thought are directly or indirectly identified by analogy with Victorian intellectual currents or groups. Classical philosophy, usually Stoicism or Neoplatonism, is seen as no more than a preparation for Christianity. One after another school is discussed, presented to the hero, and found dissatisfying. In this double education of hero and reader, we are led to surmise just how threatening philosophy, especially the two groups mentioned, was for Christianity in both historical eras.

The Victorian Church was sharply challenged by the "revival of pagan ethics and the destruction of faith in the unseen."[112] This passage of the hero from one philosophical position to another is a mark of the late Victorian historical novel in which the hero moves toward a definition of his or her own identity. Fleishman, discussing this motif of a journey as a spiritual quest for which *Marius the Epicurean* is the prime example, isolates three important strains in the late Victorian imagination—"religious doubt, the quest for spiritual discovery, and the rage for Italian culture"—and recognizes the difficulty in distinguishing such works from the novel of religious history, with which we are concerned. His stress on the prominence in the former of the inner life, apart from public incident and historical circumstance, is certainly one significant difference. In terms of the Anglo-Catholics treated here, however, the fundamental status of philosophy is critical. Unlike in novels such as *Marius*, nowhere in these works is philosophy seen as a challenge to Christianity or even as a satisfactory stage in moving to something higher. Christianity is not presented as a more fulfilling philosophy. While attuned to man's nature and reason, it is in the last analysis compelling because it is a divine revelation. The content of that revelation, as we have seen, by the end of the Victorian era mirrored the apologetical stance of Christianity to secular society in terms that were compact and yet broadly theological: the existence of God, immortality, the formation of conscience and the call of duty, and the optimistic estimation of human nature.

On the other hand, the presentation of popular paganism gave the Anglo-Catholic authors an opportunity to draw analogies with contemporary religious groups, weighing their caricaturizations—if not cartoons—with a wide range of propagandistic techniques. The Broad Churchmen and Evangelicals find themselves in Roman garb; the connections between paganism and the Romanist system are similarly drawn. The Victorian penchant for Eastern sages, occultists, and astrologers finds historic, and at times comic, precedents. A pantheon of cultic deities and rituals is presented, but pagans on this level are seldom individualized. They are the mob, *profanum vulgus*. The life they have flows from the historical experience of the nineteenth century, the popular risings and rebellions, prompted by epidemics, famine, economic disaster, as well as the mass fear and hysteria typical of such social unsettlement after the French Revolution and the revolutions of the 1830s, 1840s, and 1860s. In one way, then, the stereotyped response to Christianity and the standard form of accusation—cannibalism, infanticide, asinolatry, and witchcraft—can be seen by the modern reader as a deep psychological transference in an age of anxiety from one cultic community to another, both of which shared a mutual ignorance of the other group. The novelists do not treat this or the significant charge of atheism as the basis for the unpopularity of Christians. They never attempt to understand the roots of these pagan sentiments. These charges appear only as a stereotyped list. Applied to the Victorian context, the novelists seem to hold that the Anglo-Catholic form of Christianity is misrepresented and ridiculed by just such misinformed masses. In the same way that the *disciplina arcani* of the ancient church contributed to such misunderstanding, so the Anglo-Catholic principle of "reserve" led to similar accusations.

The Jews presented a different set of problems. Basically, messianic Judaism is defended and rabbinical Judaism is condemned. The late Anglo-Catholic novelists maintained the necessary connection between the Old and New Testaments and the theological understanding of one covenant with two dispensations that was part of the English Reformation tradition restated in the eighteenth century by H. Prideaux among others. The continuity of the covenant is also preserved in the rituals of the Church.[113] Judaism is a preparation for the Gospel such that its types, symbols, and prophecies are fulfilled in the Church, not extinguished. The rabbinical commentaries, translations, and texts, however, have subverted the clear application of the messianic passages to Jesus. Their rejection of allegorical interpretation for literal modes, passed down to modern Jews, is another evil feature. Beyond this understanding of Jews in the Victorian religious context, the figure of the Jews in the novels indicates other concerns. The Jews are the type of those "judaizers" (a label sometimes conversely attached to the High Church wing) in the Church of England who reject a high view of the Eucharist. This is a carryover, certainly, from the charges against the Jewish-Christian Ebionites and their rejection of the divinity of Jesus.

In another area, the depiction of the Jews in these novels is often the point at which apocalyptic imagery and themes appear. The reemergence of such a theme during several Victorian crises has been mentioned above. Several sources may be suggested: (1) Scripture: The Book of Daniel, whose historical validity E. B. Pusey labored to establish with what must be termed precritical results, was one often quoted source. This work was read, however, basically as an exposition of the theory of the four world empires. The Apocalypse is another source, which must have attracted considerable attention by Anglo-Catholic Ritualists because of the liturgical material present, although 2 Peter is never cited. (2) Patristic texts: In the works of various Fathers cited, especially in the

West among the Latin-speaking authors, apocalypticism recurred well into the fifth century. (3) *Acta:* The victorious agonies of the martyrs are another important font of this motif. This identification between Victorian Catholics and the martyrs is, as we have seen, an often ignored aspect of nineteenth-century spirituality. (4) Evangelical texts: Through sermons and pamphlets, characterized at times by fierce rhetoric, apocalypticism kept a foothold in the Victorian religious scene. The political schemes involving a British presence in the Levant had at their root such apocalyptic expectations. (5) The Napoleonic era: E. P. Thompson described millenarian prophecy and activity among the lower classes following the 1870s. R. A. Soloway has demonstrated that such prophetic speculation was more pervasive, affecting all levels of society. Even staunch High Church spokesmen—for example, William Van Mildert (1765–1836), later bishop of Durham (1826–36), whom Newman mentions in the *Apologia* as a major influence at Oxford—looked for "the approaching close of the Christian dispensation." Apocalyptic prophecy was often mixed up with conspiratorial theory and counterrevolutionary activity. It might be suggested that these attitudes did not die with "the vile Corsican." Whenever hysteria or actual revolution broke out, men looked once more for conspiracies of *illuminati* or the coming of Antichrist, threatening altar and throne. (6) Tractarian sources: Tract 1, written by J. H. Newman, exhorted the episcopate and presbyterate to prepare to suffer martyrdom in the eventuality—seemingly a real and present danger—that the alliance of throne and altar would collapse and a new persecution engulf the Church. Other Tractarian sermons employed imagery taken from apocalyptic sources, in which the role of the Jews in the events of the end-time were crucial. Unlike in France and on the Continent, which in the aftermath of the Dreyfus affair and the genocidal horrors of the twentieth century have witnessed the production of scholarly work examining popular anti-Semitic literature and movements, very little has been done to dissect similar tendencies in late Victorian England. What saves the Anglo-Catholic novels from the anti-Semitism of other examples of the genre is, perhaps, the highly developed sense of the continuity of the two dispensations under one unbroken covenant and the interest in the ancient ritual roots of the Anglican liturgy.[114]

Roman history and culture are the framework of the external world in which these theological and, sometimes, psychological turnings occur.

The Catholicism presented in such historical fiction differs widely, in both substance and author's intention, from the Catholicism of Gothic fiction, where the very obscurity of Catholic doctrine and ritual stimulated an eighteenth-century concern for the "sublime," "religious awe," and "melancholy sensibility." Roman society, in turn, provided the mise-en-scène that the earlier novels created through the Catholic materials.[115] The precision of technical language; the often more than mere potted history given in summaries of classical literature, philosophy, and religion; and the delineation of social customs, art and architecture, manners, employments, and characters point to a renaissance of classical learning in the Victorian period. There are important reasons for this emergence in the Victorian novel. (1) Eighteenth-century examples of this genre provided a model that was all but canonized in Bulwer-Lytton's immensely influential *Last Days of Pompeii*, especially significant for his placing a Christian community in Pompeii, a point that still vexes modern investigators. Thomas Moore's *The Epicurean* was another early influence. (2) Related to the earlier examples and Lord Lytton's work is the wider archaeological undertaking. Begun in the eighteenth century and taken up in the style and affectations of French Republicanism, archaeologists in Italy renewed their efforts with growing interest in the century of the Grand Tour and middle-class travel. English visitors joined the parade of kings, princes, popes, and czars to the sites. The novels chronicle the tremendous impact that various discoveries enjoyed. (3) The long descriptions of Roman households of various social ranks tie into the literature of domestic manners inundating the Victorian home, concerned with greater efficiency and organization. The descriptions of palaces and imperial luxuries fit into the silver-spoon variety of literature. The domestic model of an antique house exhibited at the Crystal Palace (1851) was an epoch-making event. With this understanding, critics may have to revise the estimate of the significance of the progression of a Roman character like Marius between the House of White Nights, the Aurelian palace, and Caecilia's house-church. A succession of domestic settings characterizes most of these novels, although the structures are not imbued with the personality Pater created. In particular, we might suggest, the view of Christian households owes much to the several "resort" houses that shelter Bunyan's Pilgrim on his journey; these houses are ultimately derived from the descriptions in the Book of

Acts. (4) Victorian educational practices, with their overwhelming stress on classical learning, must be seen as another factor in the use of a Roman framework. The technical precision of the military, bureaucratic, and political vocabulary, parallel to the Anglo-Catholic precision in doctrinal and ritual references, shows the pervasiveness of classical study. (5) Christian social theory, the role of the church in society and against society, is another source. Behind this is a long tradition of the theory of empire. The detailed picture of class relationships emerges from this historical framework suggesting more than mere atmospheric staging for an inward drama. No link is made by the novelists between the religious and social revolutions occurring; both seem to have a discrete existence. Christian attitudes toward the poor or the laboring poor are summed up in Philemon 12–16 and the ritual kiss of peace extended to slaves by masters. In the novels there is more of John Keble on social questions than Thomas Arnold. But there are definite strains of social concern that develop during the century; one can see marks of that development in the late works of Charlotte Yonge.[116] (6) Eighteenth-century parallel lives and histories, comparing various European nations and ancient Rome, were part of the literary canon. Although it is not explicitly stated in Gibbon's *Decline and Fall* (1776–88), such a reflexive comparison between Rome and Britain is created indirectly. But in the nineteenth century the romantic "ruins of the Capitol" that transfixed Gibbon were just as easily associated with decadence, immorality, and satanic persecution of the saints. (7) The existence of this genre of fiction, recognized as a distinct genre with many foreign and domestic examples, was in itself reason enough to explain repeated use by various authors.

From a purely literary view, none of the novels discussed succeeded in one important historical task, important at least to modern taste: recreating a genuine sense of the *romanitas*, the complex Romanness, of their characters, especially the imperial figures. That quality is found somewhat in Pater's *Marius* and more evidently in our own century in Yourcenar's Hadrian and Malouf's Ovid.[117] Luckily, our task is not to isolate such an authentic sensibility but rather to observe, in Kingsley's phrase, those Victorians in toga and tunic promenading the *via antiqua*.

4

"WHAT THE APOSTLES SAW"

Evangelical and Broad Church Novels

THE PERIOD FROM 1859 TO 1901

THE PERIOD FROM 1852 to 1859 in British history is generally referred to as the Age of Equipoise. For the churches, however, it was a time of turmoil during which the equilibrium of forces between Voluntarism and Establishment underwent critical tests.[1] The Gorham decision, the revivification of Convocation, and the prolonged debate over the Erastian relationship of Established Church and State, hinging on the demand for a spiritual court of appeal, provided the context for a wide range of controversial issues affecting not only Evangelical, Broad, and High Churchmen but also Nonconformists, Roman Catholics, and Jews. The Irish question held over from 1845, regarding the continued government subsidy of the Catholic seminary at Maynooth as a step to eventual endowment of Roman Catholic clergy, had a tangled political history.[2] Further incensed by the Ecclesiastical Titles Act of 1851 and the widespread anti-Catholic riots in England, those in Greenock and Stockport from 1851 to 1852 in particular, Irish Catholics sought to draw blood by politically assaulting the Church of Ireland.

Dissenters, as well, added their support to bills for the disendowment of the Church of Ireland as a test case for Voluntarism. The Religious Census of 1851, still regarded as a controversial report, strengthened the Nonconformist position and resulted in a number of bills to ease their political and religious disabilities: repeated measures for church-rate abolition, reform of religious instruction in schools and of the Establishment control of that system, the Burial Act of 1857 to permit the interment of Dissenters in the parish churchyard, and the proposed Oxford Bill of 1854, removing subscription to the Thirty-Nine Articles for Dissenters intent on university training, are some of the more prominent features of that political agitation. Liberal Dissenters, however, could display as much anti-Catholic fervor as Church of England Evangelicals. A number of societies formed to meet the supposed popish threat: the Scottish Reformation Society (1850), the Protestant Alliance (1851), composed of liberal Dissenters, the Scottish Protestant Society (1854), and the Tory-Erastian membership of the Protestant Association were assembled to combat popish advances, not only from Papal Aggression but also from within the English Church.

The Denison case on eucharistic worship (1853–57) and the similar prosecution in 1860 of Alexander Penrose Forbes, bishop of Brechin; litigation prompted by the revival of Anglican sisterhoods contemporary with the refoundation of Roman Catholic religious orders for women; and in the late 1850s the active prosecution of Ritualist clergy under A. C. Tait, bishop of London (1856–68), focused ultra-Protestant aversion to what was regarded as renewed popery.[3] The *Protestant Magazine* in 1857–58 claimed, as Machin's study of politics and the churches notes, that the Indian Mutiny was a divine plague visited upon England for its national toleration of pagan idolatry abroad and "popish superstition" at home. When agitation for Jewish relief culminated in Lord Russell's introduction of an Oaths Bill in 1857 to seat Jews in Parliament, a fierce debate over what was regarded as a threat to the Christian character of the nation found Jews and Roman Catholics closely compared by Anglican and Dissenting opponents. That Protestant identity of the three realms was also a principal bulwark of the revived Sabbatarian movement, brought into the national debate by plans for the Sunday opening of the Crystal Palace, the National Gallery, and the British Museum, a debate punctuated by frequent riots.

These controverted religious issues continued to foment division in the Church and nation during the 1860s. The split between Church and Chapel intensified in this decade, since it seemed to the contestants that the further extension of parliamentary democracy necessitated the dismantling of the Church Establishment. The ultimate disestablishment of the Church of Ireland in 1868 under Gladstone's government further divided religious groups. Archbishop Tait, for example, opposed it, while other Broad Churchmen supported this parliamentary action, including F. D. Maurice, Charles Kingsley, and Benjamin Jowett. The general consensus about religion had not radically changed, but an altered view of the constitutional relationship had emerged based on a developing understanding of the rights of conscience, the duty of toleration, and equity in justice.[4] The more open arena of religious discussion permitted spokesmen of religious doubt, agnostics, and free thinkers to be heard: no-religion laid claim to the rights of religion before the law.

In this decade, called by commentators the Age of Doubt, new factors were introduced into the popular debate following the publication of John Stuart Mill's essay *On Liberty* (1859), Charles Darwin's *Origin of Species* (1859), the biblical and historical criticism of *Essays and Reviews* (1860), the literature in the Bishop Colenso controversy over the historicity of the Pentateuch and biblical cosmogony (1862), and W. E. H. Lecky's intellectual history *Rationalism* (1865). Of these specific examples, *Essays and Reviews* and the Colenso affair had the most immediate effect. The Broad Church dons who channeled a moderate rendering of modern biblical criticism from the Continent into the slim volume of *Essays* and the missionary bishop of Natal were heralded alternately as demons or deliverers, shaking or preserving the foundations of biblical faith and revelation.[5] It was not until the period from 1887 to 1896 that there was widespread acceptance of biblical criticism by the churches, an acceptance that caused Fundamentalist and Modernist splits in various denominations. While the detailed working out of the implications of Darwin's theories for a natural history of the development of religion took some time to emerge—hindered by Darwin's own reluctance to make such applications—early on, the debate over science and religion found adversary champions such as T. H. Huxley and Bishop Samuel Wilberforce for the respective sides, as well as Broad Church mediators, who, whether they opted for apes, or angels as Disraeli did, were still solidly Anglicans.

The 1870s, a decade opening with the fall of the French Empire at Sedan and the rise of a German Reich, proclaimed at Versailles, and a Kingdom of Italy installed on the Quirinal, exemplify the divisive forces in European history and thought, pulled between claims of political and religious authority and greater personal freedom. The thunderous proclamation of Papal Infallibility in 1870, seen by many as the antithesis of freedom of thought, was met by Bismarck's *Kulturkampf* and ecclesiastical division on the Continent, by the assault upon "Vaticanism" in Britain, incongruously led and given status by Gladstone, and by numerous popular outbursts. The closing years of the previous decade had united religious and political zeal. The work of the Protestant Evangelical Mission and the Electoral Union, pressing for repeal of Catholic Emancipation, played a direct role in Fenian risings, such as the Murphy Riots of 1867 in the Midlands and those in Lancashire in 1868, renewed in 1874.[6] The Public Worship Regulation Act (1874) capped the popular movement against the introduction of popery into the life and practice of the English Church by Ritualists. That legislation was the government's attempt, urged by the queen herself, to end the "zoo and horror" of bloody riots in Ritualist parishes. At the same time a more expansive understanding of religion took root. The School of Theology at Oxford was opened in the 1870s, dedicated to a "scientific" study of that discipline. An Anglican moderating theology was structured there by S. R. Driver, T. K. Cheyne, W. Sanday, E. Hatch, and C. Gore, instructing a new generation of scholars and clergymen. In the Cambridge School, the earlier theological work of Herbert Marsh, Bishop Thirlwall, Julius Hare, F. D. Maurice, and Dean Alford of Canterbury, who introduced German thought to many, often suspicious, English readers, culminated in the historical and scriptural work of the theological triumvirate B. F. Westcott (1825–1901), J. B. Lightfoot (1828–99), and F. J. A. Hort (1828–92).

Max Müller, who delivered the prestigious Hibbert lectures in 1877, began publishing in 1879 his fifty-volume *Sacred Books of the East* in order to broaden the popular view of the nature of religion in general and Britain's own religious tradition in particular.[7] However, work in comparative religion raised serious questions about the finality of Christian revelation and prompted comparisons between contemporary religious history and the influx of oriental cults into the Roman Empire. An illustration of these open questions early in the decade can be seen in the heresy trial of the Reverend Charles Voysey from 1869 to 1871; clergy like Voysey, as well as agnostics and free thinkers, seriously reexamined their understanding of original sin, the Atonement, the divinity of Jesus, and the reliability of biblical sources, especially as new texts were discovered and new translations of Scripture were undertaken.[8]

In the 1880s and 1890s an anxious, even desperate, quest for authority emerged, ending in submission to the Bible and the Bible alone, or the hierarchical Church, or mystical experience, or the dearly bought integrity of a personal creed. Many currents of thought were channeled to relieve the religious drought. In 1890 William Booth's *Darkest England*, a play on H. M. Stanley's contemporaneously published *Darkest Africa*, introduced a social-gospel message in domestic missions as the kernel of primitive Christianity, reacting against the barren intellectualism of so much theological discourse. Beginning in the 1880s, a major interest in mysticism developed at the same time that statistics for the British and European churches began their downward curve, evidenced by the drop in members for ordination and church attendance. What has been called the search for the "childlike in religion," seen in the late Victorian cults of St. Francis or Thérèse of Lisieux, can be judged as a return to radical simplicity and a supposed primitive immediacy in the religious experience.[9]

Evangelical and Broad Church writers of Early Church novels, beginning with few exceptions in the 1870s, used this genre to address the pressing questions of the day. Although George Eliot found earlier examples of Evangelical fiction "vulgar," their emphasis on the personal and the importance of inner states of feeling, the deep conviction of human depravity and individual sin, the explicit accounts of repentance and conversion, and the tales of philanthropy, saintliness in the observance of ordinary duty, and missionary fervor, all recounted without reserve, provided possibilities for the Victorian novelist despite Evangelical scruples over the literary enterprise, possibilities exploited by Eliot herself in *Scenes of Clerical Life* (1858).[10] The debate over the "Higher Criticism" led inexorably to questions about the original and continuous witness of the written records of Christianity; the Protestant doctrine of plenary inspiration of Scripture appeared especially vulnerable. The Coleridgean dictum, stated boldly in his *Confessions of an Enquiring Spirit* (published posthumously in 1840), that the Bible must be read as any other book, proved a challenge during a time when vocal antagonists to the Church sought to use biblical criticism to bring down the walls of Christianity and some Churchmen used the same scholarship to cement the tottering edifice. Churchly novels, displaying a variety of responses to critical questions, were compelled to show precisely how in individual lives the Bible was to be understood as the word of life about sin, conversion, and salvation. Although there were a number of biblical conservatives such as E. B. Pusey, the new generation of Anglo-Catholics, especially the *Lux Mundi* group, appeared less shaken by the critics because their doctrines of Tradition, the Church, and the Sacraments were essentially distinct from the various points under attack, especially the Reformation stress on inspired Scripture alone. The rival Anglican schools represented in the novels ignored that developing Anglo-Catholic stance toward Scripture and focused only on older disputes: Ritualism, asceticism, and sacerdotalism.

The earlier Tractarian appeal to the Church of the Fathers lost much of its power. W. K. Clifford, a former Anglo-Catholic who died in 1879, asserted: "The spirit of the Fathers has incontestably faded. The days of Athanasius and Augustine have passed away never to return. The whole course of thought is flowing in another direction." He suggests, in a significant turn of phrase, that in order to tap Christianity's power one has only to abandon the dead letter of ecclesiastical historians and instead to "apply the exclusively moral tests which the New Testament so invariably and so emphatically enforces."[11] The Gospel can produce no false conclusions; Christian moral teaching is all that matters and is a saving antidote to the pure rationalism of W. E. H. Lecky, T. H. Huxley, Herbert Spencer, and Leslie Stephen, who have made the nation "Strauss-sick." Evangelical and Broad Churchmen did not abandon the Church of the Fathers entirely. They continued to use specific Fathers in their fiction, albeit a shorter list than Anglo-Catholic authors used; but they restored to its primacy and centrality the "primitive Church," by which they meant the Church of the apostles, the apostolic Fathers, and the Apologists. Implied in this displacement is the notion that corruption infected the Early Church, at least by the second century, dragging it down through history until the restoration of all things in the Reformation.

If the Church of the Gospels was reinstated as the model and guide for Victorian Christianity, the figure of Christ assumed an effulgent headship as the result of study of the early community. Rival Churchmen had pushed the Anglo-Catholic appeal to the doctrine, personalities, and ethos of the Church of the Fathers back to the Gospels and Acts.

In the same decades other voices questioned the "truth" of just that primitive Christianity, not the Athanasian Creed or the Fathers but Christ himself. Mrs. Humphry Ward remembered that Walter Pater in 1873 shocked the clerical guests at a dinner party by declaring that no reasonable person could govern his life by the actions and opinions of a man dead 1,800 years.[12] The attacks had initially come in the context of biblical criticism in reference to belief in New Testament miracles, linked inextricably, some thought, to belief in the miraculous person of Jesus Christ. The naturalistic argument against the sheer possibility of miracles and Humean skepticism about the probability of recorded instances coalesced with wider arguments about the trustworthiness of the documents. By a kind of special pleading, Anglo-Catholics argued that the continuous oral tradition about the divine Person of Christ precluded any difficulties dependent on texts and their transmission. But for most Anglicans the questions could not be so neatly evaded. The picture of Jesus in Scripture was also linked to varying attitudes toward the Scripture writers. St. Paul in particular was seen from different angles, either positively or negatively, as a proto-Protestant or a crypto-Catholic, the conduit of theories of justification and predestination or of Hellenistic mystery religion. St. John and the Johannine Christianity of the Fourth Gospel were used by rival schools as a restorative and alternative to Pauline extremes. The multiple lives of Jesus and St. Paul developed those several perspectives.[13] Paul makes a relatively early entrance into British novels, but it is not until the 1870s that Jesus steps, however meekly, into Victorian fiction. The general interest in the lives of Christ by D. F. Strauss and Ernest Renan, upsetting to Evangelicals, and Anglo-Catholics alike, coupled with extensive interest in the geography and culture of the Middle East, was served by numerous tourist guides and collections of photographs.

The development of historical study went hand in hand with the quest for the historical Jesus. This quest included several aspects often overlooked by scholars but represented in the novels of the period. The element of the apocalyptic was important throughout the era but especially as the century ended. The theological essays in *Foundations* (1912), a collection in the tradition of *Essays and Reviews* and *Lux Mundi*, paid special attention to apocalypticism in recognition of Albert Schweitzer's scholarly work. Connected to this eschatological tension in the novels are three interrelated questions: the continuing role of the Jews in salvation history, either introducing a different perspective on Scripture or playing a role in the arrival of the Last Days; the present danger from Roman Catholic encroachments in Britain, seen in terms of the coming of Antichrist and the premillennial battle; and the special, almost messianic, role that the British nation was called upon to exercise against the Beast "drunken with the blood of the saints." As the English Bible underwent revision in 1881, recognition was given at an earlier date to Jews in their opposition to the "mathematical" Bishop Colenso's critical work on the text of the Torah.[14] Concern for the role of the Jews in Parliament and the nation, Russian pogroms during the 1880s, and an emergent Zionism contributed to lifting the British Jew out of the stereotype of rag-picking denizen of Whitechapel and into the historic costume of Philo, Josephus, or Bar Kokhba.[15] Dispensationalist theology continued to look with growing expectation to the conversion of the Jews as a sign of the Second Advent. Various organizations and their publications carried on this work: *Trusting and Toiling on Israel's Behalf: The Organ of the Mildmay Mission to the Jews* (begun in 1896); *Jewish Intelligence, and Monthly Account of the Proceedings of the London Society for Promoting Christianity amongst the Jews* (1835–60; new series, 1861–84; new series, 1885–92), continued in *Jewish Missionary Intelligence* (1893–1946); *The Jewish Advocate for the Young* (1846–54), *The Children's Jewish Advocate* (1855–64; new series, 1865–79), *The Jewish Advocate* (1880–92), and continued in *The Jewish Missionary Advocate* (1893–1919). The image of the persecuted Jew—resonating with the history of the Inquisition—became, especially after the popular success of Eugène Sue's anti-Jesuit work *The Wandering Jew* (1844–45) and the reactions to the later proceedings of the Dreyfus affair (1894, 1899, acquitted 1906), an effective part of anti-Catholic propaganda.

It was ironic that the figure of the Jew would play such a role, because a number of Evangelicals and Broad Churchmen denounced Roman Catholics and their Ritualist imitators as "judaizers" in practice, substituting ceremonial for the Gospel and Christian morality. The uproar over the Vatican decrees was only one aspect of the growing concern about the Roman Catholic presence in Britain, as that number was swollen by immigrants. Waves of anticlericalism abroad also helped create this atmosphere. In 1874 the marquis of Ripon resigned his office as grand master of Freemasons in Britain following his conversion to Roman Catholicism. The 1870s saw two former Anglicans created cardinals and resident in England. Surely, it was felt, the Reformation faith and the Gospel were everywhere threatened. That papist threat was often expressed in the Early Church novels in terms of St. Augustine's mission to Kent. His name is a shibboleth representing either the last impulse of pure Christianity or the precursor of long-continued papal usurpation. In the latter view, Augustine's insistence on sacerdotal authority, idolatrous images and invocation of saints, confession and absolution, eucharistic devotions, and alleged miracles was in fact a restored paganism. John Bunyan's identification of the pope and the pagans in *Pilgrim's Progress* was presented in various permutations demonstrating the continuity of paganism in the modern worship and culture of papal Rome. While free thinkers charged that Christianity enslaves, antipapists blamed such bondage on the Vatican and the dogmatism and infantile credulity of pious Catholics.

This system of slavery could be overthrown only by a British Empire scripturally reinspired. The arguments about the exact date of the foundation of Christianity in Britain involved the assumption of Rome's apostasy from a scrupulously scriptural faith. The various suggestions for a founder of truly British Christianity—Simon Zelotes, St. Paul, Aristobulus, Claudia Rufina, St. Philip, Joseph of Arimathea, or King Lucius—demonstrate attempts to make claims about the apostolic, rather than Roman, tradition of the Anglican Church.[16] True Christianity, some writers insisted, was not only anti-Catholic but also ante-Catholic, predating Rome's gradual corruptions. The salvific role of the nation, depicted graphically in the contemporary republication of John Foxe's *Book of Martyrs*, likewise drew upon a sizable literature demonstrating the superiority of the English race. While Darwinism per se does not enter into the novels, there are repeated appeals to racial classifications and to an implied social Darwinism of hereditary gradations in society. The Teutons, Goths, and Anglo-Saxons, who assume the best qualities of the Greeks and Romans, are viewed as superior to the nations and peoples physically descended from those classical cultures; ranked further down the scale in differing arrangements are the "debased" Celts, Slavs, Huns, Jews, Turks, Arabs, and Africans. On the Continent this appeal to an Aryan "pure race" was being developed after 1850 in the works of

Bogineau and Herrenroth, among others. Anglo-Saxons, or the equivalent among Germanic tribes, are seen as aristocrats or as the counterpart
to a rising, although deferential, middle class. Other races are identified
with the lower orders.

There was some division among various novelists about how to
evaluate the withdrawal of Roman legions from Britain. Some national-
ists viewed this as a historical analogy to the shaking off of Roman
shackles in the Reformation. But after Edward Cardwell, the Whig-
Liberal secretary of state for war, engineered in 1868 the gradual removal
of British colonial forces from overseas dominions, some felt the passing
of a certain imperial glory. Insularity could be seen with very different
feelings; in that tradition Rudyard Kipling wrote his nostalgic *Recessional*
in 1897, the year of Victoria's Diamond Jubilee.

EVANGELICAL AND BROAD CHURCH NOVELISTS

In 1900 (American ed., 1901) the Reverend George Croly's (1780–
1860) oriental romance of the Fall of Jerusalem and the legend of the
Wandering Jew, *Salathiel* (written in 1828), was republished. The pub-
lisher's notes make it clear that increased interest in apocalyptic literature
was the cause for the reissue. In an introduction to the American edition,
Lew Wallace, who had concocted his own version of the Wandering Jew
legend in *The Prince of India; or, Why Constantinople Fell* (1893), called
Salathiel one of the six greatest novels ever written in English literature.[17]
The story of the Fall of Jerusalem was a popular one in novels of the early
Victorian era; the episode was celebrated in poetry as well, for example,
Croly's own Byronesque "Last Days of Jerusalem," William Words-
worth's "Song for the Wandering Jew," and Henry H. Milman's sequence in 1839, "The Fall of Jerusalem." By 1900, however, interest in
this historical event increased with renewed apocalyptic speculation.[18]

Croly, ordained in the Church of Ireland and presented to various
livings in England, was a frequent contributor to the *Literary Gazette* and
Blackwood's Magazine, in which his theological and literary work merged
with his social commentary. His book *The Apocalypse of St. John* (1827;
3d ed. 1838) was a treatment of Scripture as a detailed prophecy of the fall
of the Roman Church and the Inquisition, heightened by events following the French Revolution. In *The Englishman's Polar Star* (1828) he

related the Apocalypse to the British nation, aiming to create and direct politically maneuverable sentiments about the danger of Catholic Emancipation. Popery was Antichrist and, like the political claims of the Jews, a threat to the nation.[19] His pamphlets and sermons—*England, the Fortress of Christianity* (1839) and *The Bible, the Restorer of Christianity* (1849)— reflect a wider feeling in the country after 1835, the tercentenary of the translation of the whole Bible into English, that the Protestant nation and the Bible were the only remaining bulwarks against papist and Jewish encroachments and conspiracy. The later interest in *Salathiel*, though shorn of the specific political context of its authorship, retained a general connection to Croly's apocalyptic speculations.

Constructed with the opulent Romanticism of Byron (who called him "the Reverend Rowley Powley") and Moore, *Salathiel* derives its power from Croly's use of fanciful, even terrifying, situations and what has been called his "rude eloquence." The story purports to be a memoir of the sixteenth-century Venetian Jew Salathiel ben Sadi, who was cursed for unbelief by Christ on his way to Golgotha and condemned to "tarry" on earth until the Second Coming, an ironic choice of words that recalls speculation about the death of the apostle John (John 21:22). A prince of the tribe of Naphtali, Salathiel (his name means "He who calls upon God," one of the seven archangels who guided Adam and Eve and was described in Jewish apocalyptic literature) is identified by Wallace in his introduction with Israel, parallel to the corporate identification of the Suffering Servant in Isaiah. But Croly's perception is one of a dynamic, one could say demonic, individual who, after the Fall of Jerusalem, wanders through the world seeking the ruin of Rome. He stirs up Alaric and leads him "to the rock of Rome"; he "pour[s] ambition into the soul of the enthusiast of Mecca"; he inspires "a bold Genoese" in a voyage of discovery. At last he is able to find a worthy avenger: "At the pulpit of the mighty man of Wittenberg I knelt; Israelite as I was, and am, I did voluntary homage to the mind of Luther" (*SW*, 533).

The pagan empire of Rome is seen in terms of buffoon courtiers and dandies, Regency figures trading in "curls and calumny," who are "prey to tailors." They are clustered around Nero, who is seen teaching a parrot to speak Greek. Epicureans fulfill the expectation of indolence, and a Stoic is labeled as little more than a "teacher of dancing" who has risen "into the easier vocation of philosopher." The seeker after truth samples this diverse array: "He might spread the philosophic wing from the glittering creations of Grecian metaphysics, to their dark and early oracles in the East; or, stopping in his central flight, plunge into the profound of Egyptian mystery, where science lies like the mummy, wrapped in a thousand folds that preserve the form, but preserve it with the living principle gone" (*SW*, 24). Salathiel learns, without accepting it, the message that Christianity is not a philosophic dream but a divine command: "It is not a call to the practice of barren virtue, but a declaration of reward mightier than the imagination of man can conceive" (*SW*, 165).

Judaism, on the other hand, is seen as a hodgepodge of bigoted and feuding parties, brought to ruin by the "polluted license of . . . their factions." The ecclesiastical groups he describes and condemns are, of course, closely associated with certain tendencies in later Christianity and modern Roman Catholicism. Those who defiled the Temple, defile the parish church and cathedral close. Eleazor, a convert to Christianity, describes the abomination in the sanctuary: "Its courts filled with those impious traitors to the spirit of the law, those cruel extortioners under the mask of self-denial, those malignant revelers in human torture under the name of insulted religion, whose joy is crime, and every hour of whose being but wearies the long-suffering of God and precipitates the ruin of my country" (*SW*, 41). Jews are not, however, merely figures for other religious groups or adherents of an antique and distant culture; they are the impoverished inhabitants of the modern metropolis: "The name of Jew is now but another title of humiliation. Who that sees that fallen thing, with his countenance bent to the ground and his form withered of its comeliness, tottering through the proud streets of Europe in some degrading occupation, and clothed in the robes of the beggared and the despised, could imagine the bold figures and gallant bearing of the lion-hunters" (*SW*, 35). The modern Jew is thus displayed as a cautionary figure, his race reduced by divine retribution for the rejection of Christ. The glory has departed from Israel.

Salathiel, unlike Eleazor and other converts, is blind to the prophecies that the Messiah will be a suffering servant. The sacrifice of Christ is presented in a vividly symbolic scene. The high priest, having rushed back to the Temple from Calvary as if in panic, distractedly cuts the throat of a sacrificial lamb, a sin offering. Covered with the fresh blood, he rips back the outer curtain of the Temple to find the sanctuary veil rent in twain. Elsewhere, Christ is compared to the legislators, priests, moralists, sages, and conquerors of the nation. Croly asserts that the Christian claims about Jesus are impregnable, since Jesus himself had to undergo the constant scrutiny of the Jewish religious leaders: "He made His appeal to the Scriptures, in a country where they were in the hands of the nation. His miracles were brought before the eyes of a priesthood that watched him step by step; His doctrines were spoken, not to the mingled multitude holding a thousand varieties of opinion, and careless of all, but to an exclusive race, subtle in their inquiries, eager in their zeal, and proud of their peculiar possession of divine knowledge" (*SW*, 163). In effect, Croly increases the national guilt for the rejection of Jesus as the Messiah by showing the rigor in doctrine and scriptural knowledge possessed by the Israelites. Contrasted to the recalcitrant and unbelieving Jews are the compassionate and virtuous Christians, such as Miriam and the twenty-five-year-old Constantius, who resembles "Apollo" and who unselfishly rescues Salathiel from execution in Rome during the confusion of the conflagration there. These self-sacrificing individuals are also contrasted to the mob, ancient and modern: "The multitude that can still be set in motion by a wooden saint was then summoned by the stirring ceremonial of empire, the actual sovereignty of the globe" (*SW*, 145).

The powers and pomp of both Israel and Rome pale beside the "winged sons of Immortality," the angelic hosts who play a direct role in ordering destiny and the fall of nations. Visions re-create the sulfurous destruction of the cities of the plain. Epiphanies herald the "supernatural" fall of Jerusalem, forecast by meteors, lethal lightning storms, whirlwinds, showers of blood, a colossal ghost of the first Temple, and the sounds of the guardian angels of the city withdrawing. Predictions, based on a strict numerology, declare the exact time of the fall: the ninth day of Ab, the anniversary of the burning of the Temple by the king of Babylon and 1,130 years, 7 months, and 15 days from its foundation by Solomon. Spiritual gifts are poured out, even upon Salathiel: "As if the veil that separates the visible and invisible words had been rent in sunder, I saw shapes and signs for which mortal language has no name. The whole expanse of the future spread under my mental gaze" (*SW*, 3). Some of those gifts were part of the contemporary religious experience in England, demonstrated especially by the Irvingites: "I have seen men, once ignorant of all languages but their own, speaking with the language of every nation under heaven." Croly's own vision of the antagonism of Christianity with Judaism and classical philosophy and the eschatological pressure on history in the cosmic contest of Light and Darkness outlived the specific political and constitutional context that prompted his writing and was readopted at the century's close, when apocalypticism seemed once more an indispensable part of the Gospel message.

Charlotte Maria Tucker (1821–93), known by the initials "A.L.O.E." ("A Lady of England"), was the Evangelical author of over 140 books, published between 1852 and 1893, whose proceeds financed her charitable causes. Born into a family related to James Boswell, she observed leaders of fashion and society in attendance at her father's house, including the Duke of Wellington, Lord Metcalfe, and Sir Henry Pottinger. Having served as a regular visitor at the Marylebone workhouse in London, Tucker undertook the planning of missionary work in India and began the difficult study of Hindustani at age fifty-four. She arrived at Amritsar in 1875 as an independent member of the Church of England Zenana Society and moved the following year to Batala, northeast of Lahore, when she undertook her missionary work and the endowment of various schools, including a "plough" school for boys not yet Christians. She died at Amritsar in 1893 and was buried, according to her wishes, in stark simplicity without a coffin at Batala, although honored by a memorial brass at the Anglican Cathedral in Lahore.

In *Daybreak in Britain* (1880) Tucker relates the second-century story of Imogen, the orphan daughter of a British chieftain in Kent, who is Christianized by the missionary Alpheus and martyred by the "wolf-like" Druid priest Urien. This undisguised catechism, with chapter headings such as "What is the soul?" "Whom do we worship?" and "How came death into the World?" was, the author asserts, written as part of her missionary activity:

> This narrative, we may observe, was originally prepared with a view to circulation among the natives of the East; and an orientalism of style was therefore designedly aimed at, in order to introduce attractively passages of Scripture explanatory of the elementary doctrines of Christianity. The same qualities, however, that fitted it for circulation among the heathen abroad, qualify it also for the instruction of the masses in our own country and metropolis, who still require rudimentary knowledge of Divine things.[20]

Implicit is the ironic situation of writing for her missionary proselytes the story of Britain's own slow and painful conversion in antiquity and its need in the present day for reconversion. While many religious groups, especially following the Religious Census of 1851, publicly recognized the need for domestic missions, it was the Evangelicals who graphically contrasted the backward situation at home with missionary progress overseas. Britain was still seen, however, as a nursery for missionaries. The Christian Alpheus proleptically prays, "May this isle of the heathen, raised among nations, be blessed, exalted by the power of the Gospel, and herself, in future ages, send messages forth to proclaim through earth the glad tidings of salvation?" (DB, 70). One character exclaims that the spread of Christianity is evidence of a miracle. For Tucker, the missionary endeavor itself, quite apart from conversion statistics, is a "proof" of the Christian revelation: "A religion so holy must be from God; a faith which led a stranger to her race to forsake home and country, and all that he loved, to bear hardships and toils, brave suffering and death, that he might proclaim to the heathen a message from heaven, such faith could not spring from deceit" (DB, 49).

The Druid religion, priesthood, and even music are contrasted unfavorably to Alpheus' tidings. The harp song of Duw-Iou, the Druid deity, is discordant beside the mellifluous Christian hymn "Our God Is Love." Tucker does not approve of the nationalistic cult of the Druid, widespread during the late Victorian era and classically stated by William Blake in Jerusalem (1804). In that visionary song cycle the importance of Britain in sacred history is demonstrated by identifying Abraham as a Druid and the British Albion as a parent of Druids. Druidism or Bardism is called the patriarchal religion of ancient Britain, and migrating tribes are credited with founding Zion in Paddington.[21] The Druid priest, for Tucker, is a deceiving prophet who is a false guide in this world and, therefore, a totally unreliable one for the next. The basis of the Druid religion is a misguided asceticism, as in Anglo-Catholicism: "But to whom did he pray? Not to a God of mercy and love. And where was his holiness? Not in the heart. He knew not that neither fast nor sacrifice can take away sin; and that while others looked upon him as a saint, in the pure eyes of the Almighty he was a miserable sinner" (DB, 10). Tucker, who had withstood opposition to her missionary work because she was a woman, makes the hated Druid the chauvinist spokesman of a patriarchal order in society and religion: "Let woman tend the flock, and bring thatch for the roof, strike fire from the flint, and prepare the meal; she has no soul for the mysteries of religion; the low pool in the valley ascends not the mountain" (*DB*, 24–25). In an answer sounding like the response of the Syro-Phoenician woman to Christ, Imogen answers that even the low pool reflects the eternal stars.

Tucker uses nature as a manifestation of the Creator and a vestige of divine revelation, employing an allegorical method to discuss Christian doctrines. The relation of a stream and the open sea is seen as an allegory of life and the life of the immortal soul. Imogen's puzzlement over the presence of suffering and sorrow in the world, if God be truly love, is figured in her near poisoning by the venom of a dead viper in a stream. In response to a retelling of the story of the Fall and the natural depravity of Adam's race, the pagan girl inquires from her catechist, "What can we do to be saved?"

Alpheus, a Jewish convert from the land flowing with milk and honey, recounts the sacred history of the Jews and the bestowal of the decalogue, laying special stress on the proscription of idols, and then tells his own religious history. His dying sister, a convert, had urged him to "search the Scriptures for they testify of Jesus." He collected the Gospels and Epistles and compared them with the Hebrew Scriptures, "almost the complete Word of God" thus joined together. Old Testament prophecy, he discovered, was fulfilled in the New, like impression and seal. An overruling Providence placed a stranger at his door, who relieved Alpheus' last doubts by recounting the story of Paul. God had pardoned even the chief of sinners. After a year of testing Alpheus was baptized and, following further years of probation, appointed a preacher. His message is that Scripture alone proclaims "the teaching of God's Spirit." Penances could not wash away sin; the soul could not be preserved by tormenting the body, a concept seemingly shared by Catholicism and Eastern religions. God's law must be honored, but it could be borne by a substitute. Christ is that substitute, the Son of the most high God, himself very God and the only means of salvation. Mankind is washed in his precious blood, and our souls are redeemed from death; the debt has been paid and the punishment endured.

The Jews, a "nation chosen to watch over the light of truth in an idolatrous world," possessed in the inspired writings of the prophets exact details about the Messiah's family, as well as the time and place of his birth.[22] The pride of the Jews and their hatred of the "purity of His doctrine" obscured that picture, just as the pagans blindly worship idols of wood and stone. The message of Scripture, however, is clear and inspired, as Alpheus tells Imogen: "It is to thee as a buried treasure; and yet every word in these Scriptures is a life to the soul, every word has been dictated by the Holy Ghost" (DB, 63). The kernel of that message is "If ye love Me, keep My commandments." The tempest-tossed soul, like a bark on the ocean, must repent and believe; repentance means forsaking sin and faith means obedience to Christ's law. Faith alone saves, but it is "living faith, whose fruit is obedience and good works." The convert, first instructed in the Lord's Prayer, confesses sin, asks pardon, and prays for the Church and its persecutors. Baptism is seen as a means for the "soul newborn" to strengthen courage, increase faith, be marked as a servant of the Lord, and become a member of the Church. Although baptism confers an impression that believers bear forever, there is no sense in which it is discussed as a regenerative act. The Christian message to repentance and conversion is seen under the urgency of Christ's coming and the "solemn day of approaching judgment." Even the distant rumble of thunder could be the wrathful sound of his coming. Tucker's message to the world and to individuals is heightened by that expectation. The chieftain Vortimer rejects a final appeal to repent and dies unforgiven. Tucker suggests that millions who bear "the name of Christians" may in fact be lost.

The message of Evangelical novels did not change significantly after the mid-1870s.[23] Tucker's presentation of Scripture as the inspired law of God and a clarion to virtuous action, as part of her encapsulization of the Christian faith, has its roots in earlier Evangelical literature and philanthropic activity. But the portrayal of the "day-break" of the Gospel in ancient Britain, colored by her own missionary experience in India, attaches her novel to themes and concerns characteristic of the late Victorian age.

The prolific Evangelical novelist Emily Sarah Holt (born in 1836) composed her tale Imogen (1876) as a timely tract against Ritualism and the infallibility of the pope, "the Man of Sin." The novel traces the wavering fortunes of one British family from the withdrawal of Roman legions in

385 until the Synod of Whitby in 664. The fall of Rome to Alaric is also sketched. The author is more concerned, however, to show the contrast between the pure Christianity of the Early British Church and the corrupting and dissension-breeding variety imported in 597 by Augustine of Canterbury, the so-called apostle of England. The contemporary exaltation of Augustine's role, she finds, is part of the willingness of the English people to embrace or stoically endure the practices and claims of the Antichrist, foretold by "that sure word of prophecy which is the key of history." She continues:

> How otherwise can we account for men and women, gifted with ordinary intellect, believing that God is honoured by a system which seals up His revelation, and desecrates His day:—that Christ is honoured by a system which subordinates His divine fiat to the authority of His human mother's—that the Holy Ghost is honoured by a system which robes a foolish, fallible man or body of men with His prerogatives:— that the spirits of just men made perfect, are honoured by a system which would raise them to the level of Christ, and degrade Him to the level of them?[24]

The domestic story centers on the life of the holy presbyter Maur and his children, Brian, Imogen, and Nêst, and contrasts their pure brand of Christianity, centered on Scripture, with the Romanized variety of Childe Edric, the young husband of Imogen (a form of Innocentia), and his aristocratic Saxon family in Kent. A variety of Christians are represented: some who see Christianity as a supreme humanity, some who are able to blend supreme duty and supreme happiness in the tide of popularity, and some who are genuinely attracted by the central figure of Christ. One character, the princely Hrolf, whose daughter was baptized by St. Columba at Iona, is gradually led to Christianity by the Gospel, related to him by the patient Imogen, and lays down his life to rescue Edric. Christianity is seen as that kind of transforming experience, without connection to ritual or priestcraft.

Holt traces the introduction into Britain of this pure Christianity from "the far East," not from the Church of Rome, "but direct from the cradle of Christianity, the Holy Land." She discusses the historical probabilities of three major traditions: Pauline, Petrine, and Johannine. The

first tradition has the most numerous candidates as founder: St. Paul, per-
haps after a visit to Spain; Bran, the father of Caradoc and one of Paul's
converts; Eigen or Eurgain, the daughter of Caradoc and most likely the
Claudia Rufina referred to in 2 Tim. 4:21; or Aristobulus, the pupil of
Paul and companion to Bran. The legend of Joseph of Arimathea and
Mary Magdalene is dismissed as a "foolish story" and identified as a post-
Conquest fable. Petrine traditions about missions by St. Peter and Simon
Zelotes are next oldest in age to the Johannine tradition that Holt adopts,
citing the claim made at Whitby by St. Colman of Lindisfarne, whom
she identifies as an archbishop. Colman claims that the "Ephesine" tradi-
tion was a bar to conformity, a tradition uncontested by the Roman em-
issaries present. The total independence of the British Church from the
Roman was likewise affirmed in 179 by the recognition of the Celtic
King Lucius, the Lever Maur—"Great Light"—who was grandson of
Boudicca, by Pope Eleutherius (174–89) in the *Liber Pontificalis*. He was
seen as the British Church's scriptural head, since in the Bible every king
is the "vicar of God." This historical, papal recognition, she asserts, is a
stumbling block to the Infallibilists: "We are told in the present day that
the Pope is infallible only when he speaks *ex cathedra*. Bishop Eleutherius,
we may well suppose, was not seated in his chair of infallibility when he
sent this message to Lucius" (*I*, 11).

This church "from Immanuel's Land" is marked by total simplicity
and humility in liturgy and life. Maur's parish church contains only a
plain bench and table. There are no images or paintings (which are compared to the golden calf), no side oratories (i.e., chapels or chantries for
endowed masses for the dead), no painted pillars, banners, hangings,
crosses, lamps in broad daylight, or vestments of any sort. The bishops
and doctors of Britain are "clad in simple white robes" (the plain white
surplice of Evangelical parsons). The faithful memorize large portions of
Scripture, as if for a Sunday School prize. There is no kneeling, no joined
hands, no covering of the face, all of which are later Saxon customs. Britons pray standing with heads erect, faces lifted to heaven, and hands
spread forth, in the *orans* position. The entire congregation sings, as opposed to soloists or antiphonal chant by a trained choir. They have only
two hymns, instead of "the flood of the nineteenth century": the Te
Deum of Hilary of Poitiers or Ambrose of Milan and the Christological
hymn from *The Tutor* of Clement of Alexandria. These are contrasted

with histrionic Gregorian chant, "which Gregory had borrowed from
the Roman theatre." There is no division in Christianity between a
higher message for the "religious" and a lower form for the "secular."
Such a division would imply that God granted his Holy Spirit only to
priests. The Gospel is a simple message, uncluttered by dogma: "The
preacher did not once quote the holy doctors in sonorous Latin, giving
an impromptu translation for the benefit of his audience; he drew no
elaborate and hair-splitting distinctions between grace of four different
kinds, or faith of five varied descriptions" (*I*, 69). Christians do not seek a
historical hero but fellowship with a personal "Friend."

Holt does introduce two doctrinal questions: the doctrines of election and of human merit. On the subject of election she contends that all
early Christianity was Calvinistic, "almost to Antinomianism." In a footnote she discusses the doctrine of human merit held by the Celtic
Churches, which was distinct from the errors of both Rome and Pelagius
and is best exemplified in the theology of St. Patrick. She does not enter
this "blemish" directly into the novel, though, "since it is better to com-
mit an anachronism than even in appearance to inculcate false doctrine."

Contrasted to this pure Christianity is the Church of the Romanists
and Ritualists, epitomized physically by St. Martin's in Kent, where the
pious Celtic Christians are scandalized by the barely disguised use of pagan incense, idols, and vestments. Idols are "baptized" and given new
names: Thor becomes St. Peter, Odin is transformed into St. Martin, and
Hertha is the pagan counterpart of the Virgin Mary. The power of
Peter's keys as doorkeeper of heaven, a role played by a minor but important pagan god, swings the allegiance of King Oswy (Oswiu) of
Bernicia to the Romanizers. Various rites and doctrines are condemned
by Holt: priestly celibacy, services in Latin, communion in one kind,
baptism in fonts, confession, processions, image worship, "polluting"
relics, purgatory, masses for the dead, transubstantiation, pilgrimages
(which during the 1870s and 1880s gained unprecedented popularity),
extreme unction, the prohibition of the Bible, and indulgences, all "developed" from the "inner consciousness" of Rome. The language shows
her awareness of current arguments over doctrinal development. She attacks the title "universal bishop," drawn from the Vatican decrees, and
cites Pope Gregory the Great as giving this appellation to the Antichrist.
Similarly, she questions the validity of Rome's apostolic succession:

"Yet, after all, the true descent from the apostles must be less in regularity of order than in purity of doctrine" (*I*, 312). In the meetings of Augustine's Oak (602–603) and at Worcester (605), Rome's jurisdiction is extended by Augustine's pompous claim to rule over the British Church and the archbishop of London, whose see was four hundred years older than Canterbury. Sarcastically, she suggests that the stories of Augustine's miracles, produced to support those extravagant claims, had hoodwinked an infallible pope. The symbol of this papal pretension is the pastoral staff, which after the mid-1860s was adopted by more and more Anglican bishops.[25] The staff became a scepter, the presbyter's chair became a throne, and the episcopal homily was transformed into imperial law.

By the same gradual corruption, the seemingly innocuous formation of religious orders for men and women in fact perverted the Gospel. Maur's son Brian breaks off his engagement and enters the monastery at Bangor (Banchorn) because he cannot trust himself to live virtuously without rigid, external controls. As Holt concludes: "In other words, Brian felt like a man whose only hope of keeping sober lies in signing the temperance pledge. Such men cannot walk without crutches. But they are not strong, but weak" (*I*, 193). Brian, of course, meets no good end; he and the other monks are slain by the Northumbrian king Ethelfrid, perhaps at the prompting of Augustine, who is eager to punish the Celtic Church. Religious orders for women, with cloisters and a particular habit, are also criticized and, significantly, accused of undermining the traditional role of women in the home: "Did not He set her in her home at first? And is not He the best judge of the circumstances in which we may serve Him or aid others?" (*I*, 311–13).

The Ritualists are the target of some of Holt's most biting sarcasm. In describing the "Italian mission" to Kent, she comments, "Augustine's first act was to consecrate the river [the Swale]—a fact which may be commended to the notice of modern Ritualists, since the Swale thus affords them an inexhaustible supply of holy water" (*I*, 60). Holt also rejects any latter-day imports of liturgy or doctrine from Greek Orthodoxy; the gaudy pattern on a despised set of "glaring vestments" has a Greek provenance. Ritualists in their ceremonies and processions depend upon the cult of saints and relics. She ridicules especially the relics of the apostles' chains: "Paul and Peter must have been heavily chained indeed if a quarter of them were genuine."[26] This devotion, initiated by the empress Eudoxia in 436, was tremendously popular in medieval England; relics of the chains were used by women in childbirth. Wilfrid (Wilfrith I), along with St. Cedd, is likened to a modern Ritualist for his part at Whitby, where falsehoods about the universality of the Roman usage in the keeping of Easter, the form of priestly tonsure, and the administration of baptism were maintained in order to force the ignominious surrender of the British Church. At that council, the Roman Ritualists even accused St. John of judaizing. Holt concludes that if the nation had stood firm then against Roman usurpations, there would not have been the subsequent Reformation struggle.

This argument, of course, is geared to Holt's Victorian readership, who are admonished never to allow the infamy again. But there is another reason for the urgency of her message, an eschatological one. What she calls the "Protestant historical interpretation of prophecy" indicates that whereas Gregory the Great "stood upon the threshold of the dread Thousand Two Hundred and Threescore Years," she and her readers stood on the threshold of its close. Scripture had been fulfilled in the decrees of the Vatican Council. True Christians "were warned to beware of one who should teach doctrines concerning minor gods [1 Tim. 4:1], who should forbid to marry, and order abstinence from meats; who should speak lies in hypocrisy, having the conscience seared with a hot iron; who as God should sit in the temple of God, showing *himself* that he is God" (*I*, 24). The Antichrist had indeed displayed himself; the Last Days could not be far behind.

Holt had a long career of writing; her novels, like some of Kingsley's, derived their power from their anti-Catholicism.[27] The question remains why she should choose the story of the sending of Augustine to Thanet by Gregory the Great as the vehicle for her condemnation of Ritualism and Papal Infallibility. While general interest in this decade in the history of the British Church and the figure of Augustine cannot be disputed, it can be suggested that there was an even more immediate cause for Holt's characterization. In 1875 Henry Edward Manning, the archbishop of Westminster, was hastily called to Rome and notified of his election to the Sacred College of Cardinals as a belated reward for his important role at the Vatican Council and his continued championing of the cause of the pope's spiritual and temporal rights. As is the custom, the new cardinal was given a titular church in Rome: the Church of St. Gregory the Great on the Coelian Hill.[28] Holt's description of the emaciated frame and fiery temperament of Augustine was meant to depict the new cardinal and defender of infallibility. He was, in her estimation, the autocratic leader of another Italian mission from Gregory the Great and his successor.

Another Evangelical author, William Henry Giles Kingston (1814–80), used his Early Church novel to unmask papalist errors and cabals. As founder of "Missions to Seamen" in 1856, which was regarded as a significant contribution to the Evangelical awakening, Kingston was widely known as a spokesman for the emigration movement, as the author of "healthy" adventure tales for boys, usually about the sea and exploration, and as the editor of the boys' periodicals *Kingston's Magazine* and *The Union Jack* (1880–83).[29]

In his novel *Jovinian: A Story of the Early Days of Papal Rome* (1877), Kingston begins with two mysteries: What became of the pagan college of priests in Rome after Constantine's conversion? How did corruption gain a foothold in the Early Church? The questions, he finds, answer one another. Evil and hypocritical priests conspire to take over the Roman Church; Roman pontiff is but pagan flamen writ large.[30] He demonstrates this through a long series of comparisons. The use of holy water and consecrated salt, *ex voto* offerings in human shapes, wreaths of flowers, tapers in daylight, and mendicant priests with tonsures are all derived from pagan cults. Religious orders for women are as threatening to the lives of "fair damsels" as life under the high priestess of the Vestal Virgins, "a tigress without cubs." Although having no intrinsic value, relics are a means of international commerce (and robbery). But the martyrs can have no further concern for the "frail tenement" of human bodies; Christ alone heals. The *litui*, long staffs with golden crooks borne by augurs, are derided as a usage of modern Roman bishops, who also adopt the unscriptural titles of patriarch, metropolitan, and archbishop. Several Anglican bishops, such as Thomas Legh Claughton, bishop of Rochester and then St. Albans, had also adopted the custom after 1867. The statue of Jupiter Tonans is transformed into the venerated image of St. Peter, whose toe the faithful devoutly kiss. The peacock feathers fanning Juno's triumphal car become the *flabelli* used in papal processions. Statues of the gods that weep and roll their eyes soon become miraculous images of the Nazarene saints, just like the "winking Virgin" of Rimini in 1850. Flagellation and lacerations of naked flesh in pagan rites become sensual methods of ascetic holiness. Images of Isis and Horus are hailed as the Madonna and child. Astarte or Ashtaroth, the Queen of Heaven, makes a similar metamorphosis. One pagan conspirator esteems her worship as the most effective way to corrupt Christianity: "Her worship had, indeed, ever been the most popular, and provided that could be maintained, he felt sure that it would successfully oppose the two principles of the Christian faith, which he understood to consist in the belief of one God and one mediator between God and man" (*J*, 72).

This impure form of Christianity is patronized for political reasons by Constantine, who is also anxious to gain absolution for his multiple murders. The first Christian emperor's baptism is a farce, since on his deathbed he commanded Constantius, his successor, to execute six other family members he suspected of poisoning him. Their murders were plotted only moments after Constantine had been baptized. The only legal acts of Constantine were the abolition of crucifixion, the encouragement to emancipate slaves, the prohibition of gladiatorial shows, and the prohibition on infanticide. "[These] Nazarenes seem to require no priests nor sacrifices, and worship without any forms or ceremonies, as they declare that this Jesus is their sole priest, and that He is at the right hand of their great God, pleading His own sacrifice, whereby all their sins were purged away" (*J*, 18). Penances, abstinence, purgatory, fasting, and flagellations are worthless; only faith in the risen Lord saves. Foolish fables about the power of other mediators (the martyrs, Mary, or the saints) are in fact as ineffective as the rationalizing in "the false teaching of the philosophers." The sacrifice of the cross is the full, perfect, and only satisfaction of God's justice. The true light of Christ is revealed in Scripture, "the fountain head." The characters in the novel hand over to one another a scroll containing the Gospel of John. Along with portions of the Torah, the prophets, and the Epistles, the Gospels and gospel hymns constitute the Christian liturgy, simply expressing "the plan of salvation offered by God to sinful man." The "president" of the assembly takes an ordinary loaf of bread and cup of wine and reads the institution narrative of the Last

Supper: "As Christ's body was broken for us on the accursed tree, and as His blood was shed for us, so do we eat this broken bread and drink this wine in remembrance that he died for our sins, offering thereby a full and sufficient propitiation, and that He rose again, and ascended into heaven, to take His seat at the right hand of God and there to plead His death for the remission of the sins of all who believe in him" (*J*, 41–42). This loose paraphrase of and gloss on the Prayer Book communion service emphasizes that the Eucharist is purely a commemorative rite; significantly, however, it stresses the continuing intercession in heaven of the ascended Lord, a theme stressed in other Evangelical novels.[31]

The impure form of Christianity, its system of penances and absolution, had totally undermined the conscience and morals of its adherents so that they indulged in the grossest crimes without shame or remorse. In an obvious attack on the popularly conceived notion of Catholic moral theology, one character crudely describes what is meant to be the Jesuit principle of double effect: "Know you not that it is one of our chief maxims that deceit of any sort is lawful when the result is likely to prove beneficial, and that evil may be done provided a good object is to be attained?" (*J*, 89–90). In another throwback to pagan practice, however, a murderer with "a sword dripping gore in his hand" claims sanctuary at a newly converted shrine, once dedicated to Mars and now to Mary, and immediately becomes a monk there. Damasus, educated by recluses at Mt. Carmel (Kingston means the successors of the Baalim) and one of the chief promoters of the idolatrous worship of the Virgin, urges his faction, aided by monks who are really pagan priests in cowls, to slaughter the forces of his rival for the office of bishop when Pope Liberius dies. The combat, staged inside a basilica and described in such a way as to recall the era of Ritualist riots in England, leaves 137 dead. Jovinian, who is never actually identified as the theological opponent of St. Jerome regarding the question of virginity, is branded a heretic and retires from Rome to a place in the western spur of the Alps. It is not clear exactly where this new center of pure-Gospel Christianity is located; perhaps it is meant to be a reference to the area later associated with the Waldensians. Like other Evangelical writers, Kingston ends his diatribe with a hint that the rapidly approaching Last Day will see the restoration of the Gospel: "The time will come when the simple Gospel will be again faithfully

preached, and the practices of the apostolic age be restored even in
Rome itself, where the mystery of iniquity has begun its fearful reign"
(*J*, 263–64).

Frederic William Farrar (1831–1903), the dean of Canterbury (1895–
1903), is a bridge between Evangelical and Broad Church perspectives.
Educated at London University and Trinity College, Cambridge, where
he was a member of the Apostles' Club, like Tennyson a generation earlier, Farrar was greatly influenced by F. D. Maurice but never lost the
Evangelical heritage of his father, a Church Missionary Society chaplain
in India, where Frederic was born. Having taught at Marlborough College (where he was eventually headmaster) and Harrow, he was ordained
priest in 1857 and the next year, while at Harrow, published his best-selling tale of school life, *Eric; or, Little by Little*.[32] Farrar's evolutionist work
on philology, the basis of much of his scriptural commentary, helped create a friendship with Charles Darwin, at whose instigation he was elected
to the Royal Society (1866). The clergyman's forward-looking but reverent *Life of Christ* (1874) underwent some thirty-odd editions in his life-
time and was followed by an equally successful *Life of St. Paul* (1879) and
a sequel, *The Life of Lives: Further Studies in the Life of Christ* (1900). His
Early Days of Christianity (1882) and *Lives of the Fathers: Church History in
Biography* (1889) surveyed the writings of the New Testament and those
of the Apologists and patristic authors. As canon of Westminster he restored St. Margaret's Church to its long-neglected role as parish to the
House of Commons and led the local Temperance movement. During
November and December of 1877 his set of five sermons on the doctrine
of eternal punishment (published in 1878 as *Eternal Hope*), a subject current in the periodicals of the day as well as in many religious novels, elicited violent protests. E. B. Pusey's *What Is Faith as to Everlasting Punishment:
In Reply to Dr. Farrar's Challenge* (1880), in which Pusey uses several arguments suggested by Newman about the Catholic view of "purification," caused Farrar to modify his stance in *Mercy and Judgment: A Few
Last Words on Christian Eschatology with Reference to Dr. Pusey's "What Is of
Faith"* (1881).[33] He was also attacked in Charles F. Childe's *The Unsafe
Anchor; or, "Eternal Hope" a False Hope* (1879). The Evangelical Childe
accused the canon of misreading Bishop Joseph Butler, who did in fact

maintain that punishment of the wicked was judicially inflicted, agonizing, and eternal. Both Scripture and Catholic doctrine in the Athanasian
Creed (attacked by Broad Churchmen throughout the 1870s) declared
that the true nature of God was not inconsistent with eternal punishment. Life was a period of probation, the next world a time of retribution
or reward; any probation after death would be necessarily incomplete.
Childe and other fundamentalists found Farrar's Mauricean doctrine, not
compassionate and hopeful, but an aid to the "German Socialist, French
Communist, or English Secularist." While still a canon, Farrar was able
to suggest to T. H. Huxley that Darwin, who died in 1882, could be
buried in the Abbey.

Appointed archdeacon of Westminster in 1883, Farrar delivered the
Bampton lectures at Oxford in 1885, entitled *History of Interpretation*. He
held for a progressive revelation; the Bible was not so much a revelation
as the record of a revelation that is beyond harm by modern criticism because it also corresponds to the external facts of nature and the internal
experience of the heart. Disputes over inspiration cause it to be confused
with mere verbal infallibility by ignoring the evident facts of language
and history. Christ alone is Truth and free from error. In 1895 the earl
of Rosebery (prime minister, 1894–95) raised Farrar to the deanship
of Canterbury, where he set about improving the cathedral fabric
and services. He was buried in the cathedral close to Archbishop Frederick Temple, a contributor to *Essays and Reviews*, who had died the previous year.

Farrar composed two historical novels. The first was *Darkness and
Dawn: A Tale of the Days of Nero* (1891; 8th ed., 1898), a popular theme at
the time.[34] In the novel Seneca delineates the moral decay of Rome under his pupil Nero, while recognizing that Christianity shines forth in
purity and righteousness. These two forces contend against each other,
Christianity's "irresistible might of weakness" against the genius, religion, philosophy, and imperial power of paganism. The title is a typical
example of the vocabulary of an Evangelical writer: Christianity is depicted by these authors as a "Dawn" or "Daybreak" or "Dayspring."
Farrar is cognizant, however, of the historical ambiguities, as his next
title, *Gathering Clouds*, demonstrates. Research in various classical authors
had shown him that non-Christians also had some kind of access to
divine truth. In *Seekers after God* (1868), he weighed the useful spiritual

insights of Seneca, Epictetus, and Marcus Aurelius, the pagan "saints." And in *Seneca and St. Paul* (1883) he made not unfavorable comparisons between the Stoic and the last apostle.

Gathering Clouds (1896)[35] is in some respects a subtler statement of the contention by Evangelicals such as Holt and Kingston that paganism had, in dialectical fashion, reasserted itself after its apparent defeat and had emerged anew to corrupt Christianity. The older novelistic theme of the luxury, sensuality, and decay of Rome has been transferred, mutatis mutandis, to the new Rome, Constantinople. Farrar vividly portrays the "voluptuous splendours," the "gorgeous criminals," and sensuous corruption of Byzantium, attempting to achieve in his portrait, "not an imaginative landscape, but an absolute photograph." He adopts Lecky's estimation that this was an age of treachery and dissolution (as complete as that of the Sublime Porte), when there were "many fanatical ascetics and a few illustrious theologians." This is a note Farrar struck earlier in his *Lives of the Fathers*, surveying the first Christian centuries:

> Again, we shall stand by the cradle of many superstitions which infected the pure faith of Christendom. We shall be forced to watch the painful deterioration of a clergy exalted into pride of power and forced into compulsory celibacy; to see the Pagan world profoundly alienated by the worship of spurious martyrs and their yet more spurious relics; to observe the strong stream of unconscious Manichaean sentiment which surrounded virginity with ecstatic admiration and depreciated marriage as a miserable concession; to deplore the furious outbreak of ignorant fanaticism among the monks of Asia or the Circumcellions of Africa. We shall see the encroachments of episcopal autocracy, and the reintroduction into Christianity of Jewish formalism and Jewish bondage.[36]

Farrar had a special fascination with the "fiery and eloquent" John Chrysostom, the real center of his novel. The dean's somewhat ambiguous appreciation of the Fathers was governed by two factors: their respective modes of life and their interpretation of Scripture. Summing up the monumental exegetical work of the Alexandrian Fathers, so similar to the rabbinic hermeneutic of Philo, Farrar said: "They do but systematize the art of misinterpretation. They have furnished volumes of baseless application without shedding upon the significance of Scripture one ray of genuine light."[37] Chrysostom, however, presented an entirely different approach, although Farrar concluded that the patriarch was not as learned as Jerome, as conversant with the mysterious aspects of the Gospel as Origen, as profound theologically as Augustine, or as adept a textual critic as Julius Africanus. Chrysostom, as a pupil of Diodorus of Tarsus at Antioch, was, nevertheless, a bishop who loved his flock, who preached eloquently, hence his honorific name, who based his exposition of Scripture on scholarly study and eminent common sense, and who stressed the literal interpretation of the text as a plain guide for conduct rather than as the ground of controversy or metaphysical speculation.[38] The secret of Chrysostom's exegetical method, Farrar said in the Bampton lectures, was his insistence that each passage be studied as a whole, within its context; that the human element in Scripture, the interaction of living human beings, be recognized; and that the varying personalities of the scriptural writers be taken into consideration. These humanistic and humanitarian guidelines would spur modern exegetes, the dean concluded, to stress the practical message of the Gospel and prevent too idolatrous a regard for the text or its human authors. Illustrating this, he quoted St. Augustine on St. Jerome: "Inspiratus a Deo, sed tamen homo."

Farrar also recognized that Chrysostom was a figure of controversy and not above criticism. Of special interest was the reluctant, yet dynamic, political role played by the patriarch when he "spoke before kings and was not ashamed." For this reason Dante (*Paradiso* 12:136) placed him in the heavenly circle between Nathan the prophet, who denounced David, and Anselm of Canterbury, who judged King William Rufus. Abducted and appointed patriarch by order of the eunuch Eutropius, "the insect of the harems," who acts much like a British prime minister, Chrysostom finds himself swept along inexorably by court intrigues swirling around the "stupid" and languorous emperor Arcadius and the empress Eudoxia, who is marked by her external religiosity: "It impelled her to give alms, to build churches, to attend services, to prostrate herself to her favourite priests, and to adore the relics of martyrs; but so long as she manifested her devotion in this way she did not think it of any importance that it should regulate the passions of her heart and the duties of her daily life" (*GC*, 1:153). In such a situation, Chrysostom is a natural Savonarola, denouncing worldly vanities, just as Ambrose had condemned Theodosius I and Luther had stood before Charles V. The patriarch is supported only by the poor and a few fellow ecclesiastics, such as the anachronistically elevated Bishop Synesius, whose portrayal here owes much to Kingsley's *Hypatia*. Corrupt societies, however, precipitate the destruction of such reformers; Farrar's list of similar prophets includes Gregory Nazianzus, John [Jan] Hus, Luther, and George Whitefield (GC, 1:211). Chrysostom's views on the lower classes generate Farrar's only criticism of his hero's practical sense and biblical exegesis. The patriarch's effulgent praise of the "poor" is a mistaken reading of the references to the "poor in spirit" in Scripture, whom even the rich can be. Farrar is especially critical of the "atrocious impostures of the lowest classes in begging." His own role as chaplain to the House of Commons, moving easily among power magnates and royalty, and as an observer of the denizens of the Westminster slums at the very porch of the Abbey seems to color his view of Chrysostom's social gospel.

There is the usual list of items needing regulation under a program of reformation and beneficence at home and missions abroad (in this case to the Persians, Phoenicians, and barbarians). Farrar condemns those who desert the church service just before the Holy Communion, as well as those who give the "Holy Table" the "unscriptural and unprimitive designation of 'altar.'" In all things he seeks the via media. Sinners ask pardon, but the abuses attached to auricular confession are broadly hinted at. He berates the theological shibboleths of those who claim to speak for "the Church," an authority used to assert every superstitious accretion. Reflecting some of Chrysostom's own polemic against increased proselytism by Jews, the novel ridicules the judaizing use of vestments. "We have no High Priest but Christ . . . nor are we Jews," Chrysostom warns. Wealth has corrupted the Church: "In former days golden priests had used chalices of wood; now wooden priests used chalices of gold" (GC, 1:96). Farrar classifies as idolatrous the theology that had turned the Holy Supper into a "magic sacrifice and material idol," the "vulgar debauchery" of pilgrimages to the Holy Land, the use of pictures in churches as a "Bible of the laity," an innovation introduced by Paulinus of Nola, processions, and the veneration of relics, such as "kissing and hugging" the bones of Noah or Methusaleh.

He is also cautious about too meticulous a devotion to credal formulas. He defends, as part of his view of the "nobler, stronger, purer race" of

Goths, to whom the future belongs, the missionary work and vernacular Bible translation of Wulfila, the servant of "the White Christ," who "never meant to be otherwise than orthodox." Goths are superior to indolent Greeks, "ugly" Huns, and treacherous Franks; Kingsley's vision of the union of the Teuton and Roman in a future race, the English, is adopted by Farrar. Against those who question the Christology of "the little wolf," the narrator states that the world needed saints more than Catholics. In soteriological questions Farrar himself had rejected any ransom theory of the Atonement, along with any substitutionary, expiatory, vicarious, or Anselmian forensic view; we can know nothing of its operative cause, only that it was a voluntary intervention of suffering and love.[39] The craftsman Michael of Nazareth, one of the Desponsyni (direct relations to Joseph and Mary) asks: "Did Christ come to affirm a creed, Bishop, or to create a character?" Christian character is under particular assault from those who declare the inherent sanctity of clerical celibacy, a doctrine Farrar finds erroneous and unscriptural. He had written earlier about monasticism, acknowledging that it had once done "its work" but had fallen into decay, idleness, and pollution, documented in the "annals of Westminster Abbey" (meaning the reports of the official visitors under Henry VIII, prior to the dissolution of the monasteries). Farrar was a fervent, if at times muddled, defender of the early Franciscans (among whom he mistakenly placed Thomas Aquinas), identifying works on St. Francis by Mrs. Oliphant and the Catholic reformer A. F. d'Ozanam. But celibacy and harsh ascetic practices were rejected:

> Not indeed in celibacy, but if God permits us, in honourable marriage, or in the hope of a pure and faithful betrothal; not in self-torture, but yet in earnest watchfulness; not in extreme fasting, but in habitual and careful moderation; not in morbid self-introspection, but in thorough and vigorous occupation; not in enfeebling the body by maceration, but by filling its hours of work with strenuous and cheerful activity, and its hours of leisure with bright thoughtfulness, and many a silent prayer.[40]

In *Gathering Clouds*, celibacy leads to many abuses, especially sacerdotalism. Haughty priests combine "the privileges of angels with the temper of executioners," and virgins use their distinctive habits, like broadened phylacteries, as a passport to immodest freedom. The only fasting approved is that recommended in the newly rediscovered text of the *Shepherd* of Hermas, that is, for forgiveness of injuries and advance in godliness. Ascetics and hermits, afflicted with "unsocial passion," bring upon themselves through their austerities evil and carnal thoughts, while at the same time basking in a "halo of sham sanctity which is to this day enjoyed in the East by many a semi-idiotic yogi or repulsive fakir" (*GC*, 1:54).

Gathering Clouds should also be considered another example of Farrar's novels of school life. Chrysostom in Antioch and Constantinople surrounds himself with a sixth form of students and young friends. Philip, a kind of head of school character, is rescued at age fifteen by the bishop (who disguises him as a girl) after the boy has inadvertently caused the deaths of two young friends, Achillas and Eros, beaten with "lead whips" before execution. Chrysostom holds the boy's hand while he is scourged and then through the nights following; their friendship grows as the boy is led gradually to conversion. Anyone who has read *Eric* will recognize the intimate connection in Farrar's work between the lash and the conversion experience. There is also the blond chorister Eutyches, half Gothic and "as good as he is beautiful," who later is condemned for his Monophysite views on the nature of Christ. There was, he maintains, one nature after the union of the human and divine in Christ (a view derived from the orthodox Cyril of Alexandria but condemned by the Council of Chalcedon in 451). And there is David of Nazareth, one of the Desponsyni, who resembles the beautiful, youthful Christ painted in the catacombs of St. Callistus. In contrast, the reader is shown Simeon (later the Stylite) as an unwashed and verminiferous lad whose pretentious visions are caused by indigestion and whose megalomania underlies his claims as a miracle worker. There are also the "imperial boys": the "stupid" Arcadius, the "half imbecile" Honorius, and the "pure and innocent" Valentinian II, who are shown being educated as princes. Among the Goths are the "young Apollo" Thorismund and the fifteen-year-old Walamir, "beautiful as a young god," who formed "so romantic an affection" for Eutyches. The chorister rescues the youngest Goth from a massacre and holds his hands as they weep on each others' necks; Walamir, seeing the "angel-face" of Eutyches, asks if this celestial being can really love a "wretched, wounded, dying Gothic boy?" Farrar depicts the household of Chrysostom as the scene of disciplined study, boyish pranks, and sentimental male romantic attachments. Violence, sickness, and physical injury draw the schoolboy inhabitants closer together. One could say that Farrar has translated Eric's Roslyn School to the banks of the Bosphorus.

William Boyd Carpenter (1841–1918), a liberal divine and Broad Churchman of some renown, was selected in 1884 by Gladstone to be the third incumbent (1884–1911) of the see of Ripon (new foundation, 1836).[41] Born at Liverpool into a clerical family (his father was a clergyman and his mother's brother was dean of Exeter), he was educated at Cambridge and ordained in 1864. In his early years in Liverpool he had witnessed a parade of conflicting religious groups: Calvinists, Unitarians, Mormons, Roman Catholics, and Anglo-Catholics. Reading Stopford Brooke's influential *Life of F. W. Robertson* (1865) made him broaden his theological views. That Broad approach was at the heart of his foundation of Ripon clergy college (later removed to Oxford and renamed Ripon Hall) in 1898. He also helped create the new urban sees of Wakefield (1888) and Bradford (1920). Highly regarded as a preacher and pastor by Queen Victoria, he was appointed a royal chaplain in 1879 and canon of Windsor in 1882. Carpenter was to serve as clerk of the closet to Prince Albert Edward, later Edward VII, and to George V, enjoying in that duty a close relationship with Emperor Frederick III and Kaiser Wilhelm II. He formulated his religious liberalism in the Hulsean lectures at Cambridge in 1878, in which he argued that the study of psychology was useful to religion, the Bampton lectures at Oxford in 1887, and the Noble lectures at Harvard in 1904 and 1913. After resignation from his bishopric, he became canon and subdean of Westminster, in whose cloister he was later buried.

Carpenter's novel *Narcissus* (1879) depends heavily on the contemporary scholarship of J. B. Lightfoot's *Apostolic Fathers* (published in successive installments from 1869 to 1890) and the translations of the Ante-Nicene Library of T. and T. Clark of Edinburgh. The opening chapters, dealing with Ignatius of Antioch, Clement of Rome, Quadratus, and Justin Martyr, follow in line from Lightfoot's study. Carpenter's extracts from the *Octavius* of Minucius Felix, Athenagoras' work on the *Resurrection of the Dead*, the two epistles and other material ascribed at that time to Clement of Rome, Justin's *First Apology* and *Dia-*

logue with Trypho the Jew, quoted at length, and the various *martyria* of Ignatius, Polycarp, and Justin show not only that Carpenter was aware of recent work on the Apostolic Fathers and Apologists but also that by the late 1870s he deemed that Britain needed a restatement of Christianity by a new preacher and apologist of faith and reason.

The story begins with Narcissus as a youth amid the licentious splendor of Herculaneum and Pompeii. The "president" of the local Christian assembly orates about the coming of the Day of the Lord, which will punish vice as the elements are melted, a vision that terrifies his listeners. A good part of the novel is spent refuting this apocalyptic emphasis in Christianity. Elsewhere, Carpenter, who as a youth had been frightened and fascinated by John Martin's apocalyptic painting *The Opening of the Sixth Seal*, approves the many Christians in Victorian England who had at last "abandoned the hazardous policy of dogmatic interpretations of unfulfilled prophecy. We are content to express our faith in some Second Advent, but we can leave times and season, methods and order, in the wiser Hand."[42] Those who preach with "hot and self-ignorant zeal" the approaching day of doom and the rise of Nero as Antichrist are called fanatics and imposters. Justin, who cautiously observes that the sacred books "seem to me to teach this" notion of apocalypse and millennialism, nevertheless prudently warns that "extravagant and unbridled talkers do us more harm than good" (*Ns*, 239). One such overbearing fanatic, given to the "ecstatic and rambling utterances" of the Montanists, is tested in the arena and hastens to perform the required sacrifice. The fundamentalist was the most likely to become the apostate.

Narcissus quickly learns the true Christian message. Christ is Love, an "undying Friend" who "bindeth up the broken in heart." Christianity calms, makes gentle, subdues nature, and nerves for endurance. Christian lives are lovely and their deaths glorious: "The power of no sect, philosophy, or system could work such wondrous changes in men" (*Ns*, 37). But Antoninus Pius, Marcus Aurelius, and Epictetus are warmly referred to and Christians are called the "veriest philosophers." There is, on the other hand, a taint of wrong in all, and all have let that taint spread in their lives. Religion, then, has a necessary transforming function: "Life is an education: we may make it help us to grow nobler, and more fair to God" (*Ns*, 168). That education has its practical side in the world. A pandering Jew, a caricatured substitute for Justin's Trypho, curses the

Nazarenes' meddlesomeness over a girl's virtue; the Victorian philan-thropic anxiety about increased prostitution is at the root of this episode, as are stereotypes of Jews as sexually aggressive. Carpenter also claims that Christians contribute to civilization more than do the "Indian Brah-mins" who live naked in the woods. Christianity is superior to these other religions because of its social gospel. It is also superior to philoso-phy, which can merely "sing a lullaby by our sick-bed." Christians will-ingly suffer martyrdom because they love Christ; that is their secret power (and conversely, the only rational meaning Carpenter can con-struct for such voluntary deaths). Christians are strengthened by their commemoration of the savior's death through Holy Communion, in which they feed their hearts on Christ, who was the bread of life. Car-penter uses the wording of the 1552 Prayer Book service of Holy Com-munion to suggest his position on eucharistic theology. There is no value in material offerings or sacerdotalism. One hypocrite exclaims: "I have played the priest in my time—a face of sphinx-like gravity and mystery, the muttering of a few incoherent words,—and to see the crowds look-ing on with wonder; it is a rare way of making a livelihood" (*Ns*, 123).

A major part of the novel is spent with the gradual conversion of the young man Felix by the aged Narcissus. The old man declares to his proselyte that "God seeks, yet would be sought." Felix is the spokesman for a view that religion is purely a social construct: "It really matters nothing, then, what rites, or what religion you adopt, for all are equally false; but expediency should teach you to give outward respect to some religion, for all are equally useful" (*Ns*, 99). Religion binds people to-gether, stabilizes society, maintains order among the masses, and provides controlled outlets for the emotions. These rational grounds for religion, however, are powerless to aid the stricken characters in the novel's fre-quent deathbed scenes, charged with pure Victorian sentiment. Felix himself finds it hard to relinquish the lovely myths and language that are the "poetry of paganism." Carpenter in his *Permanent Elements in Religion* (1889) explored the various facets of religious belief, recognizing the in-tricacies and inherent ambiguities of belief. Although convinced of reason's proper place in the religious quest, he also recognized, as did other Victorians in the 1870s and 1880s, the tremendous appeal of mysti-cism, historically and in the present age. In Narcissus he affirms that God dwells not only in the light but also in the "gloom and clouds of Sinai and the Wilderness." He frequently describes visions and dreams among other religious experiences in the novel; one long tale of the quest for a priceless pearl by the pilgrim Alfez (a kind of comparative-religion gloss on the New Testament parable) receives as much attention as the Apologists or Scripture. Felix's conversion, his beginning to look at Christian belief "with broader thought," is made agonizingly slow for a purpose:

> It is characteristic of different ages of the world that Felix did not glide, without rigorous thought and attentive reasoning, into sympathy with the Christian creed. It was reserved for a later and so-called more enlightened age to present mankind with the humiliating spectacle of men, endowed with good and even surpassing abilities, drifting aimlessly and helplessly from creed to creed. Christianity had not then dwindled into a morbid and maudlin self-introspective sentiment—it had then some bones to give strength to its framework. To believe in Christ was then to act—it was a reality, which needed not only moral courage, but sturdy conviction to support the moral courage of those who avowed the worship of Jesus of Nazareth. (*Ns*, 214)

This liberal divine found the kernel of Christianity in the call to action. Revelation was still necessary, otherwise mankind could not see clearly the reason and cause for such action: "God is love" is the summation of Revelation. The "silver-tongued" bishop of Ripon took his own gospel to heart; he was instrumental in forming the old-age pension scheme and played a leading role in passage of the Children Act of 1908. The finest apology for Christianity, he felt, was the realization of practical love for one's neighbor.

"As the Apostles Saw Him": Fictional Lives of Jesus

Biographies of Jesus were first tentatively essayed in England during the 1860s. D. F. Strauss's two-volume *Life of Jesus* (*Das Leben Jesu*, 1835–36), translated by George Eliot (1846), was more theology than biography and too much a learned analysis of sources to appeal to the British public. It had, however, unsettled many. The young Friedrich Engels found that it shattered his pietist biblicism and doomed for him belief in any sort of absolute religion.[43] The attempts to show the human Jesus, invariably startling to Victorian readers, were not confined to literature. Using a realism initially shocking to delicate sensibilities, Pre-Raphaelite paintings such as J. E. Millais's *Christ in the House of His Parents* (1850) and D. G. Rossetti's sexually charged *Ecce Ancilla Domini* (1850) are other examples from the arts. Beginning in the 1850s tourism and exploration in the Holy Land advanced this feeling for the human Christ; the Palestine Exploration Fund (established in 1866) and the Palestine Pilgrim's Text Society (1887), providing historical guides to travelers, are later examples of the organized interest in the sacred places of Christ's earthly ministry.[44] It was the biography by the Catholic ex-seminarist Ernest Renan, *Vie de Jésus* (1863)—intended as the first volume in his massive *Origins of Christianity*, which was to extend to the death of Marcus Aurelius, and completed in 1861 in Lebanon while his devoted elder sister died close by—that had the greatest impact on the Continent, although less immediate in effect in England. Renan thought that history was transformed by genius alone and saw a "charming" Jesus as the greatest historical genius to transform society. He took Christ out of the hands of the theologians and handed him over to the historians. The vestment of piety was cast aside to show the man.

In 1865 *Ecce Homo* by J. R. Seeley, which Shaftesbury called a book "vomited from the jaws of Hell," caused as much controversy as *Essay and Reviews*. Concentrating on the bases of Christian morality rather than true biography, Seeley's austere portrait showed Christ as the supreme moralist and Christianity as the historical structure of progressive Western civilization. This picture was supplemented by Joseph Parker's subsequent response, *Ecce Deus*. The Puseyite H. P. Liddon's famous Bampton lectures in 1866, entitled *The Divinity of Our Lord*, were a conservative defense of traditional religion against the work of Renan, Strauss, and F. C. Baur (whose *Paul the Apostle*, poorly translated in 1873, was another demonstration of the linkage between the lives of Christ and Paul). *The Jesus of History* (1869) by Sir Richard Hanson, chief justice of Australia; the *Historical Lectures on the Life of Our Lord* (1860; 6th ed., 1876) by C. J. Ellicott, bishop of Gloucester and Bristol; and the article "Jesus Christ" (1863) in Smith's *Dictionary of the Bible* by William Thomson, archbishop of York, were sober productions written for the ordinary Christian. F. W. Farrar's *Life of Christ* (1874) became the best-selling biography of the age and was followed in 1879 by his *Life of St. Paul*. Uncontroversial, even prayerful, Farrar sought to address faithful Christians, but was criticized for his expansive style, for filling in the biblical silences, and for the doubt he cast on aspects of the scriptural narrative. The frantic search for new manuscripts, such as a codex discovered in 1875 by Bryennios containing the *Epistle to Barnabas*, long regarded as part of the New Testament canon; philological and textual criticism; and the insights of a developing science of comparative religion all had to be harmonized. The importance of Jewish documents for this study was recognized by Renan and his followers. Alfred Edersheim, a Jew who was an Anglican clergyman, employed the Talmud in his ponderous, scholarly *Life and Times of Jesus the Messiah* (1883).

There were in the late Victorian era other literary representations of the life of Jesus outside the scholarly investigations. There were also "fictional transfigurations" of Jesus in novels and tales, a genre used by religious writers in England only after 1878.[45] Fictionalized biographies of Christ, like modern apocrypha, were usually conscious of recent scholarship that needed simplification for the average reader or were pious restatements of the Bible.[46] Resistance to altering the biblical narrative in any way, including phraseology, was especially strong; it was not until George Moore's *The Brook of Kerith* (1916) that the biblical framework was abandoned. Some novels, such as Edwin Abbott's *Onesimus* (1882), were in the tradition of pseudepigrapha. They used archaic and "biblical" language to contribute to the aura of learnedness and to support the author's program of theological reform. Such works gave themselves an immediate "canonical" image. In an era mad with recent discoveries of hitherto unknown manuscripts, other examples of apocrypha were in fact literary forgeries. Notovitch's *Unknown Life* (1894), supposedly a record of the hidden years of Jesus in India that was then preserved in Tibet, is a prime example.[47] In another type of literature, Dostoevski's "The Grand Inquisitor" chapter in *The Brothers Karamazov* (1880) and Alphonse L. Constant's *The Last Incarnation* (1846) show the biblical Christ, *redivivus*, transplanted into later historical eras. This genre is closely related to examples of the modern *Imitatio Christi* in which Victorian heroes purposefully act in the way Christ would act in similar situations, for example, the Christlike hero of Mrs. Humphry Ward's *Robert Elsmere* (1888). On the other hand, some authors used this format to separate the social teachings of Jesus from the dogmas of the Church, using the insights suggested by modern, liberal exegetes. Eliza Lynn Linton's *The True History of Joshua Davidson, Communist* (1872) is one example that turned the Paris Communards into "Christ-men." Another type of novel used archetypal figures of the redeemer, depicting a man who was innocent of sin yet who underwent temptation and suffering, for instance, Joseph Conrad's *Lord Jim* (1900). Ministerial models of Jesus, pious country parsons or slum priests, are found in numerous Victorian novels and tales. Through scholarship, art, and literature the nineteenth century sought to ask anew, Who is this Jesus of Nazareth?

Edwin Abbott Abbott (1838–1926), himself the son of a headmaster, was educated at St. John's College, Cambridge, ordained in 1863, and took up the profession of teaching at King Edward's School in Birmingham. He soon rose to the headmastership of the City of London School, where he was known as a great moral and religious teacher with an impressive roster of students. Herbert Asquith, prime minister under Edward VII and George V, was one of Abbott's pupils. His innovations in the curriculum—in chemistry, Latin, literature, comparative philology, and mathematics—are part of a remarkable career.[48] A liberal theologian with Broad Church sensibilities, Abbott explored the textual and linguistic problems of Scripture in such works as his *Johannine Vocabulary* (1905) and *Johannine Grammar* (1906), parts of his ten-part collection *Diatessarica*. This capped his earlier work on the other Gospels in *The Common Tradition of the Synoptic Gospels in the Text of the Revised Version* (1884).

This long biblical study lies behind *Philomythus* (1891), Abbott's vehement attack on Cardinal Newman's *Essay on Ecclesiastical Miracles* (1843; re-edited in 1870 to be more anti-Protestant and reprinted in 1890).[49] Abbott found this work to be an "Abomination of intellectual Desolation." Published the year following Newman's death, Abbott's book asserted that he was in "mental and moral shock" at the "Newmanianism" of R. H. Hutton's laudatory biography, *Cardinal Newman* (1891). He was more concerned, however, to counteract the theological "system of safety" and the "conveniently Credulous Assent" that Newman represented, whereby probabilities replaced aspiration after God and faith (i.e., dogma to the papalist) overcomes history. His two-volume biography, *The Anglican Career of Cardinal Newman* (1892), was meant to challenge the profuse and roseate hagiographies produced following Newman's death. Abbott was not the first to question miracles or even to criticize Newman on the issue, but he was the first to suggest that Newman's whole life was a product of degraded love and a "Gospel of fear."[50] When Abbott was attacked by Wilfrid Ward for having called Newman's essay "slatternly," he likened himself to Newman being called a liar and knave in 1864. Abbott's central position was clarified in his work *The Kernel and the Husk, Letters on Spiritual Christianity* (1886), thirty-one brief letters composed to a youth whose faith was severely shocked after "a single term at the University" and dedicated "To the Doubters of this Generation and the Believers of the Next." The miraculous in the story of Christ casts doubt over his acts, doctrine, character, and very existence; belief in miracles is really equivalent to belief in an infallible Church, a connection similarly made in Abbott's comparative study (1898) of the miracles of St. Thomas Becket. Abbott was haunted by a theological domino theory; for many modern Christians, when their credulity in miracles evaporates, the Bible falls and they lose their belief in Christ. Miracles, suspensions of a law of nature or acts not explicable by any natural law, are quite distinct from the "mighty works," not necessarily suspensions of the laws of nature, described in the Bible. While recognizing that there might be some element of reality in the occurrences at Lourdes or in the "Faith-healing" of the Salvation Army, Abbott asserts that Christ performed "mighty works," not miracles.

Abbott lists those doctrines that require demythologizing. The essence of the resurrection of Christ was that his spirit really triumphed over death, and not that his body rose from the grave. Pauline language about resurrection of the body, in the same manner as the apostle's statements about the Apocalypse, was meant to be understood as poetry, of the type used in *Pilgrim's Progress*. The miraculous birth from a virgin was a later addition to the Gospel and designed to sanction a "false and monastic" ideal of life. In fact, this doctrine cut Jesus off from a real share in our common humanity. Abbott retains prayers for the dead because they give him personal comfort in remembering a beloved brother who drowned. He retains Heaven and Hell as metaphors for the operation of the Eternal on the dead, "one thing for St. Francis and quite another for Nero." But Purgatory and Limbo are merely hyperbole for purification; a concept of a "material Hell has probably contributed largely to insanity." Abbott finds that the Athanasian Creed can conveniently be explained away on no less an authority than that of the public statements of the archbishops and bishops. In contrast, Ritualism materializes and sensualizes religion in an "ecclesiastical battalion drill." Broad Church-men, "the more intellectual among the clergy," must direct the corporate hope for "new spiritual truth from the progress of the ages." Word-faith, book-faith, and authority-faith will collapse before the natural worship of the Spirit of Jesus: "Perhaps this collapse will be precipitated by the discovery of a copy of some Gospel of the first century turned up when Constantinople is evacuated by the Turks." If Broad Churchmen do not lead this glorious revolution, "it may be reserved for the semi-Christian or non-Christian working man, for the heretics or agnostic socialist, to guide orthodox and religious England into a higher and purer and more spiritual form of Christianity."[51] Abbott expresses the conviction that Christianity is on the eve of creating a new world order and captures the revolutionary fervor of several groups at the time, including the Christian socialists, who predicted an age of liberation and progress after the publication of their new version of the New Testament (1898–1901), *The Twentieth Century New Testament*.

In his *Apologia* (1907), still verbally boxing with Newman, Abbott explained that his novels *Philochristus* (1878), with which his later *Philomythus* resonates; *Onesimus* (1882); and *Silanus* (1906) were imaginative expansions of his primary argument that modern believers would find it easier to worship Christ without miracles. *Philochristus*, dedicated to J. R. Seeley, purports to be a memoir, a reflection on Christ like the Gospels, by Joseph bar Simeon, a "sin-fearer" who recalls his early discipleship under Christ from his home in Londinium, where he has accompanied the Roman legate Julius Plautius (the husband of Pomponia), also a Christian. Written in "biblical" language, the novel sets about giving a rational explanation to various miracles recorded in the Synoptics, remaining silent where only one or two witnesses speak.[52] The descent of the spirit at his baptism was Jesus' own vision. The feeding of the 4,000 or 5,000 is an allegory that the Bread of the Master, the leaven of the soul, increases in the hands of the Twelve. The Transfiguration was a dream. Thomas "touches" Jesus after the Resurrection by handling the loaf of broken bread, the body of the Lord. The Pentecostal tongues are a sign that all mankind should be one family. Although the Gospel of John is unknown to Philochristus, Abbott's passing comment on its late composition, the doctrine of the Gospel with a thoroughly modern interpretation, is given by Quartus (his name means "the Fourth," i.e., the Fourth Gospel). The essence of Christ's message is the Fatherhood of God, brought about in the New Kingdom by the Holy Spirit: "For his spirit was a spirit of sonship of God, and of brotherhood to men; and except the world should receive this spirit into itself, the world could not be quickened, and the nations of the earth could not pass into the family or kingdom of God."[53] Victorian commentators turned this message into the derogatory acronym "BOMFOG," Brotherhood of Man, Fatherhood of God.

The same basic message, this time relating controverted points in the writings and travels of St. Paul, is found in the pseudepigraphic *Onesimus* (1882), the memoirs of Paul's slave companion and the later Christian bishop of Beroea.[54] Christ, and then the apostles, gave sight to those blind by sin and ignorance, made souls crippled and maimed to walk straight in the path of virtue, and raised the dead in sin. Many incidents reported in the Scriptures are shown to be additions to the tradition as "supplements" (of which Mark has the fewest). William Sanday similarly uses this term in his *Outlines of the Life of Christ* (1905). Alleged miracles are in reality misinterpreted figures of speech, for example, Christ walked on the water in the same sense that one walks on the beach, and Jesus lifted Peter from a "sea of temptation." The "Great Figure" in Rome, numerous earthquakes, and the destruction of Jerusalem led Christians, as Paul himself had been led astray by his own expectations, to exaggerate the imminence of the Last Day. The novel reproduces the writings of Epictetus and puts the words of Maximus of Tyre, Aelius Aristides, Apuleius, Celsus, Justin Martyr, and Irenaeus in the mouths of fictional characters. The description of the martyrdom at Smyrna of Trophimus and Onesimus, who had gone to Asia to obtain the recent writings of John the Disciple and John the Elder to supplement the three other Gospels, is borrowed from the "Passion of St. Perpetua," an account admired by countless Victorians including J. H. Newman.

Silanus (1906) is dedicated "To the Memory of Epictetus. Not a Christian but an Awakener of Aspirations that could not be satisfied except in Christ."[55] The story, supposedly recorded in the reign of Marcus Aurelius in A.D. 163, concerns Quintus Junius Silanus, born in A.D. 90, who leaves Rome at the urging of his older friend, Marcus Aemilius

Scaurus, to hear Epictetus lecture in Nicopolis in 118. In order to defend Epictetus from criticism, Silanus obtains Paul's Epistles and then the "scriptures" from which Paul quotes, so as to understand the character of Christ. In the Epistles, unlike in Epictetus' work or the Synoptics, Silanus finds a sense of spiritual strength and "constraining love" that promises forgiveness. Clemens the Athenian, whom readers later recognize as Clement of Rome, lends a copy of John's Gospel, although admitting doubts about its authorship and accuracy. Even those who reject its principles admit that Jesus cannot be understood except through a disciple "whom he loved." Silanus is gradually converted and undergoes a saving experience by faith as he sails toward Italy to rejoin his friend, who is, unknown to him, already dead, a situation similar to that of Abbott's relationship with his own drowned brother. Silanus knows that Clemens is praying for him at the very moment that the ship for Rome loses sight of the Asian hills and sails through the encircling deep. The conversion of Silanus is one of the few in this story by saving-faith, otherwise so frequently recurrent in novels of this kind. Pliny, Plutarch, Josephus, Clemens, Hermas, Irenaeus, and Justin are all introduced; but it is Epictetus who plays the role of "tutor" leading Silanus step by step to Christ.

The kind of "enthusiasmos" that Abbott required in any true study of Christ characterized other "passionate" portrayers of the Redeemer. One such enthusiast was Marie Corelli—Minnie Mackay (1835–1924)—the tremendously successful novelist who produced a steady stream of best sellers. Her *Sorrows of Satan* (1895) was praised by Queen Victoria, the Baptist preacher Charles Spurgeon, the Roman Catholic Father Bernard Vaughan, and the Anglo-Catholic Father Ignatius Lyne. Another book, *The Master Christian* (1900), sold 260,000 copies in just a few years.[56] Her tale of Christ, *Barabbas* (1893), was praised by the prince of Wales and others but soundly condemned as a "horrid book" by the seventy-year-old Charlotte Yonge: "When one recollects that every word in the Gospels is sacred, and that the history is the direct Inspiration of God the Holy Ghost, it seems to me too terrible to twist them into suiting a person's own ideas of a tragedy."[57]

The gospel narrative is expanded in the novel and several connections between characters and events are made. Melchior, one of the Magi and Corelli's image of the seer/scientist, acts as a narrator and interpreter of the events; the novel ends with his leading Simon of Cyrene off beyond the pyramids to become the first Christian hermit. Judas' father is introduced as a usurer and friend of Caiaphas and is driven from the Temple by Christ along with the money changers. A sexual motivation is provided for various events by the character Judith Iscariot, whom Caiaphas wildly desires; Barabbas had been one of her lovers and on that account is rearrested by the High Priest, only to die in prison after a visionary meeting with Christ. Peter is shown as a total weakling and a faulty spiritual guide. Melchior prophetically observes, "Alas for thee and those that take thee for a guide for verily this fatal clinging of the soul to things *temporal* shall warp the way for ever and taint thy mission."[58] This is an attack on the Petrine tradition of papal claims, based on the quicksand of Peter's denial, as Corelli sees it, rather than on the rock of Peter's confession.

The picture of Christ is a startling one. In theological terms, one could call it either Docetic or Monophysite: Christ is simply a divine being. He is "the Figure" whose features are universal, "neither Greek nor Roman nor Egyptian." Stripped to carry the cross, he has the physique of Hercules and the beauty of a naked Apollo. During the interrogation by Pilate, this tension of potent Divinity in a frail human vessel or the appearance of one is vividly described: "No verbal answer was vouchsafed to him [Pilate],—only a look, and in the invincible authority and grandeur of that look there was something of a darkness and light intermingled,—something of the dread solemnity of the thunder-cloud before the lightning leaps forth, sword-like, to destroy" (*B*, 41–42). This is the heart of Corelli's "electric" Christology. In *The Romance of the Two Worlds* (1886) the scientist Heliobas discovers that with the powers of personal electricity he can summon the soul from the body and teleport it to distant worlds. Electricity is the key to ecstasy. Holy Scripture is a monumental power station and the cable laid between earth and heaven is the person of Christ. This wild speculation is grounded upon Victorian investigations in mesmerism and animal magnetism as a way of reconciling materialist and spiritualist philosophies.

A more familiar allegorical method is used by Corelli in describing the Resurrection on Easter morning. After initial transports of language to sketch the power of the angels, very much Pre-Raphaelite "Beings," Corelli contrasts the prostrate Barabbas, "animal man," with the "creative Soul of the Universe": "In strange contrast, stood the pure and stately embodiment of the Spirit of God made human,—the example of a perfect manhood; the emblem of life and the symbol of Genius, which, slandered and tortured, and slain and buried, rises eternally triumphant over evil and death" (B, 254). The physical reality of the Resurrection is affirmed, but spiritualized at the same moment. There is really little difference between Christ's glorified body after the event and the perfect body assumed in the Incarnation. The body is at best a convenient vehicle for the spirit. Some religious writers of the time faulted Corelli's often bizarre vocabulary, but those criticisms had little consequence for the former Minnie Mackay as she glided in her later years in a gondola imported from Venice near her home in Stratford-upon-Avon.

Later in the century the Jewish point of view about Jesus was finally articulated for the general reader. Joseph Jacobs (1854–1916), the folklorist and literary critic who wrote extensively on fairy tales, composed in his documentary novel *Jesus as Others Saw Him* (1895) an "anti-Gospel," against what was regarded as the preposterous legends and myths about "Jesus of Nazara."[59] The Dreyfus affair had prompted Jacobs to write this fictional memoir of Meshullam ben Zadok, a scribe at Alexandria, addressed to Aglaophonos, a Greek physician at Corinth, who had met Saul of Tarsus. Jacobs wanted to show Jesus as "a Jew of the Jews" whose sayings, including various *logia* and apocrypha, embedded in the early Church Fathers and unearthed in recent finds, recalled the sayings of contemporary rabbis, and whose ethical system was based on the Jewish catechetical "Two Ways," reproduced in the novel. Interest in the "Two Ways" was also probably raised by the similar material found in the *Epistle of Barnabas* (chaps. 18–20), whose text was contained in the important *Codex Sinaiticus* in the British Museum. The image of Jesus as a compassionate refuge from harsh Jewish law is refuted, since rabbinic law, the author insists, had already modified the Levitical decrees, as in the case of the woman taken in adultery. She would not have been stoned; it was only an opportunity to test Jesus.

Jacobs judges that the time is ripe for an exercise such as his own, since what "is known as the modern or critical view is ever approaching nearer the Jewish protest against the Christian claims in these regards." Those controverted claims are the concept of a blood covenant, in which Jesus is a kind of demigod, and the various miraculous narratives surrounding his birth, temptation in the wilderness, and death. That modern critical view Jacobs identifies as dependent upon the Synoptics; John's Gospel, regarded as anti-Jewish, is abandoned as "entirely apocryphal." Jews, prompted by crimes committed against them by Christians, had rejected the figure of the Pauline Christ and thus subsequently ignored the Jesus of the Synoptics. Jacobs was trying to rescue the historical Jesus for both Christians and Jews. He shows Jesus as a typical rabbi of his time, one who was tender to the poor, who bore the yoke of the Law willingly, and who was the obedient Son of the ever-present Father, as the righteous can all be called Sons of God. On the other side, Jesus disregarded the beauty of nature, never smiled, and taught only by rebuking. In an "Apologia for the Jews" Jacobs concludes that Jesus' death was in reality a "sublime suicide" because during Holy Week he had systematically alienated the priests, Pharisees, and people and did not properly explain himself, keeping a sullen and arrogant silence, which was broken only by his false confession of guilt. Jacobs placed much importance on the incident of the coin of tribute, adorning the front cover of the first edition with its image. Jesus' refusal of the role of Messiah, symbolized in his willingness to pay the tribute to Rome, alienated his followers and sealed his death.

If there is a key to Jacobs's portrayal, it is in Jesus' shame over his own illegitimacy. His antagonists knowingly yell "Mamzer!" at him. This unlocks the visionary experience of Jesus at his baptism, the experience of "Bath Kol" conferred in the words "Thou art my son." It is the inner protest of his soul against the slur on his birth and his transforming recognition of the eternal Fatherhood of God. The silent shame shown by Jesus when he is cruelly asked to judge the woman taken in adultery is really caused by the insensitive inquiry in front of the accused woman. There is the implication, however, that Jesus' embarrassment is due equally to shame over his own dubious birth. At his trial, wearing a wreath of roses of some reveler instead of the legendary crown of thorns (which Jacobs thought was rationally improbable), the crowds demand the release of the revolutionary Jesus Bar Abba (Barabbas, the "son of the father") instead of the once arrogant Jesus Bar Amma ("son of his mother") (*AO*, 199).

Jacobs has blended in a fascinating and provocative account basic elements that concerned the authors of lives of Jesus late in the century:

comparisons with a Jewish perspective on the documents and serious regard for recent biblical scholarship. To this he added an attempt to understand the psychological makeup of Jesus, not only how others saw
him but how he saw himself.

"The Sunday School Set": Children's Literature and Religious Issues

In the same measure as Early Church novels for adults, those written es-
pecially for children, besides addressing the fundamental truths of religion and morality, also recounted the topical issues in the Anglican
Church from the particular ecclesiastical stances of their authors: Low,
Broad, and High. The multiple tales of John Mason Neale and Charlotte
Yonge, discussed in chapter 3, are examples of what have been called
novels "for the Sunday School set."[60] A variety of Evangelical and Broad
Church clergy and religiously motivated laity also contributed to this
genre of juvenile literature.

Elizabeth Rundle Charles (1828–96), best known for her *History of
the Schönberg-Cotta Family* (1862), in which Martin Luther is a main character, was a novelist of latitudinarian interests, although usually categorized as an Evangelical.[61] Her works on the Early Church, for the most
part martyrs' tales, depict many lands and ages: *Tales and Sketches of Christian Life* (1850); *The Cripple of Antioch, and Other Scenes from Christian Life
in Early Times* (1856); *Sketches of Christian Life in England in the Olden
Time* (1864), showing the continuity of martyrs from St. Alban up
through the victims of the Marian persecution; *The Victory of the Vanquished: A Tale of the First Century* (1870); *Conquering and to Conquer: A
Story of Rome in the Days of St. Jerome* (1876); *Lapsed, but Not Lost: A Story
of Roman Carthage* (1877), a tale of the Decian persecution in which
Cyprian figures prominently; *Martyrs and Saints of the First Twelve Centuries: Studies from the Lives of the Black Letter Saints of the English Calendar*
(1887); and *Attila and His Conquerors: A Story of the Days of St. Patrick and
St. Leo the Great* (1894). The hagiographies she constructed were meant
to show the proper place of remembrance of the saints in the devotions
of the English Church and to link, much like the martyrologist Foxe,
the latter-day Reformation martyrs with the "true Church" of saints
throughout the ages.

Another Evangelical, the Reverend Gerald Stanley Davies (1845–1927), a product of the Charterhouse in London, published only two Early Church novels: *Gaudentius: A Story of the Colosseum* (1874) and *Julian's Dream: A Story of A.D. 362* (1875). The first is an expansion of the legend of Gaudentius, the architect of the Flavian amphitheater in Rome and a martyr there himself, somewhat like Monsieur Guillotine. It recounts the final moments of the martyrs who died there under Domitian in A.D. 93 as "soldiers of the cross" for the Christian "FAITH." Most of this short novel is given over to a physical description of the Colosseum itself. The centrality of the cross in Davies's theology is evident also in his work *St. Paul in Greece* (1877).

Julian's Dream is a cautionary tale of the corruption and "black deeds" of the age in which emperors raised Christianity from the "cottage and the catacomb" to "the palace and the cathedral." Using Julian's own writings, Davies attempts to show, as a warning to his own age, how Christianity failed to win this sensitive soul to Christ. One benefit of Julian's treatment of the Church was that her "false auxiliaries" deserted her and her true sons, whether "Athanasians" or Arians, showed themselves ready to suffer for Christ. He obviously is referring to Anglo-Catholics who deserted the English Church for Rome, and he voices a Broad Church position in regard to doctrinal differences. Davies, by attacking Julian's restoration of paganism, is similarly attacking Victorian advocates of Ritualism, Spiritualism, and Apocalyptic enthusiasts who were predicting the Last Day just as at the time of Julian's apostasy.

Annie Molyneux Peploe (1805–80), the wife of the Reverend John Birch Webb, the vicar of Weably, Herefordshire, published twenty-five works from 1841 to 1879. In *Naomi; or, The Last Days of Jerusalem* (1841), the heroine, a young Jewess searching the Scriptures for prophecies of the Messiah, learns from Mary of Bethany, the sister of Lazarus, that man is justified by faith alone. Christ had "borne His Father's wrath." Man proceeds through repentance and conversion to that faith, "founded on the Rock of Ages." No man can be pure and holy except through Jesus, who is the "power of God." Those who turn aside or slip away are warned by the fiery fate of Jerusalem in its fall, "a faint representation of that eternal punishment where those who resist in rebellion will suffer and blaspheme forever, but repent not." Converts are told to read the Book of Life, in this case the Gospel of Matthew, and believe. Mrs.

Webb admonishes her young readers, lest they become only "nominal Christians": "[Let] us beware that with all the light of the Gospel, and all the advantages of a Christian education, we do not practically reject the Saviour, and in our lives deny Him."[62] In *Julamerk* (1849) she traced the story of the Nestorians in Persia in the early fifth century. *The Martyrs of Carthage: A Tale of the Times of Old* (1850) is an expanded version of the story of St. Vivia Perpetua, written to set the Christian on guard against Satan's wiles "in these latter days." It is also an appeal to experience Christianity for oneself: "Oh, *try it*, all you who now doubt its power, and you will find that *true religion* and *true happiness* are synonymous terms."[63]

In *Alypius of Tagaste: A Tale of the Early Church* (1865) Mrs. Webb delineates the parallel histories of the historical Alypius and Augustine and their gradual movement toward faith. After many vicissitudes, including a romantic attachment between Alypius and a priestess of Isis in Egypt, both young men finally recognize the limits of reason and philosophy as the ground of morality and discover that purity and holiness can be preserved "only in the strength of ANOTHER." These devoted friends, more like twin brothers, disagree only on the issue of Augustine's monasticism, which Alypius deems a "useless and unprofitable sacrifice." On the other hand, Webb concludes, it was useful at that early period, just as enforced celibacy had a continuing place in "schools and depositories of learning." She was not sympathetic to the current agitation to remove ordination and celibacy as prerequisites for dons at Oxford and Cambridge. Her *Pomponia; or, The Gospel in Caesar's Household* (1867) introduced the Christian wife of Plautius, the Roman legate in Britain. Nero, the burning of Rome, and the first persecution of Christians all figure prominently in this novel, combining interest in British locales with the apocalyptic images of the Great Fire.

Like Mrs. Webb, other writers provided short works to meet the seemingly insatiable thirst for martyrs' tales and romantic accounts of Church history: M. Selina Bunbury's *Stories from Church History, from the Introduction of Christianity to the Sixteenth Century* (1828), Annie Field Elsdale's *Tales of the Martyrs; or, Sketches from Church History* (1844), the work of the Roman Catholic "MFS" (Mrs. F. Seamer, afterward Seymour), *Stories of Holy Lives* (1875), and those of "G. W.," *Martyr Tales and Sketches: For the Young* (1884) were brief accounts to be used by children as models for conduct and character.

On the Broad Church side, the Reverend Alfred John Church (1829–1912) was a prolific writer of juvenile literature. A pupil of F. D. Maurice at King's College, London, and a disciple of Mark Pattison at Lincoln College, Oxford, Church taught at several distinguished schools, eventually rising to the headmastership at Henley before becoming professor of Latin at University College, London. *Stories of the Last Days of Jerusalem* (1880) is actually a transcription of the works of Josephus for use in schools. His tales, no matter what the initial locale, invariably bring the hero and the reader safely back to Britain. Set mostly in the region of the Isle of Wight, *The Count of the Saxon Shore; or, The Villa in Vectis* (1887) recounts the withdrawal of the Roman legions by Stilicho, leaving Aelius "the Count of the Saxon Shore" behind to maintain the imperial presence, the subsequent devastation by the Picts, and the arrival of the Angles and Saxons as allies to the inhabitants below Hadrian's Wall. The novel ends with an account of Arthur's legend-filled victory over the Saxons in 451. *To the Lions: A Tale of the Early Christians* (1889) describes Christian life in Bithynia in A.D. 112 under the governor, Pliny the Younger, who is accompanied by his historian friend, Cornelius Tacitus. The martyrdom of Flavius Clemens in A.D. 95 is recalled. Interestingly, Church denies that Domitilla, Flavius' wife, was a Christian, but does not state his reasons for rejecting that traditional ascription. His Broad Church position is evident in his recounting of the story of the collapse of a statue, struck only by a martyr's blood, "one of those strange occurrences which we may or may not call miracles, but which are certainly signs; so full are they of meaning, and not the less truly signs because they come from causes strictly natural."[64] Equally striking is a scene in which two sisters, one a deaconess, celebrate the Holy Communion "through the simple ritual which St. Paul describes in his first letter to the Corinthians." This is the only example in all the Early Church novels of women performing any liturgical function.

The Christians at the center of the story finally flee to safety in Britain, their escape arranged by Pliny himself. Behind this novel is Church's work on schoolboy editions of both the letters of Pliny and the histories of Tacitus. *The Burning of Rome: A Story of Nero's Days* (1891) repeats the familiar events of that epoch while stressing the British origin of Claudia Rufina, whom Church identifies as the wife of Pudens. In chapter 9 of his *Stories from English History*, vol. 1: *From Julius Caesar to the Black Prince* (1895) he states that there were a few Christians in England before the mission of Augustine, a comment designed to contradict those who in the 1880s and 1890s argued for a highly organized and visible Celtic Church. *The Burning of Rome* is also prominent as one of the bitterest attacks on the Jews, associated with Poppaea, contained in any of the novels. Church's last Early Church novel, *The Crown of Pine* (1905), is a story of St. Paul's mission in Corinth and the contemporaneous Isthmian Games, interweaving Christian and athletic imagery evident in the apostle's epistles.

Breaking away from a Calvinistic background, the Reverend Augustine David Crake (1836–90) composed a series of martyrs' tales and stories of Christianity in early Britain. *Aemilius: A Tale of the Decian and Valerian Persecutions* (1871) is set principally in Antioch and Rome from 250 to 269; *Evanus* (1872) retells major events in the days of Constantine; stepping back to a slightly earlier period, *The Camp on the Severn* (1875) depicts Britain in the reign of Diocletian in 303–4, including an account of the martyrdom of St. Alban. Constantius Chlorus, the father of Constantine, is shown ruling as Augustus from his capital at York. Using the age of Diocletian as a focus, *The Victor's Laurel* (1884) blends the stories of school life and the Tenth, and final, Persecution at Puteoli near Naples and in North Africa, around A.D. 302. The story ends at the time of the Council of Nicaea (325), when the confessors who had been maimed or tortured for the faith were venerated by the assembled bishops and the emperor. Britain was again the focus of Crake's interest in *The Doomed City; or, The Last Days of Durocina* (1885), which depicts the capture by the Saxons of Dorchester, one of the three ancient episcopal sees in Britain, and the mission of Augustine. A similar patriotic interest enlivens his *Stories of the Old Saints and the Anglo-Saxon Church* (1890).

A Broad Churchman who sympathized with "advanced" Anglo-Catholic views about ritual and who had an interest in the history of Christian art, the Reverend Edward Lewes Cutts (1824–1901) composed several Early Church novels and ecclesiastical biographies. *The Villa of Claudius: A Tale of the Roman-British Church* (1861) is set in A.D. 383 in the vicinity of Colchester, a region where Cutts had done extensive archaeological work. In this novel he makes a careful distinction between England and Rome in liturgy: "'The differences are small,' said the bishop, 'but that there are differences is important, and that those differences are small is also important.'"[65] He views with a critical eye the election of Pope Damasus, Jerome's position on asceticism, and Ambrose's polemics before the imperial court. In contrast to them, he urges that British Christians have only to hold fast to the faith once for all delivered to the saints. *St. Cedd's Cross* (1872) narrates the conversion of the East Saxons by Cedd, the bishop of London (ca. 654–64), and shares much in common with Cutts's ecclesiastical biographies *Saint Jerome* (1878), *Constantine the Great* (1881), *A Devotional History of Our Lord* (1882), and *Augustine of Canterbury* (1895), in which Cutts rationalizes the accounts of miraculous healings and repeats his assertion that Christianity was not introduced into Britain until A.D. 250 and did not constitute a viable ecclesiastical structure until Augustine and his monks landed at Thanet. In 1876 the archbishops selected Cutts to investigate the Syrian and Chaldean Churches, an assignment that resulted in the archbishop's Mission to the Assyrian Churches; a novel, entitled *Amina: A Tale of the Nestorians* (1882); and his own travel account, *Christians under the Crescent in Asia* (1887). Cutts was careful throughout his writing to shelter his own High Church sympathies behind strong denunciations of the pretensions of Rome.

Another Broad Church novelist having a taste for things "Catholic" (e.g., publicly displaying a crucifix) was Emma Marshall (1830–99). Her mother was a Quaker, but she herself grew up as an Anglican and was an ardent admirer of Charles Kingsley and Dean Arthur Stanley, both "muscular" Broad Churchmen.[66] Her biographer recorded that she always wished to live within sight of the Gothic roof of an ancient minster. Marshall was a natural Romantic, nostalgic for the "dreaming spires" of English country churches, candlelit choral services, and the ethos of the Book of Common Prayer. Her novel, *No. XIII; or, The Story of the Lost Vestal* (1885), depicts life under Diocletian and Constantine in Britain, Rome, and Alexandria. The protomartyr of Britain, St. Alban, is the center of the story. He was born at Verulamium (St. Albans) late in the third century and was a veteran of the legions under Diocletian in Rome. The new foundation of the diocese of St. Albans in 1877, having as its first bishop Thomas Legh Claughton, who was one of the first Anglican bishops to readopt pontifical regalia, was a timely incentive for this fictional biography. Marshall, like many of her colleagues writing for the young, was able to weave heroic stories of historical martyrs into descriptions of the local background, stories based on a general religious and patriotic appeal but usually prompted by some more immediate controversy or event. The British Church appeared to late Victorian believers as the nursing mother of a white-robed army of martyrs and saints.

LOOKING BACKWARD

The novels in this last chapter constitute a library of comment around one book, the Bible. Evangelicals sought ways to defend and spread the Gospel at the same time that secularists and Broad Churchmen were adopting a more critical understanding of the Gospels. Free thinkers sought to use this scholarship against the Christian faith, while Broad Churchmen employed it in their new program of Christian apologetics. These latter-day apologists adopted the Coleridgean view of religion as a "higher reason" through the imagination, in the face of the broader claims of science, and agreed that the Bible must be read with other books as an equal, with due regard, of course, to its venerability and its greater concentration of revealed truth. Revelation and inspiration, they confessed, were operative everywhere in nature and in the mysteries of inner experience, but Revelation spoke with clearer accents in the Bible. It was there that the Eternal articulated its own identity: God is love. Evangelicals undervalued the creeds as impositions on the biblical message, whereas Broad Churchmen found in the formal and controversy-forged formularies none of the living spirit revealed through the biblical text and ethos. The discovery of new texts and fragments spurred those interested in preserving basic Christianity to seek the "kernel" of that message, apart from the husk of controversy and what they called "bookishness."

Questions about the nature and function of Christ naturally arose. Whether authors accepted or rejected the Reformation stress on justification *sola fide* in literature for children and adults, it was universally accepted that devotion to the person and simple message of Jesus was a transforming experience for individuals and nations. Writers disagreed about the sense in which Jesus was to be understood as "Son of God";

they all agreed, however, that he was a compassionate "Friend." They worshiped the "gentle Jesus" figure, warm and human. They supposed this "winning humanity," a product really of their own idealism and humanitarianism, to be the picture supplied by the Synoptics and the reason for the early expansion of Christianity. To this was added their rendering of the popular Johannine message: Jesus is love. The numerous martyrs' tales were then seen as the tokens of the victory of faith; since Christians loved Jesus so much, they were willing to die for him. This in itself was a further "proof" of Christian Revelation.

While stalking through the dense thicket of biblical criticism, however, questers for the historical Jesus rediscovered the importance of eschatology in the primitive Gospel and early Christian ethic. This insight was developed contemporaneously with the implied eschatology of a transformed future social order of Marxism and socialism. Apocalyptic tensions had been present in the novels throughout the century; now investigators voiced uneasiness that those unfulfilled expectations might undercut Christianity. Their study of the roots of Christian apocalyptic literature, as well as work on the texts and new translations of the Bible, led them back to the Jews. These continuing witnesses of God's covenant, degraded socially and racially in portrayals in most Victorian fiction, began to be considered seriously, apart from being the object of Evangelical missions, at a time when pogroms abroad and Zionist fervor at home created an uneasy national interest. The novelists circumvented those tensions by the simple expedient of mass baptism. Discussion of a Jewish state, likewise, was viewed simply in the apocalyptic terms of the Fall of Jerusalem under Titus and then Hadrian, providing images for a Christian understanding of the Last Day.

Coupled programmatically with the Jews were the Roman Catholics, who, with their Anglo-Catholic sympathizers, were seen as ceremonial judaizers. This renewed attention to the religion of the Recusants also occurred when Roman Catholics were taking a more prominent role in the nation. The first Catholic member of the cabinet took office almost fifty years after Catholic Emancipation, at a time when the Irish question was again dividing the country. For many writers, Roman Catholicism was not Christianity at all but a Hegelian synthesis of pagan cult and atheism with a glittering veneer of the Gospel. After the decree on Papal Infallibility, more and more writers felt that Antichrist, the new

Nero in Rome, had been unmasked, just as the "liberal" Pio Nono (Pius IX) had been unmasked in 1848. Vaticanism was seen as a new slavery, and Protestant England, the great abolitionist, was the appointed deliverer for the free-thinking, yet Christian, civilization of the modern world. The novels dealing with the Early British Church are really the miraculous-birth narratives of an English messianism proclaimed in the latter days of Victoria's imperial reign.

APPENDIX A

COLLECTIONS OF SAINTS' LIVES

Adams, D. C. O. *The Saints and Missionaries of the Anglo-Saxon Era*. 2d series. Oxford, 1897–1901.

Baring-Gould, Sabine. *The Lives of the Saints*. 16 vols. London, 1897–98.

Bedjan, Paul. *Acta martyrum et sanctorum Syriace*. 7 vols. Paris, 1890–97.

Bell, Mrs. Arthur George. *The Saints in Christian Art*. 3 vols. London, 1901–4.

Butler, Alban. *The Lives of the Fathers, Martyrs, and Other Principal Saints*. 4 vols. London, 1756–59.

Challoner, Richard. *Britannia Sancta; or, The Lives of the Most Celebrated British, English, Scottish, and Irish Saints*. 2 parts. London, 1745.

Faber, F. W., et al. *The Saints and Servants of God*. 42 vols. London, 1847–56.

Forbes, Alexander P. *Kalendars of Scottish Saints*. Edinburgh, 1874.

Godescard, J. F. *Vies des pères, des martyrs, et autres principaux saints, traduit librement de l'anglais d'Alban Butler*. 12 vols. Paris, 1763–.

Guérin, Paul. *Les Petits Bollandistes*. 7th ed. 18 vols. Paris, 1876.

Hyvernat, H. *Les Actes des martyrs de l'Égypte*. Paris, 1886–.

Mabillon, J., et al. *Acta Sanctorum ordinis S. Benedicti*. 9 vols. Paris, 1668–1701.

Martinov, J. E. *Annus ecclesiasticus Graeco-Slavicus*. Brussels, 1863.

Newman, J. H. *Lives of the Irish Saints*. 12 vols. Dublin, 1875–.

Owen, Robert. *Sanctorale Catholicum, or Book of Saints*. London, 1880.

Pétin, Abbé. *Dictionnaire hagiographique*. 2 vols. Paris, 1850.

Räss, A., and N. Weiss. *Leben der Heiligen*. 23 vols. Mainz, 1823–.

Rees, W. J. *Lives of the Cambro-British Saints of the Fifth and Immediat Succeeding Centuries*. Llandovery, 1853.

Stadler, J. E., and F. J. Heim. *Vollständiges Heiligen Lexikon*. 5 vols. Augsburg, 1858–.

Stanton, Richard. *A Menology of England and Wales*. London, 1887, 1892.

APPENDIX B

THE JERUSALEM BISHOPRIC

IN OCTOBER 1841 the British government and King Frederick Wilhelm IV of Prussia together erected (5 Vict.c.6) a bishopric of Jerusalem having episcopal jurisdiction over Palestine, Syria, Chaldea, Egypt, and Abyssinia but subject to future limitations or alterations. The plan was conceived to secure British and German interests in the Levant as the joint protectors of the small group of Protestants there to balance the presence of France and Russia as protectors of the Roman Catholics and Orthodox, respectively; see A. L. Tibawi, *British Interests in Palestine, 1800–1901* (London: Oxford University Press, 1961). Beyond these political and commercial interests the scheme was motivated by theological considerations. The king of Prussia desired the union of Protestant churches and wished to install bishops in Germany, seeing this cooperative venture as a means of securing episcopal consecration from the Anglicans. English Evangelicals in the London Society for Promoting Christianity among the Jews—one of the "six societies," among whose members was Lord Ashley, the seventh earl of Shaftesbury—saw this as a step in the necessary order of premillennial events, inaugurating the Second Coming; see Georgina Battiscombe, *Shaftesbury, The Great Reformer, 1801–1885* (Boston: Houghton Mifflin, 1975), 101–3, 137–40; S. C. Orchard, "English Evangelical Eschatology" (Ph.D. diss., Cambridge University, 1968). In July 1841 Archbishop Howley of Canterbury and Bishop Blomfield of London accepted the proposals of Chevalier Bunsen, the Prussian special envoy; Ashley, an unofficial participant in the negotiations, selected the first incumbent, Michael Solomon Alexander, born a Prussian Jew in Posen, professor of Hebrew at King's College, London, although he had "no Greek and little Latin." The bishopric was not in British territory, so Parliament empowered the archbishops of Canterbury and York to consecrate British subjects or citizens of any other State to be bishops in any foreign country; their episcopal jurisdiction was to extend over British subjects and "such other Protestant congregations as may be desirous of placing themselves under his or their authority." Consecration was to be by Anglican bishops, and candidates were to be nominated alternately by the two crowns, the archbishop of Canterbury retaining a veto over the Prussian nominee; the king of Prussia and an English subscription list split the costs of the bishop's stipend. German congregations could retain their own form of worship, but ordination of clergy was to be by the Anglican ordinal.

Under the same statute a bishop of Gibraltar was named, his jurisdiction extending to Malta, where the Roman Catholic archbishop had been formally recognized by the British government as the "Bishop of Malta," and over Italy, where the incumbent, Dr. Tomlinson, carried out episcopal functions in Rome. The sultanate of Turkey protested under pressure from the French and the Orthodox. Lord Aberdeen, the new foreign secretary, less than enthusiastic about the plan, told the Turkish envoy, while Archbishop Howley assured the Orthodox, that the new bishop was limited to evangelizing the 10,000 Jews and the few Protestants resident there and that his title was to be Bishop of the United Church of England and Ireland in Jerusalem. Aberdeen gradually impressed Howley with his apprehension over the plan.

Newman, who circulated a protest at the time, identified the plan as one of the three events that broke his confidence in the bishops and the Anglican Church; see *Apologia*, 144–49. The two main theological objections Newman advanced were (1) that it allied the Anglican Church with the "heresies" of Lutheranism and Calvinism, mentioning specifically the threat to the doctrine of Baptismal Regeneration such an alliance posed, and (2) that it was schismatical, appointing bishops in ancient sees where there were already bishops functioning. Reformed Germans, on the other hand, objected to this cooperation with the "corrupt" Church of England and to the royal scheme for introducing bishops into the Prussian Church. The Tractarians were divided. Pusey, under Gladstone's influence, initially supported the plan but later sided with Newman. Gladstone, Hook, and Palmer of Worcester College, among others, defended it, some fervently, seeing it as a means of extending the blessings of episcopal government to the bishopless Prussians. Keble was "almost unmoved" by the entire affair; see Battiscombe, *John Keble*, 226–27. When Alexander died in 1845, his successor, Bishop Samuel Gobat, was appointed amid protests, which increased because of his personal style and his active proselytizing. The joint bishopric lasted for forty-five years and was eventually placed under purely British auspices; see Chadwick, *Victorian Church*, 1:189–93; R. W. Greaves, "The Jerusalem Bishopric, 1841," *English Historical Review* 64 (July 1949): 328–52.

Appendix C

THE GORHAM CASE AND BAPTISMAL REGENERATION

IN 1835 BAPTISMAL regeneration became a party badge for the Tractarians. In that year E. B. Pusey published his lengthy "pamphlet" on baptism (Tracts 67, 68, 69) as an attack on the antisacramental character of Evangelical belief and as a defense of the unity of Anglican formularies with the "primitive view," that is, the New Testament and the Fathers. He maintained that baptism was the sole means of regeneration and of salvation itself, that postbaptismal sin required a life of penitence, and that the sacrament not only was a sign but conveyed "the grace annexed to it." He denigrated the "low" view of Zwingli that baptism was merely a sign of entrance into the Christian community, and tendentiously linked Calvin and Luther to this position. Calvin, contrariwise, maintained that baptism gave man assurance of pardon but was efficacious for the elect alone, while Luther viewed it as a promise of divine grace necessary to salvation. Offended by Pusey's views, F. D. Maurice published in 1837 a "Letter on Baptism," which became part of the first edition of his *Kingdom of Christ* (1838). He rejected both the Evangelical stress on personal faith as the instrument of justification and the High Church stress on baptismal regeneration and lifelong penitence. Both parties, he felt, ignored the transforming power of Christ and man's continual corporate union with Christ. Maurice described baptism as a "sacrament of constant union," which did not create the already established relationship of God and man in Christ but was necessary as a convenant for man to become a member of Christ's Body. Other writers reacted to the popular view of Tractarian principles. Charlotte Brontë caricatured in *Shirley* (1849) the Puseyite position when she imagined with horror infants "undergoing regeneration by nursery-baptism in wash-hand-basins."

The action of Bishop Phillpotts of Exeter in refusing to institute G. C. Gorham to the living of Bramford Speke, because of the vicar's Calvinistic understanding of baptism, and the ensuing litigation embroiled the High Church party. A decision for the bishop, it was generally agreed, would have resulted in widespread disaffection among Evangelicals and Broad Churchmen, who for the most part, while not strictly Calvinistic, considered the Prayer Book service's language about regeneration to be conditional rather than descriptive. In 1850 the Privy Council ruled in favor of Gorham. The decision, as understood by High Churchmen, seemed to argue against Phillpotts's interpretation of Articles 25, 27, and 29 on baptism and the sacraments and to advance the Royal Supremacy as the ultimate authority over the teaching office of the Church. This latter aspect, the Erastian question, soon eclipsed the sacramental question. Tractarians, convinced that Scripture, the Fathers, the Prayer Book, and Articles were unanimous in supporting them, wrote extensively on both aspects of the issue, but their sacramental concerns had already during the 1840s shifted away from this point about baptism to a developing theology of the Eucharist and a sacramental understanding of the Incarnation. Baptismal regeneration was pushed out of the arena of controversy by more pressing issues; in 1864 the Evangelical Lord Shaftesbury reflected on this when he wrote to Pusey acknowledging that baptismal regeneration was no longer a crucial topic, because all parties realized that the understanding of the Atonement itself was being dramatically eroded by the work of liberal theologians and secularists.

ABBREVIATIONS

PRIMARY MATERIAL

A	James, *Attila: A Romance*
Ac	Farrie, *Acte: A Novel*
An	Collins, *Antonia; or, The Fall of Rome*
AO	Jacobs, *Jesus as Others Saw Him: A Retrospect*, A.D. 54
Ap	Neale, *The Farm of Aptonga: A Story of the Times of St. Cyprian*
B	Corelli, *Barabbas: A Dream of the World's Tragedy*
BG	Pottinger, *Blue and Green; or, The Gift of God*
C	Newman, *Callista: A Tale of the Third Century*
D	Baring-Gould, *Domitia*
DB	Tucker, *Daybreak in Britain*
E	Moore, *The Epicurean: A Tale*
EH	Neale, *English History for Children*
Es	Mossman, *Epiphanius: The History of His Childhood and Youth as Told by Himself*
F	Wiseman, *Fabiola; or, The Church of the Catacombs*
G	Whyte-Melville, *The Gladiators*
GC	Farrar, *Gathering Clouds: A Tale of the Days of St. Chrysostom*
H	Kingsley, *Hypatia; or, New Foes with an Old Face*
HC	Mossman, *A History of the Catholic Church of Jesus Christ from the Death of Saint John to the Middle of the Second Century*
I	Holt, *Imogen: A Tale of the Early British Church*
J	Kingston, *Jovinian: A Story of the Early Days of Papal Rome*
M	Hoppus, *Masters of the World*
N	Graham, *Neara: A Tale of Ancient Rome*
Ns	Carpenter, *Narcissus: A Tale of Early Christian Times*
O	Mercier, *Our Mother Church: Being Simple Talk on High Topics*
P	Bulwer-Lytton, *The Last Days of Pompeii*
Pp	Baring-Gould, *Perpetua: A Story of Nîmes in* A.D. 213

R	Wilberforce, *Rutilius and Lucius; or, Stories of the Third Age*
S	Yonge, *The Slaves of Sabinus, Jew and Gentile*
SW	Croly, *Tarry Thou till I Come; or, Salathiel, the Wandering Jew*
V	Lockhart, *Valerius: A Roman Story*
Z	Smith, *Zillah: A Tale of the Holy City*

JOURNALS

AQ	*American Quarterly*
BNYPL	*Bulletin of the New York Public Library*
MLR	*Modern Language Review*
PQ	*Philological Quarterly*
VN	*Victorian Newsletter*

NOTES

INTRODUCTION

1. Frederic Rogers (Lord Blachford), quoted by Raymond Chapman, *The Victorian Debate*, 258.

2. Raymond Chapman, *Faith and Revolt*, 147, 148.

3. See Samuel Pickering Jr., *The Moral Tradition in English Fiction, 1785–1850* (University Press of New England, 1977). The Evangelical tales of Hannah More, Rowland Hill, and Mrs. Sherwood are considered important precursors of the Victorian religious novel: Margaret Maison, *The Victorian Vision: Studies in the Religious Novel*, 89.

4. Maison, *Victorian Vision*, 5.

5. George P. Gooch, *History and Historians in the Nineteenth Century*, 333.

6. Avrom Fleishman, *The English Historical Novel*, 27; Christopher Hill, "The Norman Yoke," *Democracy and the Labour Movement: Essays in Honour of Donna Tor*, ed. John Saville (London: Lawrence & Wishart, 1954).

7. E. A. Freeman, *The Growth of the English Constitution* (London: Macmillan, 1872), 17–21, quoted in H. J. Hanham, ed., *The Nineteenth-Century Constitution, 1815–1914: Documents and Commentary* (Cambridge: Cambridge University Press, 1969), 20.

8. Vernon F. Storr, *The Development of English Theology in the Nineteenth Century, 1800–1860* (London: Longmans, 1913). Brilioth also points out unhistorical methods employed; see Yngve Brilioth, *Evangelicalism and the Oxford Movement* (London: Oxford University Press, 1934).

9. John Henry Newman, Papers on Development: Newman MSS in the Oratory of St. Philip Neri, Birmingham, B2.I and B2.II, batch 135, cited by Jaroslav Pelikan, *Development of Christian Doctrine: Some Historical Prolegomena* (New Haven: Yale University Press, 1969), 37.

10. Maison, *Victorian Vision*, 1, 6, 224–25; Chapman, *Victorian Debate*, 261. Randall T. Davidson, later archbishop of Canterbury (1903–28), while yet dean of Windsor, described Mrs. Humphry Ward's best-seller *Robert Elsmere* (1888) as a "boiler down," attacking her misinterpretation of B. F. Westcott's understand-

ing of the affinity of Christianity to its Jewish and Hellenistic antecedents and her "Unitarian" idea of a "New Gospel of Brotherhood": Davidson, "Religious Novels," *Contemporary Review* (November 1888), 674–82. *Elsmere* remains a classic statement of the religious doubt and upheaval of the late Victorian period.

11. William Palmer, *A Narrative of Events Connected with the Publication of the Tracts for the Times* (Oxford, 1843), 44. In a later edition Palmer was more sharply critical of attitudes and personalities connected with the early tracts.

12. Chapman, *Faith and Revolt*, 146. Newman creates these titles in his first novel, *Loss and Gain* (1848); see 1962 ed., 199.

13. F. L. Cross, *The Oxford Movement and the Seventeenth Century* (London: SPCK, 1933). For a more recent introduction to the question, see Owen Chadwick, *The Mind of the Oxford Movement*. Ecumenical discussions among Anglicans, Lutherans, and Roman Catholics have generated some important surveys: Gareth Bennett, "Patristic Tradition in Anglican Thought, 1660–1900"; and Stanley Greenslade, "The Authority of the Tradition of the Early Church in Early Anglican Thought." An early ecumenical essay from the Roman Catholic perspective is provided by George Tavard, *The Quest for Catholicity*.

14. Vincent of Lerins, *Commonitorium*, ed. R. S. Moxon (Cambridge: Cambridge University Press, 1915), [2.3] 10. The original reads: "quod ubique, quod semper, quod ab omnibus." The Tractarians placed the test of "antiquity" first as part of their anti-Roman argumentation.

15. Richard Pfaff, "The Library of the Fathers"; "Anglo-American Patristic Translations 1866–1900," *Journal of Ecclesiastical History* 28 (January 1977), 39–55. The first Hampden controversy occurred in 1836 when Melbourne appointed the Whig clergyman Renn Hampden Regius Professor of Divinity at Oxford, a man Tractarians and Evangelicals alleged was doctrinally unorthodox. The second controversy involved Hampden's election as bishop of Hereford in 1848. See Owen Chadwick, *The Victorian Church*, 1:112–21.

16. Chadwick, *Victorian Church*, 2:80–81.

17. Chapman, *Faith and Revolt*, 143.

18. Frederic Rogers (Lord Blachford), quoted in Chapman, *Faith and Revolt*, 281. Piers Brendon, *Hurrell Froude and the Oxford Movement*, 71; see also 76–77.

19. John McNeill, *Modern Christian Movements*, 113.

20. Alf Härdelin, *The Tractarian Understanding of the Eucharist*, 121, 186. Keble developed this theme of "security" later in Tract 52.

21. Georgina Battiscombe, *John Keble*, 99, 105. By 1873 it had sold 379,000 copies.

22. See W. J. A. M. Beek, *John Keble's Literary and Religious Contributions to the Oxford Movement* (Nijmegen: Centrale Drukk., 1959). Keble's Tract 89, "On the Mysticism of the Fathers" (1840, although writing had begun by 1837),

showed the influence of the Alexandrian school and Samuel Taylor Coleridge on imagination; Battiscombe, *John Keble*, 214–15. See also John Coulson, *Newman and the Common Tradition: A Study in the Language of Church and Society* (London: Oxford University Press, 1971).

23. Battiscombe, *John Keble*, 211, 242. Pfaff assigns Keble a very little part in the work of the Library of the Fathers series ("Library of the Fathers," 341 n. 27).

24. McNeill, *Modern Christian Movements*, 128. See *The Works of . . . Mr. Richard Hooker: With an Account of His Life and Death by Isaac Walton*, ed. John Keble, 3 vols. (Oxford: Clarendon, 1836).

25. Quoted by Brendon, *Hurrell Froude*, 149.

26. Letter to Robert Isaac Wilberforce (10 July 1850), criticizing the latter's Archdeacon's Charge. In 1854 he criticized Wilberforce again for adopting "a philosophical dream," quoted in Battiscombe, *John Keble*, 306–7.

27. Letter to Mrs. Armstrong (12 January 1863), quoted in Battiscombe, *John Keble*, 335.

28. Letter of John Keble to Bishop Samuel Wilberforce (13 June 1851), quoted by Anonymous (author of "Charles Lowder"), *The Story of Dr. Pusey's Life*, 2d ed. (London: Longmans, Green, 1900), 363.

29. Letter of E. B. Pusey to John Keble (18 February [1848?]), quoted in *Pusey's Life*, 336.

30. Quoted in Meriol Trevor, *Newman*, vol. 1: *The Pillar of the Cloud*, vol. 2: *Light in Winter* (Garden City, N.Y.: Doubleday, 1962–63), 1:216.

31. W. Tuckwell, *Reminiscences of Oxford* (1900), quoted in W. L. Burn, *The Age of Equipoise: A Study of the Mid-Victorian Generation* (New York: W. W. Norton, 1965), 72. In 1898 William Temple, archbishop of Canterbury, declared that prayers for the dead were lawful but not compulsory; see Chadwick, *Victorian Church*, 2:356.

32. Letter of E. B. Pusey (1881), quoted in *Pusey's Life*, 534.

33. Wilfrid Ward, *Life of Newman*, 2 vols. (London: Longmans, 1912), 1:444. See the important article that sets this biography in the context of the Modernist controversy in the reign of Pius X: Sheridan Gilley, "Wilfrid Ward and His Life of Newman," *Journal of Ecclesiastical History* 29 (April 1978), 177–93.

34. Charles Stephen Dessain, *John Henry Newman* (London: Nelson, 1966), 10–11. The late Father Dessain of the Oratory gives an admirable, brief survey of Newman's grounding in Scripture and the Fathers. He relates how Newman later inserted references in pencil in the first edition copies of his sermons, showing how dependent he was on these sources (17). Coming late to the Caroline divines, Newman found the immediate "standard of Christian doctrine" in Ambrose, Augustine, Jerome, John Chrysostom, the Cappadocians (especially on the question of celibacy), Athanasius, Cyril of Jerusalem, the Alexandrians,

Lactantius, and Sulpicius Severus. For a helpful survey of articles concerning Newman's use of the Fathers, especially the Alexandrians, in the formulation of his educational theories, see Martin Svaglic, "John Henry Newman, Man and Humanist," *Victorian Prose: A Guide to Research*, ed. David DeLaura, 115–65, esp. 138 ff.

35. John Henry Newman, *Lectures on Certain Difficulties Felt by Anglicans in Submitting to the Catholic Church*, 293; "The Church of the Fathers" (1833), *Essays and Sketches*, ed. Harrold, 3:3.

36. Newman followed this manner in both his Anglican and Roman Catholic careers. Archbishop Laud was Cyprian, Jeremy Taylor was Chrysostom, and conversely Augustine against the Donatists was a recapitulation of the Non-Juror dispute ("Primitive Christianity" [1833–36]); William Palmer writing on the Jansenists in his *Essay on the Church* (1838) was a "Nestorian" writing on the relationship of Rome and the Monophysites (*Certain Difficulties*, 249); and Anglicans in general were Nestorians, Monophysites, Eutychians, Eusebians, Donatists, and Arians. It was not a matter of doctrinal identity in this final list but a question of the relationships of the rival religious bodies of the fourth and fifth centuries to the State.

37. John Henry Newman, *Via Media*, vol. 1, rev. ed. (1877), 38, quoted in Thomas Bokenkotter, *Cardinal Newman as an Historian*, 41 n. 1.

38. Newman, *Certain Difficulties*, lecture 5.

39. J. Derek Holmes, "Newman, History and Theology," *Irish Theological Quarterly*, n.s., 36 (January 1969), 34–45, 42–43. See John Henry Newman, *An Essay on the Development of Christian Doctrine*, 99–121; Owen Chadwick, *From Bossuet to Newman* (Cambridge: Cambridge University Press, 1957), 144–49. Later Newman characterized the differences between Rome and the Early Church as being only "in a few matters of discipline and tone," while Protestants differed in "all"; see Newman, *Certain Difficulties*, 287.

40. See David Knowles, "The Maurists," *Great Historical Enterprises* (London and New York: Nelson, 1963), 34–62; Robert Aubert et al., *The Christian Centuries*, vol. 5: *The Church in a Secularised Society* (New York: Paulist Press, 1978), 165–85; Aubert, "Un demi-siècle de revues d'histoire ecclésiastique," *Rivista de storia della Chiesa in Italia* 14 (1960), 173–202; and G. Fereto, *Note storico-bibliografiche di archeologia cristiana* (Vatican City, 1942).

41. Gooch, *History and Historians*, 552. The English translation of *The First Age of Christianity* was completed in 1866 by Henry N. Oxenham and dedicated to Newman.

42. Ibid., 556.

43. See H. G. Schenk, *The Mind of the European Romantics*, 95 ff.

44. Jaroslav Pelikan, *Historical Theology*, 56. Newman, while making similar

analogies, politicized the context in which his identifications are made; Church/ State relations rather than doctrinal content were the key.

45. Johann Adam Möhler, *Die Einheit in der Kirche oder das Prinzip des Katholizismus dargestellt im Geiste der Kirchenväter der drei ersten Jahrhunderte* (Tübingen, 1825), quoted in Gooch, *History and Historians*, 549–50.

46. Chadwick, *Bossuet to Newman*, 119; see Johann Adam Möhler, *Symbolism; or, Exposition of the Doctrinal Differences between Catholics and Protestants as Evidenced by Their Symbolical Writings*, trans. J. R. Robertson, 2 vols. (London: Charles Dolman, 1843).

47. David Newsome, *The Wilberforces and Henry Manning*, 286. In the 1840s Edward Manning was reading up on Möhler and other Roman Catholic polemicists (ibid., 328). Ward's insistence on experiential religion sounds quite similar to John Wesley's abandonment in 1738 of "Primitive" for "real" Christianity; see Eamon Duffy, "Primitive Christianity Revived, Religious Renewal in Augustan England," *Studies in Church History 14: Renaissance and Renewal in Christian History* (Oxford: Basil Blackwell, 1977), 287–300.

48. Thomas Mozley, *Reminiscences Chiefly of Oriel College and the Oxford Movement*, 2 vols. (London: Longmans, 1882), 1:356.

49. Peter Sutcliffe, *The Oxford University Press: An Informal History* (Oxford and New York: Oxford University Press, 1978), 8–11.

50. Brendon, *Hurrell Froude*, 192. See H. Gough, *A General Index to the Publications of the Parker Society* (Cambridge: Parker Society, 1855), preface; and also Sutcliffe, *Oxford University Press*, 8–11.

51. Chapman, *Faith and Revolt*, 261.

52. Charles Kingsley, *Yeast* (1848), quoted in Chapman, *Faith and Revolt*, 142. The name Vieuxbois may indicate "old-fashioned timber," something quite obsolete.

53. Andrew Drummond, *The Churches in English Fiction*, 173.

54. Chapman, *Victorian Debate*, 286–90.

55. Newman, *Certain Difficulties*, 310.

56. Drummond, *Churches in English Fiction*, 21–22.

57. See Thomas Arnold, *The Life and Correspondence of Thomas Arnold D.D.*, ed. Arthur P. Stanley (1844), quoted in Chapman, *Faith and Revolt*, 144.

58. Meriol Trevor, *The Arnolds: Thomas Arnold and His Family* (London: Bodley Head, 1973), 41, 101–2, 195.

59. The German *patristisch* was in use before Taylor's time, but in England *patrological* or *patrologic* was the commonly used adjectival form (*OED*).

60. Isaac Taylor, *Ancient Christianity and the Doctrines of the Oxford Tracts*, 1: preface, vi–vii.notes to pages x–xnotes to pages x–x

61. See ibid., 1:413. Taylor, accusing the Tractarians of judaizing, quotes

Erasmus' *Antidote* on ascetic practices: "Quae magis ad judaeos pertinent, quam ad Christianos, et superstitiosum facere possunt, pium non possunt." See also ibid., 2:402–22.

62. Newman refers to Taylor's work in his "Prospects of the Anglican Church" (1839), *Essays and Sketches*, 1:364. Taylor's reference (2:367) to "a few astute and sinuous minds" who want to subvent the intention of the framers of the Thirty-nine Articles and who thus forgo "the comforts of a 'good conscience'" is clearly aimed at Newman and Tract XC.

63. Bouchier Wrey Saville, *The Primitive and Catholic Faith*, vi.

64. Ibid., 6. See Saville's other works: *The First and Second Advent, with Reference to the Jew, the Gentile, and the Church of God* (1858); *Turkey; or, The Judgment of God upon Apostate Christendom under the Three Apocalyptic Woes* (1877); and *Prophecies and Speculations Respecting the End of the World* (1883).

65. Saville, *Primitive and Catholic Faith*, 84.

66. Review in the Anglo-Catholic periodical *Christian Remembrancer* (July 1860), quoted in Chapman, *Faith and Revolt*, 87. See also John O. Waller, "A Composite Anglo-Catholic Concept of the Novel, 1841–1868," *BNYPL* (1966), which traces changing perspectives in the Anglo-Catholic periodicals *Christian Remembrancer* (1851–68) and the *Ecclesiastic* (1845–68).

67. Newman, quoted in Bokenkotter, *Newman as Historian*, 41.

68. Brendon, *Hurrell Froude*, 71; Trevor, *The Arnolds*, 101–2.

69. The lectures of Charles Lloyd, bishop of Oxford (1827–29), played a vital role in demonstrating to the movement's leaders the importance of liturgical study and its use in apologetics for the Church of England; see Tract 85, treated in Härdelin, *Tractarian Understanding*, 228. Even in his early ministry at St. Clement's, Oxford, Newman preached about the "visibility" as well as the "Catholicity" and "Apostolicity" of the Church; see Dessain, *Newman*, 8.

70. James Anthony Froude, *The Nemesis of Faith* (1848), quoted in Robert Lee Wolff, *Gains and Losses*, 399–400; R. W. Church, *Occasional Papers*, 2 vols. (London: Macmillan, 1897), 2:470–74, quoted in Dessain, *Newman*, 86. The observation by Church, made two days after Newman's death, implies that Newman left the English Church because of this endemic worldliness, a view with which Newman himself was not in agreement, according to Dessain. But one should remember the famous scene in Newman's *Loss and Gain* in which the hero is physically sickened by the sight of a married curate who had sworn celibacy (198). For a balanced psychological interpretation of this often discussed scene, see Wolff, *Gains and Losses*, 46–47.

71. Bennett, "Patristic Tradition," 79.

72. Letter to Mrs. John Mozley (19 January 1837), quoted in Baker, *Novel and the Oxford Movement*, 67.

73. Letter to Frederich Capes (28 February 1849), quoted in ibid., 55.

74. Newman's comments in 1874 on "The Catholicity of the Anglican Church" (1840), quoted in Dessain, *Newman*, 83.

75. *Apologia*, chap. 2, 87; Bokenkotter, *Newman as Historian*, 46.

76. Newman, *Essays and Sketches*, 1:355.

77. *Apologia*, preface, 16.

CHAPTER 1

1. J. C. Simmons, *The Novelist as Historian,* 33, 35–36; an incisive critique of Simmons's short work is provided in a review by Robert Lee Wolff, "Present Uses for the Past," *TLS* (13 December 1974), 1404. Wolff points out the problem in Simmons's rigid chronological scheme, prematurely burying the historical novel in 1850, and in his failure to view the novels as commentary on Victorian issues.

2. Andrew Lang, quoted in Maison, *Victorian Vision*, 297.

3. No comprehensive list of Early Church novels exists. The following provide partial and selective bibliographies: Ernest Baker, *History in Fiction*; Oliver Elton, *A Survey of English Literature, 1830–1880*, 2 vols. (London: E. Arnold, 1932); James Kaye, *Historical Fiction*; Doris Kelly, "A Checklist of Nineteenth-Century English Fiction about the Decline of Rome"; J. Marriott, *English History in English Fiction* (London: Blackie & Son, 1940); Jonathan Nield, *A Guide to the Best Historical Novels and Tales.*

4. Hugh Walpole simply divides the post-Scott genre into four periods: "simple romancers" (1830–40), "serious Victorians" (1840–70), the "real romantic spirit" (1870–1910), and "modern realism" (1910–30); see "The Historical Novel in England since Sir Walter Scott," *Sir Walter Scott Today: Some Retrospective Essays and Studies*, ed. H. J. C. Grierson (London: Constable, 1932), 161–88. Curtis Dahl sketches the literary history of this tradition using more formal literary categories, dividing the subgenre into two basic types: (1) the Gothic novel of violent action and terror with little ideological content, and (2) novels directly concerned with philosophy and religion, a type with four permutations, each of which approaches culmination in Pater's *Marius*; see his "Pater's *Marius* and Historical Novels on Early Christian Times." I am deeply indebted to Dahl's categories and analysis in this chapter, but diverge from him in stressing the specific relationships of the novels to the nineteenth century and in separating religious controversialists from nonchurchly writers, in contrast to the homogeneous groupings he employs. Fleishman makes a distinction between novels of conversion, e.g., *Fabiola* and *Callista*, and disinterested "meditative" historical fiction,

e.g., *Marius* and *Romola* (*English Historical Novel*, 151). Dahl sees this as a "valid though difficult" distinction, since both types are part of one encompassing tradition (7 n. 11).

5. E. Cornelia Knight, *Marcus Flaminius; or, A View of the Military, Political, and Social Life of the Romans* (London, 1792). See Dahl, "Pater's *Marius*," 2–3. Dahl lists the following examples of novels dealing with young men coming of age amid the adventures of antiquity and pursuing a philosophical view of life that is anachronistically Christian, at least in its Enlightenment interpretation: François de la Mothe Fénelon, *Les Aventures de Télémaque* (1699) (Fénelon was the great spiritual author and adviser of seventeenth-century France whose *Spiritual Letters* were read avidly throughout the Victorian era); Jean Tarrasson, *Séthos, histoire ou view tirée des monuments anecdotes de l'ancienne Egypte* (1731); Claude-Prosper Jolyot de Crébillon, *Letters atheniennes* (1771); J. J. Barthélemy, *Voyage du jeune Anarcharsis en Gréce* (1788); Etienne-François de Lantier, *Voyages d'Anténor en Gréce et en Asie* (1798); Christoph Martin Wieland, *Geschichte des Agathon* (1766–67); *The Athenian Letters; or, The Epistolary Correspondence of an Agent of the King of Persia Residing at Athens* (1741–43). Other pedagogical views of daily life in antiquity include Karl August Böttiger, *Sabina, oder Morgenszenen im Putzenzimmer einer reichen Römerin* (1803); W. A. Becker, *Gallus; or, Roman Scenes of the Time of Augustus*, trans. F. Metcalfe (London, 1849), and *Charicles: Illustrations of the Private Life of the Ancient Greeks*, trans. Anonymous (London, 1854), which were popular translations in the Victorian period; and the American religious tract *Onesimus; or, The Run-Away Servant Converted* (Philadelphia, 1800).

6. See John Henry Newman, "The Theology of St. Ignatius" (1839), *Essays and Sketches*, 12.

7. See Marion Lochhead, "Lockhart, the *Quarterly*, and the Tractarians," *Quarterly Review* 291 (April 1953), 197.

8. Gilbert Macbeth, *John Gibson Lockhart: A Critical Study* (Urbana: University of Illinois Press, 1935), 14–15. He mentions as sources Christoph Martin Wieland, *The History of Agathon*, 4 vols. (London, 1773); "Meiszner," August Gottlieb Meissner, *Alcibiades*, 4 vols. (Leipzig, 1781–88); "Feszler," Ignaz Aurelius Fessler, *Marc Aurel*, 3 vols. (Breslau, 1791–93); Caroline Pichler's *Agathokles* (1801); François René de Chateaubriand, *Les Martyrs, ou le triomphe de la religion chrétienne* (Paris, 1809); Jean Jacques Barthélemy's *Anacharsis* (1779); and Thomas Hope, *Anastasius; or, Memoirs of a Greek* (London, 1819).

9. *Valerius* had little following; in 1841 Lockhart rewrote it to improve its style and reduced it by one half. It went through three more editions by 1868 (Macbeth, *Lockhart*, 17). The text used here is *Valerius: A Roman Story* [abbr. *V*], 2 vols. (Boston: Wells & Lilly, 1821).

10. *V*, 2:276 ff. The Christian priest Aurelius Felix does not take a sword

(*V*, 2:247). His death scene, imitating Christ's cry of despair from the cross, could have been dramatically effective; Lockhart reduces it to bathos by having the priest momentarily revive and confirm his own salvation (*V*, 2:281–82).

11. Macbeth, *Lockhart*, 82.

12. Lockhart uses St. John Chrysostom, *De Adorat. Crucis*, and the canons of the Council of Nicaea, *Conc. Nic.* 2 *act.* 4, as evidence for communion (*V*, 2:13–15). For the passionflower, see *V*, 2:195–96. Newman must have used Valerius as the source for his own anachronistic use of this flower, discovered in the New World, in his novel *Callista*.

13. *Apologia*, chap. 1, 21–22, 53.

14. *A Letter to the Hon. Pierce Somerset Butler, Occasioned by His Speech at the Lisdowney Meeting on the Subject of Tithe, Together with Observations on J.K.L.'s Defense of His Vindication by a Munster Farmer* (Dublin: R. Milliken, 1824). *J.K.L.'s Defense* was written by James Warren Doyle, O.E.S.A., Roman Catholic bishop of Kildare and Leighlin (1819–34), a defender of the religious and civil principles of Irish Catholics.

15. The text used is *The Epicurean: A Tale* [abbr. *E*] (Philadelphia: Carey, Lea, & Carey and R. H. Small, 1827). In its first year it went through four editions. Eugene J. Brzenk argues against the comparative importance of the tale in relation to Pater's *Marius*: "The 'Epicureans' of Pater and Moore," *VN* 14 (Fall 1958), 24–27.

16. Howard Mumford Jones, *The Harp That Once: A Chronicle of the Life of Thomas Moore* (New York: H. Holt, 1937), 262–63. J. M. W. Turner illustrated the 1839 edition. It was unusual enough for a Dissenter to read Moore's *Epicurean* that when Emma Tatham, the young poetic daughter of an upholsterer, read it the deed prompted rebuke in their Dissenting chapel; see Amy Cruse, *The Victorians and Their Reading* (1935; Boston: Houghton Mifflin, [1962]), 68.

17. *E*, 15. Whyte-Melville uses the titles "Eros" and "Anteros" as two of the three divisions of his novel *The Gladiators* (1836).

18. For Marsh's role in reform issues, see R. A. Soloway, *Prelates and People*, 371–75.

19. His first novel, *Brambletye House* (1826), was occasioned by a trip to Penshurst, the old country seat of the Sidneys; *The Tor Hill* (1826) was a historical romance about Henry VIII. Smith returned to the historical novel with *The Involuntary Prophet* (1835), having published a collection of stories of early Christian times in *Tales of the Early Ages* (1835). *The Involuntary Prophet*, a short tale, concerns Aaron, a Jew who witnesses the burning of Rome and the fall of Jerusalem. He dies at Pompeii, where his remains were discovered, the author states, in 1775.

20. The text used is *Zillah: A Tale of the Holy City* [abbr. *Z*], 4 vols. (London:

Henry Colburn, 1828). It had few editions, but it was translated into French in 1829. Poe parodied *Zillah* in "A Tale of Jerusalem"; see James Southall Wilson, "The Devil Was in It," *American Mercury* 24 (1931), 218.

21. Sargent Epes, ed., *The Poetical Works of Horace Smith and James Smith*, repr. of 23d London ed. (New York: Mason Brothers, 1857), xi.

22. Paul Chatfield [pseud.], *The Tin Trumpet; or, Heads and Tales: For the Wise and Waggish*, ed. Jefferson Saunders, Esq. [pseud.], 2 vols. (Philadelphia: E. L. Carey and A. Hart, 1936), 1:33.

23. See Curtis Dahl, "Recreators of Pompeii," *Archaeology* 9 (1956), 182–91; "Bulwer-Lytton and the School of Catastrophe," *PQ* 32 (1953), 428–42; and "The American School of Catastrophe," *AQ* 11 (1959), 380–90. A summary of the literary background is provided by Erich Zimmermann's *Entstehungsgeschichte und Komposition von Bulwers "The Last Days of Pompeii"* (Berlin: Nicolai, 1914), reflecting the German interest in classical sites and literature.

24. Preface to the first edition (London: George Routledge & Sons, 1834), vii. The text used here is *The Last Days of Pompeii* [abbr. *P*] (London: J. M. Dent & Sons, 1910). The novel went through dozens of editions. For a survey of the reception of the book, particularly in America, see Arthur B. Maurice, *The Bookman* (New York, 1930).

25. Preface, 1834 ed., x–xi.

26. S. B. Liljergren, *Bulwer-Lytton's Novels and Isis Unveiled* (Uppsala: Lundequistska Bokhandeln, 1957).

27. Fleishman, *English Historical Novel*, 184, 109.

28. The French artists Charles Gleyre (1806–74), Thomas Couture (1815–79), Ary Scheffer (1795–1858), and Jean-Léon Gérôme (1824–1904) joined the British painters of this genre. Lord Frederic Leighton (1830–96), president of the Royal Academy, and Sir Lawrence Alma Tadema (1836–1912) are the most familiar.

29. For martyrs, see the works of Czech painter Gabriel Cornelius von Max (1840–1915) and the Royal Academician Edwin Long, famous for his work *Diana or Christ?* (1881). Evariste-Vitale Luminais (1822–96), the "Augustin Thierry of Painting," excelled in depictions of Rome's devastation.

30. A. T. Sheppard, *The Art and Practice of Historical Fiction*, 59.

31. Margaret Dalziel, *Popular Fiction 100 Years Ago*, 81.

32. Fleishman, *English Historical Novel*, 32. See G. P. R. James, *The History of Chivalry*, 2d ed. (London: Henry Colburn and Richard Bentley, 1830), 15. Robert Louis Stevenson was a later admirer; Sheppard, *Art and Practice*, 106–7.

33. See Louis James, *Fiction for the Working Man*, 90. Thackeray parodied his work in "Barbazures by G. P. R. Jeames, Esq., & c.," in *Novels by Eminent Hands* (1847).

34. The text used is G. P. R. James, *Attila: A Romance* [abbr. *A*], 2 vols. (New York: Harper & Brothers, 1838), 1:vii. The dedication is to Walter Savage Landor. See also Elizabeth R. Charles, *Attila and His Conquerors* (1894).

35. Fleishman, *English Historical Novel*, 150.

36. The first edition was *Antonia; or, The Fall of Rome: A Romance of the Fifth Century*, 3 vols. (London: Richard Bentley, 1850). The text used here is an illustrated edition: *Antonina; or, The Fall of Rome* [abbr. *An*] (New York and London: Harper & Brothers, 1898). Kaye erroneously says it was published in 1852.

37. S. M. Ellis, *Wilkie Collins, Le Fanu, and Others* (1931; London: Constable, 1951), 7.

38. *An*, 15. Auricular confession was a popular topic, figuring prominently in religious novels of the period; see Grace Kennedy, *Father Clement* (1823); and Lady Georgina Fullerton, *Ellen Middleton* (1844).

39. *An*, 62. Collins's portraits of the clergy are interesting and varied: *Mad Monkton* (186?) has an austere father superior; *The Dead Secret* (1857), a domesticated country parson; *Armadale* (1866), the patriarchal and wise Mr. Decimus Brock; and *The Black Robe* (1881), a Machiavellian Jesuit Father Benwell. The Victorian vogue for anti-Jesuit feeling was satirized by Frank Smedly, *Lewis Arundel* (1852), in such supposed titles as "Loyoliana, or the Jesuit in the Chimneycorner."

40. Quoted in Walter de la Mare, "The Early Novels of Wilkie Collins," *The Eighteen-Sixties: Essays*, ed. John Drinkwater (Cambridge: Cambridge University Press, 1932), 58.

41. Other treatments of the age of Justinian include Felix Dahn, *The Struggle for Rome*, 3 vols. (London: Bentley, 1878); George Gissing, *Veranilda* (London: Constable, 1904); and A. Conan Doyle, "The Home Coming," *The Last Galley: Impressions and Tales* (London: Smith, Elder, 1911). Gaetano Donizetti's opera *Belisario* (1836) can also be mentioned.

42. The text used is Sir Henry Pottinger, *Blue and Green; or, The Gift of God: A Romance of Old Constantinople* [abbr. *BG*], new ed. (London: Chapman & Hall, 1880), ix–x.

43. *BG*, viii. Pottinger mentions as sources Procopius' *Persian Wars* and *The Secret History*, which were available in various editions and translations; "Lord Mahon," Philip Henry Stanhope, Viscount Mahon, *Life of Belisarius* (London, 1829); Edward Gibbon, *The History of the Decline and Fall of the Roman Empire*, 6 vols. (London, 1776–88); and Barthold Georg Niebuhr's edition of Byzantine historians, *Corpus Scriptorum Historiae Byzantinae*, 50 vols. (Bonn, 1828–97).

44. See E. R. Norman, *Anti-Catholicism in Victorian England*, 105–21; Chadwick, *Victorian Church*, 2:308–27.

45. See George Alfred Henty, *For the Temple: A Tale of the Fall of Jerusalem*

(London: Blackie & Son, [1887] 1888), Jane M. Strickland, *Adonijah: A Tale of the Jewish Dispersion* (London, 1856); and Mrs. J. B. Webb, *Naomi; or, The Last Days of Jerusalem* (London: Routledge, 1840). See also Florence Morse Kingsley, *The Cross Triumphant* (London: Ward & Lock, 1900); H. Rider Haggard, *The Pearl Maiden* (London: Longman, 1902); and Frank Cowper, *The Forgotten Door* (London, 1909).

46. George Eliot, *Essays*, ed. Thomas Pinney (New York: Columbia University Press, 1963), 320–22.

47. The text used is *The Gladiators* [abbr. *G*] (London: J. M. Dent & Sons, 1911). The novel was scheduled for publication in 1863 but actually appeared in January 1864, backdated. Other prominent novels by Whyte-Melville were his study of the Crimean campaign, *The Interpreter* (1858), and his depiction of Cavaliers in the Civil War, *Holmby House* (1860). See James C. Freeman, "George John Whyte-Melville (1821–1878): A Bibliography," *BBDI* 19 (1950), 267–68. Whyte-Melville also treated early Christianity in a series of narrative poems: *The True Cross: A Legend of the Church* (1873).

48. J. M. Robertson, *History of Freethought in the Nineteenth Century*, 2 vols. (1929), quoted in Warren Smith, *The London Heretics, 1870–1914*, 2.

49. Winwood Reade, quoted in Smith, *London Heretics*, xvii.

50. Dean Inge, quoted in ibid., 200. See also Owen Chadwick, *The Secularization of the European Mind in the Nineteenth Century*, 239–40.

51. Dahl, "Pater's *Marius*," surveys many of the most important participants in this debate (1 n. 1). See also Hedwig L. Glücksmann, "Die Gegenüberstellung von Antike-Christentum in der englischen Literatur des 19. Jahrhunderts"; David DeLaura, *Hebrew and Hellene in Victorian England*, 305–44; Martha Salmon Vogeler, "The Religious Meaning of Marius the Epicurean," *Nineteenth-Century Fiction* 19 (December 1964), 287–99; U. C. Knoepflmacher, *Religious Humanism and the Victorian Novel*, 149–223; and Wolff, *Gains and Losses*, 175–90. Other fictional accounts of Marcus Aurelius include those by Georg M. Ebers, *The Emperor*, 2 vols. (New York, 1881); Frederic Carrel, *Marcus and Faustina* (London, 1904); and Antonine Baumann, *Martyrs de Lyons* (Paris, 1906). The text of *Marius* used here is *Marius the Epicurean* (London: J. M. Dent & Sons, 1968).

52. Wolff, *Gains and Losses*, 185. Arnold's "Marcus Aurelius" is suggested by several critics as a source for Pater's characterization.

53. Chapman, *Victorian Debate*, 264.

54. Dahl summarizes the literature, opting himself for a true conversion; see Wolff, *Gains and Losses*, 179–81.

55. T. S. Eliot, "Arnold and Pater," *Selected Essays, 1917–32* (New York: Harcourt, Brace, 1932), 356.

56. See Vogeler, "Religious Meaning of Marius," 287–99, which summarizes the debate.

57. Chadwick, *Victorian Church*, 2:468–70.

58. The relationship of Newman and Pater is often discussed, so that *Marius* has been called Pater's *Grammar of Assent*; see, e.g., Chapman, *Faith and Revolt*, 166; Wolff, *Gains and Losses*, 177–78. Their respective views of the role of the institutional Church fundamentally divide these two authors.

59. *Edinburgh Review* 165 (1887), 248–67; Dahl, "Pater's *Marius*," calls attention to this idea (2 n. 1). The text used is *Neaera: A Tale of Ancient Rome* [abbr. *N*] (London: Macmillan, 1886).

60. Elizabeth Longford, *Queen Victoria*, 327–29, 334–39.

61. See, e.g., Lydia Maria Child, *Philothea: A Romance* (Boston: Otis, Broaders, 1836).

62. The text used is *Masters of the World* [abbr. *M*], 3 vols. (London: Richard Bentley & Son, 1888).

63. Several Anglo-Catholic authors treated Titus Flavius Clemens as a Christian and his historically unexplained execution as a martyrdom. In the list of martyrs executed with Flavius Clemens, Hoppus turns the "presbyter" Nicomede into "Nicodemus."

64. See the bibliographies in Martha Vicinus, ed., *Suffer and Be Still: Women in the Victorian Age* (Bloomington: Indiana University Press, 1973), 200–202.

65. The text used is *Acte: A Novel* [abbr. *Ac*], 3 vols. (London: Richard Bentley & Son, 1890). See also Ernst Eckstein, *Nero: A Romance* (1899); Henryk Sienkiewicz, *Quo Vadis?* (1895); and Emma Leslie, *Glaucia* (1904).

66. See the review of this interest in nationhood and imperialism in Alan Sandison, *The Wheel of Empire: The Study of the Imperial Idea in Some Late Nineteenth- and Early Twentieth-Century Fiction* (London: Macmillan, 1967); and Richard Faber, *The Vision and the Need: Late Victorian Imperialist Aims* (London: Faber & Faber, 1966).

67. The important passages used were from Tacitus, *Annals* 14:31–37; *Agricola* 16:1–2; and Dio Cassius, *Roman History* 60:19–62:12, 76:11–13. See W. Bonser, *A Romano-British Bibliography (55 B.C.–A.D. 449)* (Oxford: Basil Blackwell, 1964).

68. George Alfred Henty, *Beric, the Britain: A Story of the Roman Invasion* (London: Blackie & Son, 1893). See also Ernest Protheroe, *For Queen and Emperor* (1909).

69. Sir Herbert E. Maxwell, *A Duke of Britain* (London: Blackwood, 1895). Maxwell was the editor of the letters and papers of Sir Henry Pottinger.

70. For a summary of the British homoerotic literary tradition, see Paul

Fussell, *The Great War and Modern Memory* (London: Oxford University Press, 1975), 279–86. Modern historians speculate that the youths in question were probably Batavian, in any case.

71. This same material was treated by the Anglo-Catholic Mrs. Jerome Mercier, *By the King and Queen* (1886).

CHAPTER 2

1. See Chadwick, *Victorian Church*, 1:271–309; Gordon Albion, "The Restoration of the Hierarchy," *The English Catholics, 1650–1950*, ed. G. A. Beck (London: Burns & Oates, 1950), 86–116; G. F. A. Best, "Popular Protestantism in Victorian England," *Ideas and Institutions of Victorian Britain: Essays in Honor of George Kitson Clark*, ed. Robert Robson (London: Bell, 1967), 115–42; Thomas P. Joyce, "The Restoration of the Catholic Hierarchy in England and Wales, 1850: A Study of Certain Public Reactions" (Ph.D. diss., Gregorian University, Rome, 1966); Norman, *Anti-Catholicism in Victorian England*, 52–79; Walter Ralls, "The Papal Aggression of 1850: A Study in Victorian Anti-Catholicism," *Church History* 43 (June 1974), 242–56; and R. A. Soloway, "Church and Society: Recent Trends in Nineteenth Century Religious History," *Journal of British Studies* 11 (1972), 142–59. See also Wilfrid Ward, *The Life and Time of Cardinal Wiseman*, 2 vols. (London: Longmans, Green, 1897), 1:538–69. A study remains to be done on whatever benefits from the agitation in terms of increased inquiries and conversions accrued to the Roman Church. For example, Henry Manning's immediate reason for conversion was found in the "No Popery" outburst, which proved to him that the nation and the national church were not Catholic.

2. Ralls, "Papal Aggression," 249, suggests four main issues: (1) the Irish question, including immigration, the political threat of the militant Young Irelanders, and the continuing stalemate over religious policies in national education; (2) the belief that Catholicism was totally alienated from true English values, a belief intensified by the politics of the 1830s and 1840s; (3) the publicity given to Wiseman and to the reestablishment of convents; and (4) the unsettled disarray of Protestantism in the face of a revivified Catholicism.

3. Ward, *Wiseman*, 1:547–48. Following 10 November 1850, "No Popery" riots regularly disrupted services at St. Barnabas, the Anglo-Catholic parish in London where W. J. E. Bennett presided (ibid., 2:11 ff.). See also Chadwick, *Victorian Church*, 1:301–3.

4. Longford, *Queen Victoria*, 226. See also Ralls, "Papal Aggression," 245 n. 10. Newman ridiculed this apocalyptic hysteria by cleverly showing that Queen Victoria could be identified by numerological manipulation with the mark of the

beast, 666; *Lectures on the Present Position of Catholics in England*, ed. O'Connell, 26–27.

5. Novels reacting to "Papal Aggression" include M. E. S. B___, *Experience; or, The Young Church-Woman: A Tale of the Times* (1854); George Borrow, *Lavengro: The Scholar—The Gypsy—The Priest* (1851); and W. M. Thackeray, *The Newcomes: Memoirs of a Most Respectable Family* (1853–55).

6. Ward, *Wiseman*, 2:92. The dogma of the Immaculate Conception of the Virgin Mary was defined by the Bull "Ineffabilis Deus," 8 December 1854. See H. Denzinger, ed., *Enchiridion Symbolorum*, rev. ed., Karl Rahner, S.J., 31st ed. (Barcelona: Herder, 1957), 458–59. Ultramontanists saw this definition as a reaffirmation of papal privilege and supremacy, overcoming the political setbacks attendant on the revolutions of 1848. The document itself stresses the "unity of the Church," of which the pope was the effective sign.

7. Ward, *Wiseman*, 2:220; 2:207–52. See also Ronald Chapman, *Father Faber* (London: Burns & Oates, 1961). Alphonsus Liguori (1696–1787) is a major influence in the history of English spirituality. "St. Alfonso" is, of course, especially important in the study of John Henry Newman. See his *Apologia*, "Note G: Lying and Equivocation," 320–30, answering the charges that Liguori's moral casuistry allowed Catholics to play fast and easy with truth. Newman backed off from many of the Italianate forms he adopted immediately after conversion: in architecture, however, he remained a confirmed "Pagan," explaining reasonably that as an Oratorian the Gothic style would be an anachronism.

8. Chadwick, *Victorian Church*, 1:505–11.

9. Ward, *Wiseman*, 2:85; Chadwick, *Victorian Church*, 1:509. The nuns of Scorton were accused of forcibly detaining young girls. Connolly sued for restoration of marital rights from his former wife, who had entered a convent.

10. No comprehensive study of this movement has been done for England. For America, see Jay P. Dolan, *Catholic Revivalism: The American Experience, 1830–1900* (South Bend, Ind.: University of Notre Dame Press; New York: Harper & Row, 1978).

11. Chadwick, *Victorian Church*, 1:283, 2:408–9.

12. Ward, *Wiseman*, 2:35. *Punch* first described Wiseman by this telling phrase. Opponents of Wiseman invariably were surprised by his "English manner," appearance, and speech.

13. Chadwick, *Victorian Church*, 1:305–8; C. S. Dessain, *John Henry Newman* (London: Nelson, 1966), 101–2. See Trevor, *Newman* (cited intro., n. 30), 1:546–637. For the Achilli trial, see W. F. Finlason, *Report of the Trial and Preliminary Proceedings* (1852); Giacinto G. Achilli, *Dealings with the Inquisition, or Papal Rome* (1851; 2d enl. ed. 1851); Newman, *Letters and Diaries*, vols. 14, 15. Newman's important polemical work *Lectures on the Present Position of Catholics in*

England (1851) began the contest with Achilli and his supporters in the Protestant Alliance.

14. Newman, *Apologia*, 79–85; Abbé Jean Nicolas Jager, *Le Protestantisme aux prises avec la doctrine Catholique ou controverses avec plusieurs ministres Anglicans* (Paris, 1836); N. P. S. Wiseman, *Lectures on the Principal Doctrines and Practices of the Catholic Church* (1836); Ward, *Wiseman*, 1:240 ff.

15. *Apologia*, 121. Newman expanded his argument in his *Lectures on Certain Difficulties Felt by Anglicans in Submitting to the Catholic Church* (1850), his ad hominem assault on the remnants of the Tractarians. The parallel lay not primarily in the doctrines professed but in the relation of the various parties, factored by the role of papal power and Monophysite schism. For Newman, Rome then was in the position of Rome at the present day, and the Monophysites, the via media on the question, were in the position of the Anglicans. The form of the debate was also crucial, since the Orthodox party introduced terminology and descriptions that were *extra scripturas*, the charge laid against the decrees of the Council of Trent by contemporary Anglicans.

16. Whether he read it in August or September 1839 remains in question; see *Apologia*, 123, 125; and Ward, *Wiseman*, 1:321.

17. *Apologia*, 142–49. See Appendix B of this book.

18. Kingsley to his wife, Fanny, quoted in Susan Chitty, *The Beast and the Monk*, 59; John Henry Newman, "Catholicity of the Anglican Church" (1840), *Essays and Sketches*, 2:105. Newman repeats this in the *Apologia*, 132, but significantly adds: "It certainly diminishes my right to complain of slanders uttered against myself, when, as in this passage, I had already spoken in disparagement of the controversialists of that religious body, to which I myself now belong" (132–33).

19. Walter E. Houghton, "The Issue between Kingsley and Newman," *Victorian Literature: Selected Essays*, ed. Robert O. Preyer (New York: Harper & Row, 1967), 22–23. Houghton catches only the praise given Newman in Kingsley's *Alexandria and Her Schools*. Newman's art and "knowledge of human cravings" are favorably compared to Proclus, a Neoplatonist author whom Kingsley despised. Further, the subject of Newman's art and knowledge is "daemonology," the darker side of religion contrasted with the spiritual illumination of true Platonism and the study of the ordering and creating God. Kingsley is, in fact, damning Newman with this association. See Charles Kingsley, *Alexandria and Her Schools* (Cambridge: Macmillan, 1854), 117–18. In the often neglected work *Present Position of Catholics*, which shows his polemical tenacity, Newman attacks the assertions of a certain Mr. Seely in much the same terms in which he later cast his contention with Kingsley. More important, he urges the charge of untruth and lying on Protestants: "To Protestantism False Witness is the principle of propagation. . . . Errors indeed creep in by chance,

whatever be the point of inquiry or incidental or of attendant error, but I mean that falsehood is the very staple of the views which they have been taught to entertain of us" (lecture 4, pp. 1, 98).

20. Kingsley essayed this duel of Darkness and Light once again in *Westward Ho!* (1855), where the events around the repulsion of the Armada in 1588 became another example of separating the "sheep from the goats." Its virulent attack on Roman Catholicism, at face value an attack on Jesuitry and the Inquisition, appalled many Anglicans. James Anthony Froude (1818–94), whose article on Elizabethan seamen and whose later work on English history inspired two of Kingsley's anti-Catholic forays, is another link with Newman. It was James, younger brother of R. Hurrell Froude (1803–36), who broke with the Anglo-Catholic party and the Church altogether after finishing the writing of the life of St. Neot in Newman's series of saints' lives (1834–35).

21. For example, Baker, *Novel and the Oxford Movement*, 54–68, 88–100; Chapman, *Faith and Revolt*, 149–64; Chitty, *Beast and Monk*, 151–54; Allan J. Hartley, *The Novels of Charles Kingsley: A Christian Social Interpretation* (Folkestone: Hour-Glass Press, 1977), 84–103; S. W. Jackson, *Nicholas Cardinal Wiseman: A Victorian Prelate and His Writings* (Gerrards Cross: Five Lamps Press, 1977); Robert B. Martin, *The Dust of Combat: A Life of Charles Kingsley* (London: Faber & Faber, 1959), 141–47; Wolff, *Gains and Losses*, 60–65, 273–82.

22. Charles Kingsley, *Hypatia; or, New Foes with an Old Face*, 13th ed. (New York: Macmillan, 1882). Kingsley used the subtitle again as heading of chap. 6 in *Two Years Ago* (1857); see Chapman, *Faith and Revolt*, 303 n. 27.

23. Chitty sees in the novel an abandoning of Christian socialism in fiction. On the other hand, Hartley argues convincingly that the novel is a continuation of Christian socialist concerns, and even though Maurice rejected the book's proposed dedication to him, he directed its composition closely (*Novels of Kingsley*, 84–103).

24. Cardinal Wiseman enjoyed *Water-Babies* and used it for bedtime reading; see Ward, *Wiseman*, 2:173.

25. The subject was a popular one. Articles on St. Elizabeth of Hungary had appeared in the *Dublin Review* after 1836, and Montalambert completed a well-known *Life of St. Elizabeth*; see Ward, *Wiseman*, 1:252, 298. Kingsley later used some of his research on the Middle Ages in his tale *Hereward the Wake* (1866); see Hartley, *Novels of Kingsley*, 150; and Wolff, *Gains and Losses*, 282.

26. Letter to F. D. Maurice (16 January 1851), quoted in Baker, *Novel and the Oxford Movement*, 95.

27. Chadwick, *Victorian Church*, 1:481–84, 439.

28. See Hartley, *Novels of Kingsley*, 84–85, for a brief discussion of the sources. Those identified are John Toland, *Tetradymus* (1820); Edward Gibbon, *Decline and Fall of the Roman Empire* (1776–88), chap. 47; *The Letters of Synesius of*

Cyrene, trans. Augustine Fitzgerald (Oxford: Oxford University Press, 1926); Isidore of Pelusium's letters (no complete modern edition exists); Augustine's *Confessions* and *The City of God* (a translation of the former was done by E. B. Pusey for the Library of the Fathers [1838]); Philostratus, *The Life of Apollonius of Tyana* (Newman did the article on Apollonius for the *Encyclopaedia Metropolitana* [1823]); Philo; Clement of Alexandria; Origen; and Athanasius, *Against the Gentiles* (*Contra Gentes*), Migne *PG* 25.

29. Nestorius was patriarch of Constantinople (428–31); the Nestorian position attempted to interpret the person of Christ so that discourse concerning the place of the Logos in the Trinity was buffered from statements about the sufferings of the crucified. See Pelikan, *Catholic Tradition*, 194–205. For the complex political, as well as theological, shifts involved, see H. Chadwick, *Early Church*, 194–205.

30. See Chapman, *Faith and Revolt*, 154–60; Hartley, *Novels of Kingsley*, 99; and Wolff, *Gains and Losses*, 274–77. Bran, it should be remembered, was the chieftain father of Caractacus, who was baptized and asked for Christian missionaries to return with him to Britain. Cyril is a sketch of Cardinal Wiseman, Hypatia a symbol of that "Emersonian Anythingarianism" Kingsley had excoriated in *Alton Locke*. Synesius may be a portrait of Kingsley himself, although there is no indication he shared the bishop's reservations about the doctrine of the Resurrection. Chapman makes a connection between Kingsley and James Anthony Froude with this figure (*Faith and Revolt*, 303 n. 28). Victoria, saved from a nunnery, may be Kingsley's own wife, Fanny Grenfell. Raphael may be Benjamin Disraeli; his *Contarini Fleming* (1832), *Coningsby* (1844), *Sybil* (1845), and *Tancred* (1847) were already popular.

31. Baker, *Novel and the Oxford Movement*, 96.

32. *Hypatia* [abbr. *H*] (13th ed. 1882; originally published 1853, 2d ed. 1856), 87. This 1882 ed. is based on the famous Eversley edition of Kingsley's works (1881). *Hypatia* went through many English editions and was translated into Czech, German, Spanish, and Swedish. The novel won both friends and enemies; see Chapman, *Faith and Revolt*, 158, 160; Wolff, *Gains and Losses*, 282; and Drummond, *Churches in English Fiction*, 162–63.

33. Charles Kingsley, *Yeast* (New York: Harper, 1851), chap. 4, 79, 80.

34. "Still, surely the idea of an Apostle, unmarried, pure, in fast and nakedness, at length a martyr, is a higher idea than that of one of the old Israelites sitting under his vine and fig-tree, full of temporal goods, and surrounded by sons and grandsons" (Newman, *Loss and Gain*, pt. 2, chap. 5, 112).

35. Charles Kingsley, *Alexandria and Her Schools*, 139. For his attraction to monasticism, see Chitty, *Beast and Monk*.

36. Kingsley, *Alexandria*, 141. He continued the attack on celibacy in his lectures on Salvian (1864); see Kingsley, *The Roman and the Teuton*. The lectures

were criticized by Freeman, who called them "rant and nonsense" in the *Saturday Review*, and by critics in the *Times*; see Chitty, *Beast and Monk*, 248–49; and Martin, *Dust of Combat*, 265. The same subject occupied four sermons on David in 1865; see Chapman, *Faith and Revolt*, 107.

37. Svaglic, "John Henry Newman" (cited intro., n. 34), 126; Chapman, *Faith and Revolt*; and Chitty, *Beast and Monk*. See S. M. Ellis, *Henry Kingsley, 1830–1876: Towards a Vindication* (London: Grant Richards, 1931); and William H. Scheuerle, *The Neglected Brother: A Study of Henry Kingsley* (Tallahassee: Florida State University Press, 1971).

38. Hartley, *Novels of Kingsley*, 49; Chitty, *Beast and Monk*, 67. See Macario Marmo, *The Social Novels of Charles Kingsley* (Salerno: DiGiacomo, 1937); Marmo traces the path of conversion in Kingsley's characters, from love of a woman to service of their fellow men. Even when this love is removed, the religious vision of their social duties remains. In his sermons on David (1865) Kingsley commented that "monks had aimed at copying female virtues and succeeded only in attaining female vices" (quoted by Chapman, *Faith and Revolt*, 107).

39. For Kingsley "emancipated women" were "a class but too common in the later days of Greece, as they will always be, perhaps, in civilizations which are decaying and crumbling to pieces, leaving their members to seek in bewilderment what they are, and what bonds connect them with their fellow-beings" (*Alexandria*, 17).

40. Ibid., 140.

41. "If any of you ever comes across the popular Jewish interpretations of the Song of Solomon, you will there see the folly in which acute and learned men can indulge themselves when they have lost hold of the belief in anything really absolute and eternal and moral, and have made Fate, and Time, and Self, their real deities" (ibid., 77).

42. Wolff, *Gains and Losses*, 277; Hartley, *Novels of Kingsley*, 91. In his work *The Epistle to the Hebrews* (1846), Maurice described the role of the latter-day prophet, the "true teacher," who received not only "divine communications" but also the energy from God to disclose the revelation to his countrymen (see Hartley, 13).

43. *Charles Kingsley: His Letters and Memories of His Life*, ed. Frances Kingsley, 5th ed., 2 vols. (London: Henry S. King, 1877), 1:354.

44. *H*, 307. In *Yeast* Kingsley has the unsympathetic Lord Vieuxbois declare: "I do not think that we have any right in the nineteenth century to contest an opinion which the fathers of the Church gave in the fourth" (quoted in Chapman, *Faith and Revolt*, 142). For Kingsley and Maurice the appeal to the Fathers is in some sense an impossible reversion to infancy. They fail to see the appeal as cumulative, not a retrogression to the fourth century, but an appeal to the tradition preserved for 1,500 years.

45. Kingsley, *Alexandria*, 138–39.

46. Baker, *Novel and the Oxford Movement*, 89.

47. Quoted in ibid., 93.

48. Ward, *Wiseman*, 1:64, 123, 328.

49. Nicholas Cardinal Wiseman, *Fabiola; or, The Church of the Catacombs* [abbr. *F*], Jubilee ed. (New York: P. J. Kenedy & Sons, 1901), viii. The original edition was published in 1854 as the first number in the Catholic Popular Library. It went through many English editions and was translated into French, Spanish, Portuguese, Hungarian, Danish, Polish, Dutch, Slavonian, Romansch, and Russian. There were seven Italian versions before 1897 and four German editions by 1856; see Ward, *Wiseman*, 2:101. It was dramatized in English, French, and Spanish. The novel was composed after 24 October 1853 and before September 1854, during which time the author was mostly resident in Rome or Monte Porzio, the country house of the English College outside the city; see ibid., 2:75 ff. Wiseman was encouraged to do a companion volume on the basilicas by Denzinger, Rio, Overbeck, and Hergenröther (later cardinal) among others. Newman turned down the chance to do such a volume for Wiseman. Basilicas did not have the symbolic value for Newman that they had for Wiseman. Unlike Rome, the "basilicas" in England were in the hands of the State Church.

50. Ward, *Wiseman*, 1:10, 28–29.

51. Richard Altick, *The English Common Reader*, 384. Kingsley maintained a basic difference between Latin slavery and Teutonic, the latter more moral; see *Roman and Teuton*, 19 n. 1.

52. *F*, 148–52. The month of October is thus described, recalling the day (7 October) in 1850 when Wiseman announced to the English people by his pastoral letter the "restoration" of the Roman Catholic hierarchy. It was the calm before the tempest.

53. Ward, *Wiseman*, 1:216.

54. Ibid., 1:326, 519.

55. Ibid., 1:360.

56. Ibid., 1:56–59. See Wiseman's "Philosophical Contributions to the History of the Syriac Version of the Old Testament" and *Horae Syriacae* (1827).

57. Maison, *Victorian Vision* (cited intro., n. 3), 158–59.

58. Ward, *Wiseman*, 1:45; J. H. Newman, *The Second Spring: A Sermon*, ed. F. P. Donnelly, S.J. (New York: Longmans, Green, 1931), 40. It is the first line of the hymn by Prudentius for Lauds on the Feast of the Holy Innocents.

59. Ward, *Wiseman*, 1:273.

60. Newman, *Second Spring*, 37. A MS note for *Callista* concerns the idea of Agellius hung up by his heels, beheaded, skinned, and dissected with the blood streaming; see Ryan, *Callista*, 2:68 (full citation below, n. 70).

61. Newman, *Present Position of Catholics in England*, 307.

62. The second stanza originally read: "Our fathers chained in prisons dark, / were still in heart and conscience free: / How sweet would be their children's fate, / if they like them, could die for thee! *Verse:* Faith of our fathers, holy faith! We will be true to thee till death." See *The Hymnal 1940 Companion*, 3d rev. ed. (New York: Church Pension Fund, [1956]), 250–51, 431.

63. Trevor, *Newman*, 1:603.

64. Ward, *Wiseman*, 2:35.

65. Ibid., 2:94. The Boyle affair stemmed from Wiseman's attempts to discipline one of his clergy and extend the archbishop's powers over the financial and administrative aspects of the newly formed dioceses.

66. Elaine Showalter, *Literature of Their Own*, 138.

67. Mary Sharp, *A Traveller's Guide to the Churches of Rome* (London: Hugh Evelyn, 1967), 170.

68. In a letter to Canon Walker of Scarborough, quoted in Ward, *Wiseman*, 2:101.

69. *Callista: A Tale of the Third Century* [abbr. *C*] (1856 ed.), advertisement, vii. Some recent editions maintain the earlier date: *Callista: A Sketch of the Third Century* (1855), intro. by Alfred Duggan (London: Burns & Oates, 1962). Newman actually finished work on the novel between 22 July and 31 August 1855 (*Letters and Diaries*, 18:xvii). *Callista* was to have had two volumes but was limited by Burns to one, for which Newman was initially offered £30 (18:256, 285). Between 1856 and 1890 there were eight English editions and several corrected impressions. Four editions appeared in French (17:259, 18:40). A planned Italian edition fell through, but a Czech edition was successful (17:207 n. 4). In 1857 H. C. Husenbeth dramatized it in *The Convert Martyr*. See S. Dorman, "*Hypatia* and *Callista*"; A. G. Hill, "Originality and Realism in Newman's Novels"; and Ian Ker, *John Henry Newman: A Biography* (New York: Oxford University Press, 1988), 419–22. In 1839 Newman revealed only to two friends—Henry Wilberforce and Frederic Rogers—the vista of eventual conversion to Rome that Wiseman's article in the *Dublin Review* opened for him. Wilberforce hoped Newman would die rather than become a Roman Catholic. He himself, however, converted in September 1850. See *Apologia*, 124–25; and Chadwick, *Victorian Church*, 1:179–80. In 1855 Henry was instrumental in obtaining for the *Rambler* Acton's defense of Döllinger against the latter's critics in the *Dublin Review*. This dedication, certainly reflecting close personal affection of long standing, is even more telling on this other account. See Newsome, *The Wilberforces and Henry Manning*, 405.

70. See Sr. Mary Paton Ryan, R.S.M., "Newman's *Callista*: A Critical Edition," 2 vols. (Ph.D. diss., Yale University, 1967). The first volume contains a short introduction and an appendix in which are transcribed Newman's MS

notes: diary entries, fragmentary versions from 1848 and 1855, plot sketches, descriptive passages, Newman's own transcriptions of ancient and modern travel literature, and a list of books cited referring to historical detail of Christian and secular life in second- and third-century North Africa. The second volume presents a corrected text of *Callista* and apparatus criticus. See also Dessain, *Newman*, 93–94, 105–8.

71. *C*, postscript, vii–viii; Baker, *Novel and the Oxford Movement*, 55.

72. J. J. Reilly, *Newman as a Man of Letters* (New York: Macmillan, 1932), 91–93. Note Newman's defense in the postscripts of the editions dated 2 February 1881 and October 1888.

73. "Art. VII," *Dublin Review* 80 (1856), 431, quoted by Ryan, *Callista*, 1:6.

74. Wiseman, *Fabiola* (1854 ed.), vii. *Callista* was the twelfth entry in the Catholic Popular Library, published in two series (1854–61). See Charlotte E. Crawford, "Newman's 'Callista' and the Catholic Popular Library," *MLR* 45 (April 1950), 219–21.

75. An extensive bibliography of sources and works cited in the preparatory MSS of Callista is proved by Ryan, *Callista*, 1:286–92. In a letter (1 January 1853) Newman provided a short reading list of historical sources for Lady Georgina Fullerton, who was planning a novel treating the third century in France and Rome. This plan collapsed and she eventually wrote a life of St. Frances of Rome that appeared as the third entry in the Catholic Popular Library. See Ryan, *Callista*, 1:9 ff.; Crawford, "Newman's 'Callista,'" 220; J. H. Pollen, "Letters of Cardinal Newman to Lady Georgina Fullerton," *The Month* 129 (1917), 331–33; and Newman, *Letters and Diaries* 15:235–38.

76. See Dessain, *Newman*, 109; Ryan, *Callista*, 2:ii. "Who, again, would quarrel with Mr. Lockhart, writing in Scotland, for excluding Pope, or Bishops, or sacrificial rites from his interesting Tale of Valerius?" (*C*, preface, 1881, and subsequent editions). See, e.g., Maison, *Victorian Vision*, 145–47. Maison stresses those equivalencies. Svaglic, "John Henry Newman," 127, mentions a work that touches on the autobiographical material in *Callista* by Eric M. Zale, "The Defenses of John Henry Newman" (Ph.D. diss., University of Michigan, 1962). Ryan argues that such attempts are "unprofitable" and "self-defeating" (*Callista*, 1:30).

77. Vargish, 195; Wolff, *Gains and Losses*, 68–71. Many of the proper names used in the novel were derived by Newman from Horace, Sallust (e.g., Juba), Lockhart, and Neander; "Agellius" appeared in the library catalogue at the Birmingham Oratory only one line above "Africa v Marcelli" (Ryan, *Callista*, 1:24). Juba was originally named "Mago" in the MS notes. The heroine's name was derived from the catacombs of San Callisto outside Rome where the excavations

had impressed him (*Letters and Diaries* 11:290, 296). Callista, after her martyr-dom, called to mind the famous recumbent statue of St. Caecilia in Rome. A turn in the Achilli case on St. Caecilia's Day (22 November 1852) had given Newman hope of vindication. Caecilia was a special patron of the Oratory, and Newman wrote a friend in Rome asking for a small copy of her statue (Trevor, *Newman*, 1:613–15).

78. Maison, *Victorian Vision*, 21. For examples of such madness, see Robert Armitage, *Ernest Singleton* (1848), and Francis Edward Paget, *Caleb Kniveton, the Incendiary* (1833). For the exorcism, see the Reverend Edward Peach, *A Circum-stantial Account of a Successful Exorcism Performed at King's Norton, Worchestershire, in the Year 1815* (Birmingham: R. P. Stone, 1836); this volume was in the Little-more library. In a MS note Newman remarks that Juba became an "ideot" [*sic*] "serving the church." The pun is most likely on the Greek term for "layman."

79. Vargish, 174–75.

80. *C*, 263. The figure of the witch is derived from Apuleius and Robert Southey, *The Curse of Kehama*; see Ryan, *Callista*, 1:25. In 1842 Newman preached a sermon on the crucifixion and attempted to bring home Christ's suf-ferings to his listeners by paralleling the cruel killing of an animal, the humiliation and violence done to an old, revered man, and torture of a child; see Trevor, *Newman*, 1:233.

81. See Joel 1–2:17; Paulus Orosius, *Historiarum Libri VII. Lib. V. cap. xi*, in Andreas Gallandius, ed., *Bibliotheca Veterum Patrum Antiquorumque Scriptorum Ecclesiasticorum*, 14 vols. (Venetiis: Joannes Baptista Albritius, 1765–81); and Robert Southey, *Thalaba the Destroyer*, 2 vols. (London: T. N. Longman and O. Rees, 1801). See also Newman, *Letters and Diaries*, 13:449; *C*, 232–34, cf. 344 ff. The slaughter of this mob, common to both *Callista* and *Hypatia*, is derived from descriptions in Sallust; see Ryan, *Callista*, 1:26.

82. Trevor, *Newman*, 2:68; cf. the rejection of liberal attitudes toward the common people in the *Apologia* ("Note A," 216–25).

83. Wolff, *Gains and Losses*, 69. Selden and Vossius, following Herodotus and Strabo, derived "Sicca veneria" from the Punic "Succoth-Benoth" (i.e., "Tents of the Daughters"); see 2 Kgs 17:30. On the other hand, the Victorian travel accounts concerning Keff or El Kaf, the more recent names for Sicca, stress the abundant water from a crystal spring in the town; El Kaf also indicates that the town is on the declivity of a hill; see Ryan, *Callista*, 1:187–226, esp. 226. Ryan suggests that the physical features of the town in the novel were borrowed from Castra Giovanni, the ancient Enna, in Sicily, where Newman's illness in 1833 reached its crisis (2:38). If the Punic name is retained, one may posit a contrast between Callista's choice of celibacy and the ways of the wide world, the "Tents

of the Daughters," where they marry and are given in marriage, and while paying homage to the Lord, still serve the images of their own gods (2 Kgs 17:33).

84. His resources included articles by J. M. Capes in the *Rambler* on "Celebrated Sanctuaries of the Madonna"; see Ryan, *Callista*, 1:13 ff.; *Letters and Diaries*, 12:153, 156; 14:260.

85. In a letter dated 23 May 1848 (*Letters and Diaries* 12:209–10). Newman also used the following works: Capt. J. Kennedy, *Algeria and Tunis in 1845: An Account of a Journey Made through the Two Regencies by Viscount Feilding and Capt. Kennedy*, 2 vols. (London: Henry Colburn, 1846); and G. N. Wright, *The Shores and Islands of the Mediterranean, Drawn from Nature by Sir Grenville Temple Bart., W. L. Leitch, Esq., Major Irton, and Lieut. Allen, R. E.* (London: Fisher, Son, [1840?]), 109–11.

86. Ryan, *Callista*, 2:37.

87. A favorite word of Newman's. "Reality" is the epigraph to the novel, lines from a poem by Aubrey de Vere; see Ryan, *Callista*, 1:31. The phrase is also used in *Loss and Gain*, pt. 2, chap. 12; Newman chose as his own epitaph "Ex umbris et imaginibus in veritatem" (quoted in Vargish, 171–72).

88. A detailed study of the citations of poetry in the novel, breaking the fabric of the work into poetry and prose, has never been undertaken. The canon of verse he draws upon and the style and function of his own verse could be used as a practical index of Newman's literary theory when read in conjunction with his articles on literature in *The Idea of a University*, being composed at this time (1852–59).

89. *C*, 211. The cross is designated as "the symbol of redemption"; it is also termed "the dread symbol of his [Agellius'] salvation" (*C*, 29). The circumlocution shows Newman's historical sensitivity in not identifying it as a crucifix. The cross plays a dominant role in the penitential side of Newman's spirituality; see *Loss and Gain*, pt. 2, chap. 17; the cross/crucifix is also used in a miraculous exorcism of the demonic Dr. Kitchens (pt. 3, chap. 8).

90. Newman called Pusey's doctrinal notes "grossly unfair"; the work in question was the *Treatises of S. Cyprian* (Oxford, 1839). This included Pontius' life of Cyprian and portions of the *Acta* on which Newman drew for his novel; see Crawford, "Newman's 'Callista,'" 221. For a survey of works on Newman as patristic biographer, see Svaglic, "John Henry Newman," 148.

91. Cyprian, *Ep.* 64.5 (*CSEL* 3:720–21). Since baptism brought remission of sins, infant baptism for Cyprian was defended by a doctrine of original sin, not as elaborate or developed as Augustine's later position but hedged about with reference to apostolic tradition and sacramental validity; see Pelikan, *Catholic Tradition*, 291–92.

92. Ryan, *Callista*, 1:32.

93. *C*, 26, 338, 126–27, 354–56. See also Showalter, *Literature of Their Own*, 112–13.

94. *C*, 338. For a discussion of Newman's mariological stance, see Dessain, *Newman*, 135. Newman compared the moderate Catholic teaching on Mary with the Anglo-Catholic and concluded that both were in agreement with the Fathers. See Newman's answer (1865) to Pusey's first *Eirenicon* (1865) in *Certain Difficulties Felt by Anglicans in Catholic Teaching*, 2 vols. (London: Longmans, Green, 1875), 2:78. Newman's inclusion of the term *immaculate* calls to mind the dogmatic definition of the Immaculate Conception in 1854.

95. *C*, 336. Newman's use of sources for the liturgy is extensive and shows once again the importance he placed on such worship; see Charles Dessain, "Newman's Philosophy and Theology," in DeLaura, *Victorian Prose*, 166–84, on 182.

96. Ryan, *Callista*, 1:30.

97. Ibid., 1:26.

98. *Apologia*, 16.

99. For example, George Levine, "Newman's Fiction and the Failure of Reticence," quoted by Svaglic, "John Henry Newman," 146.

100. Hartley, *Novels of Kingsley*, 90; Kingsley, *Alexandria*, 131.

101. Newman, *Certain Difficulties*, quoted by Baker, *Novel and the Oxford Movement*, 60.

102. Quoted by Hilda Graef, *God and Myself: The Spirituality of John Henry Newman* (New York: Hawthorn Books, 1968), 112–13.

CHAPTER 3

1. Chadwick, *Victorian Church*, 1:189–93. Perhaps because of the Evangelical roots of Manning and Newman, apocalyptic imagery plays a significant role in their sermons, as in the rampant adventism of much contemporary Evangelical literature; cf. Thomas Newton, *Dissertations on Prophecy* (1754), especially Diss. 27. Newman cites this in his *Apologia*. Little work has been done on this although the phenomenon has been noticed; see Newsome, *The Wilberforces*, 10–12, 206–7, and Christopher Dawson, *The Spirit of the Oxford Movement* (London: Sheed & Ward, [1933] 1945), 52. A study should be done linking Tractarian exegesis of Revelation to the widespread fascination with dreams, visions, and portents. Geoffrey Faber records one famous example of a dream in his lopsided psychological study *Oxford Apostles* (London: Penguin, 1954), 46. See also Newsome, 370, for another example.

2. Wilberforce's first wife, Agnes Everilda Wrangham, was the old archdeacon's daughter. They were married in 1832; she died in November 1834 after bearing two sons, William and Edward. In 1837 he married Jane Legard. Wrangham, an old High and Dry Churchman, is appropriately cited as translator of Horace's drinking ode "Persicos odi," in Wilberforce's *Rutilius and Lucius* (see n. 6), 103–4.

3. See Mozley, *Reminiscences Chiefly of Oriel College and the Oxford Movement,* 1:225. See also Andrew C. Mead, "J. B. Mozley and the Development of Doctrine" (B.Litt. thesis, Keble College, Oxford, 1973). Cited is Gladstone's opinion of him in a letter (4 September 1854), quoted in Newsome, *The Wilberforces,* 382–83.

4. For the few lengthy studies of this undervalued theologian, see Newsome, *The Wilberforces,* 370–83; E. R. Fairweather, *The Oxford Movement* (New York: Oxford University Press, 1964), 283–367; and A. Härdelin, *Tractarian Understanding of the Eucharist,* esp. 111–222.

5. Newsome, *The Wilberforces,* 271. Wilberforce also touches upon the role of church courts in his novel: "'If ever our faith should be adopted by princes,' said Pamphilus, 'and the authority which you now exercise should be publicly recognized, we may expect to see the bishop's court as regular a part in the judicial system of the state as the court of the emperor'" (*R,* 93–94). See also the case of the exclusion of an adulterer (*R,* 242–44).

6. R. I. Wilberforce, *Rutilius and Lucius; or, Stories of the Third Age* [abbr. *R*] (London: Edward Lumley, 1842).

7. Wolff, *Gains and Losses,* 114–16. In this early stage Gresley contributed *Portrait of an English Churchman* (1838); *Charles Lever; or, The Man of the Nineteenth Century* (1841); and *Church Clavering; or, The Schoolmaster* (1843). Paget produced *St. Antholin's; or, Old Churches and New: A Tale for the Times* (1841) and *Milford Valvoisin; or, Pews and Pew-Holders* (1842).

8. See *R,* 171–74. Marriage is in no way denigrated, but celibacy is presented as a better way for the evangelical ministry. It is closely connected to moral views about the Christian in the world, asceticism, and holiness.

9. The revival of interest in Plato can be illustrated from the work of the Noetics of Oriel College, Oxford, culminating in the next generation in Benjamin Jowett's *Plato* (1871). Various texts and translations were available: *Arguments of Celsus, Porphyry, and the Emperor Julian against the Christians,* ed. Thomas Taylor, "the Platonist" (London, 1830); *Plotini opera omnia,* ed. G. H. Moser, 3 vols. (Oxford, 1835); *Select Works of Plotinus,* trans. T. Taylor (London, 1817); *Select Works of Porphyry . . . ,* trans. T. Taylor (London, 1823); *The Substance of Porphyry's Life of Plotinus* (London, 1817); *Translations . . . of the . . . treatises of Plotinus,* trans. T. Taylor (London, 1834).

10. *R*, 63. The language and imagery are certainly drawn from the early Fathers. Newman, discussing the "position" of his mind since 1845, says in his *Apologia*, chap. 5: "I have been in perfect peace and contentment; I never have had one doubt . . . it was like coming into port after a rough sea." Other Tractarians used such ocean imagery. Raymond Chapman remarks on it in the novels of Charlotte Yonge (*Faith and Revolt*, 86). The image of the Church as the Ark is a telling one: static, besieged, self-contained, exclusive, and a refuge from general destruction. This was pointed out by Augustine to the Donatists, who frequently employed this image; see Peter Brown, *Augustine of Hippo: A Biography* (Berkeley and Los Angeles: University of California Press, 1969), 221.

11. *R*, 64. Here is an early foray into an area Wilberforce would treat at length in his systematic study of the Incarnation: *The Doctrine of the Incarnation of Our Lord Jesus Christ* (London: Derby, 1848).

12. Newsome, *The Wilberforces*, 373.

13. *R*, 172–73. The identification of celibacy with "angelic nature" should call to the reader's mind Newman's own identification with the angelic order in the *Apologia* (chap. 1, 22, 47). See also *R*, 161–62, where the angelic imagery is borrowed from Augustine's Sermon 132.

14. *R*, 195–96. In *Loss and Gain* (1848) Newman satirized those young men of "advanced" theological views who proposed rigorous asceticism, including celibacy, for the ideal Christian, yet themselves married and were given in marriage. The marriages of John Keble and Henry Wilberforce were particularly grievous for him. But it was not to Newman's brand of asceticism that men like Robert Isaac looked in the early 1840s, but Manning's. It should also be noted that Manning's wife, Caroline Sargent, had died in 1837; he never remarried.

15. *R*, 86. A similar viewpoint may be seen in H. E. Manning's sermon *The English Church, Its Succession and Witness for Christ* (London, 1835).

16. *R*, 79–80. The concern for miracles was a constant one with the Tractarians, especially Newman. His *Essay on Miracles* (1826) and its radical revision in 1842 are important sources to consider. See his *Apologia*, chap. 1, 42. Later Tractarians were more guarded in their attitude.

17. *R*, 107–30, 139–68. Wilberforce refers in passing to "Bingham, Antiquities, XIII, VIII.4.1" (Joseph Bingham, *Origenes ecclesiasticae; or, The Antiquities of the Christian Church* . . . , ed. Richard Bingham, 9 vols. [London, 1821–29]); "S. Ambrose, ad Virgin. Laps." (several early editions available; see *Liber de Lapsu Virginis consecratae*, bk. 1, Migne *PL* 16:383–400 [Paris, 1845]); "Apostolic Constitutions" (numerous early editions; see *The Constitutions of the Holy Apostles by Clement* . . . , ed. William Whiston [1711]); "Bingham & Bp. Rattray, Litur. of ancient church of Jerusalem" (Thomas Rattray [bishop of Brechin, Dunkeld, Primus of the Episcopal Church of Scotland], *The Ancient Liturgy of the Church of*

Jerusalem . . . , rev. by T. Rattray [London, 1744]); "Card. Bona, Res Liturgicae i.20.1" (Giovanni Cardinal Bona, *Rerum liturgicarum libri duo* . . . [Rome, 1671]); and "S. Augustine, Sermon #132" (numerous early editions; see *Opera*, Migne *PL* 32–47 [Paris: 1841–49]). See also *R*, 111 n. 1, where Wilberforce discusses the custom of lights (i.e., candles) on the altar. He also discusses how the Church's sacrifice is parallel to the Jewish ritual (*R*, 150).

18. R. I. Wilberforce, *The Doctrine of the Incarnation of our Lord Jesus Christ, in Its Relation to Mankind and to the Church* (London: Derby, 1848); *The Doctrine of the Holy Eucharist* (London: Derby, 1853); *R*, 147.

19. Härdelin, *Tractarian Understanding*, 216.

20. Cf. *Racovian Catechism* (1605/1609). See David Clark, "The Altar Controversy in Early Stuart England" (B.A. thesis, Harvard University, 1968).

21. Härdelin, *Tractarian Understanding*, 217; see the whole of the argument, 217–19. Also Newsome, *The Wilberforces*, 380.

22. Discussing Justin Martyr on the Eucharist, Wilberforce maintains the old High Church position vis-à-vis the "novel doctrine" of Rome on the question of transubstantiation. By this date Newman and others seriously questioned their own understanding of Rome's belief. "He [Justin] speaks of the elements after consecration as being still bread and wine,—the specific point which the Romanists deny. His words assert the doctrine of the real presence in no other sense than that in which it is taught in the Catechism of the Church of England" (*R*, 166 n. 1).

23. *R*, 185–86. Cf. R. I. Wilberforce, *The Doctrine of Holy Baptism* (London: Derby, 1849), which anticipated many of the questions in the Gorham case. For a discussion of Baptismal Regeneration, see Appendix C.

24. Letter of R. I. Wilberforce to H. E. Manning (1 December 1848), quoted in Newsome, *The Wilberforces*, 277: "Probably you go further than I do in thinking confession desirable as a general and constant practice. I hardly see how it can be made so, and I am inclined to think that it would be one of those things which when it became a form might be very injurious. I say this without having altered my policy about its great uses, how could I, as an occasional thing; for those who voluntarily seek it. But counsels of perfection don't suit for general use, any more than Folio vols. for ordinary pockets."

25. *R*, 181; cf. 183. As an example of the deceit of private judgment, Wilberforce mentions the story of Maximilian, a Christian youth beheaded for refusal to serve in the army (*R*, 177–79). The story was drawn from Theodoricus Ruinart's *Acta Primorum Martyrum sincera et selecta* (Amsterdam, 1713), 300; it is used by other Anglo-Catholic novelists, e.g., Sabine Baring-Gould, *Perpetua* (1897), who also condemned the youth's action. Wilberforce's literary twist is in making Maximilian Rutilius' brother.

26. *R*, 90. In referring to Paul of Samosata, Wilberforce has left a vivid picture of the flamboyant type of Evangelical preacher: "Indeed, he was a sensual, worldly man, whose life was as bad as his teaching. They say that he used all sorts of worldly arts to make himself highly thought of. He would stamp and strike his thigh when he was preaching, to astonish our simpler brethren. Then he took great pride in the state and pomp of his office" (*R*, 90–91).

27. Newsome, *The Wilberforces*, 378. The incarnation, baptism, and Eucharist are all part of the same phenomenon, one that is "real" and that has "power" (*virtus*). To deny one is to deny all.

28. For example, Keble had this attitude. See Battiscombe, *John Keble*, 314. Kingsley, on the other hand, suspected the Puseyites of disloyalty; see Chapman, *Faith and Revolt*, 103–4.

29. And not, as Raymond Chapman suggests, for attempts to restore the conventual life (*Faith and Revolt*, 166). It was not until after the riots at Lewes (1857), during the funeral of Miss Scobell, that Bishop Gilbert of Chichester withdrew his recognition of the community at East Grinstead; see Chadwick, *Victorian Church*, 1:510.

30. A. G. Lough, *The Influence of John Mason Neale* (London: SPCK, 1962), 107–42. Several novels deal with the Eastern Church at later periods: *The Lazar House of Leros* (1859) and *The Lily of Tiflis* (1859). The most important novel in this line is *Theodora Phranza* (1857, reprinted from *The Churchman's Companion*, 1853–54), linking England and Constantinople; cf. Chapman, *Faith and Revolt*, 160–68.

31. *Triumphs of the Cross: Tales of Christian Heroism*, Juvenile Englishman's Library (1845); *A Mirror of Faith: Lays and Legends of the Church in England* (1845); *Stories of the Crusades* (1846); *Triumphs of the Cross*, 2d ser., *Tales of Christian Endurance* (1846); *Deeds in Faith: Stories for Children from Church History* (1850), 2d ser. (1851); *Victories of the Saints: Stories for Children from Church History* (1850); *The Followers of the Lord: Stories from Church History* (1851); *Evenings at Sackville College: Legends for Children* (1852); and *Lent Legends: Stories from Church History* (1855). One should also mention that curious attempt at literary revisionism: *Bunyan's Pilgrim's Progress for the Use of Children in the English Church* (1853).

32. *Agnes de Tracey: A Tale of the Times of St. Thomas of Canterbury* (1843); a contemporary tale—*Ayton Priory; or, The Restored Monastery* (1843); *Herbert Tresham: A Story of the Great Rebellion* (1843); *Shepperton Manor: A Tale of the Times of Bishop Andrewes* (1845)—Neale had translated the private *Latin Devotions of Andrewes* (1843); *Poynings: A Tale of the Revolution* (1847); and *Duchenier; or, The Revolt of La Vendee* (1848).

33. *English History for Children* (1845), preface, x.

34. J. M. Neale and J. Haskoll, eds., *Sir Henry Spelman's History and Fate of*

Sacrilege (London, 1846); a new edition was edited by S. J. Eales (1888). G. R. Elton, in various works, has pointed out the propaganda value of this claim and attempted to refute its basis by showing that numbers of Roman Catholics bought or were given such property, without apparent loss of life or issue.

35. Lough, *Influence of Neale*, 143–54. In the early 1850s Neale was engaged in two other major controversies: the Gorham case and the continuing debate over the Jerusalem bishopric. *A Few Words of Hope on the Present Crisis of the English Church* (1850) and *A Letter to the Ven. Archdeacon Hare with Respect to his Pamphlet on the Gorham Question* (1850) formed his response to the Gorham case. He did not agree with the secessionists, however much the actions of the Judicial Committee of the Privy Council and its Erastian power upset him. The formularies of the Church were clear, he thought: the decision of a civil court in matters of doctrine or discipline were not binding on the Church. Also in 1850 he collected and edited *Documents Connected with the Foundation of the Anglican Bishopric in Jerusalem, with the Protest against Bishop Gobat's Proselytism*. Samuel Gobat, the second occupant of the Jerusalem see, was charged with proselytizing among Christians in the Holy Land. Neale collected the signatures of over a thousand English clergymen to a protest, and composed a Greek version to be sent to the Eastern patriarchs. Neale was especially sensitive to this problem. He had begun publishing his vast *History of the Holy Eastern Church* in 1847, the first two volumes dealing with the patriarchate of Alexandria and a *General Introduction* in two volumes (1850), followed by an *Appendix* (1851). Neale had some difficulty securing access to material in Eastern depositories because of Orthodox animosity to the Jerusalem bishopric. It is interesting that the Reverend George Williams, Neale's friend who completed the volumes in the *History* dealing with the Patriarchate of Antioch (1873, 1878), had been chaplain to the first bishop of Jerusalem in the 1840s.

36. J. M. Neale, *Victories of the Saints: Stories for Children from Church History* (London, [1850] 1870), xi. See the Reverend Edward A. Monro, *Claudian* (London, 1862), a tale of a boy's conversion at Vienne in A.D. 174, which is imitative of Neale.

37. J. M. Neale, *The Farm of Aptonga: A Story of the Times of St. Cyprian* [abbr. *Ap*] (London: Cleaver, 1854). The *DNB* incorrectly gives 1856 as the date of publication.

38. Anglo-Catholics were especially active in work on Cyprian. George A. Poole is a good example: *The Testimony of St. Cyprian against Rome: An Essay towards Determining the Judgment of St. Cyprian Touching Papal Supremacy* (London, 1838); *The Life and Times of St. Cyprian* (Oxford, 1840); and no. 9 in the Lives of the Saints series: *The Life of Saint Cyprian, Bishop and Martyr* (Oxford, [1855]). Cyprian appears as a central character in J. H. Newman's *Callista: A Sketch of the Third Century* (London, 1855).

39. Neale's last tale treated this subject explicitly: *The Sea-Tigers: A Tale of Medieval Nestorianism* (London, 1860). In depicting the condition of medieval Christian Asia in A.D. 1250, Neale sketches a picture of the Nestorian Church stretching from Siberia to Ceylon, pointing out that in that century Christians outnumbered "most seats of idol worshippers," whereas in the nineteenth century Christians were far less populous than the Buddhists alone. He does not go further than making that sobering comparison.

40. Neale, *Victories*, chap. 3. In the preface he lists the primary and secondary works consulted: the second hymn of the *Peristephanon* of Prudentius; the *Epistle* 80 (82) of St. Cyprian; the sermons of St. Augustine (in the later work he most likely used the sermons on St. Perpetua and her companions); Arevalius' edition of Prudentius; Pamelius' notes on *Epistle* 82 of St. Cyprian; Mariettis; Gallonius' *Torments of the Martyrs*; and an ancient hymn included in Cardinal Thomasius' *Opusculi* 2.393. This is another indication of how much research was masked in his stories.

41. Cyprian to Aspasius Paternus, quoted in W. H. C. Frend, *Martyrdom and Persecution in the Early Church*, 317. Cyprian, as a Christian, in the formal charge was "diis Romanis et religionibus sacris inimicus" (ibid., 321).

42. Sabine Baring-Gould's novels (see below) do introduce some other startling material—explicit charges of child murder and mutilation, perhaps picking up the theme from Newman's *Callista* or from his own work in folklore and supernaturalism.

43. *Ap*, 45. Other writers of the 1850s drew on the *Acta Perpetuae* as authentic contemporary accounts; Sts. Perpetua and Felicity and the dream sequence in their *Passio* were employed by Newman in *Callista*.

44. Bishop Longley almost refused to consecrate the structure until he was assured that the subject of the inscription, "Pray for the sinner who built this church," was still alive. The "sinner" was Pusey himself. The bishop refused to use a donated chalice because of a similar inscription: a letter of J. B. Mozley to his sister (14 November 1845), quoted by Anonymous, *Pusey's Life* (cited intro., n. 28).

45. Chadwick, *Victorian Church*, 1:451. Although Evangelicals such as Dr. William Marsh of St. Thomas in Birmingham—"Millennial Marsh"—are the ones usually cited (see Chadwick) for such visions, the piety and preaching of diverse groups within the Church of England were affected by such heightened expectations.

46. George Anthony Denison, vicar of East Brent in Somerset and archdeacon of Taunton, precipitated a legal battle over his extreme Tractarian view of the Eucharist. See Chadwick, *Victorian Church*, 1:491–94; Härdelin, *Tractarian Understanding*, 166–68, 175. Denison held that all who receive—worthy and unworthy alike—receive the sacred body and blood of Christ.

47. Chadwick, *Victorian Church*, 1:494–95. R. I. Wilberforce had antici-
pated events and published *The Doctrine of the Holy Eucharist* (1853); E. B. Pusey,
*The Real Presence of the Body and Blood of Our Lord Jesus Christ the Doctrine of the
Church of England* (1857); and John Keble, *On Eucharistical Adoration . . .* (1857).

48. A letter to the Reverend William Russell, quoted in Lough, *Influence of
Neale*, 11.

49. Neale, *Victories*, x.

50. *Ap*, 52. Another bit of antiquarian knowledge he includes is that in antiquity sea sickness was an unknown malady (*Ap*, 150).

51. Quoted in Eleanor A. Towle, *John Mason Neale, D.D., a Memoir* (London: Longmans, 1906), 89. The D.D. was awarded to Neale in 1850 by Harvard
University.

52. Neale, *A History of the Holy Eastern Church: General Introduction*, vol. 1
(1850), 1 ff., quoted in Lough, *Influence of Neale*, 121–22.

53. Letter of J. H. Newman to R. I. Wilberforce (11 December 1853),
quoted in Newsome, *The Wilberforces*, 384.

54. J. H. Newman, *An Essay on the Development of Christian Doctrine*, introduction, sec. 8, pp. 11–12; sec. 13, p. 19.

55. Letter to Earl Granville (3 December 1870), quoted by H. J. Hanham,
ed., *The Nineteenth-Century Constitution, 1815–1914: Documents and Commentary*
(Cambridge: Cambridge University Press, 1969), 33–34.

56. See the discussion in Norman, *Anti-Catholicism in Victorian England*,
80–104, 212–28.

57. Thomas W. Mossman, *A History of the Catholic Church of Jesus Christ*
[abbr. *HC*] (London: Longmans, Green, 1873), xi–xii.

58. *HC*, cv. He cites an article "Church and Dissent" in the *Edinburgh Review* (January 1873), pp. 201, 202, which states that to suppose any exclusive external organization of the Primitive Church, corresponding exactly to modern
forms, was unhistorical.

59. *HC*, Appendix B, 491–502. The episcopate had long been a particularly
sore point in controversial works; Lightfoot and Zahn responded defensively
to Baur's repudiation of the Ignation epistles and episcopacy as authentic early
elements.

60. The quotation from Augustine is "Securus judicat orbis terrarum, bonos
non esse qui se dividunt ab orbe terrarum in quacumque parte terrarum" (*Contra
epistolam Parmeniani* 3.24). It plays a prominent part in the *Apologia*, chap. 3,
123–24.

61. Thomas W. Mossman, *Epiphanius* [abbr. *Es*] (London: J. T. Hayes,

1874). He based the novel on the Greek life by Metaphrastes, a work without "any intrinsic historical value," he finds.

62. The silence over the "Origenist" controversy is unusual, especially because of the continued controversy surrounding the removal of F. D. Maurice in 1853 from his professorship at King's College, London, because of his Origenist position denying eternal punishment.

63. *Es*, 135–39, esp. 136. Mossman is the only Anglo–Catholic novelist to give such a full description of early ordinations, basing the tripartite ritual on the works of specific apostles: Thomas (for subdeacon), Philip (for deacon), and John (for priest).

64. H. Chadwick, *Early Church*, 281.

65. O. Chadwick, *Victorian Church*, 2:468.

66. Ibid., 2:31. In the *Life of S. Elizabeth of Hungary* by Miss C. A. Jones (London: J. T. Hayes, 1874), the "most astounding miracles" are recorded, along with an extract by J. M. Neale insisting that it is a Christian's duty to believe medieval (or ecclesiastical) miracles. An anonymous reviewer for the *Literary Churchman* describes that as "a duty which must sometimes be a very hard one."

67. The Reverend Frederick George Lee, *The Church under Queen Elizabeth: An Historical Sketch*, 2 vols. (London: W. H. Allen, 1880), dedication. A miraculous cure of two small boys after a blessing with water from the shrine at Lourdes on 19 April 1879 is recounted and defended (xiii–xiv).

68. "The Keys of the Kingdom of Heaven, a Sermon by the Rev. T. W. Mossman, O.C.R. [Order of Corporate Reunion]" (London, 1879).

69. Ibid., quoted by Lee, *Church under Queen Elizabeth*, frontispiece. Lord Shaftesbury and the two archbishops in 1873 had warded off recent attempts to overthrow the Reformation in the Church of England; see Chadwick, *Victorian Church*, 2:324.

70. Lee, *Church under Queen Elizabeth*, 324 n.

71. Ibid., 382.

72. Quoted by L. E. Elliott–Binns, *Religion in the Victorian Era* (Greenwich, Conn.: Seabury Press, 1953), 474. The letter is incorrectly dated January 1879; Lightfoot was nominated in March and consecrated in April.

73. Yonge, *The Pupils of St. John*, 60. Other traditions in English historiography point to the apostle Paul or Joseph of Arimathea as the founder of Christianity in Britain.

74. Letter to W. J. Butler (28 October 1868), given in Christabel Coleridge, *Charlotte Mary Yonge: Her Life and Letters* (London: Macmillan, 1903), 237–48. Yonge's identification with the apostolate of the Church during her retirement

calls to mind a roughly contemporary French Catholic figure, Thérèse de Lisieux (1873–97), patron saint of Catholic missions.

75. Ibid., 227. Yonge's family's interest in church building was the impetus for her first novel: *Abbeychurch; or, Self-Control and Self-Conceit* (1844). The goals of home and foreign missions were often combined in such activities.

76. S. Neill, *A History of Christian Missions* (Harmondsworth: Penguin, 1975), 352–53.

77. C. M. Yonge, *In Memoriam, Bishop Patteson: Being with Additions, the Substance of a Memoir Published in the Literary Churchman* (1872); and the later biography, *Life of J. C. Patteson, Missionary Bishop of the Melanesian Islands*, 2 vols. (1873; 6th ed., 1878); see Yonge's *New Ground*, a tale about mission work in South Africa, in the *Magazine for the Young* in 1863. See also *The Making of a Missionary or Day Dreams in Earnest* (1900); *Pioneers and Founders, or Recent Workers in the Mission Field, etc.* (1871); and a *Preface to the History of the Universities' Mission to Central Africa* (1897). Her character Norman May appears as a missionary in New Zealand in *The Trial: More Links of the Daisy Chain* (1864; 4th ed., 1868; 2 vols., 1870); Neill, *History of Christian Missions*, 353.

78. Battiscombe, *John Keble*, 164–65; cf. Chadwick, *Victorian Church*, 2:214–15; Wolff, *Gains and Losses*, 117–18; Chapman, *Faith and Revolt*, 61–62, 70–71, 79.

79. Publication statistics for *The Christian Year* are found in Altick, *English Common Reader*; comments on the *Lyra* are found in Battiscombe, *John Keble*, 281–85; and Newman's essay "John Keble" in *Essays Critical and Historical*, 2 vols. (1848). See R. W. Rhodes, "John Keble—Grammarian of Piety," *This Sacred History*, ed. D. S. Armentrout (Cambridge, Mass.: Cowley, 1990), 47–60.

80. C. M. Yonge, *Musings over the Christian Year and Lyra Innocentium, Together with a Few Gleanings of Recollections of the Rev. J. Keble, Gathered by Several Friends* (London: Parker, 1871); *John Keble's Parishes: A History of Hursley and Otterbourne* (London: Macmillan, 1898); *Old Times at Otterbourne*, 2d ed. (Winchester: Warren & Son, 1891).

81. Quoted in Coleridge, *Yonge*, 221–22. The quotation is from John 5:35.

82. Letter to Marianne Dyson (9 August 1869), in Coleridge, *Yonge*, 247. The "Mrs. Keble" she refers to is most likely Bessie Clarke Keble, the wife of Tom Keble.

83. Quoted in Coleridge, *Yonge*, 308. Some of Yonge's feelings about German criticism were grounded in her aversion to the political advances of Prussia. In a letter to Dean Butler of Lincoln at the time of the Franco-Prussian War, she observed: "I confess that I have not personally been able to get into the stream of sympathy with Prussia, for Bismarck's policy does seem to me that of the ambi-

tious conqueror and I never could forgive him for Holstein. German unity does not seem to me a rightful cause, though I can perceive that it may so seem to Germans themselves, who have a sort of fanaticism for that Vaterland of theirs" (ibid., 305).

84. Chadwick, *Victorian Church*, 1:451.

85. Even careful observers, such as James E. White, have a tendency to dismiss the important role played by liturgy in the early formulation of Tractarian principles. In White's case this attitude is understandable, since he wished to stress the importance of Neale, Bennett, and other Ecclesiologists as the "fathers" of the Ritualists. See also Y. Brilioth, *The Anglican Revival: Studies in the Oxford Movement* (London: Longmans, 1925); Horton Davies, *Worship and Theology in England*, vol. 3: *From Watts and Wesley to Maurice, 1690–1850* (Princeton: Princeton University Press, 1961), 244. Cf. John H. Overton, *The English Church, 1800–33* (London: Longmans, 1894), 188 ff. This interpretation has often caused the two movements to be viewed as adversaries in some sense, governed by spirits alien to each other. See Härdelin, *Tractarian Understanding*, 226.

86. Newman's *Apologia* comments on how the market for Roman breviaries in Oxford was fierce because of Lloyd's lectures; in *Loss and Gain* Charles Reding is shown rummaging about for Catholic prayer books, while a satirical catalogue of books is introduced by the author to mock this newly inflamed Anglican fervor for apostolic liturgy. Frederick Oakeley also cites Lloyd's lectures for making the Prayer Book "more deeply valued." See F. Oakeley, "The Church Service," *British Critic* 27, no. 54 (1840), 250 ff.

87. Yonge, *Pupils*, 320.

88. Letter to Annie Cazenove (April 1865), quoted in Ethel Romanes, *Charlotte Mary Yonge: An Appreciation* (London: A. R. Mowbray, 1908), 31.

89. The attitude of the early Tractarians is brilliantly outlined by R. Greenfield, "The Attitude of the Tractarians to the Roman Catholic Church, 1833–1850" (D.Phil. diss., Oxford University, 1956, typed MS in the Bodleian Library, Oxford).

90. Chapman, *Faith and Revolt*, 70.

91. C. M. Yonge, *The Slaves of Sabinus, Jew and Gentile* [abbr. *S*] (London: National Society's Depository, 1890).

92. See Yonge, *Pupils*, 60–61; *S*, 98, 100, 109, 120. Pudens is the senator Quintus Cornelius Pudens, whose home was on the Viminal Hill. His wife, Priscilla, gave her name to the catacombs to the northeast of the Capitol. Tradition identifies their one son, Pudens, as the husband of Claudia Rufina, daughter of Caractacus. The identification has some importance for an English writer, since Nicholas Cardinal Wiseman took his title from the church of Pudens, built

on this site in the Via Urbana. The reference seems even stronger because the neophyte Telamon receives the kiss of peace from Pudens and is sent back home "by the great Flaminian Road" (*S*, 140).

93. See Newman, *Essay on Development*, pt. 1, chap. 2, sec. 2, par. 3: "This need of an authoritative sanction is increased by considering, after M. Guizot's suggestion, that Christianity, though represented in prophecy as a kingdom, came into the world as an idea rather than an institution, and has had to wrap itself in clothing and fit itself with armour of its own providing, and to form the instruments and methods of its prosperity and warfare" (1968 ed., p. 77). Also Lord Morley, quoted in Elliott-Binns, *Religion*, 113: "[J.S. Mill] used to tell us that the Oxford theologians had done for England something like what Guizot, Villemain, Michelet, and Cousin had done a little earlier for France."

94. *S*, 137. Yonge follows Tractarian historians who place the pontificate of Clement before Cletus. See, e.g., Mossman, discussed above. Likewise, the fourth-century identification of Flavius Clemens, consul in 95, and his wife, Domitilla, as Christians is pushed back and made definite in the first century; the reference to the office of Cletus and Clement as "Pope" prompted a typical Tractarian definition from Yonge: the pope is termed "no great ecclesiastic then, but truly the servant of servants, the Christian bound to be in chiefest peril in all Rome" (*S*, 233). Gregory the Great and the Roman martyrology are in the back of her mind. She makes no verbal distinction beyond this term between the bishops of Rome and other bishops, such as Trophimus, who are called "holy Father" or the "Great Shepherd," surrounded like the pope by the same protocol and college of seven deacons.

95. G. M. I. Blackburne, preface to Yonge's pamphlet, *Reasons Why I Am a Catholic and Not a Roman Catholic*, 1901 ed., p. iii, quoted in Chapman, *Faith and Revolt*, 71. She also held this position concerning Newman's defection; see Romanes, *Charlotte Mary Yonge*, 192–93.

96. Chadwick, *Victorian Church*, 2:102. Yonge's own attitude toward miracles is highly reserved. There are no miracles in this novel. One could compare the novels of Sabine Baring-Gould written in the 1890s, which for a Tractarian display quite an ambiguous, if not skeptical, attitude toward miracles. In *The Pupils of St. John* Yonge raises questions about two miracles but asserts finally "neither wonder was impossible" (*Pupils*, 74). Perhaps her own sense of reserve and standards of veracity explain her attitude in this novel: she does not want to manufacture false miracles. For the same reason, we might suggest, she does not identify any of the characters—Telamon, Sabinus, or Eponina—as a Christian martyr. In fact, she asserts that they were not (*S*, 172), although she says in the case of Telamon "assuredly the lot of such a one was among the saints" (*S*, 175).

97. Chadwick, *Victorian Church*, 2:102–4.

98. Chadwick, *Mind of the Oxford Movement*, 37.

99. His *Lives of the Saints* in 15 volumes occupied him from 1872 to 1877; his *Lives of the British Saints* was composed at the behest of the Cymmrodorion Society (1907). Baring-Gould wrote several historical novels not considered here. In 1856 he published *The Chorister*, the story of how the stained glass of King's College, Cambridge, was rescued from Cromwell's rampaging troops by a chorister of King's who was killed in the mission. The tale was complete fiction, of course, but was long regarded as factual. See William Purcell, *Onward Christian Soldier: A Life of Sabine Baring-Gould, 1834–1924* (London: Longmans, 1957), 35. In 1870 his novel *In Exitu Israel* treated the French Revolution at the time of the Paris Commune. His most famous hymn is probably "Onward, Christian Soldiers," written in 1864 for a children's festival at Horbury Bridge, Yorkshire. A bibliography of his work (1856–1925) is found in B. H. C. Dickinson's appreciative biography, *Sabine Baring-Gould: Squarson, Writer, and Folklorist, 1834–1924* (Newton Abbot: David & Charles, 1970), 176–85.

100. S. Baring-Gould, *Perpetua: A Story of Nimes in A.D. 213* [abbr. *Pp*] (London: Isbister, 1897), 49–50; *Domitia* [abbr. *D*] (London: Methuen, 1898), 125–26.

101. *Pp*, 89. Sts. John and Paul were brothers in the imperial service, martyred under Julian. The church itself, incorporating a portion of the fourth-century facade, has the distinction of being over a martyr's tomb within the city walls. Extensive improvements were made to the church in 1158 by Adrian IV (1154–59), the only Englishman ever to be elected to the papacy. The excavations to which Baring-Gould refers were begun in 1887 by Father Germano de San Stanislaus. See Mary Sharp, *A Traveller's Guide to the Churches of Rome* (London: Hugh Evelyn, 1967), 98–101.

102. *Pp*, 213. Various newer editions and translations of the *Apostolic Constitutions*, including work by the Chevalier von Bunsen, were available by the late nineteenth century. Baring-Gould does not comment on the Arian content of much of this section (viii); perhaps he was using the ancient bowdlerized version reprinted by Brightman. See G. Dix, *The Shape of the Liturgy* (London: Dacre Press, 1970), 280 n. 1. The Greek form of the Nunc Dimittis, used in the vernacular in the Prayer Book Evensong service, was included in the *Apostolic Constitutions*; see H. Chadwick, *Early Church*, 173.

103. *Pp*, 122. He dwells on the case of a boy, aged six (i.e., before the age of reason), who was allegedly sacrificed by sectaries using needles; parts of the corpse may have been eaten by rats, giving the impression of cannibal rites. Other Victorians, as we have seen, were drawn to this motif. Perhaps one may suggest psychological transference, a linkage to repressed attitudes toward the Jews and

the recurrent accusations of ritual murder associated with the Passover meal. The classic literary source is the Prioress's Tale in Chaucer's *Canterbury Tales*, a theme picked up and exploited by the Pre-Raphaelite painters. The cult of the boy-martyr, a complicated blend of eucharistic piety and anti-Semitism, was perennially popular in England, especially during periods of rising sentiment against Jews, in the twelfth century for example. The late nineteenth century saw the re-emergence of this popular cult, not without definite pedophile overtones. Frederick Rolfe (Baron Corvo) is a figure associated with this.

104. *D*, 166. In the Christian assembly they also use candles ("lights") only when needed to see by, a significant point used against the Ritualists in their use of lighted candles on the altar at all times; see *D*, 344. This is another indication of the eclectic, subjective quality of much Anglo-Catholic churchmanship late in the century, and the difficulty investigators must face in determining the distinguishing elements of Anglo-Catholicism based on any one usage, such as crucifixes, candles, incense. See J. E. B. Munson, "The Oxford Movement by the End of the Nineteenth Century: The Anglo-Catholic Clergy," *Church History* 44 (September 1975), 382–95. Munson attempts to isolate the use of incense to trace the fate of the extreme High Church party.

105. See Chadwick, *Victorian Church*, 1:509 n. 1; Juliana Wadham, *The Case of Cornelia Connelly* (London: Collins, 1956). Connelly is now a candidate for canonization by the Roman Church.

106. Mrs. Jerome [Anne] Mercier, *Our Mother Church: Being Simple Talk on High Topics* [abbr. *O*], 4th ed. (New York: E. P. Dutton, 1882). Mercier was also the author of two historical novels: *By the King and Queen: A Story of the Dawn of Religion in Britain* (London: Rivingtons, 1886), which describes Bran as the first Christian preacher in England; and *Under the Palmyras; or, Marial's Story* (London: SPCK, 1889).

107. See R. F. Littledale, *A History of the Church: From the Day of Pentecost to the Great Schism between the East and West* (London: J. T. Hayes, 1874). While for many Anglo-Catholics the events surrounding the excommunication of the patriarch Michael Cerularius are stressed, to the disadvantage of the Roman Church, others, under the influence of Freeman and historians exalting Anglo-Saxon and Germanic superiority (as well as recent Prussian conquests), emphasized the intrusion of the Norman (i.e., Roman) Church on the native population of Britain.

108. *O*, 19. Other Anglo-Catholics used similar historical arguments against the Vatican Council. An interesting analogy was made by R. F. Littledale, *Pharisaic Proselytism: A Forgotten Chapter in Early Church History* (London: J. T. Hayes, 1874), in which the arguments of the Jewish proselytizers in the Early Church are compared to the Ultramontanists. He parallels the arguments of the Jews in rela-

tion to the Catholics in Arian times with those of Manning's "insolent and aggressive faction" in relation to Anglicans in his own day.

109. *O*, 3. Sometimes a more critical note of Anglican laxness appears. *Only a Ghost* by Irenaeus the Deacon (London: J. T. Hayes, 1874) depicts a deacon of the fourth century inspecting London churches, discovering that Anglican practice is hardly as "primitive" as some claim.

110. Chadwick, *Victorian Church*, 2:109.

111. Ibid., 2:150. The boundaries of the quarrel over the Athanasian Creed were far-ranging, involving even the field of art history. A virulent exchange of scholarly opinion developed over the dating, provenance, and interpretation of the Utrecht Psalter, since this exquisite MS contained what was believed to be the earliest extant copy of the Athanasian Creed. This was only a small part of a much larger struggle for revision of the Prayer Book.

112. Wilfred Ward, *Last Lectures*, xxv, quoted by Elliott-Binns, *Religion*, 469.

113. See J. H. Newman, "The Principle of Continuity between the Jewish and the Christian Churches," sermon 15 (11 November 1842), *Sermons Bearing on Subjects of the Day* (London and Oxford: Rivington, 1843); and W. G. Ward, "The Synagogue and the Church," *British Critic* 34.67 (1843), 1–43.

114. See A. J. Church, *The Burning of Rome: A Story of Nero's Days* (London: Seley, [1891] 1892); and Marie Corelli, *Barabbas: A Dream of the World's Tragedy*, 3 vols. (London: Methuen, 1893). Attitudes toward the Jews were complex and at times ambiguous, even in more secular novels. See R. L. Wolff, "The Way Things Were," *Harvard Magazine* 77 (March 1975), 44–50. One should investigate the critical response to Eliot's *Daniel Deronda* (1876) or Trollope's *The Way We Live Now* (1875).

115. Sr. Mary Tarr, *Catholicism in Gothic Fiction*, 113, 99, 122.

116. E. P. Thompson, *The Making of the English Working Class* (London: Victor Gollancz, 1965), 116–19; R. A. Soloway, *Prelates and People*, 34–45.

117. Marguerite Yourcenar, *Memoirs of Hadrian* (1951; London: Penguin, 1955); David Malouf, *An Imaginary Life* (New York: George Braziller, 1978).

CHAPTER 4

1. G. I. T. Machin, *Politics and the Churches in Great Britain*, 252–98.

2. Norman, *Anti-Catholicism in Victorian England*, 23–51.

3. See W. Perry, *Alexander Penrose Forbes, Bishop of Brechin* (London: SPCK, 1939); A. M. Allchin, *The Silent Rebellion: Anglican Religious Communities, 1845–1900* (London: S.C.M. Press, 1958); James Bentley, *Ritualism and Politics*

in Victorian Britain: The Attempt to Legislate for Belief (Oxford: Oxford University Press, 1978); and Chadwick, *Victorian Church*, 1:497–507.

4. Chadwick, *Secularization of the European Mind*, 27–28.

5. For a survey of this contemporary debate see Chadwick, *Victorian Church*, 2:40–111.

6. Machin, *Politics and Churches*, 371.

7. Chadwick, *Victorian Church*, 2:36–38.

8. W. S. Smith, *London Heretics*, 176.

9. Chadwick, *Secularization*, 18, 92, 239–40, 251.

10. Maison, *Victorian Vision*, 90–91.

11. Quoted in A. O. J. Cockshut, *Anglican Attitudes*, 28.

12. Trevor, *The Arnolds* (cited intro., n. 58), 173.

13. See, e.g., Benjamin Jowett, *St. Paul* (1855); Matthew Arnold, *St. Paul and Protestantism* (1870); Dean Charles Merivale, *St. Paul at Rome* (1877); Frederic Farrar, *Life of St. Paul* (1879), *Life of Christ* (1874); and Lewis Page Mercier, *Outlines of the Life of the Lord Jesus Christ* (1871–72).

14. See, e.g., Maxwell M. Benoliel, *Prophecy, as Evidence of Inspiration* (1891); and David Baron, *Types, Psalms and Prophecies* (1900).

15. See Edward N. Calisch, *The Jew in English Literature* (Richmond: Bell, Book and Stationery, 1909); Rebecca Schneider, *Bibliography of Jewish Life in the Fiction of America and England* (Albany: New York State Library School, 1916); and Alexander Baron, "The Jew in Victorian Literature," *Jewish Quarterly* 2 (1955), 10–12.

16. See Henry Soames, *The Latin Church during Anglo-Saxon Times* (London: Longman, Brown, Green, and Longmans, [1844] 1848). He indicates that the founder was Joseph of Arimathea, accompanied by Mary Magdalene, Lazarus, and Martha, or "some others of the very earliest Christians." Cf. Hugh Williams, *Christianity in Early Britain* (Oxford: Clarendon Press, 1912), who places the date of foundation between 180 and 200 without naming an identifiable missionary.

17. The novel appeared under various titles: *Salathiel: A Story of the Past, the Present, and the Future*, 3 vols. (London: Henry Colburn, 1828), and *Salathiel, the Immortal, or the Wandering Jew* (London, 1853). The text used is *Tarry Thou till I Come; or, Salathiel, the Wandering Jew* [abbr. *SW*] (New York and London: Funk & Wagnalls, 1901), v. Wallace also cites *Ivanhoe, The Last of the Barons, A Tale of Two Cities, Jane Eyre,* and *Hypatia*. An interesting response to Wallace's *Ben Hur* and Sue's *The Wandering Jew*, this time a Wandering Gentile, is found in Herman M. Bien's *Ben-Beor: A Story of the Anti-Messiah* (Baltimore: I. Friedenwal, 1891).

18. See John R. Carling, *The Doomed City* (New York: E. J. Clode, 1910); Sir Henry Rider Haggard, *Pearl Maiden: A Tale of the Fall of Jerusalem* (New York: Longmans, 1902); Mrs. Florence Morse Kingsley, *The Cross Triumphant* (Phila-

delphia: Altemus, 1899); Rudyard Kipling, "The Wandering Jew," *Life's Handicap* (London: Macmillan, 1891); Elizabeth Jane Miller, *City of Delight: A Love Drama of the Siege and Fall of Jerusalem* (Chicago: Bobbs-Merrill, 1908); Sir Benjamin Ward Richardson, *Son of a Star: A Romance of the Second Century* (New York: Longmans, 1888), recounting the Bar Kokhba revolt; Mrs. Anna Pierpont Switzer, *Nehe: A Tale of the Time of Artaxerxes* (Boston: Wilde, 1901), on the rebuilding of the Temple; and Joseph Spellman, *Lucius Flavius: An Historical Tale of the Time Immediately Preceding the Destruction of Jerusalem* (St. Louis: Herder, 1904).

19. See G. Croly, *Popery the Antichrist* (1848); *Papal Rome: The Principles and Practices of Rome Alike Condemned by the Gospel* (1849); *The Miracles of Scripture Contrasted with the Fictions of Popery* (1852); and *The Claims of the Jews Incompatible with the National Profession of Christianity* (1848).

20. See Constance Savery, "A.L.O.E.," *TLS* (1 January 1949), 9. The text used is *Daybreak in Britain* [*DB*] (London: Religious Tract Society, n.d.), 22 n. 1.

21. See A. L. Owen, *The Famous Druid: A Survey of Three Centuries of English Literature on the Druids* (Oxford: Clarendon Press, 1962). Authors divided over such speculation: John Toland, *A New Edition of Toland's History of the Druids*, ed. R. Huddleston (1814), which was an oblique attack on Christianity; D. James, *The Patriarchal Religion of Great Britain* (1836); Anonymous, *The Identity of the Religions Called Druidical and Hebrew* (1829); and Algernon Herbert, *An Essay on the Neodruidic Heresy in Britannia* (1838), which attacks Druidism, Mithraism, and Free Masonry.

22. Tucker cites the following passages: Ps. 16:10; 22:7–8, 16–18; 47:5; Isa. 11:1; 35:5–6; 53:3, 5; Daniel 9:25; Micah 5:2; Zechariah 13:7.

23. Wolff, *Gains and Losses*, 248.

24. The text used is *Imogen: A Tale of the Early British Church* [abbr. *I*], new ed. (London: John F. Shaw, 1875), v–vi. The early British Church was not the exclusive domain of Anglican authors. The Roman Catholic Francophile Mrs. J. C. Bateman, in her *Ierne of Armorica: A Tale of the Time of Chlovis* (London: Burns & Oates, 1873), pitted the Druids of Armorica, "little Britain," under the banner of Arthur Pendragon and the Arian Germanic tribes against the civilized and Catholicized Franks. Processions, relics, devotions to Mary and the Sacred Heart, the Sacrifice of the Mass, and Papal Sovereignty are proclaimed in this tale, and Chlovis and Chlotilde are meant to suggest Napoleon III and the empress Eugénie. In a Spiritualist novel, *One Traveller Returns* (New York: Longmans, Green, 1888), David Christie Murray and Henry Herman describe the spiritual combat of Druids and Christians in the second century—anachronistically introducing St. David of Wales, amid domestic murder, nude pageants and orgies, human sacrifice, and martyrdom in the Colosseum—as a tract for reincarnation (10).

25. Chadwick, *Victorian Church*, 2:310–11.

26. *I*, 163. Cf. Mrs. Bateman's use of the story from the hagiographer Alban Butler about the miraculous filings from these chains, used to hallow the sword of Chlovis (*Ierne* 344–46).

27. See *The Slave Girl of Pompeii* (1887); *John de Wycliffe, the First of the Reformers* (1884); *Mistress Margery: A Tale of the Lollards* (1868); *Minster Lovell: A Story of the Days of Laud* (1890); *Robin Tremayne of Bodmin: A Story of the Marian Persecution* (1872); and *Sister Rose; or, St. Bartholomew's Eve* (1870).

28. Edmund Sheridan Purcell, *Life of Cardinal Manning, Archbishop of Westminster*, 2 vols. (New York and London: Macmillan, 1896), 2:532–34.

29. G. R. Balleine, *History of the Evangelical Party in the Church of England* (London: Longmans, 1908); M. R. Kingsford, *The Life, Work, and Significance of W. H. G. Kingston* (Toronto: Ryerson Press, 1947). See, e.g., Kingston's *How to Emigrate* (1850); *The Life of Capt. Cook* (1871); *A Popular History of the Navy* (1876); and *Livingston's Travels* (1886). He also translated several works by Jules Verne.

30. The text used is *Jovinian: A Story of the Early Days of Papal Rome* [abbr. *J*], 3d ed. (London: Hodder & Stoughton, 1890), v–vi.

31. For example, "[Christ] is not dead, but is alive for evermore: the Living One in Heaven—not the dead one bound on a silver cross" (*I*, 163).

32. Wolff, *Gains and Losses*, 220–24. Wolff cites the recent scholarship on Farrar's school novels (221 n. 1). Farrar also developed the material in *Julian Home* (1858); *St. Winifred's; or, The World of School* (1862); and *The Three Homes* (1872).

33. Anonymous, *Pusey's Life* (cited intro., n. 28), 529. For changing attitudes toward Hell, see Chadwick, *Secularization*, 104–6.

34. See, e.g., Ernest Eckstein, *Nero: A Romance* (1889); Wilhelm Walloth, *Empress Octavia* (1892); and Henryk Sienkiewicz, *Quo Vadis?* (1895).

35. The text used is *Gathering Clouds: A Tale of the Days of St. Chrysostom* [abbr. *GC*], 2 vols. (London: Longmans, Green, 1895). Farrar used various sources for his study of Chrysostom: G. F. Böhringer, *Chrysostom* (Gotha, 1853); W. Cave, *Lives of the Fathers*, ed. Henry Cary (Oxford, 1850); Albert de Broglie, *L'Eglise et l'empire romain au 4me siècle*, 4th ed. (Paris, 1868); Theodor Förster, *Chrysostomus in seinen Verhältnis zur antiochenischer Schule* (Gotha, 1869); J. H. Newman, *Church of the Fathers* (Oxford, 1840).

36. F. W. Farrar, *Lives of the Fathers: Sketches of Church History in Biography*, 2 vols. (Edinburgh: Adam and Charles Black, 1889), 1:xv.

37. Quoted by Helen Gardner, *The Business of Criticism* (Oxford: Clarendon Press, 1959), 89.

38. F. W. Farrar, *History of Interpretation: The Bampton Lectures 1885* (New York: E. P. Dutton, 1886), 220–21.

39. F. W. Farrar et al., *The Atonement: A Clerical Symposium on What Is the Scripture Doctrine of the Atonement?* (London: James Nisbet, 1883).

40. F. W. Farrar, *Saintly Workers: Five Lenten Lectures* (London and New York: Macmillan, 1878), 112.

41. W. B. Carpenter, *Some Pages of My Life* (London: Williams & Norgate, 1916); *Further Pages of My Life* (London: Williams & Norgate, 1916); and H. D. A. Major, *The Life and Letters of W. B. Carpenter* (London, 1925). The text used is *Narcissus* [abbr. *Ns*] (London: SPCK, [1879]).

42. Carpenter, *Some Pages*, 75. Carpenter as a boy also remembered Turner's "Ancient and Modern Italy" (*Further Pages*, 15).

43. Chadwick, *Secularization*, 70.

44. See Chadwick, *Victorian Church*, 2:62. This survey is deeply indebted to his work (2:60–75).

45. See Theodore Ziolkowski, *Fictional Transfigurations of Jesus* (Princeton: Princeton University Press, 1972). He isolates five distinct varieties: fictional biography, Jesus *redivivus*, the *Imitatio Christi*, "pseudonyms" of Christ, and the ministerial Christ.

46. See, e.g., the American novels William Ware, *Julian; or, Scenes in Judea* (1841); the Reverend J. A. Ingraham, *The Prince of the House of David* (1855); Lew Wallace, *Ben Hur* (1880); William Forbes Cooley, *Emmanuel* (1889); Elbridge S. Brooks, *A Son of Issachar* (1890); and Robert Bird, *Jesus, the Carpenter of Nazareth* (1899).

47. Chadwick, *Victorian Church*, 2:38–39.

48. Abbott's mathematical fantasy *Flatland* (London: Seeley, 1884) is still reprinted. Cf. Dionys Burger, *Sphereland: A Fantasy about Curved Spaces and an Expanding Universe*, trans. C. J. Rheinholdt (New York: Crowell, 1965).

49. E. A. Abbott, *Philomythus: An Antidote against Credulity*, 2d ed. (London: Macmillan, 1891). See the discussion of this work in Bokenkotter, *Newman as Historian*, 98–109.

50. Abbott, *Philomythus*, xxxvi. See also the contemporary criticism of Newman and Wiseman reproduced in Robert C. Schweik, "Bishop Blougram's Miracles," *Modern Language Notes* 71 (1956), 416–18; and Julia Markus, "Bishop Blougram and the Literary Men," *Victorian Studies* 21.2 (1978), 171–95.

51. The quotations are from Abbott's *The Kernel and the Husk* (London, Macmillan, 1886), 291, 295, 365, 367.

52. Abbott cites several of his sources: J. B. Westcott, *Introduction to the Study of the Gospels* (London, 1860); C. Taylor, ed., *Sayings of the Jewish Fathers* (Cambridge, 1877); J. Knappert, *The Religion of Israel* (London, 1877); and the works of Philo.

53. *Philochristus: Memoirs of a Disciple of St. Paul* (Boston: Roberts Brothers, 1882), 206.

54. The text used is *Onesimus: Memoirs of a Disciple of St. Paul* (Boston: Roberts Brothers, 1882).

55. The text used is *Silanus the Christian* (London: Adam and Charles Black, 1906).

56. See Brian Masters, *Now Barabbas Was a Rotter: The Extraordinary Life of Marie Corelli* (London: N. Hamilton, 1978); Cruse, *After the Victorians*, 182–83; Maison, *Victorian Vision*, 339, 40; Altick, *English Common Reader*, 386.

57. Letter to Mrs. Annie Moberly (12 April 1894), quoted in Coleridge, *Yonge* (cited chap. 3, n. 74), 324.

58. The text used is *Barabbas: A Dream of the World's Tragedy* [abbr. *B*] (Philadelphia: J. B. Lippincott, 1898), 143–44.

59. The text used is *Jesus as Others Saw Him: A Retrospect A.D. 54* [abbr. *AO*], intro. by Harry A. Wolfson (New York: Bernard G. Richards, 1925). The sources Jacobs cites are *The Book of Enoch*, ed. and trans. R. H. Charles (Oxford, 1893); J. Derenbourg, *Histoire de la Palestine* (Paris, 1867); J. Drummond, *Jewish Messiah* (London, 1877); J. Halévy, various contemporary works; A. Harnack, ed., *Die Apostellehre und die jüdischen beiden Wege* (Leipzig, 1886); the *Dialogues* of Justin Martyr; I. Loeb, *La Litterature des pauvres dans le Bible* (Paris, 1893); E. B. Nicholson, ed., *The Gospel According to the Hebrews* (London, 1879); Alfred Resch, *Agrapha*, Texte und Untersuchungen, ed. O. Gebhardt and A. Harnack (Leipzig, 1889), 5:4; S. Spitzer, *Das Mahl bei den alten Hebräern* (Pressburg, 1877); and Tatian's *Diatessaron*.

60. See the discussion of the introduction of party affiliations into a consideration of this literature by Robert Lee Wolff, "Some Erring Children's Literature: The World of Victorian Religious Strife in Miniature," *The World of Victorian Fiction*, ed. Jerome Buckley, Harvard English Studies 6 (Cambridge, Mass.: Harvard University Press, 1975), 295–318. See also Maison, *Victorian Vision*, 115; Dahl, "Pater's *Marius*," 7 n. 10.

61. Wolff, *Gains and Losses*, 244–48.

62. Mrs. J. B. Webb, *Naomi; or, The Last Days of Jerusalem* (London: S. W. Patridge, 1841), 371, 72.

63. Annie Peploe, *The Martyrs of Carthage: A Tale of the Times of Old*, new ed. (London: Richard Bentley, 1850), 343.

64. Alfred J. Church, *To the Lions: A Tale of the Early Christians* (London: Seeley, 1889), 148.

65. The text used is *The Villa of Claudius: A Tale of the Roman-British Church* (London: SPCK, [n.d.]), 60.

66. See Beatrice Marshall, *Emma Marshall: A Biographical Sketch* (London: Seeley, 1901).

BIBILIOGRAPHY

PRIMARY MATERIAL

Abbott, Edwin A. *The Kernel and the Husk: Letters on Spiritual Christianity*. London: Macmillan, 1886.

———. *Onesimus: Memoirs of a Disciple of St. Paul*. London: Macmillan, 1882.

———. *Onesimus: Memoirs of a Disciple of St. Paul*. Boston: Roberts Brothers, 1882.

———. *Philochristus: Memoirs of a Disciple of the Lord*. London: Macmillan, 1878.

———. *Philochristus: Memoirs of a Disciple of the Lord*. Boston: Roberts Brothers, 1878.

———. *Philomythus: An Antidote against Credulity*. 2d ed. London: Macmillan, 1891.

———. *Silanus the Christian*. London: Adam and Charles Black, 1906.

"A.L.O.E." [Charlotte M. Tucker]. *Daybreak in Britain*. London: Religious Tract Society, 1880.

"An Antiquary." [___Rennie]. *Saint Patrick: A National Tale of the Fifth Century*. 3 vols. Edinburgh: A. Constable, 1819.

Anonymous. *The Story of Dr. Pusey's Life*. 2d ed. London: Longmans, Green, 1900.

Arnold, Matthew. *St. Paul and Protestantism*. London: Smith, Elder, 1870.

Baring-Gould, Sabine. *Domitia*. London: Methuen, 1898.

———. *In Exitu Israel: An Historical Novel*. 2 vols. London: Macmillan, 1870.

———. *The Lives of the Saints*. 16 vols. London: John Hodges, 1897–98.

———. *Perpetua: A Story of Nîmes in A.D. 213*. London: Isbister, 1897.

———. *Virgin Saints and Martyrs*. London: Hutchinson, 1907.

Bateman, Mrs. J. C. *Ierne of Armorica: A Tale of the Time of Chlovis*. London: Burns & Oates, 1873.

Bulwer-Lytton, Edward G. *The Last Days of Pompeii*. 3 vols. London: George Routledge, 1834.

———. *The Last Days of Pompeii*. London: J. M. Dent, 1910.

Bunbury, Selina. *Stories from Church History: From the Introduction of Christianity to the Sixteenth Century.* London: R. B. Seeley & W. Burnside, 1828.

Carpenter, William Boyd. *Narcissus: A Tale of Early Christian Times.* London: SPCK, 1879.

Charles, Elizabeth. *Attila and His Conquerors: A Story of the Days of St. Patrick and St. Leo the Great.* London: SPCK, 1894.

———. *Conquering and to Conquer: A Story of Rome in the Days of St. Jerome.* London: Daldy, Isbister, 1876.

———. *The Cripple of Antioch, and Other Scenes from Christian Life in Early Times.* London: J. Nisbet, 1856.

———. *Martyrs and Saints of the First Twelve Centuries: Studies from the Lives of the Black Letter Saints of the English Calendar.* London: CKS, 1887.

———. *Sketches of Christian Life in England in the Olden Time.* London: T. Nelson & Sons, 1864.

———. *Tales and Sketches of Christian Life, in Different Lands and Ages.* London: J. Nisbet, 1850.

———. *The Victory of the Vanquished: A Tale of the First Century.* London, 1870.

Church, Alfred John. *The Burning of Rome; or, A Story of the Days of Nero.* London: Macmillan, 1891.

———. *The Burning of Rome: A Story of Nero's Days.* London: Seeley, 1892.

———. *The Count of the Saxon Shore; or, The Villa in Vectis: A Tale of the Departure of the Romans from Britain: With the Collaboration of Ruth Putnam.* London: Seeley, 1887.

———. *The Crown of Pine: A Story of Corinth and the Isthmian Games.* London: Seeley, 1905.

———. *Stories from English History.* Vol. 1: *From Julius Caesar to the Black Prince.* London: Seeley, 1895.

———. *To the Lions: A Tale of the Early Christians.* London: Seeley, 1889.

Collins, William Wilkie. *Antonina; or, The Fall of Rome: A Romance of the Fifth Century.* 3 vols. London: Richard Bentley, 1850.

———. *Antonina; or, The Fall of Rome.* New York and London: Harper & Bros., 1898.

Corelli, Marie. *Barabbas: A Dream of the World's Tragedy.* 3 vols. London: Methuen, 1893.

———. *Barabbas: A Dream of the World's Tragedy.* Philadelphia: J. B. Lippincott, 1898.

Crake, Augustine D. *Aemilius: A Tale of the Decian and Valerian Persecutions.* Oxford: A. R. Mowbray, 1871.

———. *The Camp on the Severn: A ¯ale of the Tenth Persecution in Britain.* London, 1875.

————. *The Doomed City; or, The Last Days of Durocina: A Tale of the Anglo-Saxon Conquest of Britain, and the Mission of Augustine*. Oxford and London: A. R. Mowbray, 1885.

————. *Evanus: A Tale of the Days of Constantine*. Oxford: A. R. Mowbray, 1872.

————. *History of the Church under the Roman Empire, A.D. 30–476*. London: Rivington, 1873.

————. *Stories of the Old Saints and the Anglo-Saxon Church*. Oxford and London: A. R. Mowbray, 1890.

————. *The Victor's Laurel: A Tale of School-Life during the Tenth Persecution in Italy*. Oxford and London: A. R. Mowbray, 1884.

Croly, George. *Salathiel: A Story of the Past, the Present, and the Future*. 3 vols. London: Henry Colburn, 1828.

————. *Tarry Thou till I Come; or, Salathiel, the Wandering Jew*. New York and London: Funk & Wagnalls, 1901.

Cutts, Edward L. *Amina: A Tale of the Nestorians*. London: SPCK, 1882.

————. *Augustine of Canterbury*. London: Methuen, 1895.

————. *Constantine the Great*. London: SPCK, 1895.

————. *St. Cedd's Cross: A Tale of the Conversion of the East Saxons*. London: SPCK, 1872.

————. *Saint Jerome*. London: SPCK, 1878.

————. *The Villa of Claudius: A Tale of the Roman-British Church*. London: SPCK, 1874.

Davies, Gerald S. *Gaudentius: A Story of the Colosseum*. London: SPCK, 1874.

————. *Julian's Dream: A Story of A.D. 362*. London: SPCK, 1875.

Elsdale, Annie Field. *Tales of the Martyrs; or, Sketches from Church History*. 2d ed. London: Rivington, 1844.

Farrar, Frederic W. *Darkness and Dawn; or, Scenes in the Days of Nero*. 2 vols. London: Longmans, Green, 1891.

————. *Gathering Clouds: A Tale of the Days of St. Chrysostom*. 2 vols. London: Longmans, Green, 1895.

Farrie, Hugh. See Hugh Westbury.

Forrest, Thorpe. *Builders of the Waste*. London: Duckworth, 1899.

Graham, John W. *Neaera: A Tale of Ancient Rome*. London: Macmillan, 1886.

"G. W." *Martyr Tales and Sketches: For the Young*. London: G. Morrish, 1884.

Henty, George A. *Beric the Briton: A Story of the Roman Invasion*. London: Blackie & Sons, 1892.

————. *For the Temple: A Tale of the Fall of Jerusalem*. London: Blackie & Sons, 1887.

Hollis, Gertrude. *The Sons of Aella*. London: SPCK, 1900.

Holt, Emily Sarah. *Imogen: A Story of the Mission of Augustine.* London, 1876.

———. *Imogen: A Tale of the Early British Church.* London: John F. Shaw, 1875.

———. *The Slave Girl of Pompeii; or, By the Way They Knew Not: A Tale of the First Century.* London: John F. Shaw, 1887.

———. *The Way of the Cross, and Other Tales.* London: John F. Shaw, 1883.

Hoppus, Mary [Mrs. Alfred Marks]. *Masters of the World.* 3 vols. London: Richard Bentley & Son, 1888.

Jacobs, Joseph. *As Others Saw Him: A Retrospect, A.D. 54.* London: W. Heinemann, 1895.

———. *Jesus as Others Saw Him: A Retrospect, A.D. 54.* Introduction by Harry A. Wolfson. New York: Bernard G. Richards, 1925.

James, George P. R. *Attila: A Romance.* 3 vols. London: Longman, 1837.

———. *Attila: A Romance.* 2 vols. New York: Harper & Bros., 1838.

Kingsley, Charles. *Alexandria and Her Schools: Four Lectures.* Cambridge: Macmillan, 1854.

———. *Historical Lectures and Essays.* London: Macmillan, 1889.

———. *Hypatia; or, New Foes with an Old Face.* Reprinted from *Fraser's Magazine.* 2 vols. London, 1853.

———. *Hypatia; or, New Foes with an Old Face.* 13th ed. New York: Macmillan, 1882.

———. *Plays and Puritans, and Other Historical Essays.* London: Macmillan, 1873.

———. *The Roman and the Teuton: A Series of Lectures Delivered before the University of Cambridge.* Preface by F. Max Müller. London: Macmillan, 1887.

Kingsley, Frances E. (Grenfell), ed. *Charles Kingsley: His Letters and Memories of His Life.* 2 vols. London: Henry S. King, 1877.

Kingston, William H. G. *Eldol the Druid; or, The Dawn of Christianity in Britain.* London, 1874.

———. *Jovinian; or, The Early Days of Papal Rome: A Tale.* London, 1877.

———. *Jovinian: A Story of the Early Days of Papal Rome.* 3d ed. London: Hodder & Stoughton, 1890.

Lee, Frederick G. *The Church under Queen Elizabeth: An Historical Sketch.* 2 vols. London: W. H. Allen, 1880.

Lockhart, John G. *Valerius: A Roman Story.* 3 vols. Edinburgh, 1821.

———. *Valerius: A Roman Story.* 2 vols. Boston: Wells & Lilly, 1821.

Marshall, Emma. *The Life of Our Lord Jesus Christ; or, Little Sunny's Sweet Stories of Old, for Very Young Children.* London: J. Nisbet, 1886.

———. *No. XIII; or, The Story of the Lost Vestal.* London: Cassell, 1885.

Maxwell, Herbert Eustace. *A Duke of Britain: A Romance of the Fourth Century.* Edinburgh: W. Blackwood & Sons, 1895.

Mercier, Mrs. Jerome [Annie]. *By the King and Queen: A Story of the Dawn of Religion in Britain.* London: Rivington, 1886.

———. *Our Mother Church: Being Simple Talk on High Topics*. 4th ed. New York: E. P. Dutton, 1882.

———. *Under the Palmyras; or, Marial's Story*. London: SPCK, 1889.

"MFS" [Mrs. F. Seamer, afterward Seymour]. *Stories of Holy Lives*. London: R. Washbourne, 1875.

———. *Stories of Martyr Priests*. London: R. Washbourne, 1876.

———. *Story of the Life of St. Paul, the Apostle*. London: R. Washbourne, 1877.

Monro, Edward A. *Claudian: A Tale of the Second Century*. London: Masters, 1862.

Moore, Thomas. *The Epicurean: A Tale*. London, 1827.

———. *The Epicurean: A Tale*. Philadelphia: Carey, Lea, & Carey and R. H. Small, 1827.

Mossman, Thomas W. *Epiphanius: The History of His Childhood and Youth Told by Himself: A Tale of the Early Church*. London: J. T. Hayes, 1874.

———. *A History of the Catholic Church of Jesus Christ From the Death of Saint John to the Middle of the Second Century: Including an Account of the Original Organisation of the Christian Ministry and the Growth of Episcopacy*. London: Longmans, Green, 1873.

Mozley, Thomas. *Reminiscences Chiefly of Oriel College and the Oxford Movement*. 2 vols. London: Longmans, 1882.

Murray, David Christie, and Henry Herman. *One Traveller Returns*. London: Chatto & Windus, 1887.

———. *One Traveller Returns*. New York: Longmans, Green, 1888.

Neale, John M. *The Daughters of Pola: Family Letters Relating to the Persecution of Diocletion, Now First Translated from an Istrian MS*. London and Oxford: J. H. & J. Parker, 1861.

———. *Deeds of Faith: Stories for Children from Church History*. London: Mozley, 1850.

———. *The Egyptian Wanderers: A Story for Children, of the Great Tenth Persecution*. 1854. London: Masters, 1879.

———. *English History for Children*. 1845. 9th ed. London: Burns, Masters, 1878.

———. *The Exiles of the Cebenna: A Journal Written during the Decian Persecution, by Aurelius Gratianus, Priest of the Church of Arles; and Now Done into English*. London and Oxford: J. H. & J. Parker, 1859.

———. *The Farm of Aptonga: A Story of the Times of St. Cyprian*. London: Cleaver, 1854.

———. *The Farm of Aptonga: A Story for Children, of the Times of St. Cyprian*. Burntisland: Pitsligo Press, 1856.

———. *The Followers of the Lord: Stories from Church History*. London: Masters, 1851.

———. *The Quay of the Dioscuri: A History of Nicene Times: Written in Greek, by*

Macarius, Merchant of Tunnies and Balamydes; and Now Translated from Two Alexandrian Manuscripts. London and Oxford: J. H. & J. Parker, 1860.

———. *The Triumphs of the Cross: Tales and Sketches of Christian Heroism.* London: Masters, 1845.

———. *Victories of the Saints: Stories for Children from Church History.* London: J. T. Hayes, 1870.

Newman, John H. *Apologia pro Vita Sua.* Edited by A. Dwight Culler. Boston: Houghton Mifflin, 1956.

———. *Callista: A Tale of the Third Century.* London, 1855.

———. *Callista: A Sketch of the Third Century.* London: Burns & Oates, 1962.

———. *The Church of the Fathers.* London: Rivington, 1840.

———. *An Essay on the Development of Christian Doctrine.* 1845. Westminster, Md.: Christian Classics, 1968.

———. *Essays and Sketches.* Edited by Charles F. Harrold. 3 vols. New York and London: Longmans, Green, 1948.

———. *Historical Sketches.* 3 vols. London: B. M. Pickering, 1872–73.

———. *Lectures on Certain Difficulties Felt by Anglicans in Submitting to the Catholic Church.* Rev. ed. Dublin: James Duffy, 1857.

———. *Lectures on the Present Position of Catholics in England.* 1851. Edited by D. M. O'Connell, S.J. New York: America Press, 1942.

———. *Letters and Diaries.* Edited by C. S. Dessain et al. 31 vols. London and New York: T. Nelson; Oxford: Clarendon Press, 1961–.

———. *Loss and Gain: The Story of a Convert.* 1848. London: Burns & Oates, 1962.

Ogle, Nathaniel. *Mariamne: An Historical Novel of Palestine.* 3 vols. London: G. B. Whittaker, 1825.

Pater, Walter H. *Marius the Epicurean: His Sensations and Ideas.* 2 vols. London: Macmillan, 1885.

———. *Uncollected Essays.* Portland, Maine: Thomas B. Mosher, 1903.

Pottinger, Henry. *Blue and Green; or, The Gift of God: A Romance of Old Constantinople.* 3 vols. London, 1879.

———. *Blue and Green; or, The Gift of God: A Romance of Old Constantinople.* London: Chapman & Hall, 1880.

Saville, Bourchier W. *The Primitive and Catholic Faith, in Relation to the Church of England.* London: Longmans, Green, 1875.

Sienkiewicz, Henryk. *"Quo Vadis?": A Narrative of the Time of Nero.* Translated by J. Curtin. Boston: Little, Brown, 1897.

Smith, Horatio. *The Involuntary Prophet: A Tale of the Early Ages.* London: Richard Bentley, 1835.

———. *Zillah: A Tale of the Holy City.* 4 vols. London: Henry Colburn, 1828.

Taylor, Isaac. *Ancient Christianity and the Doctrines of the Oxford Tracts for the Times.* 2 vols. London: Jackson & Walford, 1839–42.

―――. *True Stories from the History of the Church.* London, 1843.

Tucker, Charlotte M. See A.L.O.E.

Wallace, Lew. *Ben-Hur: A Tale of the Christ.* New York, 1880.

Webb, Mrs. J. B. [Annie Molyneux Peploe]. *Alypius of Tagaste: A Tale of the Early Church.* London: Religious Tract Society, 1865.

―――. *Julamerk: A Tale of the Nestorians.* 3 vols. London, 1849.

―――. *The Martyrs of Carthage: A Tale of the Times of Old.* 2 vols. London, 1850.

―――. *The Martyrs of Carthage: A Tale of the Times of Old.* London: Richard Bentley, n.d.

―――. *Naomi; or, The Last Days of Jerusalem.* London: S. W. Partridge, 1841.

―――. *Pomponia; or, The Gospel in Caesar's Household.* London: Religious Tract Society, 1867.

Westbury, Hugh [Hugh Farrie]. *Acte: A Novel.* 3 vols. London: Richard Bentley & Sons, 1890.

Whyte-Melville, George J. *The Gladiators: A Tale of Rome and Judaea.* 3 vols. London: 1863 [1864].

―――. *The Gladiators.* London: J. M. Dent & Sons, 1911.

―――. *The True Cross: A Legend of the Church.* London: Chapman & Hall, 1873.

Wilberforce, Robert I. *The Doctrine of the Holy Eucharist.* 3d ed. London: Derby, 1853.

―――. *Rutilius and Lucius; or, Stories of the Third Age.* London: Edward Lumley, 1842.

Wiseman, Nicholas Cardinal. *Fabiola; or, The Church of the Catacombs.* London: Catholic Popular Library, 1854.

―――. *Fabiola; or, The Church of the Catacombs.* Jubilee edition. New York: P. J. Kenedy & Sons, 1901.

Yonge, Charlotte M. *The Pupils of St. John the Divine.* London: Macmillan, 1868.

―――. *The Slaves of Sabinus, Jew and Gentile.* London: National Society's Depository, 1890.

SECONDARY MATERIAL

Altick, Richard D. *The English Common Reader: A Social History of the Mass Reading Public, 1800–1900.* Chicago: University of Chicago Press, 1957.

Baker, Ernest A. *History in Fiction: A Guide to the Best Historical Romances, Sagas, Novels, and Tales.* 2 vols. London: George Routledge & Sons, 1907.

Baker, Joseph E. *The Novel and the Oxford Movement*. Princeton: Princeton University Press, 1932.

Battiscombe, Georgina. *John Keble: A Study in Limitations*. New York: Alfred A. Knopf, 1964.

Baumgarten, Murray. "The Historical Novel: Some Postulates," *Clio* 4 (February 1975), 173–82.

Bennett, Gareth V. "Patristic Tradition in Anglican Thought, 1660–1900." *Oecumenica* (1971–72), 63–87.

Berger, Morroe. *Real and Imagined Worlds: The Novel and Social Science*. Cambridge, Mass.: Harvard University Press, 1977.

Bokenkotter, Thomas S. *Cardinal Newman as an Historian*. Louvain: Bibliothèque de l'Université, 1959.

Brendon, Piers. *Hurrell Froude and the Oxford Movement*. London: Paul Elek, 1974.

Buckley, Jerome H., ed. *The Worlds of Victorian Fiction*. Harvard English Studies 6. Cambridge, Mass.: Harvard University Press, 1975.

Butterfield, H. *The Historical Novel: An Essay*. Cambridge: Cambridge University Press, 1924.

Chadwick, Henry. *The Early Church*. Harmondsworth: Penguin Books, 1976.

Chadwick, Owen. *The Mind of the Oxford Movement*. London: Adam and Charles Black, 1960.

―――. *The Secularization of the European Mind in the Nineteenth Century*. Cambridge: Cambridge University Press, 1975.

―――. *The Victorian Church*. 2 vols. New York: Oxford University Press, 1966, 1970.

Chapman, Edward M. *English Literature in Account with Religion, 1800–1900*. Boston and New York: Houghton Mifflin, 1910.

Chapman, Raymond. *Faith and Revolt: Studies in the Literary Influence of the Oxford Movement*. London: Weidenfeld & Nicolson, 1970.

―――. *The Victorian Debate: English Literature and Society, 1832–1901*. London: Weidenfeld & Nicolson, 1968.

Chitty, Susan. *The Beast and the Monk: A Life of Charles Kingsley*. New York: Mason & Charter, 1975.

Church, R. W. *The Oxford Movement, Twelve Years, 1833–1845*. Edited by G. F. A. Best. Chicago: University of Chicago Press, 1970.

Cockshut, A. O. J. *Anglican Attitudes: A Study of Victorian Religious Controversies*. London: Collins, 1959.

Cruse, Amy. *After the Victorians*. London: George Allen & Unwin, 1938.

―――. *The Victorians and Their Books*. London: George Allen & Unwin, 1935.

Cunningham, Valentine. *Everywhere Spoken Against: Dissent in the Victorian Novel*. Oxford: Clarendon Press, 1975.

Dahl, Curtis. "Pater's Marius and Historical Novels on Early Christian Times." *Nineteenth-Century Fiction* 28 (June 1973), 1–24.

Dalziel, Margaret. *Popular Fiction 100 Years Ago: An Unexplored Tract of Literary History*. London: Cohen & West, 1957.

Darton, F. J. H. *Children's Books in England: Five Centuries of Social Life*. Cambridge: Cambridge University Press, 1958.

Davies, Horton. *Worship and Theology in England*. Vol. 3: *From Watts and Wesley to Maurice, 1690–1850*. Princeton: Princeton University Press, 1961.

DeLaura, David J. *Hebrew and Hellene in Victorian England: Newman, Arnold, and Pater*. Austin: University of Texas Press, 1969.

————, ed. *Victorian Prose: A Guide to Research*. Essays by Fellows of the Royal Society of Literature. New York: Modern Language Association, 1973.

Dorman, S. "*Hypatia* and *Callista*: The Initial Skirmish between Kingsley and Newman," *Nineteenth Century Fiction* 34 (1979), 173–93.

Drinkwater, John, ed. *The Eighteen-Sixties*. Essays by Fellows of the Royal Society of Literature. Cambridge: Cambridge University Press, 1932.

Drummond, Andrew L. *The Churches in English Fiction: A Literary and Historical Study*. Leicester: Edgar Backus, 1950.

Elliott-Binns, L. E. *Religion in the Victorian Era*. Greenwich, Conn.: Seabury Press, 1953.

Fleishman, Avrom. *The English Historical Novel: Walter Scott to Virginia Woolf*. Baltimore: Johns Hopkins University Press, 1971.

Frend, W. H. C. *Martyrdom and Persecution in the Early Church*. New York: New York University Press, 1967.

Glucksmann, Hedwig L. "Die Gegenüberstellung von Antike-Christentum in der englischen Literatur des 19. Jahrhunderts." Inaugural dissertation. Hannover, 1932.

Gooch, George P. *History and Historians in the Nineteenth Century*. Boston: Beacon Press, 1959.

Greensalde, Stanley L. "The Authority of the Tradition of the Early Church in Early Anglican Thought." *Oecumenica* (1971–72), 9–33.

Härdelin, Alf. *The Tractarian Understanding of the Eucharist*. Uppsala: Studia Historico-ecclesiastica Upsaliensa, 1965.

Hill, Alan G. "Originality and Realism in Newman's Novels," *Newman after a Hundred Years*, ed. Ian Ker and A. G. Hill, 21–42. Oxford: Clarendon Press, 1990.

James, Louis. *Fiction for the Working Man, 1830–1850*. London: Oxford University Press, 1963.

Kaye, James R. *Historical Fiction: Chronologically and Historically Related*. Chicago: Snowdon Publishing, 1920.

Kelly, Doris B. "A Checklist of Nineteenth-Century English Fiction about the Decline of Rome." *BNYPL* 72 (1968), 400–13.

Knoepflmacher, U. C. *Religious Humanism and the Victorian Novel: George Eliot, Walter Pater, and Samuel Butler.* Princeton: Princeton University Press, 1965.

Kumar, Shiv K., ed. *British Victorian Literature: Recent Revaluations.* New York: New York University Press, 1969.

Longford, Elizabeth. *Queen Victoria: Born to Succeed.* New York: Harper & Row, 1974.

Lukács, Georg. *The Historical Novel.* London: Merlin Press, 1962.

McAdoo, Henry R. *The Spirit of Anglicanism: A Survey of Anglican Theological Method in the Seventeenth Century.* New York: Scribners, 1965.

Machin, G. I. T. *Politics and the Churches in Great Britain, 1832 to 1868.* Oxford: Clarendon Press, 1977.

McNeill, John T. *Modern Christian Movements.* New York: Harper & Row, 1968.

Maison, Margaret M. *The Victorian Vision: Studies in the Religious Novel.* New York: Sheed & Ward, 1961.

Newsome, David. *The Wilberforces and Henry Manning: The Parting of Friends.* Cambridge, Mass.: Harvard University Press, Belknap Press, 1966.

Nield, Jonathan. *A Guide to the Best Historical Novels and Tales.* London: Elkin Mathews & Marrot, 1902 (rev. ed., 1929).

Norman, E. R. *Anti-Catholicism in Victorian England.* New York: Barnes & Noble, 1968.

Pelikan, Jaroslav. *The Emergence of the Catholic Tradition, 100–600.* Vol. 1 of *The Christian Tradition.* Chicago: University of Chicago Press, 1971.

―――. *Historical Theology: Continuity and Change in Christian Doctrine.* New York: Corpus; Philadelphia: Westminster, 1971.

Pfaff, Richard W. "The Library of the Fathers: The Tractarians as Patristic Translators." *Studies in Philology* 70 (1973), 329–44.

Rance, Nicholas. *The Historical Novel and Popular Politics in Nineteenth-Century England.* London: Vision Press, 1975.

Roth, Cecil. *A History of the Jews in England to 1858.* 3d ed. Oxford: Clarendon Press, 1964.

Sadleir, Michael. *Excursions in Victorian Bibliography.* London: Chaundy & Cox, 1922.

Schenk, H. G. *The Mind of the European Romantics: An Essay in Cultural History.* London: Constable, 1966.

Sheppard, A. T. *The Art and Practice of Historical Fiction.* London: Humphrey Toulmin, 1930.

Showalter, Elaine. *A Literature of Their Own: British Women Novelists from Brontë to Lessing*. Princeton: Princeton University Press, 1976.

Shuster, George N. *The Catholic Spirit in Modern English Literature*. New York: Macmillan, 1922.

Simmons, James C. *The Novelist as Historian: Essays on the Victorian Historical Novel*. The Hague: Mouton, 1973.

Slack, Robert C., ed. *Bibliographies of Studies in Victorian Literature: For the Ten Years 1955–1964*. Urbana: University of Illinois Press, 1967.

Smith, Warren S. *The London Heretics, 1870–1914*. New York: Dodd, Mead, 1968.

Soloway, R. A. *Prelates and People: Ecclesiastical Social Thought in England, 1783–1852*. London: Routledge & Kegan Paul, 1969.

Stang, Richard. *The Theory of the Novel in England, 1850–1870*. New York: Columbia University Press, 1959.

Stevenson, Lionel, ed. *Victorian Fiction: A Guide to Research*. Cambridge, Mass.: Harvard University Press, 1964.

Steward, Herbert L. *A Century of Anglo-Catholicism*. New York: Oxford University Press, 1929.

Tarr, Sr. Mary Muriel. *Catholicism in Gothic Fiction: A Study of the Nature and Function of Catholic Materials in Gothic Fiction in England, 1762–1820*. Washington, D.C.: Catholic University of America Press, 1946.

Tavard, George H. *The Quest for Catholicity: A Study in Anglicanism*. London: Catholic Book Club, 1963.

Templeman, William D., ed. *Bibliographies of Studies in Victorian Literature for the Thirteen Years 1932–1944*. Urbana: University of Illinois Press, 1945.

Vargish, Thomas. *Newman: The Contemplation of Mind*. Oxford: Clarendon Press, 1970.

Wolff, Robert L. *Gains and Losses: Novels of Faith and Doubt in Victorian England*. New York: Garland Publishing, 1977.

Wright, Austin, ed. *Bibliographies of Studies in Victorian Literature for the Ten Years 1945–1954*. Urbana: University of Illinois Press, 1956.

Ziolkowski, Theodore. *Fictional Transfigurations of Jesus*. Princeton: Princeton University Press, 1972.

INDEX

INDEX

369

Studies in Victorian Life and Literature

The Presence of the Present
Topics of the Day in the Victorian Novel
Richard D. Altick

George Eliot's Serial Fiction
Carol A. Martin

Toward a Working-Class Canon
Literary Criticism in British Working-Class Periodicals, 1816–1858
Paul Thomas Murphy

The Imagined World of Charles Dickens
Mildred Newcomb

A World of Possibilities
Romantic Irony in Victorian Literature
Clyde de L. Ryals

The Night Side of Dickens
Cannibalism, Passion, Necessity
Harry Stone

Carlyle and the Search for Authority
Chris R. Vanden Bossche